Ste Brigette de Suède
Catherine de Suède

THE BORGIAS

CLEMENTE FUSERO

THE BORGIAS

Translated from the Italian

by

PETER GREEN

PRAEGER PUBLISHERS

New York - Washington - London

Praeger Publishers, Inc.
111 Fourth Avenue, New York, N.Y. 10003, U.S.A.
5 Cromwell Place, London, sw7 2JL, England

Published in the United States of America in 1972

Originally published as *I Borgia*
© 1966 by dall'Oglio, Milan
Translation © 1972 in London, England, by The Pall Mall Press

Library of Congress Catalog Card Number: 71–154354

Printed in the United States of America

CONTENTS

CONTENTS

INTRODUCTION

*T*HE Borgia name has held inexhaustible interest for people throughout history. In no other age, perhaps, can we find a family which has so dazzled the world with its abundance of energy and brilliance in such short space of time, or has left such an incendiary a trail behind them. Most dynasties have covered a lengthy span of history and the leading figures have usually been widely spaced in time. But the House of the Borgias burst upon the European scene and in a few years it grew from an obscure fief to a position of supremacy, throwing up in a little over a century four such men as Callistus III, Alexander VI, Cesare and St Francis Borgia.

They fascinate because they are men of action and their traits of personality go to make up the supreme example of the Renaissance type of individualism: vigorous instincts, gifts of character and intelligence, capacity for calculation and splendour of ideals and ideas. Along with this went a sumptuous and violent life-style, and an element of mystery and enigma to do with various individual Borgias' lives. No one, for instance, has solved the obscurity of Rodrigo's love life and his presumed offsprings or has solved the murder of the Duke of Gandia, or the manner in which the Duke of Bisceglie was done away with. It is also a fact that for none of the crimes ascribed to individual members of the Borgia family can there be produced sufficient evidence to make a guilty verdict certain.

It is in their qualities as men of action in politics that the Borgias have really left their mark for posterity. Historically speaking, their policy resulted in an end to the crisis of the Papal State and led to the establishment of a temporal authority that was destined to keep a firm grasp on the reins of power in Central Italy for the next three hundred years. The prestige and indeed the very authority of the Roman See had been threatened by continual troubles, heretical movements, conciliar dissension, internal anarchy and ill-veiled hostility on the part of the emerging nation states of Europe. It was therefore necessary and timely for the Church's authority that a vast and powerful lay state (the 'Kingdom' of Cesare) be created which buttressed and disciplined the Ecclesiastical State and which set about a programme of sealing the Italian frontiers against foreign aggression and evolving a policy of Italian national recovery. This is the pattern which emerges from a serious study of the Borgias' actions and even though their programme was barely begun before it was cut short this pattern shows all the distinguishing marks of an unfinished masterpiece.

Pope Julius II, whose good fortune it was, in Machiavelli's words, to be heir to the labours of the Borgias, lacked the intelligence to continue the policy that had been his predecessor's brainchild. Unfortunately he was a spiteful and envious man, incapable of rising above the level of his own prejudices and sentiments. To avenge himself on his dead enemy, and to ruin that enemy's son, he was determined to secure for the Church the territory which Cesare had wrested from local lords and had turned into a model state—thus shattering for centuries to come the idea and the possibility of a sufficiently strong national state. He destroyed Cesare, but he also destroyed Italy.

When writing about this family it is hard to avoid enthusiasm, but the aim throughout has been sober and rigorous objectivity, free from partisan apologia. All the statements made in these pages rest on firm and specific evidence in so far as the present state of research on the Borgias will permit. In the interests of easier and quicker reading I have refrained from giving a source reference for each individual assertion.

This book differs from other modern works on the same theme in devoting much fuller space to an examination of the family's origins and subsequent decline and to the history of the Dukes of Gandia, and, in particular, of Callis-tus III, a Pope of great character and vision whose life and times are less well known than that of Alexander VI, but are equally rich in drama. If this book succeeds in thinning the ranks of those who continue to look on the Borgias as a brood of monsters rather than as men not substantially different from their contemporaries then it will have served its purpose. The family was richer than others in both virtues and failings, more resolute for good and ill alike—a family, then, in which black and white were strongly contrasted and which could produce both the sinner, Alexander VI, and a saint, his great-grandson Francis.

CLEMENTE FUSERO

THE ORIGINS

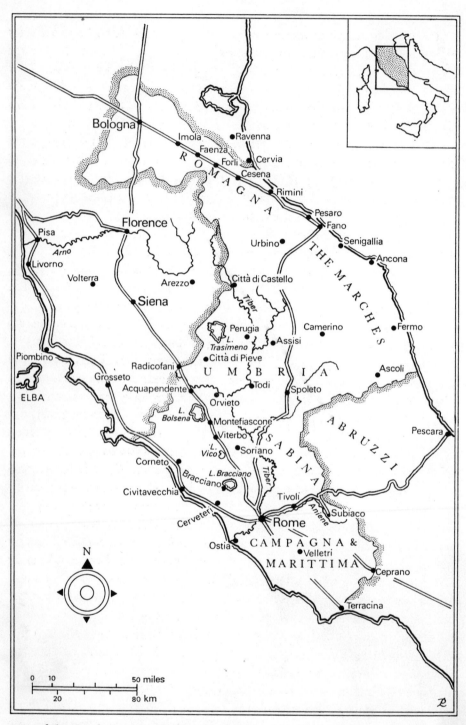

Map of the Papal States in the fifteenth century

*F*ROM the glacis of the frowning castle, Pedro de Atarés could see the houses of Borja descending the hillside, with their white walls and red roofs, huddled close together as though in self-defence against enemy attacks and the blazing heat of the sun. Down below in the valley flowed the waters of the Rio Huecha. As far as the eye could see at high noon, in any direction to the furthest horizon, all this territory formed part of Aragon.

In the immediate vicinity of rivers or mountain torrents, a number of *huertas* spread their lush greenery under that brazen sky: fertile oases of almonds and olives, figs and vines, vegetable gardens and wheatfields. But elsewhere the chequered landscape of Aragon displayed the parched and blinding aridity of the desert. Burnt hillsides, their soil crumbling away into dust, and bare escarp-ments ranging in colour from pale grey to yellow ochre, provided the sole touch of variety in this depressing panorama. During summer the *calina* stood idle in the airless fields, like so many crouching beasts. The only sign of life in this timeless, still world—moving slowly along the roads that furrowed its surface, plodding through scattered and sleepy towns, by scrannel pasturage or steppe-like expanses of halfa or among the bare rocky foothills—was the occasional peasant on muleback, eyes set and frowning in his swarthy, sunburnt face.

Borja, however, lay at some distance from this scene of torrid desolation, and thus had escaped its depressing influence. It was situated on the southern edge of the Ebro plain, and little more than twelve miles from the main road that made its way along the right bank of the river from Saragossa to Logroño, and thence by a roundabout route to the sea, with the river and its lush vegetation always on hand to provide refreshment. To the north-west the near-barren upland plateau of the Bárdenas, and in the south-west the Sierra de Moncayo—a steep sandstone barrier the highest peaks of which rise to over 6000 feet, divid-ing the Ebro basin from the highlands of Castile—formed the backdrop to a harsh and rugged landscape which aptly reflected the character of its inhabitants.

Though it did not as yet enjoy the title of city (this was not conferred upon it until 1438, by Alfonso V, the Magnanimous), nevertheless Borja could boast of an extremely long history. Its actual foundation went back to 930 B.C., and was the work of the Celtiberi, who called it Borsa or Bursa, meaning 'healthy spot'. Seven centuries later it witnessed the arrival from the South of the dark-skinned warriors of Carthage, who pushed the frontiers of their domains this far north, and emphasized their ascendancy by installing some extremely tough garrisons. But before the generation that had been put down by the might of Carthage had passed away, Rome's legionaries were already disembarking on the shores of Spain. After completing their own leisurely and very different conquest, the Romans took the Ebro as the boundary-line between the two provinces into which they had divided the peninsula thus acquired. They also, as we know from the deathless pages of Livy and Pliny the Elder, changed the town's name to Burao. The collapse of the Roman Empire under barbarian onslaughts brought down from the North a series of invaders with long blond hair and fierce blue eyes: the Vandals, the Suebi, the Alemanni and, finally, the Visigoths, who having seized the legacy of Rome held on to it for three hundred years, until it was wrested from them by the invading Moors. At this point the ancient Celtiberian village changed its name yet again. Borja, or 'castle tower', was in fact the title bestowed on it by these warriors from Africa, with their guttural speech and curved scimitars, who had come hither under the command of the terrible Musa ibn Nursair. The latter's sinister reputation had preceded him: there were dark rumours of cannibalism, of general massacres in the name of Allah.

In the central and southern parts of Spain Moorish rule evolved a most magnificent culture, and reached fantastic heights of opulence. The heady winds of Arab poetry spread throughout the land. Everywhere there sprang up white fretted houses set amid fountains and nodding palm-trees. But these lands in the North, which remained austerely Roman and stubbornly Christian, had suffered a long period of decline, during which they witnessed the complete destruction of their Latin culture, plumbing the very depths of poverty, and only redeeming their abject condition of servitude by spasmodic attempts at revolt.

In truth, the invaders here had a hard time of it. As happened throughout the mountains of the North, from Galicia to the Asturias, from Biscay to Cantabria and Navarre, ever since the time of Pelagius the Visigoth there had developed a constant series of resistance movements in this area. These had not merely prevented the Moors advancing further, but had frequently compelled them to pull back their frontiers.

The process of transformation which had led so large a part of Spain to acquire Arab characteristics—literally allowing the soft tentacles of Moslem culture to drain away its very lifeblood—could, in fact, show one or two fairly notorious examples in this region as well. Nevertheless the inhabitants as a whole remained basically unchanged, stiffening their will by assuming, as it were, a cloak of silent expectation. And every time the hour of insurrection struck, this unassimilable people took up arms in the name of the Christ they had so steadfastly refused to deny. A permanent state of war with the Moslems gradually developed. The Spanish activists took advantage of any occasion when the Sultan of Cordova was hard-pressed by internal rebellions; sudden attacks were their speciality, and they regularly carried out commando raids of the kind they had learnt from the invaders themselves.

Even so, the Spaniards in the North were no better off than those of their fellow-countrymen who had been subjected to Islam. If the latter endured the yoke of the Sultan, the Emirs, and the Cadis, the former groaned under the iron hand of a tyrannical nobility and the fleshly rule of a mean and grasping clergy, so that their existence was miserable in the extreme. There could be no rest or security or enjoyment of life for these lean peasants, working their parched, thirsty soil; hunger and battle were their lot, and unending struggle against the foreigners who had settled down in their most fertile region. This fierce war was further exacerbated by famines, embittered by rapacity, and rendered still more bloody by the general thirst for reprisals, religious fanaticism, and sheerly bestial hatred that characterized both sides alike.

Nor should it be imagined that the champions of Christendom were inspired or sustained by a high ideal of unity. Even the North was split up into a number of minuscule states, no less jealous and quarrelsome than those of the South: here too the Spaniard revealed his basically individualistic nature, his irremediably separatist attitude to life.

Yet a species of higher logic nevertheless guided the course of events. The various independence movements were gradually drawn together, so that they flowed in wider common channels. Their leaders had no option but to amalgamate with one another; and this inevitably brought them, sooner or later, within the orbit of the great landowners. Such a process of absorption steadily increased and strengthened the latter's holdings, till a time came, rather before the turn of the millennium, when the Christian kingdoms of León, Navarre and Aragon—among other minor States—took solid shape and acquired more or less permanent boundaries. By now the Moors had finally renounced their scheme of opening a corridor through to the Pyrenees, and invading the 'Great Territory', as they termed France. They contented themselves with keeping up their terrifying raids along the frontier, to which the Christians retaliated with equally bloody and predatory offensives of their own. Ordoño II of León, for example, carried his trail of devastation as far as the outskirts of Cordova. Sancho I of Navarre descended on Najera and Viguera, thus inciting al-Mansur ibn Amir-Mohammed to launch a punitive expedition which resulted in the invasion, sack, and all but total destruction of his colourful capital.

Internal anarchy—Arabs against Berbers, renegades and Christians against the central government—led, about the beginning of the new millennium, to the final decay of the Caliphate: in 1031 the Vizirs formally declared it abolished. From this dismemberment of Moslem Spain there sprang up a whole galaxy of small autonomous Moorish kingdoms.

Great historical occasions create great men of action. In the North, the most conspicuous character during this period of transition—which lasted for a whole century, until the Almoravide and Almohade invasions—was Sancho III, known as El Mayor. King of Navarre for about thirty years, he made a military alliance with Aragon, a highly advantageous alliance-by-marriage with Castile, and came within an ace of seizing León. On his death, which took place in 1035, he was in a position to bequeath each of his four sons a kingdom.

Aragon went to Ramiro I, though in fact he had already acquired it before proclaiming himself king, under the title of the earldom of Jaca, this appellation being derived from the identically-named hilltop stronghold above the Rio Aragon. Jaca was a city of modest proportions but illustrious traditions. At this period it was encircled by a splendid towered fortification-wall, adorned with a beautiful cathedral, and had a strong citadel to strengthen its defences.

Ramiro, who founded the first Aragonese dynasty, proved to be a highly enterprising character. He consolidated his own kingdom, projected various ambitious building schemes, and in 1042 attempted to filch Navarre from his brother García III, through a far from edifying war which—to the great comfort of the moralists—went very badly for him. His mania for territorial aggrandizement later led him to become involved in a conflict that broke out between three Emirs of Saragossa and Huesca. Again, his intervention had most unfortunate results for him, of which he scarcely had time to repent before his death. In fact he died fighting (1063) before the walls of Graus, an obscure little town in the Pyrenees, near the confluence of two minor rivers. Among the Castilian troops who fought beside Saragossa's Moorish battalions, and inflicted defeat and death upon Ramiro, the most distinguished warrior was the twenty-year-old Rodrigo Díaz de Bivar, the future Cid Campeador.

PEDRO DE ATARÉS

It was to the incontinent habits of Ramiro I of Aragon that the Borgias owed their origins. Ramiro, himself the illegitimate son of Sancho el Mayor, had brought into the world a bastard who, far from being abandoned to a miserable destiny, grew up—as was then the custom with ruling Houses—in Court circles, and in due course was granted titles and rank. From this scion was descended Pedro de Atarés, the first Lord of Borja.

Few events worthy of note took place during this period within the territories of Aragon and under Spanish skies. A succession of monarchs had ascended Ramiro's throne: first Sancho Ramírez, who in 1076 had realized his father's dream by usurping the rule of Navarre, and had suffered a very similar death, falling at the siege of Huesca in 1094; then Peter I, a valiant warrior, friend and comrade-in-arms to the Cid, who had continued his father's policies and avenged his death—beating the Moors at Alcoraz and Barbastro, wresting lovely Huesca from them and making it the capital of his kingdom; then his brother, Alfonso I, known as The Champion, who first grasped the sceptre in 1104, and was destined to hold it for thirty years. Pursuing his family's policy of aggrandizement, in 1109 he married Urraca—daughter of the King of Castile and León, and Raymond of Galicia's widow—who appears, in legendary guise, in the famous *Romancero de Zamora*; but he never managed to get his claws into the lands and throne of Castile, since Urraca's right to inherit was sharply contested on the battlefield. Finally the marriage itself was dissolved, on the initiative of the Bishop of Santiago: a prudent move, which sought to curtail such deadly vendettas at a time when the Kingdoms of Christendom needed to fight side by side if they were to stem the new incursions of Islam.

A warrior of high renown, Alfonso the Champion in 1118 conquered Saragossa, the 'white city', which from then on replaced Huesca as the capital, and entered on a period of quite exceptional magnificence. Alfonso took up residence in the splendid castle of Aljafería, formerly occupied by the Beni Hud princes, and had good grounds for feeling that he had raised his dynasty to an apogee of power and fame. (In 1809 an earthquake almost completely des-troyed this castle, leaving for our admiration little but the ruins of one or two reception chambers, with marvellous ceilings, and a small oratory adorned with flowery arabesques.) Saragossa—the ancient Caesaraugusta, jewel of the *huerta* on the Ebro, perhaps the most strikingly Islamicized city in the entire peninsula, and a Moorish frontier stronghold against which the Kings of Castile had in vain expended all their military might and cunning strategy— was indeed a formidable feather in his cap. The dynasty had, as they say, arrived.

From his King and kinsman Alfonso Pedro de Atarés received the lord-ship of Borja. This was a key appointment, since the little town stood near the frontier, at the crossing-point of two major trunk-roads: one from Castile, which continued towards the Pyrenees, and another from Navarre, which went on up to Saragossa. The importance of this grant stands out clearly when one realizes that Borja was only captured from the Moors in 1120, two years after the fall of Saragossa itself. Thus the grandson of King Ramiro's bastard took possession of a strategic stronghold still hot from the flames of battle—and one to the conquest of which his own sword must surely have contributed.

Contemporary evidence has very little to tell us about Pedro. Nevertheless, it is still possible to sketch a 'presumptive portrait' of him.

Pedro de Atarés came from a line of warrior-kings—men largely governed by their instincts, impetuous, avid for power, much given to fratricidal quarrels, open-minded and tenacious—which in little more than a century had irresistibly forced its way to the forefront of the new Spain now coming into being. There can be no doubt that in his vigorous blood he carried the virtues and vices of the stock from which he was sprung: courage, determination, pride, a lightning-swift readiness for action, and perhaps the family's coarse and turbid sensuality as well. These are characteristics which reappear in the Borgias, when their rich humanity unfolds itself in the full midday brilliance of their history. We cannot envisage him otherwise than stamped in the warrior-mould of his age: a steel-clad man, lean as his own land, and similarly full of hot and hidden impulses.

He was a young man—or at least scarcely past his youth—when he first climbed the crag of Borja and took up residence in the castle which the Moors had evacuated; he had another thirty years of life left to him.

More than once the inhabitants of the little town saw him mount his horse and ride away to fight in his King's campaigns—or better, *para ir a tierra de Moros*, as people used to say at the time: a phrase that hinted broadly enough at the object of such incursions, namely plunder and devastation. During those periods when Pedro was resident at Borja, life in the castle knew spells of hearty liveliness and good cheer. He was, after all, a gentleman in the Spain that had acquired luxurious and pleasure-loving tastes from its Arab conquerors; he was also a man of his time when it came to that robust capacity for enjoyment which the warrior evinced in his hours of leisure, between yesterday's surmounted perils and those that still threatened on the morrow.

A tough warrior, then, and—as a true Spaniard—a man of pious faith. One day it so happened that he was caught by a hurricane among the crags of the Sierra de Moncayo, and lost his way in its wild gorges; the fact that he managed to come through safely he regarded as a miraculous intervention on the part of the Almighty, and he repaid his debt by building a monastery in these mountains, about eleven miles from Borja. This was the Cistercian foundation of Veruela, which stood above the village of Vera, famous for its red wine.

When Alfonso I died, in 1134, without leaving any sons, Pedro de Atarés could presumably have made his blood-relationship an excuse for attempting to seize the throne. Those few historians who refer to him at all pay him tribute because he refrained from doing so.

The fortunes of the Aragonese dynasty were in danger of foundering through lack of immediate heirs. Ramiro II, the brother of the deceased King, made it his business to remedy this state of affairs. He was a monk and a bishop, but lost no time in divesting himself of his ecclesiastical vestments. Having obtained the necessary Papal dispensation, he hastily contracted a proper marriage in order to assure himself of a successor. His wife only managed to give him a daughter, Petronilla. But for him that was good enough. His task thus discharged, Ramiro II yielded to nostalgia, and reassumed the habit of a Benedictine. In the three years of his reign he had found time to prove that a monastic garb had by no means killed in him those native gifts of energy which characterized his stock, nor indeed dimmed his knowledge of the skills essential for good government. In a hall belonging to the University of Huesca, he promised the rebellious nobility 'a bell capable of making itself heard from one end of the country to the other'. Then, illustrating his sober statement with the touch of a first-class draughtsman, he proceeded to build the said bell on the marble floor. Fifteen heads of decapitated gentlemen went to make it, with a sixteenth hung from them in the guise of a clapper. This episode made a splendid impression on all parties concerned, and was remembered, right down to our own times, as the affair of the 'Huesca bell'.

Though he returned to his monastic life in 1137, Ramiro II nevertheless retained the title—and prerogatives—of sovereign. He died in 1154, and was buried in the same city that had witnessed his persuasive oratorical gambit; his tomb can still be seen there, in the cloister of the Church of San Pietro.

Nor by then did Pedro de Atarés any longer look out from Borja Castle at the bold outlines of the Sierra and the Aragonese countryside; he had closed his eyes for ever on 21 February 1151, and slept, his hands folded across his breast, in the monastery he had founded at Veruela.

GENEALOGICAL UNCERTAINTY

In the same year as the first Lord of Borja died, the daughter of the monk-king married Raymond-Berengar IV, Count of Barcelona. This union, which enabled the Kingdom of Aragon to get a foothold in Catalonia, marked the beginning of the second Aragonese dynasty. Their realm now had an outlet on the coast; they saw opening up before them those prospects which properly belonged to a Mediterranean power.

Nothing is known about the immediate descendants of Pedro de Atarés. An impenetrable cloud descends upon the fortunes of his family. The Lords of Borja do not re-emerge into history until 1240, at the time of their emigration to the Kingdom of Valencia.

This series of missing links in the chain has led some people to suppose—often, indeed, to assert with peremptory conviction—that there was no real connection whatsoever between the Borgias and the family tree of Pedro de

Atarés, to which (it is argued) they attached themselves in a purely arbitrary fashion, by way of manufacturing a princely pedigree for their house. It remains true, however, that no solidly clinching arguments are advanced in support of this thesis; and that (while declaring the version of a direct descent from Atarés unfounded) its adherents can find no testimony which would direct research on the family's origins to some other quarter, and help to clear up the mystery. In default of such documentary evidence, those who deny a line of descent between the grandson of King Ramiro's bastard and the Borgias of the Valencia region can do no better than point to the fact that the latter— though undisputably immigrants from Borja—no longer called themselves 'de Atarés', did not figure as Infanti of Aragon, and (as far as is ascertainable) did not hold the lordship of their place of origin.

They forget, however, that during the ninety years which elapsed between Pedro's death and the appearance of the Borgias on the shores of Valencia, enough could happen to provide a perfectly adequate explanation for these changes. They also forget that, in the absence of any testimony capable of exploding the 'ancient roots' tradition, it is only fair to accept it. Above all, they forget that the Borgias had no need to manufacture themselves a dis﹍ tinguished pedigree. When the Duke of Ferrara was contemplating marriage with Lucrezia, he dispatched a confidential agent to Spain with the task of checking on her family's claims to gentility. On 18 October 1501, this agent wrote to the Este Court that after conducting exhaustive investigations in every quarter (which included a scrutiny of the relevant documents as well as the interrogation of those persons best qualified to judge) he could guarantee that the family was 'of great age and nobility in Spain'.

This is not the end of the matter. A manuscript account from the monastery at Veruela (*Registro universal de todas las escrituras que se hallan en el archivo de este santo y real monasterio*), compiled from original sources in 1671 by a monk called Atilano de la Espina, provides a by no means unlikely explanation for the change of name. After the conquest of Jativa, it reports, the victorious troops acclaimed the eight *hidalgos* of Borja—whom we shall discuss further in a moment, and who were traditionally supposed to have been distant descendants of Atarés—with the cry *Viva Borja!* Hence their adoption of the name. Far from the nest on their ancestral rock, they must have felt naturally driven, by sentiments of pride and nostalgia, to assume—or rather to preserve—the name of their town of origin; never for one moment envisaging the genealogical doubts which their decision would later arouse.

One could certainly regard the Borgias with a sceptical smile when, some﹍ what over﹍enthusiastically, they added to their lineage no less an ancestor than

Julius Caesar, who (it was alleged) while quaestor in Spain, had contracted a liaison with a lady of their family. Yet even this enormity can be excused when we recall how Sandoval later worked out a genealogy for Carlos V which—without skipping a single generation—traced him right back to Adam by way of Caesar, Aeneas, and Hercules. One could smile at their absurd presumption on this occasion; but one could not reasonably accuse them of boasting when they claimed descent from that by no means exalted figure Pedro, the lord of a tiny frontier town. Had their assertion been false, not only the House of Aragon (with which they were often at loggerheads) but any Spanish nobleman (and Rome swarmed with such) could readily have refuted it.

On the other hand this version found acceptance and confirmation in Spain. Even in the seventeenth century, José Pellicer, author of a *Seyano Germánico*, supported it categorically, adding that the first person to assume the cognomen 'de Borja' was in fact a son of Pedro de Atarés, Gimen Garcez. This would seem perfectly logical and natural, seeing that from henceforward his family was linked to the place over which it held sway, and that the name of the place itself (recalling as it did a victory over the Moors) constituted an honourable title. However, those who challenge this line of descent retort that the simple name of Gimen Garcez is 'improbable'[1] for the period, and—once again—support their thesis on a mere hypothesis, arguing that Pedro de Atarés 'probably' departed this life without leaving any sons behind him. This last conjecture, indeed, really cuts the Gordian—or in our case Borgian—knot by excluding any possibility of true descent.

JATIVA

It was during the great flight of the Reconquest that the family fortunes of these landed gentry from Borja really spread their wings.

Santiago, y cierra España! Eight knights of the clan fought under the banner of that powerful, rubicund monarch James I, the sovereign who first led the emergent Catalan-Aragonese power on the high seas, wresting the Balearics from Moorish domination.

When the King moved on to the conquest of Valencia, the 'magnificent eight'—notable amongst them being one Esteban, a huge, hulking fellow said to be capable of lifting a horse—went with him, and showed such lion-like prowess in battle that they earned rich recompense at his hand; he enrolled them amongst the *caballeros de la Conquista*, and assigned them territories in the occu-pied kingdom—Jativa, Canals, and some other neighbouring localities.

This may not have been a lavish fief, but it was nevertheless of considerable value. Jativa, the 'second jewel' in the crown of Valencia, was at that time huddled against the harsh flank of Monte Bernisa, though later it descended and spread out over the sunlit plain. Above it, the shrub-clad peaks of the Sierra offset the massy bulk of the two castles, linked by an indented line of fortifications which extended their stony arms on either side of the city, and on 7 February 1240 had given its besiegers a great deal of trouble.

The countryside around Jativa displays considerable contrast and variety. The Sierra de Enguera is a bare, angular mountain, with peaks that stand out sharply against the blood-red sunset sky, creating a most impressive scene. From the more massive of the two castles one still seems to hear the lament of the princes and nobles who suffered imprisonment there. Further inland, towards Puerto de Almansa, is Canals, with its idyllic-looking houses, dominated by the bulk of the castle where the future Pope Callistus III was born. Beyond Canals lies Alcudia de Crespins, with its ruins, and Montese, which in 1318 gave its name to the famous Order of Knights founded by James II as a sub-stitute for that of the Templars, and destined to have a Borgia as its last Grand Master; and beyond these is Vallada, hard by that enormous *piedra encantada*, or 'magic rock', which can be made to oscillate by the mere touch of a child's hand. Harsh jagged ridges and gloomy jutting crags dominate the horizon.

But where the countryside trips, as though dancing, down to the sea's embrace—even inland you can smell the salt breeze—the vegetation is luxuri-ant, Mediterranean, ranging through every shade of green under a blindingly azure sky. This is the great sun-drenched *huerta*—fields and gardens, palms and orange-trees, with strips of reddish earth, white arrow-like bell towers, crosses standing out high on cypress-clustered knolls, and, facing the sea, the bright enchantment of Gandia; while over this entire Eden—unforgettable for anyone who has surveyed it from the eminence of the San Feliu hermitage, close by the castle—there shines a vibrant, crystalline, plangent light.

Twice, in 1707 and 1936, Jativa has suffered devastations and fires which destroyed precious relics of the past. But it is still possible, here and there, to find images and suggestions of bygone ages. There are the *solares* that once housed proud and splendid noblemen; there is the fascinating Almudin, jewel of the most ancient quarter; there are numerous fountains, that carry the cheer-ful sound of running water into every remote corner; the Borgia mansions on the Calle de la Triaca and the Calle de Moncada, which with their flowery, well-shaded patios, quiet rooms, and armorial bearings preserve the memory of long-lost magnificence; the great house on the Plaza de Aldomar, which though sadly crumbling and decayed still tells us of an age which saw the birth of the future Alexander VI; and the collegiate church, where various mementoes of the family are displayed—the Borgia chapel (commissioned by Isabel, sister of the first Borgia Pope and mother of the second) with its 'Virgin and Child among Angelic Musicians', by Reixach, and the 'Triptych' by Jaume Jacomart Baço, Alfonso V's court painter, who brought a breath of the Italian Renaissance into this far corner of Spain, and the sacred vessels donated, as a token of their affection, by the two Popes.

After the occupation of Valencia and Jativa, the southward advance rolled on with vigorous determination, weakening the Moors and driving them back along the narrow coastal strip, reaching Albaida, with its *alcázar*, liberating Cocentaina (its Roman walls restored by the invaders), crossing the beautiful Alcoy and the swift Jijona, to reach the sea at Alicante, and press inexorably on towards Murcia. At the storming of Orihuela—set in a proverbially rich countryside on the left bank of the Segura—a certain Rodrigo de Borja distinguished himself.

Power, like wealth, contains a dynamic quality that leads to its own increase. It was inevitable that a kingdom in so vigorous a process of expansion, overflowing from the lower slopes of the Pyrenees till it reached the southern shores of the peninsula, should pursue its development at all costs, surmounting every physical obstacle, forcing every line of lesser resistance. Little more than forty years after the conquest of Valencia, Peter III (The Great), who in 1276 succeeded his father James I, turned his gaze from the shores of Valencia towards Sicily, where Charles of Anjou's Frenchmen, with blind industriousness, were toiling to bring about their own ruin through an endless sequence of tyrannical and overbearing acts: fiscal oppression, despoliation of the feudal landowners, corruption in office, outrageous behaviour that offended the island modesty of the local women. Peter, who had married Manfred's daughter, Constance of Hohenstaufen (Dante's 'mother of the honour of Sicily and Aragon') not only welcomed notable Sicilian exiles at his court, lending a sympathetic ear to their anti-French and pro-Ghibelline proposals, but also sent out agents to win over the island, and—camouflaging his plans for a landing by an ostentatious expedition against Tunis—established contact with those who looked back wistfully to a time before Benevento fell to Charles of Anjou.

The Sicilian Vespers spared him the risks attendant upon such an undertaking. It was but a little time after the cries of 'Death to the French!' on 30 March 1282 that a Sicilian parliament acclaimed him sovereign of the island. He arrived there from Tunisia in August, on the heels of the last French fugitives. In the war that followed, the Kingdom of Aragon made its first, and highly successful, appearance on the chess-board of Europe, fearlessly standing up to the fulminations of the Holy See, shattering the impetus of the crusade

led by Philip IV, the Bold, and beating hostile naval forces in the waters off
Malta (June 1283), Naples (June 1284), and the Scogli delle Formiche (Sep-
tember 1285), with a fleet under the inspired and brilliant command of Admiral
Ruggero di Lauria.

Another forty years, and the banner of Aragon flew over Sardinia; a century
later it had reached the shores of Naples. And just as the descendants of Atarés
had been borne from Borja to Jativa on the tumultuous wave of the Recon-
quest, so via the bridge of Aragonese expansion thrown across the Mediterranean they now passed into Italy.

THE BULL AND THE CROWNS

Meanwhile in the recently occupied territories their social status remained that
of lesser provincial nobility, and their life—when they were not fighting for
some still-unsubjugated area—that of ordinary country gentlemen. Nor by any
stretch of the imagination could they be termed wealthy. The original partition
of the fief between those eight kinsmen had not left anyone with a substantial
holding; and subsequent increases in their numbers impoverished them still
further.

However, from the *Cronica de Valencia*, by Ramón Viciana, we know that
the King held them in high esteem. The fact that they had fought in the war of
liberation, and belonged to that circle of the Aragonese nobility which was
most closely linked with the Court, entitled them to special consideration.
Furthermore, the gifts that were a constant privilege of their stock—intelligence
courage, extraordinary physical vigour, and winning good looks—compelled
general admiration.

Neither conspicuous nor opulent, but ambitious to a degree, they were on
the look-out for any opportunity to raise the star of their fortunes still higher.
Their armorial bearings displayed an ox at pasture in a green and red field,
surrounded in the bordure by eight sheafs. This specifically agricultural emblem was also that of Borja. The city's coat of arms was divided per pale; its
left-hand side bore a three-towered castle on a rock, its right-hand side the ox.
A hypothesis has been advanced to the effect that this is an attempt at trans-
lating the name in visual terms: *bo* (ox) plus *orja* (barley).

The eight sheafs (which might have been meant to represent the eight
caballeros de la Conquista, transmuted into landed gentry, with sway over a fertile
countryside) were subsequently replaced by the same number of double crowns.
The docile ox became the formidable bull of the Borgias, a far more apt symbol
for the family's hard and rugged *virtus*: the pride, energy, and temper which this

remarkable breed of men, as fearless as they were unscrupulous, revealed to the world at every crucial phase of their history, from the time when they left their lonely crag in Aragon to set forth against—and exterminate—the Moors, to the period during which they mortified their seething ambitions on the soil of Valencia (thus offering a prime example of that 'Borgia patience' which was to shine forth so surprisingly in Cardinal Rodrigo); from the age of Callistus III and Alexander VI, when the Borgias launched their irresistible assault on the bastions of supreme worldly power, to that of Francis, Duke of Gandia and Marquis of Lombay, courtier and statesman, Viceroy of Catalonia and a figure of European stature, who committed himself to a total rejection of all human vanities—triumphing heroically over those instincts which had hitherto ruled him, to achieve a shining redemption of his past through the exercise of virtues even more difficult than those which had aided him to hold sway over the world's political destinies.

THE AGE
OF CALLISTUS III
1378 – 1458

*I*N the history of the Borgias 1378 stands out as a year of particular significance and importance. It saw the birth of the man who first set them on the road to European fame and eminence; and it brought about a good many of the factors governing those situations with which they were called upon to deal.

On the evening of 27 March there died in Rome the sixty-nine-year-old Pierre Roger de Beaufort, whose title as Pope had been Gregory XI. His last moments were troubled by shades of remorse at having failed to undertake those reforms so ardently called for by St Catherine of Siena, who had brought him back from Avignon, and by presentiments of vast perils threatening the imme-diate future of the Church. He was a weak man—though on occasion capable of exasperated gestures—who had, to his great misfortune, found himself con-trolling a helm which called for hands of steel. He had returned to Rome only on 17 January the previous year, re-establishing the Apostolic See there after its long exile in Avignon; and during the few months of his sojourn in the Vatican—broken by yet another prolonged withdrawal, for reasons of caution, to Anagni—he had had the depressing sensation of having arrived in a city where the only law was that of the jungle, and there was no way of remedying matters.

Of the sixteen cardinals who, on the afternoon of 7 April, gathered in con-clave to elect his successor, four were Italian, eleven French, and one Spanish: Pedro de Luna, whom we shall meet again as antipope. The 'ultramontanists', therefore, enjoyed an overwhelming majority, even though they were them-selves split into two factions: the French group (in the wider sense), which had the war-like Robert of Geneva as its candidate; and the Limousine party, which sought to place on the pontifical throne a man from their own region. But the violence of the mob (which burst into the Palace, shouting and waving arms, and, though driven out after three hours' fighting, proceeded to bellow ferocious threats under the windows of the hastily-sealed chamber where the conclave was gathered) played havoc with the cardinals' reasonable delibera-tions. The din which shook the walls did not form a propitious accompani-ment either to a careful sifting of candidates, or to the prelates' usual cunning electoral gambits, which amid all the hubbub outside likewise tended to go by the board.

The demonstrators wanted an Italian Pope at all costs; and not merely an Italian but a Roman. That evening the leaders of the thirteen city wards came to parley, under the window, with the sixteen dignitaries shut up inside, their object being to extort a promise that the election would be made in conformity with the will of the people. Throughout the night, by the glare of torches, their deafening clamour kept the cardinals awake. Next morning, the bells of St Peter's rang a tocsin, by way of urging them into a rapid—and subservient—decision.

Quickly enough, but with no great show of submissiveness, the conclave made up its mind. One cardinal abstained, and three voted against the candidate, but the rest were in favour of a prelate who did not belong to the Sacred College: Bartolomeo Prignano, a Neapolitan, the Archbishop of Bari. They thought that in this way they had protected themselves from the fury of the mob, and joyfully congratulated themselves on having found a solution to their dilemma. Still full of euphoria at such a narrow escape from danger, they summoned their elected candidate, and were proceeding to the chapel for the solemn proclamation of his name. At this point a sword-waving crowd burst into the building, with a noisy, half-crazy mob at their heels, all shouting that they meant to have a Roman Pope.

With the quick instinct bred of fear, the cardinals seized their decrepit colleague Francesco Tebaldeschi, who shared with Cardinal Giacomo Orsini the providential privilege of Roman birth, flung the Papal mantle round his shoulders, thrust the mitre upon his head, and hoisted him up by main force—first stunned with amazement, then protesting vigorously—to the altar. Then, while the poor man continued to struggle, and in a pitifully quavering voice (drowned by the jubilant cheers of the mob) protested that he was *not* the new Pope, they abandoned him to the homage of his fellow-citizens, and—taking quite remarkably nimble advantage of the pandemonium that was going on—vanished. Some sought refuge in the Castel Sant'Angelo, others hastily barricaded themselves in their houses; four of them did not rest until, pale and breathless, they found themselves outside Rome.

Still, what's done cannot be undone; and the flock had perforce to resign itself to accepting the Neapolitan as its shepherd. He assumed the name of Urban VI; no Pontiff had ever shown a greater sense of irony in choosing his title, and none so drastically belied its meaning.

Urban VI—a man in every other way worthy of considerable respect—lost no time in parading a harshness of manner that left those who witnessed it absolutely astounded. Having settled into the Vatican with a radical programme of reform, he set about implementing it in so patently headstrong a fashion that even Catherine of Siena was made uneasy by it. 'Carry out your plans with moderation, calmly and benevolently,' she hastened to advise him. 'For the sake of Him who was crucified, subdue, if only a little, those sudden impulses to which your nature drives you!'

But, to cut back, strike down, prune and curtail were the only actions that Urban understood. He proceeded to stride through the rank garden of ecclesiastical immorality, raising trouble right and left. Where he should have had recourse to the most delicate shears, he employed the club and the bludgeon. He gave no one an impartial hearing. He publicly proclaimed his intention of making his electors' flesh creep. Only two days after his enthronement we find him railing harshly against the prelates of the Curia, branding them as perjurors. A fortnight later, in public consistory, he reviewed the manners and morals of the higher clergy, saying such things—to borrow Machiavelli's phrase—as 'Dog does not believe in eating dog'. At another consistory, he peremptorily silenced those cardinals who tried to protest against his rough manner of speech, telling them, loudly, that they 'babbled like fools'. He called Cardinal Orsini a halfwit, and dismissed that powerful figure Cardinal Jean de la Grange, the King of France's counsellor, as a knave and rascal. When a diligent taxcollector brought him the money he had received, expecting to be complimented, Urban flung a fistful of the coins in his face, accompanying this gesture with a quotation from the New Testament, likening the wretched official to a contemptible descendant of Simon Magus.

To root out the foul weeds of ecclesiastical immorality, luxury, simony, and all the innumerable other abuses, to make a clearing in the rank growth of the forest—such was Urban's aim. He wanted to reform everything and everybody. But it soon became clear that the parties concerned would not allow themselves to be reformed so easily.

A powerful current of opposition began to develop among the muchabused cardinals, being especially strong where the French group was concerned: these made no secret of their determination to reestablish Avignon—after this disappointing Roman interlude—as the true Pontifical See.

Three months after the April election, the split between Urban and the Sacred College had widened into an abyss. There was something undeniably admirable about the persistent, not to say obsessional, way in which he stuck to his basic objective. Both his rectitude and his courage were beyond cavil. One day he calmly confronted a nearriotous mob, emerging from his palace and blandly remarking to the heated demonstrators: 'Here I am. What do you want?' If his ruthless intransigence and adamantine honesty had been combined with greater adroitness of method, he might perhaps have spared the Church a century and a half of scandal and disaster. But granted his character and the approach he adopted, he inevitably precipitated a disaster of unprecedented proportions.

The crisis finally broke one day when, confronted with a large group of sulky, scowling French cardinals, he lost control of himself and shouted that he would create so large a new batch of Italian cardinals as to reduce the 'ultra-montanists' to perpetual silence within the bosom of the Sacred College. Amongst those present was Robert of Geneva, kinsman to the King of France, and one of those prelates on whom the purple seemed out of place, an inappropriate surrogate for military and Court life: the man who had smoothed the way for Gregory XI's coming to Italy by spreading devastation and death, aided by the Breton and English mercenary forces of Malestroit and John Hawkwood. Robert of Geneva, without saying a word, turned his back on the Pontiff and strode out of the audience-chamber.

By 26 July there was not a cardinal left in Rome except for poor Tebaldeschi, who had been unable to get away; he lay in bed, panting and gasping, making ready for a far more irrevocable departure. All the others, on the pretext of escaping from the fierce summer heat, had taken their leave; and for every one of them this flight from Rome was tantamount to a crossing of the Rubicon.

On 9 August 1378, from Anagni—where they were protected by a mixed force of Gascon and Navarrese troops under Bernard de la Salle, and could thus breathe easily—they issued a proclamation declaring the election of Urban VI null and void, on the grounds that it had been forced upon them by intimidation on the part of the Roman populace. Encouraged by the French King with promises of help and money, and by a declaration of solidarity from Queen Joanna I of Naples, they took the last logical step in their rebellion: on 20 September, at Fondi, with the tacit agreement of the three Italian cardinals, they chose as Pope Robert of Geneva, who took the name of Clement VII.

Rome now became the key-centre: its possession was equivalent to a guarantee of legitimacy, and Clement VII did not despair of wresting it from his ill-tempered adversary, in as much as he knew he could count on the French garrison of the Castel Sant'Angelo, as well as on a company of Breton mercenaries and on the support of the Queen of Naples. Nevertheless, on 27 April 1379 Castel Sant'Angelo capitulated, and three days later the Breton forces were beaten at Marino. Clement VII fled to Naples, to put pressure on the Queen and try to drum up some following in Italy. Joanna was favourably disposed towards him; but the populace proved so hostile that he began to fear for his own safety, and, abandoning all hope of dislodging Urban from Rome, fell back on the safe position which the events of recent ecclesiastical history had made available for him. On 13 May 1379 he left Naples, together with the Court he had built up during these eight hectic months; and on 20 June he made his entry into Avignon, bringing back the warmth and bustle of life into the dead, silent halls of the Pontifical Palace.

Thus Christendom now found itself saddled with two Popes. Though such a situation was not without precedent (in fact it had happened on no less than thirty-two previous occasions), a completely new twist was given to events by the fact that *both* candidates had been elected by the Sacred College—and, what was more, by the same Sacred College. On each occasion the vote had been all but unanimous; and on each occasion the same cardinals had acted as electors.

Urban VI now turned into a kind of crazy, paranoid character in the best Shakespearean tradition, with the drama of his career veering wildly between hilarious farce and bloody tragedy. To begin with, he dealt with the defection of the fifteen villains, as he termed them, in the most simple and obvious way: he merely created a whole new Sacred College. The Queen of Naples he excommunicated, and declared deposed (she was later strangled to death). He now assigned the theoretically vacant Neapolitan throne to Charles III, of the Dukes of Durazzo-Anjou, and mounted a crusade against Joanna, which he financed with the proceeds acquired by plundering Church property in the most scandalous fashion.

Charles—an astute Angevin profiteer—duly acquired the Kingdom, but speedily showed his ingratitude. The outraged Urban descended on Naples to remind him of the agreements he had not as yet honoured—including the bestowal of a splendid constellation of cities on one of the Pontiff's favourite nephews. Charles heard him out, with downcast eyes and the expression appropriate to a contrite sinner, after which he went through the motions of a reconciliation. He then had Urban besieged in Nocera. Several times daily Urban would appear at his window between two lighted tapers, and, while sacristans pulled energetically at the bell-ropes, pronounce thunderous sentence of excommunication on the besiegers.

Eventually, Urban got back to Rome, where he at once set about abusing and bullying his new cardinals, just as he had abused and bullied their predecessors. Indeed, he reduced them to such a state of exasperation that some of them swore to tear the tiara from his head and assure him the peaceful tranquillity of private life in his declining years. By a stroke of bad luck the plot was discovered. Urban had the conspirators imprisoned, put to the torture, and executed.

He spent what time remained to him putting a final polish on the hatred with which he was surrounded, and died, amid universal jubilation, on 15 October 1389. But neither his removal from the scene, nor that of his opponent (which took place five years later) was destined to put an end to the Great Western Schism. In Rome and in Avignon, both the legitimate Pope and the antipope had had successors; this not only caused much confusion and spiritual bewilderment, but had most serious consequences as regards ortho-doxy, religious life, and the general moral outlook.

Europe split into two camps of allegiance. Northern and Central Italy, Flanders, Scandinavia, Hungary, Poland, and most of the German states sided with Rome. Avignon had the support of France, the Kingdom of Naples, Scotland, Austria, Savoy, Cyprus, Castile, Navarre, and Aragon.

This division, which exhibited itself in so lamentable a manner at the top of the hierarchy, was repeated at every conceivable level below it. In states and cities, villages and monasteries, bishops, priests, and abbots, the heads of religious communities no less than of knightly Orders, could be seen con-tending—by force of arms if need be—for the possession of their appointments and the right to exercise their office.

Even the saints appeared to be divided, declaring themselves for one Pontiff or the other. Within the orbit of the Roman Church we find Catherine of Siena, Catherine of Sweden (daughter of St Bridget, the visionary who died at Rome in 1373), and Blessed Peter of Aragon; under the Church at Avignon there flourished that extraordinary character Colette of Corbie, Peter of Luxem-bourg (a pathetic and touching figure), and Vincent Ferrer, a towering giant of a Dominican, whom we shall meet again shortly when his path crosses that of the first great Borgia.

In these intestine conflicts, religious authority became more than ever de-pendent on, and victimized by, the political arm, whose intervention and support it solicited at every turn. The mutual hatred and oppression existing between the two factions dictated the prince's decisions and strategy: he would crush the one, and give backing to the other. In the more propitious cases that came before him, he would appropriate the object of contention for himself; in less promising cases, he sold his support for various privileges and concessions. It got to the point where he would apply the *placet* condition—under the terms of which a Papal Bull could neither be published nor implemented without the prince's previous consent—in almost every instance.

The greatest victim of this rivalry—fated to continue, with episodes of in-sensate violence and disconcerting blindness, until 1429—was undoubtedly the authority of Rome, both in its temporal and in its spiritual aspect. The capital of Christendom had already suffered an untold amount from the long cap-tivity in Avignon. It emerged from this struggle with the city on the Rhône reduced to a mere battlefield, held by anarchic rebel forces, where the Pontiff—his prestige and power sadly diminished—had a difficult life, and found it hard to impose even a token degree of discipline.

Such is the background of the situation which the Borgias found, and in which they played their part, all of them (during the crucial period of their history) being closely bound up with the vicissitudes of the Church in Rome.

On the last day of that year during which the disaster of schism fell upon Christianity, there was born, in the castle of Canals, near Jativa, the man destined to bear the name and fortune of the Borgias beyond the confines of Spain.

His father, Domingo, belonged to one of the family's less wealthy branches. A minor country gentleman, his life bounded by the rock of his forefathers and the fields which yielded his meagre revenues, he certainly was of no great account, even in this remote corner of the kingdom. Contemporary documents refer to him sometimes as *doncel*, and sometimes as *labrador*, thus presenting a consistent picture of the well-bred but impecunious *hidalgo*, who though he might not actually cultivate his estates with his own work-roughened hands, nevertheless kept a very close eye on those who did. Of the boy's mother, Francisca Marti, we know only that she came from Valencia.

In accordance with a family tradition, the child was baptized in the collegiate church of Jativa, and given the name Alonso. He very early showed signs of a marked tendency to piety and studiousness. In adolescence, he also revealed a natural gift for teaching, becoming the schoolmaster for the town's peasant children. All this, though at first sight surprising, falls into place beside the family's other characteristics. The line runs clear through from the religious streak displayed by Pedro de Atarés, who founded the monastery of Veruela, to the saintliness which emerges in the fourth Duke of Gandia, by way of the intense (and too little emphasized) devoutness of Alexander VI.

At the age of fourteen, Alonso was sent to continue his studies at the University of Lerida, the ancient Roman Ilerda. This brought him close to the home of his ancestors, in that city which, after the marriage of Ramiro II's daughter to the Count of Barcelona, had become the official residence of the Kings of Aragon. The family's by no means flourishing circumstances tempt one to guess that there may have been some outside help—perhaps from the Court, which watched the private lives of its nobility with assiduous interest—both at the beginning and during the later stages of the boy's career as a student.

This career was a brilliant one, sustained by an acute brain, indomitable tenacity, and a wise choice of studies. Simply by concentrating on an ecclesias-tical profession and the field of jurisprudence, Alonso de Borja already showed that he had summed up his age to a nicety. The troubled state of the Church opened up many possibilities, for pastoral zeal and industrious ambition alike;

the violence of the legal battles that went on between the factions, and within each of them, as well as between the ecclesiastical authorities (who clung stub, bornly to inherited privilege) and the civil authorities (irresistibly drawn towards the assertion of each town's independence, and the development of jealous national groups), all offered vast scope for expansion to talents on the technical side of the legal profession. It is undoubtedly true that the two most marked characteristics of this period were the prevalence of hard-fought litigation, and the virtuoso brilliance of those who specialized in it.

Having graduated *in utroque iure*, Alonso de Borja returned for some while to the haunts of his childhood. His piety never faltered; he was often to be seen kneeling in prayer, either at the nearby Ermita de la Cruz, or in the collegiate chapel of Jativa, or one of the churches of Valencia. And it was at Valencia that he had the meeting which forms the only known episode of his youth; a meeting which set its mark on him, and decided his future destiny.

Also in 1378—the same year that saw the beginning of the schism and the birth of Alonso de Borja—there was ordained priest one of the epoch's greatest protagonists: Vincent Ferrer, better known to Italian hagiographers as San Vincenzo Ferreri.

Vincent was born at Valencia in 1350. Being possessed of a strong religious vocation, he donned the white habit of a Dominican; and when he issued forth from the shady seclusion of his monastery to preach throughout the cities of the kingdom, it was not long before his name acquired an immense and wide, spread fame.

We find it hard today to form any adequate idea of this great preacher, going about his business in the splendid and dramatic sunset of the Middle Ages. The great preacher of those days—idolized not only by a whole population, but by whole peoples—was a disseminator of ideas, one who discussed problems, laid down principles, aroused emotions, a master of thought and life alike.

He rode from city to city, like some spiritual adventurer, to bring each expec, tant crowd the eager fire of his spirit and the overwhelming power of his utterance. He followed the main highways, sometimes escorted by a troop of rough paladins ready to defend him against intemperate demonstrations of popular enthusiasm, and to keep public order. His arrival filled churches, cathedrals, public squares, windows, and the roofs of adjacent houses to over, flowing. When he preached in the open, a flag was always hoisted beside the improvised pulpit, so that his hearers could settle themselves in a spot where the wind carried his voice towards them. And like a wild wind itself, the force of his utterance would fall on the crowd, packed between the columns of the

cathedrals, or under the vault of heaven. His itinerary was marked by a succession of spiritual fires, which left the horizon glowing as if in a blood-red
twilight. This was indeed, the very twilight of medieval Christian sentiment,
and the spasmodic convulsions of the crowd were a consummation of its final
agony.

All the mystical suffering, all the burning religious *integralismo* of a dying age
dominated the spirit of this giant of the Word, this unwearying traveller whose
voice was like the storm, who for forty years trod the roads of Spain, France, and
Italy, preaching penitence and foretelling disasters, moving his listeners, terrifying them, converting them. Having journeyed through the history of his
times as the interpreter of a world on the very brink of change, in 1419 he
brought his extraordinary adventure to an end at Vannes, on the coast of
Brittany, where in the transept on the ancient cathedral of St Peter his tomb
seems forcibly to hold prisoner, not a body, but a mighty voice.

The renown his name enjoyed was due above all to the unprecedented
effectiveness of his intervention in the field of converting the Jews. No other
preacher brought so many Jews to the point of baptism. Yet it is precisely here,
over the matter of his incursion into the Jewish question, that history has
ambushed him, formulating certain serious reservations regarding both the
consequences and the moral validity of his work.

The movement towards Spanish unification carried with it a spirit of racial
and religious intolerance which—sedulously fomented by the old Catholic
nobility—overthrew the peaceful coexistence that had grown up over the
centuries, in various parts of Spain, between Christians, Jews, and Moslems.
Against the Jews—who possessed conspicuous wealth, had enviable social
status, and enjoyed a virtual monopoly of certain professions (e.g. medicine and
tax collecting)—there was unleashed, during the first half of the fourteenth
century, a furious wave of religious persecution, which, under an ostensible
mask of religious zeal, barely concealed feelings of hatred, envy, allied with a
fierce appetite for plunder. Very soon it was made mandatory for Jews to reside
in ghettos, or *juderías*, while various other oppressive and humiliating regulations
were enforced upon them. In 1391 the situation reached a point of open
violence, breaking out in a series of massacres that must be reckoned amongst
the most horrendous which European history has ever had occasion to
record.

The Jews had only two choices open to them. They could either go into
painful and wearisome exile (it may be that amongst these expatriate fugitives
were the ancestors of Christopher Columbus), or else accept baptism. In their
tens of thousands they flocked to enter the One True Fold of the Church; yet

though these mass-conversions seemed to solve the problem, in fact they merely created another rather more thorny one—that of the *conversos* or *marrani*, as newly-baptized Jews or Moors were termed. It was not long before they infil-trated every level of society, including Court circles. They had ties of kinship with the old aristocracy, they crept into the very highest echelons of the ecclesias-tic hierarchy, they held the most influential posts in the civil service. And from the problem of the *conversos*—Christians often of doubtful faith, if not secretly still practising Jews—there presently germinated, under the protective cover afforded by orthodoxy, the fine flower of the Inquisition.

Vincent Ferrer's preaching, therefore, found an all too favourable field for its sensational consequences. For him proselytizing was an easy matter. One of his converts was the rabbi Selemoh ha-Levi, a man brimming over with wisdom and learning who afterwards, under the name of Pablo de Santa Maria, became Bishop of Burgos, tutor to Prince John of Castile, Chancellor of the realm, a luminary of the Church and a guiding spirit behind the Inquisition: perhaps the most distinguished anti-semite to emerge from the ranks of those most ruthless champions of anti-semitism, ex-Jews who had attained to high office. The *conversos*, in fact, supplied the Inquisition not only with its victims, but also with its persecutors.

So it came about that Vincent Ferrer, kindled and stirred by a zeal of un-doubted spiritual nobility, made his own unconscious contribution to the build-up that resulted in a singularly ugly drama.

Something of the mind that cast its influence so widely over Latin Europe comes through in Titian's idealized portrait, now at Rome in the Galleria Borghese. The image it presents is one of marked robustness and sobriety; there is a basic quality about it which the black-and-white Dominican habit accen-tuates with striking effectiveness. Incisiveness of line, contrasting light and shade, and the rugged vigour with which the features are portrayed—all emphasize the man's essential *hispanidad*. Note those large, contemplative eyes under high, arching eyebrows, and the wide, tight-shut lips between bristling growths of hair. Here we have the portrayal of a sombre and burning power in repose.

Alonso de Borja was given an astonishing prediction concerning his future when he went to hear the great Dominican preach in Valencia. The excite-ment aroused by Vincent's sermon was so great that Alonso felt moved to go up to him afterwards and ask to be remembered in his prayers.

Vincent Ferrer looked at him, and seemed deeply moved. Then he raised his eyes and revealed a page of the future. 'My son,' he said, 'I rejoice with you.

Remember that you are destined one day to be the ornament of your country and your family. You will be invested with the highest authority to which mortal man can attain. I myself, after my death, will be an object of your veneration. Strive to keep yourself in your present virtuous life.'[1]

Domingo de Borja's son lowered his eyes under the friar's keen scrutiny. Vincent, smiling, nodded in confirmation of what he had said, and moved away.

A double prediction such as that which Alonso had heard was not easily forgotten; and in point of fact it accompanied him through the whole of his life. Over the years he confided the matter to various friends, who subsequently testified that he had done so. As late as 1449 we find him revealing Vincent's words to another great preacher and future saint, John of Capistrano, the Franciscan, who died a year after he had seen them fulfilled.

More than half a century was to elapse before the Dominican's prophecy came true; but from the moment of their encounter, circumstances seemed to direct Alonso de Borja's life, with sure and patient progress, towards some great climactic achievement.

RIDING THE WAVE OF SCHISM

We may assume that the friendship of the great preacher was not altogether unconnected with Alonso's debut in his professional career. It could not but introduce him to a world of political conflicts and allegiances, of plots and patronage, that was clearly bound to assist his preferment.

The University of Lerida appointed him to a lectureship in the same Faculty where, as a student, he had given evidence of such quick and penetrating intelligence; and through this post he acquired both authority and renown. In less troubled times, a professorial chair would probably have formed the permanent centre for his studious existence. However, events very soon swept him up into their machinery.

At the very beginning of the schism, Vincent Ferrer, with Cardinal Pedro de Luna's urgent encouragement, had come out strongly in favour of the Avignon Pope. In 1380, two years after the Conclave of Fondi, he had even sent King Peter IV of Aragon (known to history by the strange epithet of 'the Ceremonious') a treatise entitled *De moderno Ecclesiae schismate*. His purpose in so doing was to make Peter abandon his wavering neutrality, and declare himself openly for Clement VII. After the latter's death, in 1394, he proceeded, with positively volcanic fervour, to uphold the legitimacy of a Spanish succession, as embodied by his friend Pedro de Luna, whose confessor he was, and who in due course summoned him to Avignon. Vincent stayed there three years before leaving in disgust.

Pedro de Luna—now Pope at Avignon, with the title of Benedict XIII— had had a career which in many respects foreshadows that of the future Callis- tus III. Of noble Aragonese stock, he had been first a student and then a lecturer at the University of Montpellier, subsequently holding ecclesiastical benefits at Cuenca, Saragossa, and Valencia before his appointment as a cardinal in 1375.

When he took up residence in the city on the banks of the Rhône he did not find himself a complete stranger there. Provence and Aragon had at one time enjoyed so close a relationship that (early in the thirteenth century) the two regions had discussed the possibility of political unification. They shared a common background of culture, tradition, and customs. The dialect which Pedro spoke was clearly related to that employed by his predecessors from Languedoc.

Now in contrast to Clement VII, Benedict XIII no longer aimed at seizing the See of Rome in order to sanction his own legitimacy and eliminate the rival claimant; or rather, his ambitions in this direction remained very much *sub rosa*, though he did promise Louis d'Orléans, the French King's brother, a promi- nent fief located in territory belonging to the Papal States. His fundamental problem was, and remained, that of safeguarding the throne he occupied, while the rest of Christendom—writhing in the vice-like grip of this inadmissible dyarchy, and growing daily more scandalized and indignant—cried out for some solution to so urgent a dilemma. The top political leaders of Europe, both Colleges of Cardinals, the more famous Universities, and numerous dis- tinguished theologians all pitched in with various suggestions. These ranged from calling a general council to deposing the two rival Popes and electing a third in their place. The subtle legal quibbles which clever intellectuals brought up in the hope of finding some way out of the impasse merely served to embroil the situation still further. Amid this chaos the Spaniard—who, unfortunately for Catholic Christendom, proved quite remarkably long-lived—clung to his *plenitudo potestatis* with unshakeable tenacity, sustained by a pride worthy of Boniface VIII, a masterly gift for political intrigue, and unrivalled expertise in canon law. These gifts were reinforced by absolute purity of life, a profound belief in his own legitimacy, and the intransigent conviction that he had a duty to fulfil, a dignity to defend, and a divine investiture to uphold in his humble person. Such an attitude let him wriggle through the meshes of every attempt to make him renounce his position voluntarily, and ward off or counter all the blows aimed at dislodging him from his position of proud authority.

He had not occupied the See of Avignon for very long before the atmosphere around him became, first heavy, and then unbreathable. An assembly of the French clergy declared he 'fostered and encouraged schism'. The King turned his back on him, releasing his subjects from their obedience to him, and threatening to cut off his fiscal revenues. The cardinals, with five exceptions, left him in the lurch, even going so far as to make off with his seal. Courtiers and clerks deserted him. The inhabitants of Avignon itself and the Comtat Venaissin generally, egged on by their bishops, rose in revolt against his rule. A certain mercenary captain, Geoffrey de Boucicaut, who feared neither God nor His saints, put him under siege in his own dazzling and towered palace. But *le pape de la Lune*, as the French jokingly called him, countered the hostility of the mad Charles VI and his ministers with a vigorous political line of his own, which involved the backing of the King of Aragon. He faced the desertion of his cardinals and functionaries with the imperturbable sang-froid of a man who knows himself to be morally invincible. Against the rebellious populace, and the mercenaries who besieged him for six long months, he deployed his indomitable hardihood and tenacity.

The epilogue to this period of hostilities saw him a prisoner in his own stupendous palace-fortress (which Jean Froissart described, with justification, as '*la plus belle et la plus forte maison du monde*'), watched over by a garrison of the Duke of Orléans. By the terms agreed on, he was no longer to leave his palace without the King of France's express authorization. Yet though for all practical purposes a prisoner, he still remained Pope.

In the wake of France, Sicily, Castile, Navarre and Provence likewise repudiated his authority; and the Jubilee of 1400, which attracted masses of pilgrims to Rome, crumbled the last bastions of his spiritual prestige. But he was still there, secure in the unassailable conviction of his own dignity.

During the night of 11–12 March 1403 he escaped, in disguise, from the palace (where his virtues as a schismatic, but morally irreproachable, Pontiff had redeemed the memory of more than one legitimate, but corrupt, predecessor) and made his way to safety in the territories governed by the Count of Provence. He never returned to Avignon. The cities of Provence, Languedoc, Roussillon and Aragon all witnessed the passage of this strange figure, this indomitable fighter who emerged from the attack he had undergone stronger than ever, recovering a large part of his lost flock in the process.

His antagonists in Rome were short-lived men. Boniface IX died in 1404, and Innocent VII in 1406. Every time a conclave assembled in vigil it seemed as though the knot of the schism would be cut at last; but this wandering old man bravely deflected every blow, and his opponents struck nothing but empty air.

This was the man—doubtless to be included in a network of influences which embraced not only his confessor Vincent Ferrer, but also the Aragonese Court—to whom Alonso de Borja owed his first advancement in his career. From him he received a canon's stall at Lerida, which supplemented his in-come as a university teacher in a very welcome fashion; by him he was named vicar-general of the city. These were as yet modest enough distinctions; but they testified to the fact that this studious young man, with his lucid intelligence and measured utterance, had already begun to attract some attention.

'O happy election, O blessed return of concord, O union of peace!' cried the luminaries of the Sorbonne, when twenty-four cardinals—fourteen from Rome and ten from Avignon—gathered in council at Pisa to put an end to the schism after months of discussion (amid a dense throng of prelates and ambassadors from all the powers in Christendom), on 26 June 1409 declared the two rival Popes deposed, and nominated a new one to replace them: Pietro Filargis, a Greek, the Archbishop of Milan, who now assumed the title of Alexander V.

The cries of jubilation, however, soon ceased amid some ridicule. Both deposed Popes refused to vacate their respective Sees, since they did not recog-nize the legislators at Pisa as having any authority to deliberate on matters concerning Papal status. So instead of two Popes, Christendom in some astonishment, now found itself saddled with three.

And three there remained, even when in May the following year the Greek breathed his last, since the cardinals lost no time in electing a successor to him. This time their choice fell on that crafty and dissolute character Baldassare Cossa, who gave himself the title of John XXIII.

On the other hand it is true that the two dispossessed Pontiffs had ample excuse for dismissing as mere vain *flatus vocis* the verdict of a synod which had summoned itself, and conducted its deliberations on the gratuitous assumption that a Council—as representative and interpreter of the collective conscience—was thereby superior to the Pope. Their action had its theoretical antecedents in a widespread trend of thought supported by some illustrious names, which were quite above suspicion: a trend of thought which, as far as the actual facts went, seemed abundantly justified, not only by the Church's current plight, but also by those far from infrequent cases of 'Petrine infirmity', as the Parisian teacher Pierre d'Ailly euphemistically termed the moral unworthiness of cer-tain Pontiffs. This did not, however, prevent it from subverting traditional doctrine, and threatening the rigid hierarchical order of that monarchy which the community of the faithful had always hitherto embodied. From Bona-ventura to Albertus Magnus, from Alexander of Hales to Thomas Aquinas, the major exponents of Catholic thought, basing their arguments on a concept of Papal authority as a mandate received directly from Christ, and not from any more or less well-qualified representatives of the democratically-minded faithful, had always asserted the superiority of Pope over Council, the nullity of any synod not Papally convened, and the invalidity of all deliberations undertaken without the Pope's assent, and his express approval.

At Constance, in 1414, there opened what might be defined as the last Grand Assize of decaying medieval Europe. A vast throng of prelates and dignitaries, of experts in every kind of theological doctrine, of great aristocrats, of leading politicians and diplomats, spent whole years carrying out a stormy, verbose consultation at the bedside of that distinguished invalid, the Holy Church, under the lofty patronage of the new Emperor, Sigismond of Luxem-bourg, a handsome, bearded man, energetic of manner and somewhat too authoritarian in his views.

Of the three objectives which the Council set itself—the elimination of schism, the suppression of heresy, and moral regeneration—only the first was achieved, and even that by some very fanciful methods. In the field of reaction against doctrinal deviation, almost the only tangible result was the condemna-tion of Jan Hus, who ended his life at the stake—this being the price he paid for his naïvety in ever entering that hunter's arena to defend his propositions. If a programme of reform had been seriously and effectively implemented at this point, the Church would have been spared the disaster it suffered a century later; but nothing more solid was produced than complaints and invective (especially against the higher clergy), which may have been justified on reli-gious grounds, but merely laboured the obvious.

After a great deal of effort the Council succeeded in getting two of the three rival Popes out of the way, and in annulling the third (at least on paper). This opened the way for the election of yet another candidate. On 29 May 1415 the Council, employing all the most insulting epithets it could think of, pro-claimed the deposition of John XXIII, who shortly before had vanished from the scene. On 15 June Gregory XII, by the hand of his trusty agent Carlo Malatesta, sent the Emperor a formal Act of Renunciation regarding the Roman See; in compensation for his obliging docility, he was nominated Legate *a latere* for the Marches of Ancona, a consolation-prize which he did not enjoy for long, since in the October of 1417 death claimed him.

It now only remained to eliminate Benedict XIII, the former Cardinal de Luna. But against the bastions of his resistance all the Council's industrious efforts struck and bounced off like so many pebbles. Their exhortations, their threats, their enticing promises, all proved equally useless. The man stood rock-like in the conviction of his own righteousness. Abandoning France (where even his most faithful supporters, Armagnac and Foix, were beginning to blow cold) he sought refuge south of the Pyrenees, under the wing of the Aragonese government.

It was in these circumstances that young Alonso de Borja, on 4 May 1416, was designated to present his nation's views and demands at Constance. It is, however, quite certain that he did not go.

The Council now, in 1417, took its last step by declaring Benedict XIII deposed. For about two years the old man had been in retreat at Peñíscola, a rocky knoll standing fortress-like at the end of a tiny sandy peninsula on the Mediterranean coast, half-way between Castellón de la Plana and Tortosa. Though a peculiarly difficult place to storm, in 1233 it had been wrested from the Moors by that admirable monarch James I. It was here that Benedict, now almost ninety, received notification of the Council's decision concerning him, followed by the announcement of Oddone Colonna's election as Pope, under the name of Martin V. He treated both items of news as yet further testimony to the blindness of a misguided world. They could deliberate at Constance to their hearts' content; but the True Church was with him, and lived in him, its unique and irreplaceable bulwark.

He continued to plan for the future and busily set about seeking some way out of the awkward dilemma in which he now found himself. By the following January—a bitter month for him—his last three cardinals had defected; but not even then did he regard himself as beaten. There he stood, on that wave-beaten tongue of land, head held high, a dramatic hero uneasily balanced on the subtle dividing-line between tragedy and farce; and there, for another six years, he continued to play (in complete good faith, and for himself as much as for others) the part of the sole legitimate Pontiff, investing his performance with wonderful dignity and most impressive majesty. In this sea-girt hermitage, as he saw it, there resided the much-assailed but unsinkable Church of Peter, that rock, buffeted but indestructible, against which, by divine promise, the powers of hell could not prevail.

In the opposition camp they now referred to him as 'Signor de Luna'; but they still could not ignore him. His very existence was a thorn thrust into the general desire for peace and tranquillity: a serious stumbling-block, since in Spain (where King Alfonso was using his resistance as a lever to screw con-cessions out of Martin V) vast masses of people still swore by his name.

Alfonso V ascended the throne of Aragon in 1416. At his side there now moved the slight, industrious figure of Alonso de Borja. His native talent, his knowledge of jurisprudence, his common sense and adaptability (the two basic requirements for a good diplomat) his exceptional capacity for hard work, his ability to take a bold stand on certain occasions, and the astuteness with which he steered a prudent course on others—all these qualities had brought him out of obscurity, and advanced his ecclesiastical career still further. Two note-worthy landmarks in this advancement had been a canonry at Barcelona, and the administration of a Valencia parish. Then, in the storm-tossed surge of current affairs—which, while it may sink the improvident without trace, always bears clever, talented men, Machiavelli's *virtuosi*, far and high—by skil-ful manoeuvring he brought himself to the notice of his sovereign, who from 1417 kept him at his side as a secretary and counsellor.

Thus before he was forty, Alonso de Borja found himself the King's con-fidential adviser in all matters regarding relationships with foreign powers, the Holy See in particular: not that of Peñíscola, where the grand old man served as a mere instrument of intimidation and blackmail, but the one which Martin V was confidently preparing to transfer back to Rome.

The support which Alfonso V of Aragon ostentatiously bestowed upon Benedict was given with the intention of extracting two specific concessions from the Pope elected at Constance: first, a reluctant assent to the King's appropriating the greater part of the Church's revenues in Aragonese territory; and second, the more or less exclusive and absolute right to dispose of ecclesias-tical offices, prebends, and benefices. These two aspirations—here as in France, England, Germany, and other parts of Europe—formed a logical corollary to the gradual crystallization of the new national states. These, with their marked tendency towards centralization, and the jealous hoarding of their own re-sources, were liable to oppose any ancient communal concession that would drain national capital out of the country, or encourage interference from some foreign power.

At first Martin V gritted his teeth and made a few concessions. Then, in an attempt to eliminate Benedict from the scene and to force his hand, he sent a mission to Spain under Alamanno Adimaro, the Cardinal of Pisa, its object being to reach agreement with the Aragonese clergy, thus relegating the old man of Peñíscola to the archives while at the same time morally disarming the King.

The optimism of such a project verges on simple-mindedness. At Lerida, where a synod had been convened, Martin V's emissary found himself dealing with fanged and snarling clerics who looked down on him as an interloper, denied him the honour of the chair, and flatly refused to send delegates to disturb the self-styled Pontiff. Adimaro spoke of besieging Peñíscola; sneer-ingly they retorted that the position was impregnable. He then hazarded another suggestion: why did the Aragonese clergy not make a substantial financial gift to the King, as a way of persuading him to drive the antipope into the sea? The request was so patently idiotic that the assembly burst out laughing in his face. The course of the synod was marked by terrible storms and rows, with colourful insults being hurled to and fro; nothing whatsoever came of it, and it left the situation, if anything, more tense than it had been previously.

For Martin V—who, though elected in the Kaufhaus of Constance on 11 November 1417, only reached fickle Rome on 28 September 1420—there was now no remaining course except to wait patiently until death removed his antagonist. This event finally took place on 23 May 1423, by which time the old man was well over ninety—but not before he had, at the last moment, fired a Parthian shot by creating four new cardinals, three of whom, on 10 June, in turn elected a successor: Gil Sánchez Muñoz, the arch-priest of Teruel—who naturally reverted to Avignon tradition by assuming the name of Clement VIII.

Comically enough, the schism secretly spawned a second antipope in France, the idea, presumably, being to produce him on the day that the King of Aragon reached an agreement with Rome. On 12 November 1425, in fact, Jean Carrier—the fourth of those cardinals created by the late Benedict XIII, and his self-styled vicar-general—held a one-man conclave, in conditions of strict secrecy, at which he elevated to the pontifical dignity a completely unknown sacristan from Rodez, one Bernard Garnier. No one at the time knew about this episode; it was only some years later that Carrier revealed his astonishing action to the Count of Armagnac, with whom he had sought refuge. The ex-sacristan never gave any trouble to anybody. But over forty years later, in the territories of Armagnac, he still had some simple-minded followers who looked forward to seeing him returned to Rome in triumph.

With the defunct Benedict XIII replaced by a vigorous Clement VIII on the chess-board of his ecclesiastical policy, Alfonso V continued the game. Alonso de Borja—who, though he did not feel that the time for reconciliation was yet ripe, had foreseen it and was making his preparations accordingly—stood behind him throughout, an incomparable prompter.

The game became appallingly bitter and close-fought after Martin V—thereby disappointing Aragonese aspirations to the throne of Naples—by arrangement with the High Constable, Muzio Attendolo Sforza, declared himself for Louis III of Anjou. The King foamed with rage. He proclaimed Martin V's Papacy illegitimate, forbade his subjects to have any dealings with Rome, and tore up all Papal Bulls. He sent a warning to Cardinal Pierre de Foix, then travelling to Spain as a legate, that if he so much as set foot in the

Kingdom he would lose his head. Finally, he ordered the coronation of Clement VIII to be celebrated with all possible pomp and circumstance.

The schism flared up again with renewed fury, though on a narrower front than before. To begin with, Martin was in a cold sweat of fear. Then he recovered his nerve, and fear gave way to righteous anger. He imperiously summoned the King to Rome to answer for his acts of usurpation and his rebellious conduct, thus demonstrating that a Colonna's nerve did not fail when called upon to deal with outbursts by a sovereign of merely Aragonese ancestry.

It was at this point, when the tension had reached its peak, that Alonso de Borja produced the best evidence for his common sense and realism. He made his sovereign see the dangerously isolated position in which the nation would find itself if it pursued, *à outrance*, a schism which, with all Europe celebrating the return of unity in matters of religious discipline, was clearly a dead issue. He forced him to examine the consequences of an eventual—and by now almost inevitable—excommunication. He underlined the advantages to be gained, after that initial display of intransigence, from a reconciliation with the Pope who was now firmly established at Rome.

The Aragonese monarch was too astute to resist this bland and graceful hand which took him by the halter, and led him towards the pastures of profitable docility. Though he did not answer the summons in person, he lost no time in dispatching to Rome an embassy that was authorized to offer words of peace and homage. He showed himself most willing to embark on friendly discussions with Cardinal Pierre de Foix, who—having been threatened with decapitation—was in no hurry to complete his journey. When the cardinal at last arrived, he was greeted with smiles.

A series of talks followed, in which Alonso de Borja played a preponderant part as intermediary and smoother-out of difficulties. These discussions laid the foundations for a more formal agreement. The cardinal went back to consult with the Pope; in January 1429 he returned and the dispute was brought to a happy conclusion. The King of Aragon renounced his rebellious attitude, and cast forth the canker of schism from his bosom. In return for this favour, Martin V offered him the exorbitant sum of 150,000 florins.

Clement VIII, submitting—with a very good grace—to the exhortations which Alonso de Borja addressed to him in the Cortes of Teruel, on 14 August 1429 divested himself of the Papal mantle and obediently returned to the ranks of the Roman hierarchy, being nominated Bishop of Majorca by way of compensation. His cardinals, to save face (and in the hope of saving something more substantial from this disaster), went into conclave on the symbolic

Peñíscola, and with all due solemnity proceeded to elect as Pope the man who had already held that office for the past twelve years—Martin V.

The day after Clement VIII's abdication, Alonso de Borja, as was only just, received due reward for all his hard work and wise counsel. In smiling agree ment, his King and his new Pope bestowed upon him the rich and pres tigious bishopric of Valencia. The winding-up of this final aftermath in the split of the Church had been, in fact, all his doing.

He was not, as yet, a priest; but this stumbling-block was considerably removed five days later, when he received ordination at none other place but Peñíscola, which had been the stronghold of his old friend and protector. The next day, 21 August 1429, he was consecrated bishop by Cardinal Pierre de Foix.

It was undoubtedly a fact of some significance that this man, born in the same year as witnessed the outbreak of the Great Western Schism, should have been carried forward on the wave of events which it set in motion, from his modest post at Lerida to a confidential relationship with the King, and the episcopal seat of Valencia. Still more significant was the fact that, after long service in the ranks of the Avignon opposition (where he took several oppor tunities of advancing his career), he should now have striven so hard to give that opposition the *coup de grâce*—and by so doing have duly reaped the reward destined to open up a dazzling future for him in a now orderly and pacified Rome.

He was fifty-one years old; and that prediction by the Dominican preacher (who had died just a decade earlier, far away in Brittany) was beginning to acquire a flavour of credibility at last.

THE PASSAGE TO ITALY

Alonso de Borja's collaboration in his King's policies grew closer and deeper during the busy years that followed, till it assumed the form of a perfect partner ship. Always beside the sovereign—that man of vast ambitions, irrepressible energy, and genuinely magnanimous character—the Bishop of Valencia proved a source of acute ideas and timely moves. If in certain situations he was capable of counselling stubbornness, audacity, and carrying a trial of strength to within a hair's breadth of breaking-point, he could also (and rather more often) pro pose a friendly compromise at the precise moment when the opposition was ready to make substantial concessions. He was a master of tactics, and perhaps the brain behind a kingdom.

If Alfonso avoided forcing issues disastrously when they were most exacerbated, and if (after conflicts to which he brought all the toughness and obstinacy inherent in his nature) he reaped such conspicuous successes at the conference-tables of diplomacy, then the credit should often go to the ex-lecturer from Lerida, who always kept a watchful eye on Alfonso's impulses, and indeed on occasion seemed actually to encourage them; yet at the critical moment would lay a gentle hand on his shoulder, and move forward to interpose himself between the King and his opponent, with the smile that characterizes the man of peace.

The principal adversary (or rather the power from which he both wanted to, and could, obtain rather more) was still the Pontiff, though there was alarming internal opposition from various quarters: the restlessness of the cardinals, the threat of subversive Conciliar doctrines, and the state of permanent danger created by the anarchic arrogance of the Roman barons. These left him very weak in the sphere of foreign policy, and forced him to make many concessions to the demands, threats, and blackmailing gambits of the new young nations. The latter were impatient to shake off the yoke of servitude that belonged to a bygone age, to stand up in proud and total autonomy, and to profit by the disturbed international situation, which offered them a chance of enlarging their territories.

So on the battlefield of Conciliar debate—latterly somewhat exacerbated, after the death of Martin V, and now in its second round, with the Synod of Basle—the prelates and theologians fought fiercely, never pulling their punches, to make Eugenius IV accept the principle of his subordination to the representatives of Christendom. And behind them were other forces. There was the Emperor, who deluded himself that he could use the humiliation of the Papacy as a springboard for his own persistent—but henceforward anachronistic—striving after European supremacy. There were the kings of the new states, now in their final phase of development, peddling programmes of expansion and complete independence. There were the sovereigns of minor principalities, some of which had originally arisen as feudal domains of the Church, who now showed themselves eager to shake off, *de jure* as well as *de recto*, the last vestiges of Pontifical authority. There were the wealthy commercial republics, which often found their interests conflicting with those of the Church's temporal authority. There was the emergent bourgeoisie of Europe, now progressively taking over the leadership of political and civil life—a leadership hitherto held by the decadent nobility, tied to an obsolete system of traditional privilege. There were the pulsating, irresistible currents of a new trend in thought, a new vision of life and its realities, a new conception of the world and its problems, a new idea of man and his destiny, which countered the medieval emphasis on the wretchedness and misery of this world's creatures by magnify, ing their greatness and their dignity, setting up experience against dogma, freedom in place of constraint.

And behind the impatient longing which found expression in hammering programmes of reform, there stood one clear and urgent objective (which had already manifested itself in the more significant religious movements of the last two centuries): to bring the Church back to its original spiritual integrity, not only by purifying it, but also by dismantling its temporal power and limiting its vexatious incursions into politics.

In a certain sense, then, it can be said that the struggle lined up the Pope against Europe; the traditional prerogatives of the Holy See against the spiritual and intellectual uneasiness of an awakening world; the Church's worldly power against a new political structure (with an interest in overthrowing it), and a religious feeling which, as time went on, found increasing difficulty in accepting that power as it stood.

On the plane of spiritual authority the Pontiff had, with the Council of Florence (1439), routed the opposition in Basle, and won a victory that was afterwards to be clinched by the Lateran Council of Julius II. In matters of temporal power, however, the Church had gone against the spirit of the age, which is never, ultimately, defeated, and the march of history—that manifesta, tion of collective awareness—which in the long run overcomes all opposi, tion.

Through the strenuous, persistent, and open, minded activities, both political and military, of its Renaissance Popes, the Vatican was to succeed (at a high price, admittedly) in recovering its lost positions by force, and in consolidating its anti, evangelical territorial dominion, thus perpetuating throughout the Italian peninsula a state of affairs that was strikingly obsolete by comparison with the New Order in Europe. Nevertheless, the Church's ambitions for worldly power and rule now stood condemned, both by the conscience of Christendom and the consistent logic of events; and against that verdict there was no appeal.

The second key moment in Alonso de Borja's career arose, like the first, from his skilful exploitation of disagreement, in negotiating a peace settlement that could not fail to bring an ample reward in its wake.

Success depends on one's ability to adapt fortune to circumstances; and the most salient circumstance which presented itself to the Bishop of Valencia's shrewd diplomatic mind was a new disagreement between his sovereign and the Holy See—ruled now by the always impetuous and frequently reckless Eugenius IV—regarding the investiture of the Kingdom of Naples.

With Sicily lost after the episode of the Vespers, the Angevins (the head of the clan now being Charles I, created Count of Anjou and Maine by his brother St Louis, King of France) had nevertheless still retained their hold on the Kingdom of Naples. The throne was occupied by a succession of direct claimants, culminating in Joanna I, who might best be described as a somewhat coarse copy of Clytemnestra. Her first husband, Andrew of Hungary, who was also her cousin, she had assassinated by a hired killer. His three successors she sucked dry in turn, and was herself finally strangled, on 12 May 1382, in the castle of Muro Lucano; despite all those husbands she had failed to produce any offspring who could succeed her.

The struggle for the succession was fought out between three collateral branches of the family, those of France, Hungary, and Durazzo, and ended with the victory of the last-named. This new dynasty literally plagiarized the misfortunes of its predecessor; the line failed in 1435 with the death of another Joanna—slightly less lewd and dissolute than the first one, but disastrously inept when it came to governing a kingdom, and the unfortunate victim of favourites, intriguers, adventurers, and *condottieri*, whose consciences were as elastic as their appetites were fierce.

In 1420 this same Joanna II, with a view to frustrating the hopes and expectations of the French Angevins, had adopted Alfonso V of Aragon. Never was any act of feminine spite more laden with dramatic consequences: from it, indeed, there was destined to spring a series of wars destined to usher in the great tragedy of Italy. The first period of strife for the Queen's inheritance took place during her lifetime. Supporting her were the Aragonese forces of Alfonso V and some mercenary bands under that truculent figure Braccio da Montone. On the other side, against her, were the troops of Louis III of Anjou, and those commanded by Muzio Attendolo Sforza, the Queen's ex-favourite and High Constable of the realm.

In 1423 Joanna II performed an abrupt volte-face. Under Martin V's careful manipulation, she repudiated the adoption of Alfonso, and proclaimed French Anjou her heir. This was followed by the Aragonese monarch's defeat at Aquila, which forced him to beat a hasty retreat, shamed and furious, on to Spanish soil.

In 1434 Louis III died, and the Queen, who herself had only a few months of life left to her, now assigned her throne, as a legacy, to his brother René. And with this decision there opened the second phase of the Franco-Spanish conflict, since it goes without saying that the Aragonese monarch did not suffer from the kind of moral scruples that would force him to respect the final wishes of the deceased.

His opponent was one of the most interesting figures in this whole period: a bookish, imaginative man, contemplative and rural-minded, condemned by fate to prove himself in a world of proud ruffians, having known and savoured the perfection of happiness on his enchanted Provençal estates—pottering round the vineyards (it was he, so the story goes, who first introduced the cultivation of the muscatel grape), and browsing through his books in one of those bright, cheerful châteaux set beside a flowing stream, where his ghost still seems to linger, enjoying the sunlit stillness. Besides French and Provençal, he knew Latin, Greek, Italian, Hebrew, and Catalan. He painted, and illuminated manuscripts. He was also a composer, and could play the lute and the mandora. He wrote poetry that was not unworthy of those charming Courts of Love that were once held in the magical, rocky scenery of Les Baux, the jewel of Provence. He pursued studies in mathematics, jurisprudence, and geology. He was, in short, a sort of *homo universalis* on a small scale. Besides all this he showed himself an enlightened patron, a sovereign of simple tastes and familiar manners, a good master who enjoyed chatting with his subjects, organizing popular festivals (such as that of Tarasque, which still survives today), and recreating a vogue for ancient cavalry manoeuvres.

But to suppose that these eminently pacific tendencies had extinguished in him the warrior virtues of his race would be to do him a grave injustice. When the occasion called for it, he showed that he could put away his books, abandon his pastimes, and gird on his sword with a stout heart. At the age of nine he had lost his father, and three years later he was married to Isabella, heiress to the Duchy of Lorraine; but to take possession of his inheritance he had needed to sally forth under arms, and as things turned out his adversaries had taken possession of him instead. They continued to hold him prisoner, in defiance of an arbitration by the Emperor Sigismond; and to obtain release from captivity he had been forced to disgorge a large quantity of gold pieces—good-quality money, in contrast to the coins he minted himself, which his subjects referred to as *parpaillottes*.

Now his lucky star, by forcing him to replace his brother as claimant to Naples, once again tore him away from the sweet *otia* of poetry and scholarship, to fight for the possession of a distant domain which, in his private heart, he did not, we may assume, really care about to any great extent.

The war—a long and bitter one—was fought out with the participation of Italian *condottieri* on a large scale, and saw more than one peninsular State divide itself between either side. To begin with, the fortunes of war favoured René of Orléans, who was supported by the Duchy of Milan and the sea-power of Genoa, and also had the industrious backing of Pope Eugenius IV—an align-ment which Alfonso of Aragon repaid in kind by ostentatiously lining his own forces up behind the Council of Basle.

At one point it looked as though nothing could prevent the Neapolitan crown from adorning René's learned brow: this was when a Genoese fleet met that of Aragon in the waters off Ponza, gave the Aragonese a tremendous drub-bing, and captured Alfonso in person (August 1435). Philip-Maria Visconti had the prisoner sent to Milan. The Angevins rejoiced, Eugenius IV gave thanks to Almighty God, and the Genoese chuckled at the thought of all the rich ransom with which their coffers would soon be overflowing. They had reckoned neither with the political hard-headedness of Visconti, nor with the diabolical slipperiness of the Aragonese monarch. Alfonso, in fact, perhaps by buying the allegiance of that all-influential figure Zanino Riccio, the Duke's adviser—and certainly by dangling before the latter's eyes the bugbear of a French hegemony in Italy—contrived to obtain, not only his own freedom (at a comparatively cheap price) but also the cordial backing of Visconti; and one fine autumn day he took off from Milan, like some distinguished guest at the conclusion of a State visit. The line taken by Philip-Maria, which so enraged the Genoese that they were driven into revolt, skilfully blended generosity and common sense, since (for obvious geographical reasons) France was more vulnerable than Spain; and over the Duchy of Milan—always supposing he had no male heirs to succeed him when he died—there lay the shadow of a French claimant, fruit of his sister Valentina's marriage to Louis of Orléans. The claim was, indeed, to be lodged, openly and with some determination, on his death a couple of years later.[2]

The war went on. By the summer of 1442, when Alfonso conquered Naples, it could be regarded as over to all intents and purposes. But this event by no means marked the final sunset of Angevin hopes, which the French Court thereafter inherited, and raised to the level of a national aspiration. For many years yet René of Orléans would continue to play the pretender's role though with ever-sparser conviction and increasingly obvious detachment. Time brought white hairs to his head while leaving his royal prerogatives as platonic as ever. Yet the title of sovereign remained firmly attached to his person: his Provençal subjects still referred to him as *le bon roi René*. But King of what, now?

Alfonso of Aragon entered Naples on 2 June 1442, passing with lowered head under an aqueduct which, some nine centuries earlier, had also witnessed the

entry of that distinguished figure Count Belisarius. He made up for this enforced gesture of humility the following year, when he allowed himself a most
lavish repeat performance, for which a gap some forty ells wide was knocked in
the walls. Through this he passed in a gilded coach, wearing the costume of a
triumphant Roman general of the Imperial era, his sunburnt features shaded
under a cloth-of-gold canopy borne by twenty young noblemen. Allegorical
floats, a self-propelled tower, riders in fancy dress, and a 'Julius Caesar' (who,
in bombastic Italian verse, explained the significance of the allegories) all helped
to enrich the procession, whose proud splendour rendered somewhat futile all
those tributes to Alfonso's modesty for not having agreed to accept the crown
when Spanish-Neapolitan flattery suggested it. In point of fact, the aristocratic
opposition had played very little part in the mounting of this blown-up carnival
pageant, which sent all Italy into raptures.

So the Aragonese dynasty settled in Naples, and launched itself, with all
sails spread, upon the waters of Italian political life—thus opening a long
chapter of Hispanicization, which was not to prove among the more fortunate
experiences undergone by that supine peninsula in the course of the centuries.

Hitherto Alfonso had given numerous proofs of that skill, energy, and
tenacity which made him stand out like a giant among the leading figures of his
age; but on the stage of this new Kingdom, lit by the brightness of a culture and
a civilization which had dazzled the whole world, he proceeded to reveal other
aspects of his exceptional personality, which abundantly justified his title of 'the
Magnanimous'. *Graecia capta ferum victorem cepit*: the old tag applies. The
Spaniard (though very far, we may note, from being a barbarian) acclimatized
himself in the most breathtaking fashion to the atmosphere of Renaissance
Italy.[3] During the sixteen continuous years that he occupied the Neapolitan
throne, he showed himself a magnificent nobleman, a passionate devotee of
antiquity, an enthusiastic—and eminently well-read—patron of writers and
artists, and a monarch of affable, not to say jovial, temperament, endowed with
a natural exuberance that gladly found its outlet in hunting, entertainment, and
love-affairs. Though already elderly, he embarked on his romance with
Lucrezia d'Alagno in a spirit of youthful ardour. For the visit of the Emperor
Frederick III he did not hesitate to squander 150,000 gold florins. We find
him presenting Poggio Bracciolini with an enormous sum as compensation for
his Latin translation of Xenophon's *Cyropaedia*; sending out a humanist, in
1451, to observe the Milanese-Venetian war *in situ*, and write a commentary on
it; telling Giannozzo Manetti, on his appointment as secretary, at the most
lavish salary: 'If the need arises, I will share my last crust with you,' and when
the writer spoke, listening to him in still, almost ecstatic concentration; rap-

turously venerating every illustrious relic of Roman civilization. The esteem and admiration which he enjoyed in Italy were such that, when it looked as though there might be a chance of his extending his sway over all Italy, a man as intelligent as Aeneas Silvius Piccolomini could write to a friend, telling him to rejoice at the prospect, because of the great things which Alfonso's 'kingly nature' gave grounds for anticipating that it would bring about.

In reality, it is only fair to add, Alfonso's 'kingly nature' also had its darker side. Such generosity and luxury and downright extravagance, on the grand scale, would not have been possible without a certain inbred financial shrewd- ness which was by no means so popular with his subjects. Though he secured his revenues by means of ferocious taxation, he was always thirsty for more. After a lethal earthquake in the Abruzzi, he did not scruple to press the sur- vivors, with ruthless insistence, for the monies owed not only by the living, but also by the dead. He bulked his income with various devious and unpleasant expedients, ranging from the declaration of a crusade, which would shake con- tributions out of the clergy, to the crafty promotion of obviously covetous ad- ministrators (he waited, cat-like, until they had made their pile, and then pounced, reducing them to beggary).

His adviser Alonso de Borja remained at his side in Naples, and very soon emerged into the limelight himself. Relations with the Holy See—which had clouded over after a brief sunlit interlude in 1429, and were now once more stormy—undoubtedly called for his brand of enlightened intervention. As I have already shown, tension was heightened, during the most ruinous phase of the war, by the open pro-Angevinism of Eugenius IV, that intransigent vege- tarian Pontiff (who had been forced to flee from Rome, by boat, after a public uprising, with a hail of stones from the mob rattling about his ears, and to seek asylum in Florence). There was a moment when Alfonso made it clear that he took the rebel Council of Basle very seriously indeed—it had put up a new anti- pope in the person of the ex-Duke of Savoy—and considered the idea of dis- patching Alonso de Borja, as the man in best odour with the higher Aragonese clergy, to be his representative there. But the Bishop of Valencia had had the good sense to avoid so compromising a mission. He was a man who held firmly by that fundamental rule of diplomacy: always leave the way open for a profitable reconciliation. In any case, what secure or valid advantage was there to be obtained from that mad hornet's nest of sedition buzzing away on the banks of the Rhine?

When Naples was firmly in Alfonso's possession, and it became clear that Angevin claims were now a mere subject for academic debate, the fugitive

Pope—considering matters in the peaceful atmosphere of the Florentine monas/
tery of Santa Maria Novella—recognized the futility of further resistance. At
this point Alonso went smoothly and skilfully into action. An understanding
with the Aragonese King of Naples would suit the unfortunate Pontiff very
well just now. He was impatient to be back in Rome, and his subjects there
had themselves begun to beg for his return, since during his absence the city had
plumbed an abyss of squalor and misery. Such a pact would leave him stronger,
more secure, in a position where he could face up to the insolence of the
foundering—and by that degree the more spiteful—Council of Basle, besides
freeing himself from the molestations of Francesco Sforza, whose initial position
as vicar of the Ancona Marches had not prevented him, in due course, from
committing various acts of predatory hostility against the Church's territories.

These negotiations—conducted on behalf of the King by Alonso da Borja,
the Pope's representative being Cardinal Scarampo, a slight but steely figure,
and one of the most dynamic prelates of his age (after the fall of his colleague
Giovanni Vitelleschi he was made head of the government in Rome)—cul/
minated in a formal agreement, which was concluded at Terracina on 14 June
1443.

The Pontiff invested Alfonso of Aragon with the Kingdom of Naples as his
fief; in addition he was also granted, for the term of his natural life, two cities—
Benevento and Terracina—belonging to the Papal States. (Less than a year
later the Pope was to confirm the sovereign's bastard son Ferrante in his right
to succeed his father.) Alfonso, for his part, undertook to recognize the Pope's
legitimacy, which meant breaking off all relationship with the Synod of Basle,
and ignoring its deliberations *en bloc*; to respect ecclesiastical privileges; to pay
the Church an annual and quasi/symbolic vassal's tribute, the most striking
feature of which was the traditional white horse; to provide ships for a forth/
coming crusade against the Turks; and to send 50,000 men as reinforcements
for the Papal troops, with the object of dislodging Sforza from the Ancona
Marches.

For both the contracting parties this was an excellent agreement. The Arago/
nese monarch saw his *de facto* possession of this newly/acquired Kingdom
(originally a Church fief) given the sanction and seal of complete legitimacy.
The Pope, meanwhile, had pulled a powerful support from under the dissident
Council (which had placed great hopes in Alfonso), and could now prepare
for his return to Rome—an event which actually took place three and a half
months after the signing of the treaty, on 28 September 1443, thus putting an
end to an exile which had lasted for nine years and more.

In Naples, whether clearing up ecclesiastical affairs, or applying himself to the wearisome task of reorganizing a kingdom that was in a sadly chaotic state after so many years of war, Alonso de Borja continued to do work of the first importance, which he handled in a supremely competent manner. One of his most significant undertakings was the institution of the famous Santa Chiara tribunal. At the same time he supervised Prince Ferrante's education; this pedagogical task had somewhat disconcerting results, since Alfonso's son was later to reveal himself as one of the most cynical and ferocious individuals—if also one of the most intelligent—who ever wore a crown.

Above all, it was in Naples that Alonso de Borja reaped the reward for his work as a mediator. He received it in the spring of 1444, when Eugenius IV summoned him to Rome and there, on 2 May, invested him with a cardinal's scarlet robes, assigning him as his titular church the ancient basilica of the Santi Quattro Coronati. It was a well-earned recompense—and one which gave the Pope the added benefit of introducing to the Sacred College an excellent jurist, a wise political counsellor, a most valuable link between Rome and Naples. It would also serve to detach him from his close connection with the Aragonese monarch, whom, it might be said, he had served almost too well.

THE RISE OF RODRIGO

In Rome, Alonso de Borja very soon made his mark as a figure worthy of all respect: irreproachable in his private life, of exemplary piety, with simple and sober tastes, dignified in manner. As cardinal he remained, essentially—and more than ever now that removal from the Aragonese Court had freed him from a whole load of other duties, leaving him more or less entirely on his own—the scholarly student of his quieter years.

People praised his independent spirit, his horror of adulation and intrigue, his abstention from all political cliques. His naturally dry, reserved character helped to keep him isolated. Sharp in his estimate of a situation, intellectually precise, dry and cutting in his judgements, he was one of those individuals whose words are few and always well-considered, and who, while they win ready esteem, seldom meet with much sympathy.

For eleven years he was destined to remain in this situation, an attentive and largely silent observer of events and men—beginning, naturally, with his colleagues. The twenty-six members of the Sacred College—eleven Italians, and fifteen foreigners—fell readily into two distinct groups, one being distinguished by its pious disposition, austerity of behaviour, and sincere devotion to the good of the Church, and the other by inclinations and habits which treatises on ecclesiastical history are wont to describe euphemistically as 'worldly'.

Those prelates who could at once be assigned to the 'exemplary' group included such figures as Juan de Carvajal the Spaniard, a diplomatic of the very highest ability—made manifest during the twenty-two legateships he had held— and a shining example of every Christian virtue, not excluding that open and winning 'harmlessness of the dove' which (as we learn from the Gospel) can very well coexist with the 'wisdom of the serpent'. There was also his fellow-countryman Juan de Torquemada, a well of theological doctrine, a first-class polemicist, and an ardent champion of Papal rights. There was John Bessarion, the former Basilian monk from the Peloponnese, a famous exponent of Chris-tian Platonism, and the last Greek to achieve European status for centuries, who advocated reunion between the two Churches, and had gone over to Catholicism in December 1439, together with Archbishop Isidore of Kiev. There was Domenico Capranica, a scion of the Roman nobility, who had been unjustly held back from advancement by Eugenius IV, and whose rare humanistic learning (he had a library of over 2000 volumes, free of access to any scholar) was combined with a sense of pastoral responsibility well attested by one scheme of reform he put forward, even though this came to nothing.

Notable amongst the 'worldly' group were Scarampo, already referred to above, a man with every necessary qualification to join the ranks of the most devilish petty tyrants in the Italy of his day; Pietro Barbo, nephew to the present Pope, an outstanding and markedly cheerful prelate, much addicted to all the good things of life; and Guillaume d'Estouteville, a fabulously wealthy and blue-blooded nobleman related to the French royal family, who had a fantastic palazzo (in which he led the life of an Oriental pasha), and sometimes passed through the streets of Rome with a cavalry squadron three hundred strong to escort him.

On 23 February 1447 death ended the tribulations of the Venetian Pontiff, who on his death-bed—if we can trust Vespasiano da Bisticci—was heard to murmur self-pityingly: 'O Gabriel, Gabriel, how much better for your soul's salvation would it have been had you never become Pope or Cardinal, but had died in your Order!'

On the evening of 4 March Alonso Borja went into conclave, together with the other seventeen cardinals then present in Rome. The electors had one factor very much on their minds: the long-standing rivalry between the two most distinguished families of Rome, represented in the Sacred College by Cardinals Prospero Colonna and Giovanni Orsini of Tagliacozzo. It is to be presumed that Alonso de Borja, along with the other two Spaniards, gave his own vote to the former, who was King Alfonso's candidate. But Colonna's candidature failed by two votes, he having obtained ten only instead of the necessary twelve. At the third scrutiny there was elected—by the narrowest of margins, and to everyone's astonishment—one Tommaso Parentucelli, a man who in the space of three years had risen to the very top of the ecclesiastical tree, winning in quick succession a bishop's mitre, a cardinal's hat, and now the Papal tiara. He was a small, lean, quiet-voiced man, with piercing eyes and quick, springy movements. He took the title of Nicholas V. And his pontificate, as everyone knows, was the delight of the humanists—even those humanists who circled round the Christian *civitas* as outsiders, pronouncing the names of gods that had not been heard of for over a millennium.

Though he now moved in a Roman ambience that was lit by the vivid morning brightness of the Renaissance, Alonso de Borja had the closed mind of a Spaniard who was still basically living in the Middle Ages, and an Aristotelian head stuffed with syllogisms. He must have prepared himself to lower his eyes when confronted by the enthusiastic cultural activities of the new Pope, who now girded himself to introduce into the life of the Church all the intellectual ferment of a new era, and to throw open the whole ecclesiastical edifice to the winds of contemporary artistic change. During the eight years of his pontificate he accomplished a quite staggering range of projects, displaying in the process a breadth of vision which not only makes him the first (and, morally speaking, the best) of the great Renaissance Popes, but in certain respects would seem to rank him above even the most distinguished of his successors, including Julius II and the over-rated Leo X.

Alonso de Borja profited by his position in Rome to adapt himself to the spirit of the times; he assimilated Nicholas V's example of literary and artistic culture, and fitted smoothly into the new Roman intellectual climate. Though perhaps too old for such an effort (he was now close on seventy) he nevertheless took advantage of his position to place himself on the wheel of nepotism, which was one day to bear him aloft with majesty and momentum.

Before embarking on this subject in detail, it will be as well, right at the beginning, to make some reference to a character who—despite his mysterious origins—enjoys a certain importance in the present story. He is by no means the only member of the Borgia family to wander through the pages of history with an interrogation-mark where his father's name should be. I am alluding to Francesco—born in 1432, Papal Treasurer under Alexander VI, Bishop of Teano in 1495, Bishop of Cosenza from 1498, made a cardinal in 1500, tutor to the young Rodrigo, Duke of Bisceglie, after the Borgias' fall from power—so implacable an enemy of Julius II's that the latter had him thrown into gaol, and would have stripped him of his cardinal's robes had he not finally coun-tered this move, in 1511, by dying.

In the absence of enlightening evidence, some scholars investigating the much-debated Borgia family tree have affiliated him to Alonso, who, they claim, sired him on some unknown woman while Bishop of Valencia. Others attribute the honour of his begetting to a certain Juan de Borja y Doms, the uncle of Alexander VI, of whom literally nothing else is known.

Two considerations are normally adduced against the hypothesis of Alonso's paternity. It is highly improbable that, after an irreproachable youth, he should suddenly have embarked on some illicit and clandestine love-affair when he was coming up for fifty; and there is also the marked lack of interest which he would seem to have taken in the enigmatical Francesco, though he was other-wise given to quite shameless favouritism where his nephews were concerned.[4]

In distant Jativa and its environs, the cardinal's relatives very soon began to receive tokens of his remembrance and generous solicitude for their welfare. Alonso had left four sisters there: Juana, Francisca, Catalina and Isabel. All four now began to receive gifts of money from Italy. This beneficent balm descended rather more copiously upon Catalina and Isabel, who were married with children. Catalina, the wife of one Juan del Milá, had two children: Pedro and Luís Juan. Isabel, the favourite, had married her cousin, Jofré de Borja y Doms (whose mother belonged to a highly distinguished patrician Aragonese family), and had borne him numerous offspring: two sons, Pedro Luís and Rodrigo, and four daughters, Beatrice, Damiata, Juana and Tecla.

The boys, whose smooth brows bore the promise of their family's future fortunes, naturally incurred more solicitous attention from their uncle the cardinal; he was quite consciously and deliberately setting out to raise his line to greatness. This meant planning the future long in advance, and deciding, even at this stage, what each youngster was to do: a secular career for Pedro Luís de Borja and Pedro del Milá, an ecclesiastical one for Rodrigo de Borja and Luís Juan del Milá.

In the spring of 1449, with a favourable wind and under the auspices of their kinsman the cardinal, the Borgia clan put their first advance guard aboard ship for Rome in the person of Rodrigo, the future Alexander VI, now an adoles-cent. It is not certain whether he travelled alone, or accompanied by his brother and two cousins: we know that before his elevation to the Papacy Alonso had summoned more than one member of his family and given them patronage in his capacity as cardinal.

Rodrigo was borne at Jativa on 1 January 1431, and grew up amid the privileged conditions proper to the son of a country gentleman in the provinces. From a *Life of Alexander VI and Duke Valentino*, of which manuscript versions survive in various libraries, at Rome and other Italian cities, and which is probably to be attributed to Bernardino Babotti, 'a Spanish jurist and theologian, learned in many fields of knowledge', we learn that the boy's father, Jofré de Borja y Doms, was a person of some consequence, with connections at Court. 'He had made many journeys to the benefit of the Spanish Crown, and enjoyed the honour of discharging the greatest offices in that realm. . . . He was a remarkable person of great intelligence, and bearing much responsibility for the affairs of the kingdom, since he had risen to command many fortresses through his watchfulness and high integrity, and those other qualities which vied in his person; having for so long discharged such lofty and conspicuous tasks, he acquired much wealth and credit, and got the reputation, by current report, of being the greatest man of his day.'

After limning the father's characteristics with such complex emphasis, Babotti—who claims to have written during Alexander VI's pontificate, though all the surviving copies of his work can be dated to a later period, and contain plentiful interpolations—goes on to sketch the personality of the son: 'Rodrigo, when still a child, revealed the great intelligence he had inherited from his father; indeed the said child attracted respect and esteem because of his disposition and his abilities.'

His early education was entrusted to the guidance of Antonio Nagueroles, a local luminary whom his father had brought in to be the boy's tutor. Even then, it would seem, his natural aptitude showed itself in such bright and indeed blinding flashes that Don Jofré, 'seeing that the child's true bent was for study', had made it 'his first concern to have him properly taught, under the most learned and knowledgeable instructors'.

When Don Jofré died, prematurely, in 1441, his widow Isabel did not hesitate to move, with her children, to Valencia, so that the boy could pursue his studies in a more propitious environment. At the same time it should not be thought that Rodrigo was always bent over his books, nor that he spent all his time and energy in the company of scholars. 'Apart from his study of letters', Babotti hastens to add, 'he had a great talent for military matters and the handling of arms. From childhood onwards he would go hunting in the countryside with arquebus, pistol, and dagger; and (when the opportunity arose) he would likewise display his mettle in this sphere.'

Indeed, he displayed his mettle so well that many people predicted he would end up on the gallows. 'As Rodrigo grew in years, so he also grew in pride and haughtiness, cruelty and tyranny, showing himself stern, implacable, vindic⁄tive and unpredictable in his actions. It is said that when only twelve years old, he killed another boy in Valencia—his equal in age, but of low birth—by driving his scabbard again and again into his belly, to punish him for having uttered some indecent words. . . . This was the first test of his pride, and the first incident that forced people to recognize the stuff he was made of, the kind of spirit and temper he had.'

This horrifying episode is neither confirmed nor denied by our other sources and we may legitimately feel somewhat sceptical about it. But there is no good reason to disbelieve the moral picture which Babotti draws of the boy, after so glowing a tribute to his intelligence. In any case, the characteristics he delineated are perfectly consonant with those that more or less typify a contemporary Spanish *hidalgo*. Above all, we have the scornful pride, the despotic and aggressive toughness, the fierce instinct for a vendetta, that were all basic ingredients of the Borgia character: qualities, moreover, which the period not only tolerated, but actively encouraged.

A long period spent in the environment of the Roman Curia; experience of Vatican diplomacy (guaranteed to impart a sophisticated polish); thirtyfour years of patience and restraint, sustained even after the death of Callistus III, in a campaign to secure the Pontifical Throne; the effort of selfdiscipline, combined with an everincreasing prevalence (in his character and behaviour alike) of that sensual hedonism which formed another element in the Borgias' burdensome heritage, and which offered his more violent impulses a convenient loophole—all these things enabled the future Alexander VI to free himself from the tyranny of his wilder instincts, and to fashion himself a marvellous mask of meekness. This is not to say that the old fires did not flare up again sporadically. We have eloquent examples of this in his dealings with Giuliano della Rovere, or the ambassadors of Their Most Catholic Majesties of Spain. But this hereditary wildness, though repressed by him, was to be transmitted—in a horrifyingly undiluted form—to his son Cesare, the most typical Borgia of them all.

It is hard not to smile at the curious course of events when one sets the anecdote concerning the murder of the boy from Valencia (an event putatively dated to 1443) beside a Papal Bull of 1445, in which Nicholas V declared, substantially, that so many reports had reached him concerning the merits of the fourteenyearold Rodrigo de Borja ('probity of life and conduct', 'laudable proofs of rectitude and virtue'), as to suggest that he was eminently worthy of holding ecclesiastical benefices, both performing the office and collecting the appropriate prebend. As a first step, he was appointing him to the Chapter of Valencia. The promising young lordling of Jativa (who meanwhile had taken another necessary step by obtaining minor Orders) thus broke at a gallop into the rich pastureland of ecclesiastical benefices, blithely indifferent to the howls of protest that arose from the stalls of the infuriated local clergy. Titles and takings followed thick and fast during the next four years; he still held on to them even when, in pursuit of his destined career, he took ship for Italy.

When he reached Rome, his old uncle the cardinal must have felt his heart swell with pride at the sight of him. Rodrigo was at the full peak of his adoles-cence; his youth shone like a flower that has just opened wide in the morning sunlight. He had that full-blooded impetuosity which is often to be found in young men of Mediterranean extraction. His hair was brown and wavy, his eyes could melt languishingly or glint with proud anger at will. He had the swarthy complexion of the Valencian, a ripe red mouth, and a lithe, powerful body. With all this his manner was noble and self-assured; he bore himself like a *grand seigneur*.

The life of Rome seethed around him, offering him a spectacle that might well make him feel that this was truly the centre of the world.

The first great event was the Jubilee of 1450, which transformed the city into a vast ants' nest of indulgence-hunters, pouring in from every European country, and tramping endlessly round from one basilica to another, incom-prehensible in their speech, picturesque in their costumes, touching in their naive amazement. They bellowed their sacred hymns with deafening vehemence and their thirst for indulgences was positively ferocious. The city was crammed to bursting-point with these noisy pilgrims. In streets and on bridges, Papal troops were obliged to intervene with clubs to control the traffic of humanity. The inns were packed out, and had to turn away whole swarms of people look-ing for lodgings. No provisions could be had in the shops for love or money; the demand for victuals always exceeded the supply. Prices soared dizzily. Gold poured in torrents down the throats of merchant-speculators and rolled into St Peter's Treasury.

But presently the dog-days came, roasting streets and sidewalks, and the air filled with foul exhalations, and for a hundred miles out of Rome the roads were littered with inert, contorted wretches, who very soon were to stiffen in their final death-agony. The plague had struck Rome and her basilicas, and began to claim victims at a fearful rate. The entire Papal Court vanished like a flight of angels. Cardinals, bishops, abbots, monks and priests scattered in all directions—including ports of embarkation. The Pope scurried from one castle to another with mad excitement. Finally he shut himself up in Fabriano, whence he issued a decree of excommunication, loss of benefices, and general disgrace against anyone who, having been in Rome, let himself be seen within seven miles of His Holiness's asylum. It was nearly the end of October before the Pope returned to the Vatican. The plague had stopped, and the pilgrims were flocking back to inundate the city with their prayers and their gold. Amongst them was Roger van der Weyden, who had been in Italy since the previous year, a herald of the seductive realism and mellow splendours of Flemish painting.

On 19 December, hard on the heels of the plague, there came another tragedy to sadden the Jubilee festivities: a collision between the crowd and a herd of animals on the Ponte Sant'Angelo, which led to an outbreak of panic and violence, almost two hundred people being crushed to death.

Another much talked of event which took place in Rome under Rodrigo's eyes was the visit, in 1452, of Frederick III, who had come for his Imperial coronation—and also to claim his bride, Eleanor of Portugal. The diplomat responsible for arranging both these matters in advance was Aeneas Silvius Piccolomini, a talented and irresistible busybody who for some years had been assuming steadily greater importance on the European scene.

While the Habsburg monarch, accompanied by his modest-sized train, went from city to city, enjoying an enthusiastic reception everywhere, Nicholas V was trembling with fear lest Rome's subversive elements—inflamed by repub-lican idealism derived from classical sources, and relying on the widespread anti-clericalism of the Vatican's subjects—might take advantage of the Em-peror's presence to start a revolution, and induce him to assume the sovereignty over Rome. An attempt at insurrection had already been made, eighteen years before; and one person very possibly involved in the attempt was Stefano Porcari, a most dangerous man who, though working for the Papal govern-ment, bore it a deadly hatred, and aimed to blot it from the face of the earth. Porcari was the scion of an ancient and noble house, a brilliant humanist and vastly experienced traveller, whom Nicholas V had contrived to confine in Bologna, under the control of Cardinal Bessarion, with an annual pension that was—somewhat naïvely—meant to damp down his libertarian ardours. The Pontiff, however—always supposing that his spies did their duty properly— could not fail to be aware of some rather disturbing links between Rome and Bologna. Even had he been in doubt on this score, the ferment produced in certain Roman circles by the Emperor's approach would, equally, have warned him to be on his guard. This he most certainly was. He strengthened his defences, and garrisoned the least reliable districts with 2000 mercenaries, under the command of thirteen marshals. No one could be quite sure whether these precautions were directed against seditious elements, or betrayed very powerful uneasiness as to the intentions of the Emperor. The latter certainly thought it necessary, when he was at the top of Monte Mario, to send the Pope most ample reassurances—once again through the indefatigable Piccolomini's agency.

Rodrigo was certainly in the procession of cardinals which, on the evening of 8 March, went out to pay the Tyrolean homage on the lower slopes of the hill, together with representatives of the Papal government, the city, and the great Roman families. The next day witnessed the state entrance of Frederick and Eleanor, who had come to meet her future bridegroom with an escort 3000 strong. And on the 19th, Laetare Sunday, Rodrigo had the privilege of wit-nessing the splendid Pontifical High Mass in St Peter's, during the course of which the Pope placed the Imperial crown on the head of the thirty-seven-year-old Habsburg, and on that of the enchanting Eleanor. After five days of feasting and political discussions, the newly-married couple and their train rode off to Naples to pay a visit on King Alfonso, the bride's uncle. Neither Rod-rigo nor anyone else realized that history had chosen them as witnesses of a memorable event: this Imperial coronation, the last in a long series, had been the swan-song of the Middle Ages.

Frederick then returned to Venice, and as summer drew on recrossed the Alps, in haste and fury, to quell an Austrian rebellion led by his ward Ladis-law. He left in the memory of the Italians the image of a mean and greedy monarch, lacking in majesty. At Venice he had actually disguised himself as a small tradesman when he went shopping to avoid paying inflated prices.

During the four years of this sojourn in Rome, Rodrigo pursued his studies under the best masters, amongst whom the most outstanding was Gaspare of Verona, a famous scholar and man of letters who wrote a biography of Paul II. In the school run by this distinguished humanist, which attracted pupils from the highest levels of society, the Spaniard was able to mix with the cream of Roman youth, and learn—far more so than his uncle—to breathe the atmosphere of this new culture in an easy, effortless manner. Yet he cannot have retained any very affectionate memory of his teacher, since Gaspare later broke out in bitter lamentation over the ingratitude of his former pupil, who was [he said] so generous with others but so mean where he was concerned.[5]

Simply to live in Rome was a cultural education. The humanists were in a ferment of activity. During these years artists such as Fra Angelico, Benedetto Buonfigli, Bartolomeo di Foligno and Andrea del Castagno were painting their frescoes. The Pope himself was busy organizing a quite formidable architectural programme, based on aims and concepts which—had fate granted him a longer span of life—would have totally transformed the appearance of the Vatican area, and shown how his zeal as a builder far outstripped that shown by even his most illustrious successors in the Papacy. All this upsurge of artistic creativity must have struck Rodrigo as the revelation of a world ruled by sublime inspiration.

As the cardinal's nephew he would certainly have enjoyed free access to Vatican circles. Here there reigned the most learned and brilliant Court in all Europe, a meeting-place for such men as Leon Battista Alberti, Lorenzo Valla, Poggio Bracciolini, Giovanni Aurispa, Francesco Filelfo or Giannozzo Manetti, from 1451 the Pope's Apostolic Secretary and especial favourite.

From these leaders of the new cultural movement—whom Nicholas V had gathered under the wing of his patronage and favour, turning a blind eye to the fact that some of them were scandalously corrupt—the youth of Rome could draw an example of passionate intellectual activity, allied in certain cases with unbridled freedom of thought, open-minded artistic amorality, a cheerfully dissolute way of life, and factious envy amongst themselves.

The last noteworthy event which Rome provided for Rodrigo's scrutiny took place in January 1453. This was the abortive republican conspiracy, dis- covered at the last moment before it was due to take place, which brought Porcari and some of his companions to the gallows.

In June Rodrigo left the city, to go and study Canon Law at the University of Bologna. It was here, not long afterwards, that he learnt of the terror and consternation brought about in the capital of Christendom by the news of the fall of Constantinople, which had taken place on 29 May, and of the frantic diplomatic efforts at once initiated by the Holy See in an effort to rally Europe to the rescue. However, despite his highly painful preoccupation with the Turkish threat, the Pope did not wholly forget Rodrigo. Indeed, he gave proof of his affectionate concern in a Bull by virtue of which he conferred upon him the highly profitable deanship of Catalbano.

At Bologna life was gay and pleasurable, with hearty conviviality, and con- siderable good-natured indulgence in erotic pastimes. The men were exuberant the women endowed with solid charms and most bountiful generosity.

The city was governed, with exemplary wisdom, by Sante Bentivoglio, a man of controversial paternity with a romantic past behind him, who ruled cordially as *primus inter pares*. Recently he had shown himself a virtuoso per- former when it came to walking the tightrope of political neutrality, carefully keeping out of the conflict between Milan and Venice. Both *ordo* and *populus* had reason to be grateful to him for the agreement of 1447, through which— after a tussle with the Holy See that had lasted over half a century—he obtained on the city's behalf the maximum possible concessions in the sphere of civic liberties. The Bentivoglio family's suzerainty, which had come close to foundering after the murder of Annibale, was considerably strengthened as a result of this agreement. And another prudent move on Sante's part, the year before Rodrigo arrived in Bologna, had been the marriage he contracted with Ginevra Sforza, daughter of the Lord of Pesaro—a union which brought him into the closed circle of the top Italian families, and increased his status accordingly.

Ginevra was undoubtedly illegitimate, but the same could be said of Sante—not to mention the son who already lived at his side. She was also a mere child; but he was in no hurry. He brought her to Bologna on 19 May 1454. The city never dreamed, on this festive occasion, how strong a grip the hand of the child-bride (now entering the old Bentivoglio family mansion on the Strà di San Donato) would maintain over it for the next fifty years and more. After her husband's premature death, Ginevra married her reluctant cousin Gio-vanni. They settled down together in the new Bentivoglio palazzo, where she proceeded to give ample proof of her vigour (both moral and physical) by presenting him with no less than sixteen children, in addition to the two she had already borne Sante, and by exercising over her family, the city, and its stormy political life, both foreign and domestic, that iron control which makes her worthy of comparison with another more famous female example of Sforza *virtus*: the 'virago' Caterina.

Time went quickly by. And while the Spanish student crammed his head with legal matters, distinguishing himself in university circles by his intellectual acuity and seriousness of application, there was about to take place the event which gave a sudden formidable twist to his career.

CATALAN ROME

Infirmity, sorrow, and moral suffering had by the spring of 1455 sadly weakened the already fragile strength of this book-loving Pope. Amid the bitter atmo-sphere which marred his last days he complained that he was the unhappiest man in the world, surrounded by an evil horde of lying courtiers, cheated and deceived even by those in his most intimate private circle. Weeping, he asserted that he had enjoyed more happiness in one single day when he was plain Tommaso da Sarzana than during a whole year of his pontificate.[6] He died during the night of 24–25 March, his sunken eyes gazing at a crucifix.

Rome boiled and fermented like a vat of new wine. The pungent, heady odour of republicanism was abroad in the air. About a week earlier the leading members of the Papal Court, and other persons under the protection of the stricken Pope, seeing that his death was imminent, and familiar with the violence that generally accompanied an interregnum, had left the Vatican, hastily transferring themselves and their possessions either inside the walls of the Castel Sant'Angelo, or else to some other secure place of refuge. For some days already the cardinals on the one side, and the representatives of the various Italian and foreign powers on the other, had been engaged in their customary urgent manoeuvres to influence the Holy Spirit's choice of a successor.

This preliminary phase, before the opening of the conclave proper, repeated the situation of March 1447. The struggle for the succession—conducted by a mixture of pressures and enticements—brought as antagonists into the lists Cardinal Prospero Colonna and Cardinal Latino Orsini, in whose persons there met, and clashed, the interests of their respective families, and of the States lined up behind them.

Each of the two parties conducted its own electoral campaign behind the scenes—with its own methods. 'Colonna and his followers', Nicodemo Tranchedini da Pontremoli, Francesco Sforza's agent, wrote him on 16 March, 'build up their support by canvassing votes, by flattery, and by circumspection; whereas Orsini and *his* supporters rely on their swords or their power generally.' In other words, a policy of blandishment versus one depending on a demonstration of force. It was most people's belief that Colonna's party would have had victory within its grasp had Nicholas V died without further delay; but as he continued to linger on in a kind of no-man's-land between this world and the next, the Orsini faction had managed to gain ground on them, luring Alfonso of Aragon away from their side, and embarking on successful negotiations with Venice, the object of these manoeuvres being to make the final choice fall on a third party, either Barbo or Scarampo.

The official conclave began on 4 April, and was attended by fifteen of the twenty-one members of the Sacred College: seven Italians, four Spaniards, two Frenchmen and two Greeks. The nominations of Colonna and Orsini were both rejected *ab initio*. So were several tentative efforts involving the names of persons owing allegiance to one or other of the two groups. The electors now turned to the 'neutral candidates'. For a brief moment there emerged above the heaving waters of conflict—already haloed, as it seemed, with victory—the majestic bearded countenance of Bessarion. However, if we are prepared to stretch a point or two and believe the version of events recorded by Aeneas Silvius Piccolomini's *Commentarii*, it was (of all things) his beard which proved his undoing. The French Cardinal Alain de Coétivy inveighed against the choice of a Greek who so ostentatiously adorned himself with this heterodox facial hair, a plain reminder of his all-too-recently abandoned schismatic origins.

Day followed day, and Rome grew impatient. The general atmosphere of nervous tension was aggravated by a fear (by no means wholly unfounded) that there might be some brutal and unannounced incursion by the mercenary bands of Jacopo Piccinino, who had been discharged by the Venetians after the Peace of Lodi the previous year and looked as though he might try to sink his fangs into Church territory, and carve himself a fief out of it.

Tension reached its climax on 8 April. That morning Francesco Sforza's agent—having held up his dispatch from hour to hour in the expectation that he would shortly learn the result of the election—now finally decided to put pen to paper. To his master he communicated the heartfelt wish that in the forth-coming scrutiny they might at long last 'let their choice fall on one man, be he good or bad'. Nothing, he added, was now more likely, especially 'on account of the fear the cardinals entertain of the populace, who begin to murmur at such great delay'.

The ink of Nicodemo's dispatch had scarcely dried on its paper when the election of Nicholas's successor became an accomplished fact. The cardinals, realizing the impossibility of scraping up the required percentage of votes for one of themselves, first fell back on an unknown from the outback, Antonio of Monfalcone, a Franciscan friar. When this attempt at a compromise also broke down, they let their colleague Scarampo and the critic of Bessarion's beard talk them into postponing the trial of strength between the various groups to another conclave; for the moment, to avoid wasting yet more time, they agreed on a provisional solution to their impasse. They would elect that member of the Sacred College who—taking age and health into account—seemed destined to occupy the Holy and Apostolic See for the shortest possible time.

It was thus that Alonso de Borja, thanks to his appearance of ailing, wasted senility, emerged as Pope from a conclave which he had entered without anyone dreaming of him as an even remotely possible candidate. He was seventy-seven years old, but had the good luck to look much older; everyone thought he must be over eighty. 'The reason why these cardinals agreed on their colleague from Valencia', Bishop Bartolomeo Visconti wrote to Sforza that same day, in a postscript to Nicodemo da Pontremoli's dispatch, 'is because of his great age; each one of them hopes to get his own way more easily in the next election than proved possible in this one.'

Amid such general stupefaction, the only person not surprised by the result of the conclave was the aged man himself. For the past eleven years, ever since being created a cardinal, he had confidently looked forward to the fulfilment of Vincent Ferrer's prophecy.

A medallion, by Andrea Guazzalotti, which portrays the features of Nicholas V's successor, faithfully emphasizes that curved profile—convex forehead, strong nose, chin receding into the fleshy folds of the throat—which recurs in the iconography of Alexander VI, and clearly constitutes one charac-teristic of the Borgia 'type'. Though not so authentic, the idealized portraits of him painted by Sano di Pietro (Siena, Accademia di Belle Arti), Pinturicchio (Siena, Libreria del Duomo) and Jacomart Baço (Jativa, Borgia Chapel) all converge on the same physical type, with more or less clearly recognizable characteristics: big eyes, strong jaw, a robust neck. Age, and the scholarly life he had led, had refined and as it were chiselled his features. Under the high, bare dome of his cranium, that seamed face, with its keen gaze and the firm lines round the lips, still showed a goodly residue of vitality.

Assuming the name of Callistus III—as though to erase for ever from the palimpsests of history the antipope of that name and number whom Frederick Barbarossa had in 1168 set up against Alexander III—Alonso de Borja set out to prove that age had not weakened him, and that even during a presumably brief pontificate much could still be done.

There were few smiles of satisfaction, in Italy, to greet the *Habemus pontificem* of 8 April. With the Spaniards already occupying the southern part of the penin-sula, the elevation to the Papal throne of a candidate who was Alfonso of Aragon's friend and fellow-countryman could not but alarm a good many governments (those of Venice, Genoa and Florence in particular); it also struck at the threadbare pride of an Italy which—though as torn and multicoloured as Harlequin's costume—could still on certain occasions be pervaded by a sense of nationalistic jealousy.

'See,' Lionardo Verracci exclaimed sadly on 10 April, in a letter to Cosimo de' Medici, 'see where the hesitancy of our Italians has brought us! The Catalans have the power, and God alone knows how well-suited they are by nature to rule.' But what's done cannot be undone; and even he consoled himself with the hope that this Spanish Pope would die in the reasonably near future: 'For the present we must possess our souls in patience. I take comfort from one thing: because of his age, this situation cannot long continue.'

What the Roman populace thought of the newly-elected Pope can be deduced from a revealing incident that took place on 20 April, the day of the coronation. After the service in St Peter's, Callistus III rode off in procession to take possession of the Lateran Palace, surrounded by prelates and civic dig-nitaries. In the Piazza di Monte Giordano representatives of the Jewish com-munity were waiting—in accordance with ancient tradition—to offer him the 'Scroll of the Law'. The rabble now moved in to the attack; presumably their main aim was to make off with this valuable tome, but at the same time they did not mean to let slip so good an opportunity of showing the new Pope what scant respect they felt for him, by involving him, personally, in the alarmingly violent turmoil which now ensued. Callistus III only managed to get away with the greatest difficulty, dishevelled and flustered, panting for breath, and even then he was subjected to a second assault a little further on, and deprived of the canopy under which he had been advancing.

Great hostility was also shown him, as time went on, by the humanists, particularly in their written works. After enjoying, for eight long years, the succulent fruits of Nicholas V's favours, these ornate parasites of the Papal Court found it hard to swallow the indifference and intolerance with which they were regarded by this Spanish Pope, this Papal lawyer-cum-statesman, who could not appreciate the elegant construction of their periods or the ringing cadences of their hexameters, being accustomed to manipulate concepts rather than amuse himself with the music of words.

Not that Callistus III kicked them all out of the Vatican or condemned them to starvation *en bloc*; far from it. Rather improbably, given the circumstances, he promoted that stubbornly anti-clerical figure Valla to the post of Papal Secretary, and loaded him with canonries into the bargain. He treated the aged Poggio in a considerate fashion, and showed some favour to all the other members of this distinguished group. Yet even when he chose to take a generous line with them, he did so in the detached, off-hand manner of one throwing a morsel of meat to some bothersome domestic animal. In all his dealings with them, his expression would reveal irritation, if not actual disapproval: the irritation of a serious man who finds himself surrounded by a pack of frivolous and presumptuous day-dreamers. He too was a man of culture; but culture, for him, meant something quite different from what it did for them.

Dry, laconic, indifferent to the bitterness of those around him, careless of the fears and disappointments that his election had provoked practically everywhere throughout the peninsula, marvellously armoured in the knowledge of his supreme authority, and proudly determined to exercise it with impartial justice, he took his own highly rational convictions, and turned them into the single, unshakeable norm dictating his every course of action.

True to himself, and to the mentality he had acquired from his cultural background, he detested rhetorical flourishes. The inner need which drove him to employ clear, brief language was also that which inspired his simple, sober, efficient way of life.

He was a great worker, who personally dictated all correspondence of importance. He insisted on scrutinizing every document, and intervened directly in every problem. And at the end of his busy working day he found in study that repose which another man might have sought in some more frivolous diversion—being ambitious to keep his mind nimble and alert, intact and fertile, as he had done with his knowledge of jurisprudence during the years at Lerida.

Those people (and there were plenty of them) who at the time of his election already saw Alfonso of Aragon—the most powerful and dreaded monarch in all Italy—freely manipulating this Pontiff who had once been his secretary, were very soon forced to change their minds. When, after the coronation, the traditional embassies began to arrive in Rome, proffering the homage and obedience of the Italian States, Alfonso attempted to make that from his own realm dependent on certain conditions, subject to negotiation. Such a move was not only designed to remove the yoke of vassalage. Alfonso also wanted to find out just how amenable Alonso de Borja was. After all, the new Pope owed a great deal of his worldly advancement to Alfonso's help. Alonso de Borja promptly destroyed any possible illusions Alfonso might have on this topic by sending back a curt refusal to compromise in any way whatsoever. The King was forced to realize that not the very slightest reliance could be placed upon his condescension. The result, as we shall see, was a conflict that lasted until both of them were dead.

If no one else rejoiced over Alonso de Borja's elevation to the Papal throne, it caused Alonso himself vast exultation, for the possibilities that his election opened up regarding the future fortunes of his family.

One of his first acts as Pope was the canonization of the Dominican preacher who had prophesied his elevation. On 29 June of that same year, Vincent Ferrer became a saint; and the matter would have been concluded a month earlier had not the 'investigation of his case' taken a little longer than was anticipated.

Though quick enough to pay this debt of gratitude, Callistus III showed himself even more eager when it came to bringing his relatives forth from the shadows of obscurity. The eighth of April, 1455, marked the beginning of a staggering and absolutely unprecedented epoch of nepotism, which during the next half-century left all Europe agape.

Rodrigo was not the only member of the family to join his uncle, the cardinal, in Italy. Between 1449 and 1455 three other nephews reached Rome: Rodrigo's brother Pedro Luís, and Pedro and Luís Juan del Milá, the two sons of Catalina. Four young bulls from the Borgia *manada*, snorting with fierce energy, instinct strong in their veins, their hearts swelling with ambition: handsome youths, marvellously alert, vigorous alike in mind and body, bursting with charm and self-assurance, brave to the point of temerity. It was not long before they began to get themselves talked about. The Italians found their harshly guttural Arabic name quite unpronounceable, and took to calling them, sometimes, Borges, but more often, and in the end permanently, Borgia.

The coronation ceremony found all four of them in Rome, basking cheerfully and haughtily in the radiance spread by their uncle's tiara. Three weeks later, on 10 May, the twenty-four-year-old Rodrigo was appointed Apostolic Notary; on 3 June he was assigned the deanship of the Church of Santa Maria in Jativa, with a number of other benefices in the region of Valencia. Callistus was at pains, not only to get them to the top in their careers, but also to enrich them befittingly; these fat prebends (not to mention those previously procured for them) were further augmented during the next three years by the following: the deanship of the Chapter at Cartagena, the revenues or administration of the Cistercian monastery of Santa Maria di Chiaravalle, the Benedictine abbey of Sant'Angelo in Massa and the Cistercian convent of Fossanova, the rectorship of the infirmary of Sant'Andrea di Vercelli, and countless benefices in the dioceses of Magonza, Burgos, Palencia and Toledo.

The Pope gave precisely the same treatment to Luís Juan del Milá, the other nephew who had entered on an ecclesiastical career. By this time he was already Bishop of Segorbe, a Spanish town quite near ancient Saguntum, though vastly remote from its titular pastor: not so far distant, however, as to exempt it from sending him its annual revenues. So he too could count on a good collection of stipends and similar benefices.

When, in the second half of June, Rodrigo took the road back to Bologna, where he was to complete his studies and take his degree, Luís Juan went with him: the thirteenth, in fact, had been chosen as the day on which he was to take over the governorship of the city from Bessarion. Callistus had sent a couple of Briefs on ahead of them before they left. In the first he enjoined the authorities of those places through which they would have to pass, and in the second those of Bologna, to show all due regard and courtesy (including exemption from tolls or duties) to the *venerabilis frater episcopus Segobricensis* and the *dilectus magister Rodericus de Borgia*, his *nepotes valde cari*. From documentary evidence it appears that these two youngsters travelled with a train of at least a hundred followers.

At Bologna—which they reached on 19 June, to be given a princely welcome—Rodrigo took up residence in the Palazzo Gregoriano and resumed his studies with exemplary fervour. Andrea Barbazza the jurist, who was his tutor, had high praise for the application with which he spent three hours daily at classes on Canon Law.

On 13 August the following year he took his final examinations, with the brilliant results that were to be expected after such careful preparation—and in the light of his privileged status. *Nemine discrepante*, that is, without one objec‑ tion or reservation on any examiner's part—indeed, with the warmest all‑round approval—he was declared a Doctor in Canon Law.

In a 'secret book' belonging to the University, and still preserved in Bologna, the event is duly noted. Beside his name we find the title of Apostolic Proto‑ notary and the words 'nephew of His Holiness Pope Callistus III'; mention is also made of the fact that, almost as soon as he received his doctoral insignia from the hand of Professor Battista di San Pietro, he showed his gratitude by presenting the teachers of the Faculty with 'fine caps and gloves of chamois leather'. This Registry note recommends itself to our interest for another reason besides: in the margin, some unknown person diligently sketched the Keys of the Kingdom, and added the various dates at which this former student was made a cardinal, elected Pope, and died. The last entry takes the form of a somewhat singular epitaph: *Mortuus est 1503 augusti, et sepultus in inferno.*

But Rodrigo—together with his cousin Luís Juan—received his best gradu‑ ation present from his uncle, who, in the second half of September, informed the Senate of Bologna, through a cheerfully resonant Brief, that he had decided to make his two nephews cardinals. Invited by the Pope to share his *leticiam et voluptatem*, the Senate, with remarkable docility, duly shared it; and to prove their sincerity (though expressing private regrets) they bestowed upon each of the two nephews a thousand Bolognese *lire* as a present; they also sent four ambassadors with the task of giving them an honourable escort to Rome.

The ceremony took place on 17 November. Rodrigo, who was not yet a priest, became a cardinal‑deacon, with the title of San Nicola in Carcere. He was twenty‑five years old, and another twelve were to elapse before he was fully ordained. In actual fact, the nomination of both young men as cardinals had already been put forward at a secret consistory on 20 February; the Sacred College had approved it, in the hope that the Pontiff would die before 'pub‑ lication', but had made no secret of its hostility to such a measure. Merely by forcing Callistus to accept a delay it made no doubt about its attitude.

However, this bestowal of red hats on the two cousins was not an isolated event, but rather a new line of departure—as the Sacred College was very soon made to realize. The rhythm of Pontifical generosity was somewhat swifter than the College's reactions. Before Their Eminences had exhausted their indigna‑ tion at the arbitrary disposal of some office or prebend, they would find them‑

selves faced with another, so that their mutterings and protests had hard work keeping up with the nimble heels of the Pope's nephews. In the December of that same year (1456) the cardinals saw Rodrigo appointed Legate to the Ancona Marches; in January 1457 Luís Juan received a similar appointment to Bologna, while that autumn Rodrigo—at the age of twenty-six—landed the most prestigious and important post the Vatican had to offer: that of the Vice-Chancellor of the Church, which carried an annual stipend of 20,000 ducats, and overall responsibility (in direct collaboration with the Pope himself) for the government of Christendom. And even this was not all. In December 1457 Rodrigo was appointed Inspector-General of all Papal troops in Italy; at an *ad hoc* consistory called on 30 June 1458 he was invested with the bishopric of Valencia. This office—held for years by Callistus III himself, and henceforth to become a veritable private perquisite of the Borgia family—brought in some-where between 18 and 20,000 ducats a year. In any case, the very least the Pope could do for Rodrigo was to vacate this see in his favour.

This marked, as it were, the sixth evening of Callistus III's nepotic activities. Having got so far, he followed God's example, and rested—for ever.

The Pontiff showed himself no less markedly solicitous on behalf of those nephews destined for a lay career: in particular as regards Rodrigo's brother Pedro Luís. This young cavalier, whom contemporary accounts describe as extraordinarily handsome, and endowed with lively intelligence, was to be the champion of the Borgia family's princely ambitions. Hot-blooded, proud and dissolute, he had—in full measure—that insolence which always characterizes Fortune's favourites. Into this Roman world, dominated by ecclesiastical guile, he brought a touch of hot youth, aggressively tempered with pride, gaiety, and defiance: youth that displayed the fierce laughing expression of some piratical adventurer.

In January 1456, he became Captain-General of the Church. Late in the evening of Sunday 14 March, Callistus III suddenly summoned the com-mandant of Castel Sant'Angelo, Giorgio Saluzzo, Bishop of Lausanne, and bade him hand over the edifice entrusted to his care. Saluzzo tried to protest against this injunction, but was forced into submission by the Pontiff's threats, amongst which one in particular, that of excommunication, with all its attendant ritual penalties and consequences, and delivered in a harshly furious voice, proved most effective. Thus it came about that on the following day Pedro Luís obtained command of the Castle—which meant, in fact, the control of Rome.

The city turned surly, and roared like the sea with a squall blowing up.

Callistus III answered these demonstrations of dissatisfaction in the autumn, by adding to his nephew's other offices and prerogatives the governorship of twelve cities that were also strategic strong-points in the Papal State, and that of the so-called 'Church patrimony' in Tuscany as well. Yet even this accumulation of power (which elicited stern but vain protests from that highly upright figure Cardinal Capranica) formed no more than the modest commencement of the career which Callistus III had in mind for his nephew.

As regards that perpetual duel between the Colonna and the Orsini families which formed an unchanging background to Rome's political life, and to a great extent conditioned it, the Borgias had already made their decision: to support the former, and pitch into the latter. This was a line of policy destined to continue (with infrequent interruptions mostly occasioned by personal resentment) down to the time of Alexander VI and Cesare. In the summer of 1457, therefore, Pedro Luís launched against the Orsini family one of those campaigns—involving attacks on fortresses, with much depredation and destruction—that bore a closer resemblance to some incursion by brigands than to warfare proper: the first in a whole series of similar undertakings by future Borgias which the hills of Latium were to witness.

On his return, the warlike Pedro Luís was appointed Prefect of Rome; he also became Vicar of Civitavecchia, Caprarola, Vetralla, and sundry other places. On this occasion the official servility shown by Rome's civic authorities bore clear witness to the domesticating effect produced by two years of Borgia strong-arm methods. The guardians of the Urbs, having listened in demure and attentive fashion to the Pope's well-wrought panegyric on the virtues of his nephew, and the young man's truly Italian sentiments, besought Callistus also to entrust him with the military command over all fortresses in Rome's prefecture. At this point one of their number, impelled by a happy inspiration which the rest must have envied, spoke up to express the hope that this new young City Prefect would very soon be crowned King of Rome.[7]

A Borgia now occupied the throne of Peter; there was one Borgia in the Vatican as Vice-Chancellor of the Church, and another commanding the military forces and key strongholds of the Papal State. Other Borgias in considerable if unspecific numbers, held various positions of authority and trust, having been foisted on the Vatican's administration, or spread abroad, in plum appointments, throughout Italy and Spain; Rome and the Church were beginning to look like their family fief.

They begged, they demanded, they got what they were after. Callistus himself had occasion in due course to complain about the exorbitant greed of his sisters and of Isabel in particular, who wanted to provide her daughters with dowries and houses at the Church's expense—an aim in which she achieved a remarkable degree of success. No one had ever dreamed that the Pope had such a warren of relatives in Spain. They kept on appearing—relations, and relations of relations—and for every one of them there was a corner in the sun, for each applicant one of those countless sinecures or odd positions which the hyper-trophied development of the Papal bureaucracy had created over the centuries.

Some of these Borgias, after an initial sojourn in Rome, took off for distant parts on the winds of adventure, fully confident that their name would win them authorization for the most risky undertaking, and at the same time safe-guard them from all punishment. This is why, in 1457, we find two of the Pope's nephews, who had sailed East with the crusaders' fleet assembled on the Tiber (under the supreme command of Scarampo, the Papal Legate), sacking and pillaging towns on Cyprus, and generally revealing themselves as dyed-in-the-wool delinquents. The terrible cardinal, it is only fair to add, had no hesitation in imprisoning them.

Yet the Borgias were no more than the most obvious nucleus of this pullula-ting colony. From the Kingdom of Naples, from the shores of Valencia, from every remote corner of Spain, waves of immigrants descended on Rome. Push-ing, shameless, and arrogant, they proceeded to grab themselves positions, exhibiting the most truculent haughtiness in the process. They arrived lean and poverty-stricken, but within an incredibly short space of time contrived to line their purses. Their chattering, guttural speech was to be heard on every street. By now they had a near-monopoly of public offices, which were not infre-quently abandoned with contempt by their old occupants, in allergic hostility to the new regime. These immigrants were the masters now.

The populace referred to them generically as 'Catalans', without making any distinction as to their place of origin. At first the newcomers had been treated with good-natured indifference; but now the hatred they aroused grew greater with each passing day. It was not enough for these Catalans to lord it pom-pously over the local population and to devour Rome alive; on the slightest excuse they would bury a hand's breadth of steel in the belly of any hapless native Roman who showed himself jealous of their special privileges, or fed up with their arrogance. Hardly a day passed without blood being spilt some-where in the streets of the city.

The Pope let this state of affairs go on unchecked. He could not know everything. Besides, this was the price he had to pay for that insistence on internal security which lay at the root of his nepotism, and its logical conse-quence—the Hispanicization of Rome.

THE CRUSADING FEVER

The name of the first Borgia Pope shines out at the head of one of the most beautiful and moving pages ever written in the book of the history of human effort, effort concentrated with convulsive energy and unsparing self-sacrifice on the achievement of a particular goal. The goal was not, in fact, achieved. But the results of human endeavour are often determined by unavoidable circumstances; and just as nothing is added to the moral value of such undertakings when they culminate in victory, so does a defeat in no way detract from that value.

Though his body was withered by age, Callistus III possessed a fiery spirit; and he had ascended the Papal throne with one great and all-devouring project in mind—to free Christian Europe from the Turkish scimitar which, more especially since the occupation of Constantinople, had been pointed at her throat. All his efforts, all his thoughts, all his political activities converged on this one end.

On a medallion which he caused to be struck after the futile and delusive victory won off Mytilene, in the summer of 1457, by the crusading fleet, we read: 'I was elected for the annihilation of the enemies of the Faith.' Such a proclamation is somewhat surprising, both for the dash and self-assurance which pervade it, and for the war-like feeling it reveals. These words are not simply a paean of joy after a success which was, in sober truth, destined to prove illusory; nor are they merely an ardent outburst of enthusiasm and relief. They are an unlooked-for revelation, showing us that in this subtle jurist and consummate diplomat there was hidden a formidable underlying stratum of feeling—not to mention abundant, indeed excessive, impulsiveness.

This 'annihilation of the enemies of the Faith' was really the central purpose of his pontificate. As a Spaniard, a descendant of Pedro de Atarés and the *Caballeros de la Conquista*, a native of Valencia who had grown up amid the echoes and reverberations of an anti-Islamic epic—compounded simultaneously from tradition and living reality—he could not but regard himself as a Knight of the Cross.

Looked at from this point of view, there is some significance in the trouble he took, at the very beginning of his pontificate, to promote the review of Joan of Arc's trial, which resulted in her full and indeed glorious rehabilitation: for him she was the heroine of a war of liberation, fought in the crusading spirit, at the prompting of that ancient battle-cry, 'God's will be done'.

An ecclesiastical career had not extinguished the original Borgia qualities in him. He also displayed them, to an impressive degree, in the energy and speed with which he tackled the project, the accents with which he urged it on, and the decisiveness he brought to its execution—the extremism, one might say, that permeated his every word and action, riding roughshod over the vicissi tudes of fortune, flaying sloth, indolence, and selfishness, firing everyone and everything with his own flame hot enthusiasm.

One unmistakable Borgia trait was his open and passionate vehemence. Without ever descending to mere rhetorical exaggeration, it constantly boiled up and spilt over in an incessant emotional barrage of appeals, intimations, pleas, protests, and lamentations. Another Borgia hallmark was the courage he displayed even when things were at their worst and most disheartening, un tiringly redoubling his efforts, flinging himself into projects that seemed (and often were) doomed from their first conception. 'Only the pusillanimous', he once asserted, 'fear danger. And only on the battlefield does the palm of glory grow.'[8]

In fact it was not the pusillanimity of contemporary Christendom which made the enterprise so forlorn a hope, but rather the conflicting interests of rulers and governments, committed (with pure blind obstinacy) to the implementa tion of their selfish and nationalistic policies, and altogether indifferent to those collective problems facing the (henceforth dissolved) European community. What militated against success were the mutual enmities, the rival struggles between various States—all the jealousy and suspicion and spite; in the last resort it was the historical impossibility of resuscitating a sense of solidarity which presupposed some spiritual cohesion, an order governed by Dante's two 'suns', the Emperor and the Pope. Callistus III's appeals fell on deaf ears because not even the threat of imminent danger sufficed to recompose and restrengthen the *disiecta membra* of an irreparably divided Europe, in which each saw nothing but his own particular problems, his own immediate gambits, and had completely abandoned the concept of a collective destiny, not only transcending all individual States on the plane of moral values, but—in the long run—binding them together and modifying their aims: because on the day that the Turkish horde invaded and enslaved Europe, all those private and 'par ticular' gambits which the piously myopic rulers were playing against one another on their political chess board would be swept away by one violent backhanded blow.

Callistus III was the last medievally minded Pope, the last crusader in the traditional sense of that word, bred in a Spain still ablaze with religious en thusiasm, and badly misled by his excessive faith in the kindling power that a noble and generous cause could have on the minds of his contemporaries. His mistake, if we can so describe it, was not to despair of his own authority, the

persuasive power generated by his personal example, or the communal conscience of the age in which he lived. It was an honourable error. But his
position rather resembled that of some elderly sea-captain, who stands erect in
the bows while his vessel is under attack by pirates, shouting orders and words
of encouragement to a quarrelsome and stone-deaf crew.

For many a decade now it had been the Papacy's fate to shoulder the entire
burden of this problem, and to agitate for the defence of Europe. The Emperor,
who might have been expected to undertake the task of coordinating the
various nations' forces, and leading them in the field, could—to all practical
intents and purposes—no longer do anything. He was weak, mainly through
lack of funds, and now very largely ignored by his intractable feudal barons,
who had become a good deal more powerful than he was. Thus he already
had troubles enough without attempting—in an ever more restricted and
problematical sphere of influence—to salvage what little of his former prestige
remained.

   During this progressive dissolution of its central authority, Europe had lost
two great opportunities of freeing itself from the Moslem threat. The first had
presented itself half a century earlier (1402), when Tamerlane delivered a
tremendous blow to the Turkish forces, shattering them on the upland plateau
of Ankara. At that time the conqueror had shown signs of wanting to establish
relations with the Western powers, perhaps in the hope of cementing some vast
alliance. At all events, it was clear that his own interests gravitated so strongly
towards Asia as to prevent him representing any real threat on the shores of the
Mediterranean. In fact, he lost no time in vanishing whence he had come, back
into Asia. A prompt and vigorous campaign from Europe would undoubtedly
have helped to exploit the Asiatic barbarian's victory for the benefit of Christendom, by overthrowing the accursed Turkish empire (which was already
plunged in helpless anarchy) and driving the Turks right out of Anatolia. But
nothing in fact was done. Mohammed I was allowed time enough to rebuild
the empire's military potential, as it had been during his father's reign; and his
successor, Murad II, found it so reinvigorated that he could launch an audacious offensive for the conquest of the Balkan peninsula.

   The second opportunity to save matters offered itself in the fatal year of 1453,
when Mohammed II, that pale, slim *condottiere* of twenty-three, a fierce-hearted
prince with ideas as vast and predatory as an eagle's flight, had drawn his
siege-lines tight about Constantinople. There is no doubt whatsoever that, in
this supreme crisis, the fleets of Europe could still have freed the city and saved
the Eastern Empire. This was made abundantly clear when four galleys

belonging to the Genoese commander Maurizio Cattaneo ran the blockade as far as the Golden Horn, spreading confusion and terror in their wake. Yet Europe had allowed Byzantine to founder in a sea of blood.

And now the Turks were there at the mouth of the Bosphorus, firmly planted on European soil: 300,000 warriors, drunk on victory and slaughter, with a youthful leader, hungry for conquest and power, and determined to subjugate Christendom. They were there, and indeed they had already recom-menced the assault on Europe, advancing in two different directions. One force drove through to the Danube, and then followed it upstream, thrusting into the very heart of the continent, while the other invaded the Balkan peninsula, whence they debouched on the Adriatic and the Mediterranean.

What opposition did Europe offer to the impact of this furious tide? Little or none, except for the heroic conduct of two men: one, Janos Hunyadi, a Hun-garian, the Voivode of Transylvania, and the other, George Scanderbeg, an Albanian. The first, the galloping 'white knight', had, in some twenty years' fighting, filled the endless Danubian plains with his heroic deeds, as he resisted the advance of the Islamic hordes. His fortunes varied, but never his indomitable tenacity. The second—who grew up among the Turks as a hostage, subse-quently escaping to lead a band of tough mountaineers from his own country—for over ten years waged a desperate struggle against the invaders, with flashes of brilliance and audacity that much resembled the tactics adopted by modern partisan guerrillas.

These, however, were the enterprises of two men only. Though marvellous in themselves, such episodes could never exercise any decisive influence on events; and they took place on the frontiers of a Europe which was content to stand at the window and admire them from afar.

On the day after his election, in the letters he sent the various Christian powers notifying them officially of his elevation to the Papal throne, Callistus III explicitly announced the programme of his reign as an effort, at European level, to achieve the expulsion of the Turks.

On 15 May 1455, twenty-five days after his coronation, he presented the Catholic world with a Bull announcing the crusade: an epic medieval-style fanfare, in an age which could no longer be galvanized by such music. This document, which summoned all nations to join in the process of liberation, proclaimed most generous indulgences to those who answered the appeal, authorized the collection of the so-called 'Turkish tithe' to finance the cam-paign, and set 1 March 1456 as the date for the expedition's departure.

The Borgia Pope followed up his Bull with a powerful and well-coordinated

propaganda campaign in every country of Europe. He sent out whole battalions of travelling preachers on circuit, mobilizing for this purpose all the
really first-class religious orators, who were taken off all other tasks, and forbidden to take any text but this for their sermons (an injunction afterwards
reinforced with threats of excommunication). On every important foreign
country he unleashed, with the title of legate, his most eloquent and enterprising cardinals—Juan de Carvajal, Niccolò di Cusa, Denys Széchy, Alain
de Coétivy—to encourage and coordinate all efforts aimed at producing men
and money. The men he sent out for the purpose of collecting tithes and
offerings reached the tiniest towns and the remotest territories of Europe.

The crop—potentially at least—was very great, and there were workers in
plenty eager to scythe, stack, and thresh it. Yet in the event the harvest soon
proved all too sparse. The preachers, on the one hand, were forced to realize
that it was not much use guaranteeing plenary indulgences to anyone who went
and got himself spitted on the sabres of the Infidels. The collectors of tithes and
small offerings, on the other, soon saw that kings and republican governments,
bishops and priests, were all competing in zeal and ingenuity towards the same
end—preventing the money of their subjects, or pastoral flock, from being
diverted to Rome. Furthermore, money thus gathered very often tends to stick
to the hands of the agents collecting it, and some notorious abuses of this sort,
even though stamped out and punished in exemplary fashion by the Pontiff
himself, certainly did not help the development or growth of the project. In
addition to dishonest collectors, and the resistance encountered almost everywhere, there were certain princes who, before they were prepared to back the
scheme, bluntly demanded fifty per cent of the takings. Nor was there any lack
of false preachers and sellers of indulgences, who went about their business in a
discreetly unobtrusive way.

But the gravest and most insurmountable problem was still the indifference,
the passive opposition, the ill-concealed hostility which the Pope's project
encountered everywhere, high and low: people regarded it as an outlandish
foreign gimmick which was rapidly becoming both tedious and troublesome.
A quick glance round the scene, in Italy and abroad, will serve to illustrate
this point.

Venice offered no possible chance of illusion. The previous year—on
18 April 1454, to be precise—the Most Serene Republic had successfully
negotiated an armistice, alliance, and commercial treaty with the Ottoman
Empire. This naturally obliged her to abstain from making any contribution
whatsoever, in men, arms or money, towards a prospective crusade. Venice did
not, in the end, swerve from her carefully observed neutrality, and continued to

look favourably on the Turk. This atmosphere of mutual cordiality was such that in 1457 the Sultan went so far as to invite the Doge to his son's wedding.

Milan produced many flowery verbal promises and reassurances, but never anything more concrete. Francesco Sforza, who five years earlier had gained control of the Duchy by strangling the ridiculous puritan republic that emerged briefly during the post-Visconti period, was busy consolidating his own position, and had no inclination to go off in search of adventure.

Genoa pullulated with mistrust, inertia and impotence. The republic had sunk from one bondage to another—decaying in the East, weakened by internal discord and a series of minor but chronic campaigns against Naples—until on 15 November 1453 it made over its Black Sea possessions to the Banco di San Giorgio, and never regained them. Out of deference Genoa subscribed to the financial operation of the tithe, but did nothing more—especially after she saw the fleet that had been prepared for the crusade go into action at King Alfonso's behest.

In Florence there was much verbal manoeuvring, which never led to any sort of effective action. The Florentines, indeed—especially the merchants and the bankers—by no means regretted the fact that the Turks had already weakened Venice, and might in the long run weaken her still further.

The situation in Naples was still worse. Alfonso V, who as late as 1454 had been proudly setting himself up as a latter-day Geoffrey of Bouillon, and on 1 November 1455 was solemnly invested with the emblem of the Cross, afterwards proved the expedition's most devious saboteur, using Piccinino to keep Italy in confusion and thus force the Pope to yield over the matter of the Neapolitan succession.

Outside Italy reactions had been more or less the same. There was nothing to be got out of either France, Germany, or England. France was still exhausted from her struggle against the English; her clergy were hostile to the project generally, particularly the tithe, and permeated by those Gallican trends apparent throughout the 'Pragmatic Sanction', which the King had issued in 1438. Her legate, like Cardinal Alain, gave signal proof of laziness or indifference by his failure to react in a fitting manner to the Pontiff's urgent remonstrances, and by never sending him any money. The King made a formal declaration (May 1455) that he would much prefer to remain aloof from such an undertaking.

Germany was being shaken by a stormy blast from the North that threatened both tithes and indulgences alike. At two meetings of princes and dignitaries of the Church, held in Frankfurt on Main during February and August respectively, speeches were made which, in their fierce anti-Papal tone, clearly

foreshadowed Luther. England, meanwhile, was embittered by the defeats and
territorial losses she had suffered across the Channel, torn internally by the
Wars of the Roses, and stubbornly confirmed in her old distaste for the ex-
ploitations and interferences of the Roman Curia—a distaste which was, in its
turn, paving the way for the schism of the succeeding century.

The help that both could and actually did come from other areas of Christendom was not very considerable. The West, by and large, preferred to shell out
a little money rather than supply men, arms, and vessels. Only in the countries
of Central Europe, which already felt the hot flames of the Crescent licking
about them, did it prove possible to recruit some heterogeneous and by no
means outstanding combatant levies—and even these were bands of adventurers rather than proper companies of soldiers. 'The Pope calls for help, and
no one listens,' Aeneas Silvius Piccolomini wrote in one of his letters. 'He
makes threats, but no one fears him.'

Callistus III—who to ensure the success of his crusade had solemnly sworn
that he would sacrifice all the Church's possessions, including his Papal tiara,
and even give his life if the need arose—stormed and raved. Disgusted by the
apathy of the West, he summoned various Franciscans who had come back
from distant lands, to find out whether any reliance could be placed on these
peoples. He sent Friar Ludovico of Bologna to see whether Georgia and Persia
could be brought in. He even turned to the ruler of Caramania and obtained
from him a promise to send an army 60,000 strong—though, truth to tell, no
one ever set eyes on it.

The sacrifice of the Church's possessions was no mere rhetorical announcement. The Spanish Pope was not given to half measures: few men could
match him when it came to throwing all available resources into any undertaking. He did not restrict himself to squeezing the leathery hearts and purses of
Christendom, and taxing the cardinals by the imposition of a special tribute: he
set an example himself. He sold a large proportion of the jewels and other
precious objects in the Papal Treasury—exquisite examples of the goldsmith's
art, magnificent table services, sacred vessels and church ornaments. He introduced economies everywhere. He dismissed men of letters and other parasites.
He cut down on the building programme and the number of commissioned
frescoes. The few painters left in his service found themselves painting standards
for the crusade, while the sculptors were reduced to turning out cannon-balls.

The Pope could no longer set eyes on any object of gold or silver without at
once ordering it to be sold, or taken to the Mint and transformed into ducats. On
his table there now appeared only earthenware dishes, or those of the cheapest
metals. He displayed a quite indescribable enthusiasm for this austerity regime.

In one Brief he announced: 'We do not blush to admit that, in furtherance of the immortally glorious task of upholding the defence of the Holy Gospel and the orthodox Faith, an enterprise which we pursue even at the cost of sleepless nights, we have indeed been left with a mere linen mitre.' And again: 'For this war we have, up to the present time, contributed our gold, our silver, our *iocalia*, and our very mitre.'

Iocalia: under this label—vaguely tinged with contempt, as though it was used to designate futile bagatelles and children's favourite playthings—he included those works of art which his most recent predecessors had acquired in such numbers. This characteristic affords us an extraordinarily vivid glimpse of the man as he really was. When some officers of the Curia hurried up to him, panting with emotion, bearing the news that men digging in the Church of St Petronilla had unearthed a magnificent marble sarcophagus containing two coffins, one of an adult, the other of a child, lined with thick plaques of silver and containing two corpses dressed in gold-woven silk (it was thought this might be the tomb of Constantine and his son), the Pope was overjoyed—but not because of any enthusiasm for archaeology. He ordered all precious metals found to be sent to the Mint; from the gold in the robes alone coins were struck off to the value of a thousand ducats.[9]

THREE VICTORIES AND A DISAPPOINTMENT

The strategic plan which this elderly Borgia had worked out was, on paper, a very simple one. He intended to raise an army and fit out a fleet. With these he would make for Constantinople, and wrest it from the Turks by a simultaneous land and sea assault. If this operation were successful, and vigorously followed up, it would bring about the destruction of the Ottoman Empire.

To assume command of the army Callistus III appointed Philip, Duke of Burgundy and Count of Flanders, a bellicose Croesus whose revenues were twice as large as those of the Kingdom of Naples, and over four times as large as those of Florence. In 1451, while in Brussels, that great mystic Denys the Carthusian had told him the secret of a vision he had experienced from which Philip had learnt that God meant him to don the crusader's mantle and liberate the Holy Sepulchre. One can only suppose that on the day of ecstasy Denys was rather off-form. But the prophecy both obsessed Philip and filled him with high enthusiasm; from thenceforward he had assumed the role of the heaven-chosen hero. On 17 February 1454, at Lille, he had been responsible for a most curious episode, of which Callistus III was undoubtedly informed. He had organized a banquet, during which there appeared the allegorical figure of the Church, in deep mourning, seated on the back of an elephant and reciting a pathetic lament in verse. Afterwards he and his fellow-diners had sworn, over a gold-collared pheasant, to become crusaders.

Nevertheless, the originator of this buffoonery was a very serious man. As Philip the Bold's nephew, and the son of John of Burgundy (known as 'The Fearless'), as sovereign of a true and independent State which for centuries past had written its name in the annals of French history, as leader of a party that for some while had dominated the country, and had only resigned itself to furling sail after the defeat of the English, Philip was a match for any European monarch in terms of authority and prestige. During the career of Joan of Arc (whom he took prisoner at Compiègne) he played a leading part on the other side. He certainly did not lack familiarity with battlefields, on a number of which he had pursued his cherished ambition of seizing the French sceptre for himself. They called him Philip the Good. In actual fact he was a remarkable epicure, whose cultivation of pleasure went with a passion for risks and action, who blended tough and warlike instincts with a coolly calculating intelligence, whose respect for culture and passion for art offset the vaulting boldness of his ambitions. He founded Dol University, instituted the Order of the Golden Fleece, and proved himself an enlightened Maecenas, to the benefit of artists such as Van Eyck and Van der Weyden. He had three successive wives, but report also credited him with some twenty-four mistresses. Luxurious and lavish, affable with his friends but a terror to his enemies, a mixture of magnificence and brutality, he was, in short, one of the most typical figures of his age: the perfect embodiment of a *grand seigneur* during that transitional period when the crudely vigorous barbarism of the Middle Ages was giving way to a more refined culture, that of the Renaissance.

The Pontiff granted him substantial favours, including a part-share in the ecclesiastical revenues of the Duchy, and was at pains to ratify the peace he had concluded with King Charles VII, the Maid of Orléans' former *gentil Dauphin*, who had arranged for (or condoned, which came to much the same thing) the murder of his father.

Philip took the Cross. He also took the revenues—and not just the percentage that was his, but all the rest too, so that the Pope had to send him a letter of remonstrance, beseeching him to send on at least something. Above all, he took his time. He took it in such abundance that Callistus III could die without having seen him stir a finger. The only things he never took up were his arms, and the command of that hypothetical crusading army. As we shall see shortly, Alfonso of Aragon's conduct as supreme commander of all naval forces was equally elusive.

On 8 September 1455, at a ceremony in St Peter's, the Pope personally laid the Cross upon Cardinal Urrea, Archbishop of Tarragona, who was to take a small flotilla and bring succour to the Aegean islands, then suffering much tribulation from Turkish raids and landings. This expedition would constitute a prelude to the full-scale crusade. Those who attended the ceremony were struck by the fervour of this aged Pontiff, whose life now seemed to be hanging by the very finest of threads, and were touched with compassion when they saw him overcome by emotion.

Some weeks passed before Urrea's flotilla weighed anchor from the port of Naples, where it had been reinforced by a naval squadron of King Alfonso's, under Admiral Villamarina's command. The galleys put to sea, and steered resolutely northwards. The first news Callistus had of their activities was the report that they had gone to devastate the coast around Genoa, and that—as a kind of extra flourish to this most remarkable undertaking—they had also amused themselves by making piratical attacks on Venetian merchantmen.

The Pope's indignation and distress found outlet in lamentations, floods of invective, and violent abuse. On 17 December he convened a meeting of the Sacred College, and with its unanimous approval appointed that small, truculent, intractable prelate Scarampo *legatum apostolicum, gubernatorem et capitaneum atque ducem totius classis*, with the task of bringing his treacherous predecessor, now dismissed, back to Rome for a personal interview with Callistus, in which he would be required to explain and justify his operations.

The *classis* or fleet of which the Venetian cardinal had been appointed commander shared one characteristic with the Duke of Burgundy's crusading army: both of them were still *in fieri*—that is, not yet actually in existence. However, the process of assembling the fleet had at least begun. At Ripa Grande, on the Tiber, Callistus had set up a group of shipyards. Till a short while previously this project had been written off as a wild pipe-dream; but now the yards were loud with activity. Very often people would see the Pontiff down there, speeding up the rhythm of the workers by his presence and his exhortations.

Impatience almost took his breath away. He wanted, at all costs, to win the battle against time. There were several reasons for this. He knew the Turks were preparing a great expedition against Hungary, and by the following spring would be on the march towards the Danube. The humiliation of the Cross, and the sufferings of Christian lands that had fallen under the domination of the Crescent, tormented him night and day. Last but not least, he did not want to close his eyes for ever without having first freed the Catholic world from the terror and servitude imposed on it by the Infidel.

He worked all through the autumn and winter, and on into the spring of 1456, with tireless energy. Before the beginning of summer a fleet was ready: sixteen galleys, fully armed and manned—three hundred cannons, about a thousand sailors, and five thousand troops from various regions of Italy. The cost of all this came to something very near 150,000 ducats. The resultant fleet was a prodigy of one man's determined will.

Callistus stood on the banks of the Tiber and watched the fleet sail away, eyes damp with emotion, hope springing in his heart. As aides to Scarampo he had sent out two men: Velasco de Farinha, a Portuguese officer who held the title of Vice-Admiral, and Alonso Calatambio, from Aragon, to deal with matters concerning the judiciary.

The sixteen galleys set off, and dropped anchor in the Bay of Naples. Once there, it seems they could not conjure up so much as a breath of wind to speed their departure. King Alfonso, after promising fifteen vessels, could not bring himself to part with them. He had also employed the money extracted for the forthcoming crusade to pay his debts, throw parties, and finance the expedition against Genoa. Now he was stalling to gain time.

Meanwhile the most alarming reports kept pouring into Rome. Turkish assault forces had captured Athens. Mohammed II, with an army of 100,000, was advancing towards the Danube: he meant to invest Belgrade, the outlying fortress of Hungary, and from there penetrate into the heart of Europe. If the chance of effective intervention still existed, it had to be grasped without a day's delay. The Turks must be attacked in the Aegean, and thus stopped from spreading all over Greece. The opening of this second front would also force them to slacken their pressure against Hungary.

Callistus III sent an emissary of his, Giacomo Perpinya, post-haste to Naples, with orders to put pressure on Scarampo and force him to depart immediately, without the King's squadron: in Sicily he would find plentiful cash reserves, and the fleet until lately commanded by that villain Urrea. He also sent Scarampo an urgent message, which said, among other things: 'Victory against the infidel Turk has been promised us from on high, even with scanty forces—unless you prevent it. And bear in mind that the end of summer is already at hand. If you do not sail now, what kind of weather can you expect?'

Scarampo would not, perhaps, have dared to say openly just what he was waiting for. He belonged to the anti-Borgia, anti-Catalan party; he knew that the Pontiff's relations detested him, and was convinced that they had got him made fleet-commander, with a whole mass of titles and legateships as well— Sicily, Dalmatia, Macedonia, Greece, Crete, Rhodes, Cyprus, besides lesser islands and provinces of Asia—simply and solely to get him as far away from

Rome as possible. Now, as a result of his dealings with King Alfonso—who was using delaying tactics to force the Pope into making certain concessions dear to his heart—his envy of the Borgias had become still further exacerbated. His conduct was not much better than that of Urrea, and made it clear just how little reliance Callistus III could place on those about him—beginning with the cardinals—and how sadly right he had been, from this point of view, to surround himself with blood-relations and fellow-countrymen as some protection against betrayal and covert attacks. One can make out a solid enough case against the nepotism practised by him and other Renaissance Popes; but even though the widespread disloyalty and ever-lurking treachery of the day, and the conduct of men like Urrea and Scarampo, may not justify it, they certainly help to make it more understandable, and to mitigate the severity of one's final judgement.

It was not until the evening of 6 August that the fleet left harbour and set course for the East. Alfonso, who had continued to promise them those fifteen galleys on condition that they waited until spring of the following year, at the last moment decided to release some old ships: four or five vessels, according to some, though others mention only a single quadrireme.

On the same day as the crusading fleet passed out of Naples harbour, news reached Rome that put the whole city in a frenzy of excitement: on 14 July (1456), in the course of a five-hour battle beneath the walls of Belgrade which had left the Danube red with blood, the 'white knight' had put the Turks to rout, and liberated the city, after a fortnight's siege during which it had suffered heavy bombardment. Mohammed spent a week nursing his fury, and then returned to the attack. At the head of his janissaries he made a valiant attempt to storm the fortress. This encounter was a dark and lurid inferno, with appalling casualties on both sides; but a sortie by Janos Hunyadi finally held and broke the tide, the attackers were beaten off, and the original victory miraculously confirmed. Mohammed himself was wounded, the enemy camp in the hands of the crusaders, and the Turks in headlong flight.

The credit for these two triumphal occasions, which redeemed the shame of Byzantium and allowed Christendom to breathe in hope once more, naturally went, in the first instance, to the formidable Hungarian *condottiere*. However, if it be true that any victory is also the fruit of much organization and psychological planning, a large proportion of the credit should go to two remarkable men who served under him, and whose work had made his success possible. These were the Franciscan friar John of Capistrano, who—in defiance of his seventy years—had literally been the spirit of the liberation, giving courage, assistance and hope, moment by moment, and in the very midst of battle, to the defenders of Europe; and Cardinal Carvajal, who had been the brains of the whole campaign, donning seven-league boots to organize it, travelling tire- lessly up and down the entire length and breadth of the Danubian area to collect funds and men, and then taking up quarters in Buda, where he became responsible for the army's supply-lines. It was to these two men that the Voivode owed the influx of a whole mass of irregular troops, who provided welcome reinforcements for the army, some 7000 strong, which he had raised at his own expense: townsmen and country peasants, monks, students, roving German mercenaries, individuals of every condition and provenance, a red cross sewn on the breast of their surcoats, carrying a weird assortment of weapons, and for the most part with little or no experience of warfare. A victory won with troops like these, against an army such as that of Mohammad II—which was far larger and better-armed, with a great deal more military experience—defied rational explanation. It could only be termed a miracle: a miracle compounded from the military genius of the 'white knight', the heroism of the combatants, and the inspiring and courageous example of the old friar.

But behind all this, at the source of that flood of enthusiasm which had produced so dazzling and unforgettable a scene beneath the walls of Belgrade, at the departure-point of that sequence of cause and effect which had brought matters to so splendid a conclusion, there undoubtedly stood one man: Callis- tus III. In one area, and one only, his passion for liberation had found a response and borne fruit; but this was enough to make it quite clear that if more people had answered his appeal and given backing to his efforts, the Ottoman stranglehold would surely have been broken.

In the light of subsequent events, this victory at Belgrade was to be proved largely sterile, its sole virtue being to win a breathing-space, a period of truce. But Christendom exulted in it as though it were a guarantee that the incubus would be lifted; and none exulted more than the elderly Spaniard in the Vati- can. This success was indeed the jewel of his pontificate, and he did not hesitate to describe it as the happiest event in his entire life. He ordered the bells of Rome to ring a victory peal, and bonfires to be lit in celebration. The glad news was spread abroad through all Christendom. With his profound religious faith, he ascribed this victory to the prayers and acts of penance which he had imposed upon the entire Catholic world on St Peter's day—that is, at the very darkest point of those months, when he felt himself sorely tempted to despair of the whole enterprise—while at the same time calling, as a first step towards regaining Divine favour, for general reform in the moral sphere.

On 23 August an emissary from Francesco Sforza, one Jacopo Calcaterra, had a three and a half hour interview with him. He found the Pontiff in bed, suffering from gout, but brimming over with happiness: 'He never tired of repeating the same thing, two or three times over, exalting and magnifying the aforesaid victory, while lauding and commending to the skies the name of His Illustrious Excellency Johannes the Voivode, as one of the most glorious men who had been born in the past three hundred years, or were alive at this present time.'

During this audience, the frail but pugnacious old fighter showed his polemical side in no uncertain fashion. In mordant tones he emphasized the 'shameful and opprobrious conduct' of all those who had opposed, derided, or otherwise shown their disapproval of him, those who had expressed the belief 'that he had no idea what he was after with these crusades of his, that he was cherishing vain illusions, and wantonly squandering the Church's resources'.

This thrust was clearly directed against King Alfonso, who had taken—and continued to take—the liberty of criticizing His Holiness's policy in public. It was followed by a violent outburst against Scarampo, who had entered into a conspiracy with the King while at Naples, abetting him in his slanderous aspersions on the Pope and encouraging his grievances, and had also shown a most remarkable reluctance to put to sea. Now he was gone, and Italy had thus got rid of 'the greater scorpion' infesting it.

The Duke of Milan's envoy felt that the Pope was floating on a slightly exaggerated breeze of euphoria when he heard him express the conviction that from now on the sovereigns of Europe would hold him 'in higher esteem than they had done hitherto', and that they would show themselves 'changed men, obedient and well disposed to his will'. Yet this same envoy could not but feel a certain degree of covert uneasiness when confronted by the disturbing self-confidence which he sensed in the Pontiff when the latter emphasized that 'a thousand times this past year have I written or dictated letters to many foreign parts', or that during the course of his Pontificate 'the infidel and iniquitous Mahommedan sect would be consumed and destroyed for ever'.

Callistus III now intensified his efforts with renewed fervour. The Ripa Grande shipyards continued to turn out fresh vessels. In the Vatican Chancellery secretaries penned non-stop appeals, at his dictation, to every remote corner of the Christian world. The feeling that the crucial hour, the decisive turning-point, the final triumph were not far distant infused all his activities with 'the Nemean lion's nerve'.

When he learnt that the crusading fleet had successfully reached Rhodes (which Scarampo thereafter made his permanent headquarters) and liberated the islands of Lemnos, Samothrace and Thasos, expelling all Turkish troops from them, and setting up garrisons of their own, there could, he felt, be no further doubt about the matter: the days of the 'Mahommedan sect' were numbered.

This joy was of brief duration. Neither the victory of Belgrade nor these conquests in the Aegean sufficed to disturb Europe's massive indifference; and the various Powers paid no more attention to the Pope than they had ever done. Then two almost unbelievably cruel strokes of fortune befell him. On 11 August 1456, only a bare three weeks after his ringing achievement, Janos Hunyadi died of the plague, in a church, where he had had himself carried during his still-lucid last moments. And then on 23 October, at Villach in Carinthia, John of Capistrano also breathed his last, worn out by unremitting toil.

No man knew better than Callistus III what a tragedy these two losses were—losses that left the whole main front defenceless. No man suffered more than he did as a result. And no man reacted more vigorously against the mood of depression that once more threatened to engulf him. As evidence both for his sweating agony and for his indestructible courage we still have the correspond-ence covering this period, distributed through the forty-eight stout volumes that contain the record of his pontificate.

There were moments at which age, weariness, and disappointment drove him to reproaches and supplications. 'Night and day', he wrote to Cardinal Alain on 17 December 1456, 'we keep vigil, ready if need be to jeopardize our life for the cause, yet find but few collaborators. . . . We place great trust in your devotion, and hope for great assistance therefrom; but salvation lies in the avoidance of delay, and deferment renders the ill incurable. . . . Do not let this old Pope, who has suffered so much in defence of the Holy Gospel, be forced to endure still greater affliction than has hitherto been his lot.'

On other occasions his tone became threatening—as in the following passage, taken from a letter he wrote on 16 February 1457 to the French legate: 'Woe, woe to those who oppose us! He who troubles us shall without fail be brought to justice, whosoever he may be.' The only thing that now sustained him— holding him back from collapse, admitting defeat, giving up and dying—was that implacable inner tension of his. His features were strikingly stamped with the marks of the suffering he bore. His pain-ridden, emaciated face inspired such pity as to make one diplomat write that even a heart of stone would feel compassion at the sight of him.

He now searched the confines of the known world for the aid which Europe denied him. He sent messages to the King of Ethiopia. Carvajal, who became a kind of permanent roving pilgrim, he dispatched first to Bosnia, to urge King Stephen Thomas and his people to join the struggle, and then to the Emperor and to Ladislaw of Hungary, in an attempt to reconcile them, and to induce them to take up the idea of the crusade. He tried to whip up and canalize general enthusiasm by fixing 6 August—the day on which he had learnt the news of the victory at Belgrade—as the date for the Feast of the Transfiguration. Having got so disappointing a response from the crowned heads of Europe, he decided to appeal more directly to popular feeling. This gambit brought him some response from Germany, France and England, where bands of simple folk took the Cross and set forth—with a revival of the mood that had flourished in Peter the Hermit's day—to defend the bastions of Hungary.

Above all, he strove to support the last great fighting paladin left in Christendom: George Castriotis, better known as Scanderbeg. This romantic figure, the so-called 'athlete of Christ', who for something like a quarter of a century had stood out against the Ottoman invasion—elusive, invincible, deadly in ambush, striking and moving with the speed of light—was perhaps the most brilliant partisan leader of all time. The steep, wild, mountainous landscape of his country, rock-racked, seamed with water-courses, full of bogs and thick forests, was ideally suited to his methods of warfare. From his towering eagle's-nest at Kruja he hurled himself against the Turk with the convulsive energy of a wild beast. Ordeal by battle was his supreme pleasure.

For a long while nothing had been heard of Scanderbeg; but at the first reports of the struggle on which the Pontiff had embarked, he marched back into the limelight, dispatching letters to the Pope, Francesco Sforza, and King Alfonso. Exultant, ready for any bold undertaking, in a state bordering on the frenetic, he offered them the services of his sword, and called for help to mount a decisive campaign. Callistus III, having for the moment no other resources at his disposal, sent Scanderbeg money and promised him ships.

When he learnt of the sweeping victory which the Albanian won at the Tomoriza, on 2 September 1457—15,000 Turks killed, as many more taken prisoner, twenty-four standards captured, the entire enemy camp occupied and plundered, the Ottoman threat driven back from the shores of the Adriatic—he stepped up his financial support, and ordered Scarampo to detach part of his fleet for support and supply duties on the Albanian coast. Two days before Christmas, finally, he conferred on Scanderbeg the title of Captain-General of the Church in the war against the Turks.

The warrior of Kruja tried, in his turn, to administer a vigorous shaking-up to the apathy of the Christian Powers, emphasizing the gravity of the situation and the urgent necessity of collective intervention; but his crude language and compelling arguments had no more effect than the Bulls and Briefs of the Pontiff.

Shortly before the news of the engagement on the Tomoriza, there also reached Rome a dispatch announcing a naval victory won by the crusaders' fleet in the August of that year, off the coast of Mytilene. This island, along with five others, had since 1355 been under the rule of a Genoese family, the Gattiluzi, who were related to the Byzantine emperors. Twenty-five enemy galleys had been captured. There was now a large area of the Aegean into which Turkish ships no longer ventured.

In the shipyards of Ripa Grande work went steadily on. By early September Callistus III was able to send a further squadron into Eastern waters. With it there went yet another of his relations, Michele Borgia, whom he had chosen as a confidential agent, and given the task of plying between Rome and Rhodes: he would accompany the galleys on the outward trip, and have charge of the cash reserves aboard them. Despite their long-standing feud, the Pope con-tinued to send his cardinal-admiral letters full of glowing praise, encourage-ment, and recommendations, on each occasion repeating assurances concerning his solicitude for Scarampo's welfare.

Belgrade, the Tomoriza, Mytilene: three most glorious episodes, which con-soled Callistus's weary heart, and filled him with the hope that they might mark the auspicious beginning of a decisive campaign. Death was to spare him the realization that he had made a bad mistake. Early in 1458 it was rumoured that he meant to use this crusade as an instrument for advancing his kinsmen, and indeed for getting his nephew Pedro Luís an Eastern crown. This rumour at once scotched the last lingering possibility of any collaboration from the Italian states. These three victories, moreover, gave the Christian world the illusory notion that there would be no more trouble from Islam for a long while to come. As a result, they thought no more about it.

The fruit of success lay within their grasp, but was never plucked. A few years later all that had brought it about—the toil and suffering of the first Borgia Pope, the crushing tasks undertaken by men like Capistrano and Car-vajal, the prowess and bloodshed among the combatants—was revealed as pathetically useless, since everything that had been won was lost once more. The victories terminated in failure.

In the haven provided by the quarrels and disagreements going on between the various European Powers, the Ottomans now proceeded to lick their wounds. Then, with a fresh access of daring and ferocity, they flung themselves into a series of furious incursions, clearly bent on tearing the throat out of

Europe. Men who were young in Callistus's day had, by the time they reached their prime, seen the Turks attack the Morea, destroy Attica, shatter the Venetian fleet off Negroponte, swallow up Euboea, turn the Aegean into their own private lake, and thrust on as far north as the lagoons of Venice to beard the Lion of St Mark. On 10 August 1480, twenty-two years after the unheard preacher of this crusade was dead, Mohammed II's warriors landed at Otranto. Of 22,000 inhabitants, 12,000 were killed and left in the blazing summer sun. The remainder found themselves slaves. The archbishop and the commandant of the fortress were sawn in half. Those prisoners who refused to embrace Islam were mostly slaughtered, and fed to wild beasts. Nothing can have sounded more plausible than the Sultan's prediction, the scornful flash of white teeth in that olive-dark face, as he said: 'It will not be long before my horse is eating his oats from the High Altar of St Peter's.'

It is impossible to say what might have become of Europe, blind and crazy as she then was had Mohammed II not died in 1481. The struggle between his two sons for the succession, and the consequent civil war, temporarily brought this irresistible Turkish advance to a halt. Christendom was saved by pure accident. But through the whole of this long humiliating episode, the Spanish Pope's example shone out like some bold peak above a grey and rotting expanse of marshland.

AGAINST ALFONSO AND FERRANTE

'Priests', the King of Naples was fond of saying, 'are men of arms rather than men of prayer.' One had to concede him a certain measure of experience in the matter: he had, in fact, spent most of his life steering an adroit course through various ecclesiastical quarrels, and playing his own gambits—subtle or forceful, according to circumstance—against the Popes. One may add that in these trials of strength he was very often assisted by Alonso de Borja. It was his fate, towards the end of his life, to come into head-on collision with the 'priest' who had been his friend and collaborator: the 'priest', moreover, who could thank *him* for the career that had brought him ultimately to the pontificate.

But if the Alfonso of the old days—days of collaboration and friendship—was now King of Naples, Sicily and Sardinia as well as of Aragon, Catalonia, Valencia and the Balearics, Alonso de Borja now sat on Peter's throne, and bore himself like a man who has no time for weaknesses or complaisances of any sort. The old harmony could continue to exist only on condition that both protagonists refrained from putting a foot over the clearly marked line which defined their respective rights.

When Alfonso—whose greed for new territory was growing in him like some malign tumour—expressed a desire to be invested with the Ancona Marches as his feudal domain, Callistus III told him, in round terms, that such an aspiration was merely absurd. This was Alfonso's first intimation that he could no longer rely on this old association to expand his frontiers at the Church's expense. It was also the first time that the presumptions of Alonso's former protector were at variance with the aims of the man who had attained the very highest office.

When Alfonso later persisted in assigning certain wealthy Spanish bishoprics to patently unsuitable individuals whose only merit was that of being his relations or favourites, Callistus III (who in truth intended to bestow them on equally dubious relations of his own) went on record with a stinging reply: 'Let the King of Aragon rule his own realm, and leave the task of governing the Church to us!'[10] And this—a sacrosanct defence of independence for the spiritual arm—was in actual fact the first clash between the domestic interests of the sovereign and the Pontiff's own nepotism.

Alfonso became mean and venomous. Abruptly changing to strong-arm methods he sent a couple of letters to Rome which sinned in every direction save that of excessive reverence. They were addressed to the Pontiff's secretary, but clearly aimed at giving the Pontiff himself a spiteful dig in the ribs. Jacopo Calcaterra, who had the opportunity of reading them, informed the Duke of Milan that in one Alfonso sarcastically exhorted the secretary to 'arouse and awake' His Holiness, so that he might finally decide to go into action over the crusade, since to him, Alfonso, 'it seemed as though he slept'. The royal epistolary prose—again according to Calcaterra—was, in addition, studded with 'many strange phrases', or, in other words, a number of further impertinences. And this skilled diplomat concluded: 'I write this that your lordship may know and understand that between the two—His Holiness and the King— things are not so entirely well sorted and ordered as at first the whole world thought and believed.'[11]

'As the whole world *feared*' would be a more accurate way of putting it: Italy in particular, which could look for some disagreeable surprises when two Spaniards—the most powerful monarch in the peninsula and the sovereign of the Papal State—came to a private working agreement. Three months after the Borgia election, then, relations between Naples and Rome were not merely not 'entirely well sorted', but rapidly deteriorating into open hostility.

Alfonso's sarcastic allusion to his having urged the Pope crusadewards was doubly reprehensible: first, because during the three months of his pontificate

Callistus III had already given highly convincing signs of being anything but 'asleep', and second, because the man who was exhorting him, with such mocking arrogance, to 'wake up' was also doing his best, behind the scenes, to hamper his efforts.

The crusade was a collective undertaking, and its implementation pre-supposed as a *conditio sine qua non*, peace and concord between the States. What, we may ask, was Alfonso's contribution to calm in Italy? The answer is soon told.

In the summer of that year, 1455, Jacopo Piccinino, a professional mercenary and military contractor who now found himself out of a job, after studying the field with great care to see where he could best filch enough land to make himself a modest fief, and settle down for good, made an attack on the territory of Siena. Callistus III, on receipt of a desperate appeal from the tiny Tuscan republic, now in grave peril, sent out a punitive force to its defence, com-manded by Giovanni, Count of Ventimiglia, a Sicilian. Other States—Venice, Florence, Milan—likewise sent their watchdogs to bark at Piccinino. The Papal forces, operating conjointly with a detachment of Francesco Sforza's militia, drove the aggressor back to Castiglione della Pescaia, between the marshes and the sea: a kind of trap from which he would find great difficulty in escaping, but where it would be equally tricky to come to grips with him, let alone dislodge him from his position. The immediate result was that Piccinino got the best of it all round. Indeed, he could have held out there for the rest of his natural life, thumbing his nose at the armies which were besieg-ing him—at a respectful distance—from the landward side. He had the sea behind him, and the ships of good King Alfonso brought him plenty of supplies.

With cheerful impudence, Piccinino even went so far as to turn the supposed trap into a base for piratical operations. Darting out from Castiglione, he descended on Orbetello, captured it by a surprise attack, and proceeded to raid and sack other places along the coast. He also amused himself by boarding Genoese vessels that he found sailing the high seas.

After a while Callistus wearied of spending thousands of ducats on this inconclusive expedition against the man whom he referred to as *latrunculus Iacobus*. He therefore tried to do a deal with Alfonso, its object being to stop him giving Piccinino support and supplies. But the King of Naples put an unacceptable price on this favour. He demanded that *latrunculus Iacobus* should be given supreme command of a crusading fleet, gathered from the Powers belonging to the 'Italian League', and financed by them to the tune of 100,000 florins *per annum*. The Pope would have nothing to do with such a scheme.

At the beginning of April 1456, after an attempt by Piccinino to set fire to the Papal galleys in Civitavecchia harbour (these being earmarked for the Eastern venture), Callistus, fulminating, pronounced sentence of excommunication on the *condottiere*, and on all those who gave him support.

Of these latter the most eminent was undoubtedly Alfonso. At first he erupted in fury, threatening to expel all relatives of the Pope from his domains. Then he pulled in his horns, requested a resumption of negotiations, and finally compelled Piccinino to leave the Sienese in peace, and remove himself troops and all, to Neapolitan territory. At the same time he managed to extract 20,000 florins from poor Siena (which, paradoxically had thus to *pay* for the aggression it had suffered, rather than receive any compensation), and as much again from the Apostolic Camera. Such a solution left both protagonists embittered and sullen: neither the Roman nor the Neapolitan Spaniard could get much benefit from it.

The bad joke played by Urrea in taking his fleet on an unexpected course towards the shores of Genoa, and the artful obstructionism that was generally rife where the crusade was concerned, were hardly liable to bring about a *détente*. But the hidden core of this reciprocal hostility lay in a question which (to Alfonso's way of thinking) had top priority: a fundamental question, and one that—despite its initial avoidance—would at some point have to be faced and resolved. This was the confirmation of the investiture of the Kingdom of Naples—in theory a feudal domain pertaining to the Church—and the linked problem of the succession.

When Callistus III was still Bishop of Valencia, and the King's political adviser, he had worked most skilfully on Eugenius IV with a view to obtaining formal recognition of the conquered throne, including Benevento and Terracina (which really belonged to the Papal domains), and the Pope's agreement that Ferrante should succeed to the Kingdom. Now, however, he obstinately turned a deaf ear to Alfonso's solicitations for a renewal of the investiture, and would not even discuss the matter of Ferrante's succession. Both refusals had an ulterior motive behind them.

A year after Callistus's election, Alfonso had still received neither the confirmation of his fief, nor even a vague and general assurance on the matter. His patience exhausted, he told his ambassador in Rome to jettison all polite restraint, and made it clear that a little brutal frankness was in order, reinforced if need be with some wellchosen insults. So it came about that the Pontiff, during a stormy interview with the diplomat, found himself being taunted with his modest background, his povertystricken childhood, the shabbiness of his native stronghold, Canals, the time when he used to sing the Epistle in the Church of Sant'Antonio—all this being designed to remind him that he should not raise his head too high, since he had come up from practically nothing, and it was only the King's generosity that had picked him out of the mud in the gutter.

The conflict, as has already been noted, grew more bitter at this point because of several good fat Spanish bishoprics which both contestants wanted to bestow on their own relatives and favourites, and which neither of the two would agree to see held by the other's nominees.

In June 1457 an emissary from Alfonso presented himself at the Vatican, and in his King's name demanded the archbishopric of Saragossa for one of Alfonso's grandsons, the eleven-year-old bastard of Ferrante, who was himself illegitimate. Callistus greeted this request with a 'No' that was as firm as a block of granite. The ambassador, who had been carefully briefed, retorted with a threat: they would appeal to a future Council. Now if there was one word capable of making any Pope fly into a rage, 'Council' was it. Moreover, by sheer coincidence, only a few days before an envoy had reached Rome from the University of Paris, bearing most vehement protests against the exaction of money in France for the crusade, along with eighteen Articles that were tantamount to a direct attack on Papal authority, and a demand for the sum-moning of a Council.

Callistus III saw red. There and then he poured out a hissing diatribe against the Aragonese monarch's representative, following it up with a sentence of excommunication so thunderous that it shook the very earth and sky. Then, while the poor fellow slunk out, bent double under such a load, and muttering that he would appeal to God's own justice to be summarily freed from this imposition, Callistus summoned a secretary, and in an agitated voice dictated a Brief to the King of Naples. We do not possess its text, but we know—from a dispatch which the Abbot of St Ambrose's sent to the Duke of Milan—that it ended with the following noteworthy example of minatory concision: '*Verba papae: sciat tua Majestas quod papa scit deponere reges.*' To which Alfonso—likewise using Latin—replied with a letter in which there occurred this sentence: '*Verba regis: sciat tua Sanctitas quod, quando voluerimus, reperiemus modum deponendi pontificem.*' He could not, however, fail to observe that the Pope's threat was a good deal more consistent than his own.

In October of the same year there came to Rome the King's mistress, the exquisitely beautiful Lucrezia d'Alagno. She hoped that when she left again it would be with a Papal dispensation permitting her to become her sovereign's wife. She was given a most splendid reception, had the honour of being solemnly received in the Vatican, and held converse with the Pope and his attendant cardinals; but when she once more took the road for Naples it was empty-handed.

In the spring of 1458 various peacemakers (including the Pope's own kins-men, notably Cardinal Rodrigo) went to work with great determination, but their efforts remained entirely fruitless. Callistus's attitude had not changed one whit since August 1456, when in the course of an audience granted to Jacopo Calcaterra after news of the victory at Belgrade, he had launched into a bitter tirade against Alfonso, saying that 'God's judgement' would overtake him, threatening him with 'grievous and lengthy harassment', and showing himself acidulously sceptical regarding the likelihood of any repentance on the King's part: 'It seemed to him impossible that an old man of seventy such as the King's Majesty should be turned from his habitual ways.' The rancour and obstinacy of both had now reached such heights that each awaited the other's death, with unconcealed impatience ready, in the event, to intone an exultant private *Nunc dimittis*.

The truth—according to the shrewdest Italian diplomats accredited to the Vatican—was as follows. Despairing of being able to depose Alfonso, Callis-tus was impatiently waiting for his natural removal from the scene—an event that was essential if he was to reassert the Church's ancient rights over the Kingdom of Naples, and to bestow it upon his nephew Pedro Luís. This was why he so firmly challenged Ferrante's right to the succession.

By the late spring of 1458 a good many people were alert to this hidden but fundamental aspect of the situation. Furthermore, Callistus, knowing that his adversary was gravely ill, made certain involved speeches on the subject of Naples, which, by their very caution and reticence, merely served to heighten suspicion in those who heard them. He did not, as yet, show his hand; but it hardly required the craftiness of Ulysses to deduce the direction in which he was moving.

Giacomo Antonio della Torre, who had a series of long private discussions with him in early June, found him remarkably euphoric and talkative. 'He looks forward to the King's Death with the greatest joy,' della Torre wrote Sforza on the 11th, refraining from any comment on that highly un-Christian sentiment. The only shadow marring the Pope's great delight was the fear that, once Alfonso had gone, Piccinino would go into action and hamper the realization of his, the Pope's, plans for the future. As regards Alfonso, Callis-tus remarked that he had always been a thorn in the Church's side, causing much tribulation to no less than three successive Pontiffs: Martin V, Eugenius IV, and himself. Now he wanted 'to free this kingdom and his successors *omnino*, once and for all, from such servitude'; this was why he would fight *totis veribus* to prevent the Duke of Calabria obtaining the succession. As jus- tification for this line of conduct, Callistus adduced the Church's ancient rights over the feudal domain of Naples, and the concern of all the Italian States that the Church should reabsorb it into her own territorial patrimony, thus ensuring general peace throughout the peninsula. France, he declared confidently, would cheerfully accept such a solution. And indeed this reference to the Kingdom beyond the Alps had its own importance, and a strongly topical flavour, since Genoa—after being attacked the previous year by both Urrea's and Alfonso's fleets—had solicited aid from the French. The latter had granted them full solidarity, and had profited by the occasion to exhume the dormant but by no means defunct claims of the Angevins. Now here was the Pope asserting that France, on the death of Alfonso, would never stand for the Duke of Calabria inheriting the throne, 'and kindling such a fire in Italy as to burn each and every one of us'. There was, therefore, only one way of averting a war that would, clearly, spread through the entire peninsula: for the Church to remove the Kingdom of Naples from both contending claimants.

These arguments on the part of Callistus, who described himself as *pater et dominus pacis*, were both subtle and plausible; but behind his proclaimed con- cern for the peace of Italy, diplomats stationed in Rome had little difficulty in scenting the machinations of nepotism.

Such a gambit was audacious enough: the ambitions of the Borgias had obviously broken into a wild gallop. This, however, was typical of the moral atmosphere then prevalent. We may illustrate the latter, with perfect fairness, by means of a famous letter which Lorenzo de' Medici wrote Pope Innocent VIII, after his daughter Maddalena had married Innocent's son: 'In short, I beg Your Holiness, in all humility, that it may please you now to begin acting as a Pope should, to the benefit, I mean, of these your dependants, and not to place so much trust in your own prosperity and healthy constitution.' Men became Pope at an advanced age, and their pontificates seldom lasted more than a few years; they therefore had to act fast to assure the fortune and position of their relatives. Besides, Lorenzo added, with impudent candour, a Pope did not have to be generous with his own possessions; what he handed out was the property of the Church. . . .

To avoid any hint of anachronistic astonishment when studying Callis- tus III's immoderate proposals, we should also bear in mind the fact that these times favoured great and sudden rises in fortune. It was an age in which an ordinary mercenary captain like Francesco Sforza could, almost overnight, seize the Duchy of Milan and become one of the most eminent princes in all

Italy; this was still the period when men could win a fief or a throne by a light-ning *coup de main* or some astute political manoeuvring.

The family came above all else. Callistus was so blinded by his affections that he saw in Pedro Luís—as the ambassadors of the Italian States mockingly noted—a 'new Caesar'. He was working hard to secure as Pedro's bride a young girl from the Colonna family, the cardinal's grand-daughter; the cardinal himself, as the Abbot of St Ambrose's wrote, had lent a favourable ear to this suggestion—both ears, in fact. Nor, so far as could be judged, did the throne of Naples represent the Pontiff's ultimate ambition for Pedro Luís. It was rumoured in Rome (and the rumour was promptly recorded in dispatches written by the ambassadors of Milan and Venice) that the young Borgia would very soon leave for Cyprus, where a royal crown awaited him. The elderly sovereign of the island, like a fairy-tale king, had one daughter, and was keep-ing his kingdom, as a legacy, for whoever should be found most worthy to marry her. The Pope had already sent thither, in the role of matchmaker, a certain bearded and eloquent friar, who collected a reward of five hundred ducats for undertaking such a mission, and expressed complete confidence in his own ability to bring about the marriage. After that, with glorious Con-stantinople by God's grace reconquered, Pedro Luís would finally also don the Imperial crown. Early in 1458, according to a dispatch which Antonio of Trezzo sent Francesco Sforza, Callistus III (somewhat prematurely) conferred on him the title of Emperor of Byzantium.

At this stage it seemed a legitimate supposition that the Pope's nepotic aspirations were being coloured by a touch of senile dementia.

The summer of 1458 was heralded, in Rome, by one of the customary epi-demics. Everyone scuttled off at top speed, including most of the cardinals. But Callistus remained obdurately anchored in the Vatican, because from day to day he expected to hear the news of his enemy's death.

This reached him just before the end of June: Alfonso had breathed his last late on the evening of the 27th. He left Sicily to his brother John, and the throne of Naples to Ferrante.

Ferrante—now twenty-seven, and for the next thirty-six years destined to reveal himself a most worthy disciple of his father when it came to Pope-baiting—was a man who knew very well where his own interests lay. This knowledge was so diabolically thorough, and demonstrated, on various occasions, in so horrific a manner, that public opinion held him to have been sired by some bastard Moor from Valencia (times had changed, and it was no longer possible to believe him a child of the Devil). A sullen, bestial character, capable of displaying tremendous energy, and endowed with a most subtle political brain, he pursued one aim only from the day of the accession: the annihilation of his real or potential enemies. Sustained by a quite incredible hatred, aided by his marked capacity for dissimulation, and possessing an infallible instinct for striking at just the right place and moment, he managed to make a clean sweep of the lot of them. Notwithstanding his hot, thick blood, he was a stranger to intemperance of any sort. He both loved and respected culture. In certain respects he might almost be considered an intellectual. He was passionately devoted to hunting, and took great pride in the exotic animals he had collected for his small zoological garden. His favourite hobby, however, was catching his enemies alive, and then keeping them in cages. His normal method of capture was first to stage a cordial, but fictitious, reconciliation with the person in question, who would then receive an invitation to dinner. When they died, he had them artistically embalmed, in their best clothes. And living or embalmed, he held them in great affection, since there was no pleasure to equal that which he derived from contemplating them.

He went about their elimination with a cold ferocity that was wholly devoid of remorse, sparing not even those whose services to his family should have earnt them some consideration. In 1465 Piccinino, his father's friend and tool, came to pay him a visit: Ferrante welcomed him like a brother—but no sooner had he got him safe inside the walls of Castel Nuovo than he gave orders for his execution. Similar treatment was also meted out to a minister named Antonello Petrucci, who had damned his soul and sacrificed all hope of salvation in Ferrante's service.

With such a man, Callistus could be under no illusions. To topple him from a throne that was still warm from his father would be no easy matter. Along with the announcement of Alfonso's much-prayed-for demise, news reached the Vatican that young Ferrante, without wasting any time shedding tears over the corpse, had sprung to horse and ridden through the streets of Naples, where the populace had greeted him with cheers and smiling faces.

'The trap is sprung and we are free!' Callistus exclaimed joyously, by way of comment on the death of a man who had been his King. He at once sent men to arrest the Neapolitan ambassador, and bring him to Castel Sant'Angelo but the hired bullies chosen for this task came back, somewhat crestfallen, and informed him that they had found the house empty, with unmistakable signs of a hasty departure. The only consolation left to Callistus was to have the place ruthlessly gutted.

Next day there were family celebrations, with the handing out to relatives and friends of those benefices and posts which Alfonso's opposition had hitherto made it impossible to assign. The most precious pearl of all, the splendidly-endowed bishopric of Valencia, went—with no objections from the deceased—to Cardinal Rodrigo. 'And in this manner,' Antonio da Pistoia wrote the Duke of Milan 'the Pope hath enriched the greater part of his kin, in such a manner that the whole palace smiles thereat.'[12] So, doubtless, did the beneficiaries.

That same afternoon Callistus summoned the French Cardinals Alain de Coétivy and Guillaume d'Estouteville, and—plunging into numerous per-suasive arguments, which dragged on until nightfall—revealed to them his intention of re-establishing (in the Church's name) the right to dispose freely of the Kingdom of Naples, and to put it to such use as might best suit him. As between Ferrante of Aragon and René of Anjou, he fully recognized that the latter, beyond any doubt, could make out a better claim; however, one would see. . . . The two cardinals left the Vatican with a faint smile on their lips; they were too shrewd not to realize that the old man, with all his chatter, had one end, and one only, in view. This was to get them on his side for the struggle against Ferrante, enticing them with the prospect that the Kingdom might possibly be assigned to that somewhat bucolic figure René, though his own unshakeable intention was to bestow it upon Pedro Luís. Antonio da Pistoia, in the dispatch quoted above, claimed: 'He is determined, if perchance this domain fall into his hands, to give it to none other man save to his nephew, Messer Borges, who by His Holiness is taken for a second Caesar.' And he concluded: 'I believe that your lordship will judge these to be mere childish desires, rather than matters capable of achievement. . . . Nevertheless it is possible that this may furnish cause for a great fire to be lit.'

Meanwhile Callistus sent a large sum of money to his nephew (who at the time was raiding the wretched townships of the Papal State with his troops, and holding them to ransom) accompanied by a message warning him to hold himself in readiness for action. He rejected all Ferrante's attempts to come to some understanding, even refusing to give his envoy audience. Finally, on 12 July, he issued a Bull which was tantamount to a declaration of war: this laid claim to the territories of the Neapolitan Kingdom on the Church's behalf, and forbade its subjects to swear an oath of fealty to any person who might claim the crown. At the same time, it was rumoured, Callistus had peremp-torily demanded that Ferrante at once disburse the sum of 60,000 ducats, which his father was presumed to have bequeathed for the benefit of the crusade.

Rome trembled at the alarming prospect of another war; and Naples was terrified. In both cities men got the impression that they were dealing with a madman. Hidden threats of revolt ran through the official circles of the Urbs.

No one wanted a new conflict for the *beaux yeux* of the heartily detested 'Messer Borges'.

Callistus, undaunted, pressed on regardless. He told his nephew to recruit more troops; he sought—in vain—to win the alliance and support of Milan. During an official discussion with Francesco Sforza's spokesman he expressed himself in highly unceremonious terms on the subject of Ferrante, whom he described as a nobody, a worthless bastard sired by an unknown father.[13]

Since all his efforts to reach agreement had failed, Ferrante had no option but to stand firm and fight. He summoned his parliament, to obtain the support of those of his barons who subsequently rebelled, and paid a heavy price for doing so; he launched a whirlwind diplomatic campaign with the more important Italian States; he got Antonio Beccadelli, known as 'the Panormitan', to draft an act of accusation and protest against the Pope's conduct; and he organized a special mission to go to Rome, and there appeal to a Council. When Callistus's own envoy, whose job it was to deliver and publish the Bull of 12 July, set foot on Neopolitan territory, Ferrante demonstrated the inconsistency of that axiom according to which an ambassador is exempt from all molestation, legal or otherwise. He had the man seized, robbed of his Papal screeds, his horse, and his purse, and given a good drubbing into the bargain; so that Antonio da Pistoia could write to the Duke of Milan, a few days later: 'The officer who carried to the Kingdom of Naples those Bulls published here against the King is returned to Rome on foot, penniless, having been able neither to deliver the said Bulls nor to bring them back with him. All he has to show for his pains are certain blows and bruises.'

Callistus grew pale with anger when he learnt that Sforza and Cosimo de' Medici disapproved of his anti-Aragonese policy, and had recognized Alfonso's successor as the legitimate sovereign. This meant that he would have no allies in the armed aggression which now seemed inevitable. Scorn and fury, combined with the extreme tension of the past few months, made him fall ill. On the outcome of his sickness hung the choice between peace and war.

SUMMER OF DRAMA

It was in the cool and breeze-swept atmosphere of Tivoli (where he had retreated to recover from the heat and escape the plague) that Cardinal Rodrigo Borgia received news about the beginning of July, of the Pope's indisposition. He resisted his first impulse, which was to hurry straight back to Rome. The Pontiff's infirmity, he reflected, was due to his years: *senectus ipsa est morbus*. For some while now the old man had been in ailing health, confined to his bed for days at a time, pierced with the sharp pains of gout or burning with fever; but such infirmities did not curtail his activities. He went his way regardless, as methodically as ever: there was simply no stopping him. One might almost say that he had transformed his private apartments into an infirmary, the smell of which spread right through the Apostolic Palace. At times he led the life of an enclosed anchorite. Both his bedroom—its windows tight shut even during those suffocatingly hot summer nights—and his study (crammed with legal and ecclesiastical works) gave off that odour which sick-rooms tend to generate. Those secretaries who were obliged to fill their lungs with it, cursed their luck, while prelates called in for consultation crossed the threshold with disgust. On some occasions the Pope—a man of stout heart and stubborn temperament— would himself emerge, bright and early, with the cheerful expression and sprightly movements of one who, thanks to God, has survived yet another day.

Cardinal Rodrigo did not, therefore, hurry to tear himself away from the banks of the Anio, where—with the gay hedonism befitting his twenty-seven years—he was disporting himself amid pleasures and comforts by no means unworthy of the ancient tradition that culminated in Hadrian's residence at Tivoli, or Tibur, as it was then known.

But when a courier, still breathless after his breakneck ride, brought Rodrigo the news that the Pope had been given up for dead by his doctors, that the ordinary day-to-day administration was suspended, and that the situation looked uncommonly like coming to a critical head at any moment, he threw further delay to the winds, and called for his horse at once.

It was the evening of 25 July. The young cardinal reached Rome in the middle of the night. He made his way along the banks of the Tiber to the Vatican. When, somewhat later, he retired to his own palazzo, he found that his servants had all fled, and the house had been ransacked by the mob. On coming out again, he was confronted by a large and hostile crowd. Sustained by a courage which for the first time revealed the exceptional temper of his character, he strode through them with such imperturbable majesty that they were at once cowed and reduced to silence.

The Pontiff was holding a consistory in his sick-room, with the cardinals gathered round his bed. He spoke to them of the struggle against Ferrante, of the crusade, of questions relating to the political and religious government of the Church. His weak voice and laboured breathing, his sudden lapses into unconsciousness, the extraordinary emaciation of his body—for days now he had taken no nourishment of any sort—all emphasized, more than ever, the presence in that broken shell of a will as tense, tough, and vibrant as a steel wire.

From now on Rodrigo seldom left his side. The old man chafed continually at this illness which had so treacherously laid him low, immobilizing him at the most crucial moment of his enterprise—and which now threatened to checkmate him in the game he was playing over the Neapolitan succession. His mood remained dark and gloomy, only lightening when images and memories of Spain came up in conversation, or—even more—when reference was made to the Borgia family's splendid record hitherto, and the even greater prospects which their present achievements held out for the future. He did not give a thought to his own approaching end. He mentioned death to them, as an eventuality that should be taken into consideration, but he did not believe his own hour could possibly be at hand. On other occasions when sickness had laid him low he had always recovered. Besides, there was still so much to be done.

A sudden deterioration in his condition, on 30 July, caused a rumour to spread through the city that he was actually dead. Thereupon Rome, as though at a prearranged signal, flung itself on the Catalans. Those who were unfortu-nate enough to be caught out of doors paid dearly for the hatred which three years of oppression and tyranny had built up in the people's hearts.

The rumour was promptly denied; but this brief and violent prelude had no sequel, since all those who had possessions to safeguard lost no time in getting them away from the danger-area, while anyone still marked down as a target for public resentment very soon disappeared from circulation. The Sacred College hurriedly nominated an emergency committee for the maintenance of public order. Rodrigo Borgia had good cause to rejoice when he learnt that amongst its members—in addition to Bessarion and the two Frenchmen, Guillaume d'Estouteville and Alain de Coétivy—was his great friend Pietro Barbo, nephew of Eugenius IV. This courageous Venetian, who shared his own taste for refined pleasures and magnificent living, was a man on whom he knew he could place complete reliance.

The first measure taken by this committee of cardinals was to strengthen the armed guards at key danger-spots in the city, and thus keep the violent mob at bay. On the day following the first outbreak of anti-Catalan fury, the Pope—still hovering between life and death—put forth his final flower of nepotism, creating Pedro Luís Duke of Benevento, Count of Terracina, and Marquis of Civitavecchia. The first two cities had become available—at least in theory—on Alfonso's death; but taking possession of them was quite another matter, since Ferrante had them both solidly garrisoned. The cardinals, however reluc-tant they might feel about the matter, did not openly oppose this triple investi-ture; any effort on their part to thwart it, they feared, might lead to their incarceration in Castel Sant'Angelo. Besides, they hoped that death would very soon render it null and void.

They did, however, stick their toes in when, the next day, His Holiness made it very clear that he meant to appoint four new cardinals, including a brace of Spaniards. Obviously the dying man was still busy—between fits of uncon-sciousness—working out ways of strengthening and enlarging the foundations of Catalan power. That evening the more influential members of the Sacred College met in the enterprising Cardinal Alain's palazzo, and agreed upon two points: to withhold their consent from the appointment of the new car-dinals, and to demand that Pedro Luís hand over Castel Sant'Angelo. Until this second point in the programme had been implemented, it would be more prudent if they kept away from the Vatican and its environs, to avoid un-pleasant surprises.

Fear fomented rebelliousness: no one knew what the morrow might bring. From all parts of the Papal State alarming reports of riots and disturbances began to reach the city. On 2 August certain envoys of Ferrante nailed an appeal to the cardinals on the gates of St Peter's. *Aut, aut*: either the Sacred College negotiated an agreement with their Aragonese master, or, if they did not, he would make one himself—with the Roman mob.

Unaware of all the confusion going on around him, unaware of the moves being made by his cardinals (who had, so to speak, sung his *requiem* a week before, and were now waiting anxiously for the next conclave), unaware of the Catalan massacre that had paid off so many old scores, the grand old invalid in the Vatican kept reasserting his confident determination to survive. Only the most insistent pressure from Antonio de la Cerda, his fellow-countryman, induced him—still with great reluctance—to take the Last Sacraments. Amid groans and gasps, as death slowly tightened its grip on his throat, he continued to talk of the crusade, of the war against Ferrante, of new investitures for Pedro Luís.

Rodrigo, realizing at this point that the game was lost, and that all yesterday's crazy ambitions were now so much ballast to be tossed overboard in an effort to salvage one's skin and ready cash, exploited his influence to restrain his brother's proud but insensate dream of resistance. The latter was now barricaded in Castel Sant'Angelo with his troops, and gaining much encouragement from the intransigent attitude assumed by his officials; he enunciated sky-darkening threats, and played the public role of the *miles gloriosus*.

From the dying Pope's room there was removed to the charge of the Sacred College a strongbox which contained his savings. According to the official version put out by the cardinals, these amounted to 120,000 ducats. Unofficial rumours (collected by Sforza's spokesman Ottone del Carretto) put the sum at 300,000. From this strongbox there was now removed the sum of 22,000 ducats, representing the sum willed by Callistus III to Pedro Luís.

Their eminences made it clear to this hotheaded Spaniard that if he handed over Castel Sant'Angelo and the fortresses of the Papal State, his entire inheritance would be delivered up at once. Otherwise he would not get so much as a penny, and would run the risk of provoking a resistance which augured little good for him. At the enticing glitter of noble metal, the candidate for the thrones of Naples, Cyprus and Constantinople, with lamb-like docility, rendered up the fortress—an act that was equivalent to the shearing of Samson's locks. It was 4 August. At his orders, the troops swore allegiance to the Sacred College.

The situation rapidly worsened. While the Pope—still ignorant of the catastrophe—spent his last hours in what was presumably rage-filled silence, throughout the cities and townships of the Papal State there was unleashed against the Catalans the full fury of a populace that had become sick of the abuse of power, and was filled with that wild intoxication that always accompanies the fall of any hated political regime. At Nepi, Viterbo, Civita Castellana, Ascoli, Fabriano—just about everywhere, in fact—Spanish blood ran in the streets. Piccinino took his band into Umbria, and occupied one city after another. All the roads leading away from the territories of Peter's successor were crowded with panic-stricken Catalans, galloping for dear life, doom written on their faces.

In Rome, the sidewalks suddenly became red-hot under the feet of those who for three years now had been the masters. The great patrician houses once more found a common cause that overrode their quarrels; they not only urged on the rabble, but led the hunt themselves. The Orsini family proved especially ruthless: under the leadership of their cardinal, Latino, they tried to corral Pedro Luís within a series of concentric circles that extended from the mountains to the sea, with the object of preventing his escape, and making him pay for the campaigns he had conducted against their castles.

On the night of 5–6 August there was no sleep for the occupants of Castel Sant'Angelo. At three in the morning the great gates swung open. Pedro Luís, biting his lip till the blood came, rode out between his brother (who was dressed as a layman) and Cardinal Barbo, who by his action on this occasion furnished his colleague with one of those proofs of friendship that are not readily forgotten. Their escort consisted of three hundred cavalry and two hundred foot-soldiers.

The cavalcade made its way upstream along the bank of the Tiber, crossed the river, and proceeded as far as the Porta del Popolo; here it doubled back on its tracks, made its way right across the city through the most deserted districts, and reached the Porta San Paolo without encountering any trouble *en route*.

At the start of the road leading to the sea the two cardinals halted. Rodrigo, in the name of the Sacred College, bade the troops escort Pedro Luís—who was still Captain-General of the Church—as far as Ostia; but foot-soldiers and cavalrymen alike simply shrugged their shoulders and dispersed, abandoning the fallen despot to his fate.

There was nothing left for Rodrigo to do but embrace his brother, see him set spurs to his horse, and watch him gallop away, a dwindling black dot against the first flush of the dawn sky, till finally he vanished from sight. Then, with the Venetian riding silently at his side, he went back into the hostile city. At a certain point the two men parted, and Rodrigo returned to the Vatican.

This was where his duties now lay, beside his uncle, who lay dying in the terrible loneliness created around him by the ingratitude of his relatives and fellow-countrymen, the fear in his household, the hatred of all those who for three long years had chafed at the Catalan yoke, waiting for this moment. For Cardinal Rodrigo Borgia that long August day was a searing and unforget-table ordeal, a crucial turning-point that shaped the whole future course of his life. In that grimly silent chamber, with the fury of the Roman mob exploding in waves against the walls outside, he lived through an experience that was to weigh heavily on the larger part of his future activity.

His brother was now a solitary fugitive, travelling a road bristling with dangers towards some unknown and unpredictable fate. A proud dynastic dream had suddenly collapsed. The Roman barons—the House of Orsini in particular—were up in arms and athirst for the fugitive's blood. In the Vatican itself the old Pope had been left to die like a dog, in punishment for having attempted—by favouring his kinsmen and fellow-countrymen—to rescue Papal authority from the arrogant jungle of Roman politics. All these thoughts occupied the mind of the young Spaniard as, bursting with grief and impotent rage, he sat by the dying man, praying, weeping, lavishing upon him all the humble care which filial piety and compassion dictated. A time would come when the lesson learnt on 6 August 1458 could be reconsidered and formulated in a series of clear, self-evident truths; a time would come that was propitious for drawing conclusions from it in the field of action. Every detail was cruelly branded on his memory, like an inscription carved in stone with a steel chisel.

And indeed, I am most firmly convinced we cannot fully understand certain

aspects of the policy afterwards adopted by Alexander VI and his terrible son
if we ignore the burden of passion which accumulated that day in Rodrigo
Borgia's breast, and if we do not take into account the urge for punishment,
revenge and vendetta that was born in him under the pressure of those few
short hours.

Callistus passed away towards nightfall. 'The Pope has died within these
last twenty-four hours,' Antonio da Pistoia at once wrote to the Duke of
Milan. 'The Catalans are all in flight or in hiding, and have so great a
burden of hatred to contend with, that it is a sore matter for them if they be
found.' And he added a postscript about the anger and unpopularity which
Barbo had incurred for having 'smuggled Borges out of Rome'.

No one seemed to have noticed the curious coincidence inherent in the date
of the Pope's death. On 6 August 1456 Callistus III had watched his crusading
fleet put out from Ripa Grande for the open sea; on 6 August 1457 he had
received the news of the victory which the 'white knight' had won beneath the
walls of Belgrade; and 6 August 1458 was the day of the first Feast of the Transfiguration, which, in a triumphal moment of joy, he had himself instituted.

Not long afterwards Rodrigo learnt what had befallen Pedro Luís. He had been
lucky enough to reach Ostia without mishap. Here a galley—loaded with
money and precious objects—was supposed to pick him up, but did not
appear at the rendezvous. It would have been pointless for him to hang about
waiting for it when each moment's delay could mean his death. He therefore
entrusted himself and his remaining hopes to a small boat, and set out for
Civitavecchia, the last fief which the Pontiff had bestowed upon him.

Ten days after the death of Callistus III a conclave went into session under
an arcade of the Apostolic Palace, which had been suitably adapted for this
purpose. It proceeded to elect Aeneas Silvius Piccolomini, the humanist who
was also a diplomat with a European reputation, the sharply witty playwright
and scabrous novelist, the man, in short, of many and various talents who,
after a moral change of heart, in 1444, had with most convincing diligence
established himself as a *homo novus*. The electors had come very close to choosing
a French Pope, in the person of Guillaume d'Estouteville. The victory by
Piccolomini—who passed into Papal history with the title of Pius II and a
viaticum of marvellous suggestions (*Aenean rejicite, Pium accipite!*)—was the
result of an energetic and well-planned joint stand by Rodrigo Borgia and
Pietro Barbo.

The amazing caprice of history which led the future Alexander VI to re-
enact—with somewhat more sensational luck—certain features in Callistus III's

pontificate, and the future Valentino to recapitulate (though with far more impact) the weakly-sketched career of Pedro Luís, similarly exhibited all the features of an exact prefiguration in this final phase of Rodrigo's brother's adventure, anticipating the precise circumstances of the situation in which Cesare Borgia afterwards found himself during his flight from Rome.

At Civitavecchia, Pedro Luís wavered between hope and despair. No Papal decree had, as yet, stripped him of his titles and offices: he was still City Prefect and Captain-General of the Church. And a number of strongholds, including Spoleto, still remained in his possession, with Spanish commandants and garrisons that were loyal to him. Though fallen from his position of power, and having only by a miracle escaped assassination at the hands of his pursuers, he nevertheless still continued to inspire respect and fear. He could make common cause with Piccinino, the 'Count Lackland' who had set himself up on Church territory, aided by his band of mercenaries. He could come to a profitable agreement with Ferrante, who was willing to use any means that would secure recognition and investiture out of Rome on his behalf. In time he might, perhaps—though such a project was fraught with risk—reassemble the shattered Catalan party, and give it a new lease of life.

In the event he neither did, nor attempted to do, any of these things. Preferring to extract more immediately accessible benefits from the situation, he agreed to negotiate—on a cash basis—for the delivery of those fortresses still under his control, and for his own withdrawal from the scene. Thanks to his uncle's well-filled strongbox, this accommodating attitude proved highly advantageous to him. The agreement was confirmed on 3 September.

It is not known where he proposed to take himself off and embark on the next phase of his adventure; but we may reasonably infer that his mind was turning towards Spain, where the Borgias still had their modest family fief. There, with the substantial funds at his disposal, he could have purchased a richer and more extensive estate. Just how obsessionally the Borgias clung to the idea of acquiring a prestigious *seigneurie* in Spain is well demonstrated by Rodrigo's action twenty-five years later, when he sent thither the son whose name, predetermined career, and premature death all alike, recalled Pedro Luís. What was more, the fugitive's more famous nephew Cesare—under very similar circumstances, after sudden ruin in Italy—likewise succumbed to the natural attraction exercised by the land of his birth.

But before he could set forth from Civitavecchia, Pedro Luís was struck down by a fever, and died on 26 September, after naming his brother as his heir.

The surviving Borgias in Italy—always excepting Rodrigo—were a mediocre lot; but Rodrigo towered head and shoulders above them, and was already a figure of quite exceptional stature. Anyone with a sharp eye would have had good reason to ask himself whether the age of Callistus might not, sooner or later, be followed by that of his nephew.

During this period he was busy planning a sarcophagus for his uncle's body that should be worthy both of the man and of his work, to stand in St Andrew's rotunda, behind the basilica of St Peter's. This splendid monument (destined to be destroyed when the basilica that housed it was subsequently pulled down) also served as a kind of riposte to the spiteful exultation of the opposition party. It looked as though he had buried in it his family's dream of greatness. In fact it held a promise and a hope. In his blood there still ran undiminished, as an earnest for the future, the vitality of the old Borja bull, slaughtered in the Roman arena under that August sun.

THE AGE OF
ALEXANDER VI AND CESARE
1458 – 1507

ODRIGO was to spend thirty-four years (1458–1492) waiting and manoeuvring outside a closed door, before the door finally swung open and let him across the threshold. He was to have a protracted exercise in patience and self-control, and a political apprenticeship perhaps without equal in the history of the Church—all accomplished from a position in the forefront of events, and during a period that was extraordinarily rich in memorable incidents, crowded with exceptional characters, and with so dynamic a rhythm to its development that contemporary witnesses felt they were seeing the face of the world change from one day to the next.

It is during this lengthy interlude in Borgia history that we see Rodrigo reach full maturity, acquiring those strongly drawn features that hint at the strength of the bone-structure beneath their enveloping flesh. Calculation and pugnacity—the poles of human action—developed in him, to a quite uncommon degree, the ability to be both open-minded and stubborn, pliable in his choice of means, yet constant in his pursuit of chosen end, at once devious and decisive. For thirty-four years these talents of his were daily engaged in a continual skirmish with formidably intelligent rivals, a never-ending succession of alliances and volte-faces, an assiduous reappraisal of the way his own position was modified by changing circumstances. From this training there emerged a political *maestro*, who more than deserved the panegyric bestowed upon him by Machiavelli, in some of the most glowing pages of *The Prince* (Chs. XI and XVIII).

Besides this refined tactical wisdom, and the resolution that betokened the man of action, his experience inclined him towards that spirit of tolerance which—the age being in many respects a fiercely barbarous one—was to win him much sympathy, and mitigate the spiteful verdicts pronounced on him. Rodrigo was to demonstrate this characteristic in the political arena, over matters regarding freedom of thought, and at the level of ordinary day-to-day news—protecting Rome's Jewish refugees, showing remarkable patience in his attitude to Savonarola (though the friar's obstinacy produced a clash in the end), annulling the condemnation pronounced by Innocent VIII against Pico della Mirandola, and allowing Rome's poisonous scandalmongers to decry him as they chose. 'Rome is free territory, and Romans have a habit of saying and writing whatever takes their fancy. Even if they speak ill of His Holiness, they are not silenced'—the words are those of Alexander VI himself.

By the time his long period of waiting ended, Rodrigo would be sixty-one. Now he was in the flower of his youth, the classic embodiment of a great

Renaissance lord; he had, to perfection, the gift of blending work with pleasure, and in both spheres displayed that consummate excellence which denotes the truly exceptional person. He performed his delicate duties as Vice-Chancellor with such laudable zeal that he won recognition—and lavish rewards—from no less than four successive Pontiffs.

He was an *arbiter elegantiarum* according to the tastes and concepts of his age, which still preserved certain barbaric features from ruder and earlier centuries, and loved to spread itself, with somewhat gross ostentation, in those comforts and luxuries which wealth made possible. The Rome he knew was that of the mid-fifteenth century, moving towards the noonday splendour of the High Renaissance; and he was one of the men who lent tone to its society.

That passion for hunting which Rodrigo had brought with him from Spain continued to absorb a great deal of his overflowing energy and enthusiasm. He could often be seen riding across country, cloaked and booted, with spirited steeds and a superb hunting pack. He was immensely proud of his fine hounds. Like all high aristocrats and sovereigns of that period, he employed traditional methods of selective breeding to produce his hawks and hunting-dogs.

From Spain, too, he brought an enthusiasm for bull-fighting. There is no evidence for the *noble arte* of the *corrida* having been practised in Callistus's day, though Rome was then swarming with Spaniards. Rodrigo, however, would from time to time, as one more proof of his irrepressible *hispanidad*, regale the Urbs with splendid and spectacular bull-fights. Later, he derived even greater pleasure from the way this tradition was kept alive by his son Cesare, a dilettante *torero* of legendary powers, with cat-like elegance and an infallible blade.

Ample revenues, and the heritage bequeathed him by his brother, enabled the Vice-Chancellor to surround himself with dazzling luxury. Under Sixtus IV, when cardinals were notoriously wealthy, he was to be the richest of them all, with the possible exception of Estouteville; and in each of his successive residences he made a display of rare furniture, exquisite silverware, magnificent tapestries, top-ranking works of art, well-appointed stables, and every sort of refined comfort. When in the summer of 1460 he accompanied Pius II on his summer holiday at Corsignano—which the Pontiff had re-christened Pienza, and raised to the status of an episcopal see—Rodrigo did not hesitate to have a palazzo of his own built there. During Sixtus IV's pontificate he had another one—of quite staggering architectural grandiosity, and with showily magnificent interior decoration—erected in Rome, half-way between the Ponte Sant'Angelo and the Campo dei Fiori: now known as the Palazzo Sforza Cesarini, and at the time regarded as the finest townhouse in Rome.

Contemporary chroniclers described it in awestruck terms, adding detailed accounts of the life he led there, the treasures he had accumulated, and the banquets he gave. In a letter written to Ludovico the Moor the day after a dinner at which Rodrigo entertained some of his colleagues (21 October 1484), Cardinal Ascanio Sforza was to draw on all his meagre resources of style and language to praise the reception rooms, adorned with 'storied tapestries', the carpets 'chosen to match the other decorations', a certain bed which had a canopy 'all furnished with smooth crimson hangings', a sideboard 'crowded with fine-wrought gold and silver vessels', and then more rooms, further chambers, more beds and furniture, enough to leave anyone agape. And the Moor's brother was very far from being some penniless provincial. His wealth was not much inferior to that of the Spaniard; his palazzo near the Piazza Navona was an authentic nabob's court; his life had an atmosphere of grandeur about it. But what bewitched and seduced him in Rodrigo was the latter's refined taste and infallibility of choice, the ease and correctness that informed his opulence.

Though aristocratic by birth, the Spaniard was about as far as could be imagined from the typical epicure of his day. His banquets may have been lavish on occasion, but he himself observed the most amazingly strict sobriety. His daily fare, indeed, can best be described as austere, and was to remain so (a thing which disappointed his household) even during the years that he was Pope.

Though hardly outstanding among the great supporters and promoters of humanistic culture, Gaspare da Verona's former pupil did not share his dead uncle's indifference to literature and the arts. He collected books, and took an enthusiastic interest in the activities of the earliest printers, who had reached Italy from Germany. On his shelves were to be found some of those valuable classics which issued from the hand-presses of Schweinheim and Pannartz, who in 1467 left the Benedictine abbey of Subiaco to set up their own printing-works at Rome, in Pietro de' Massimi's palazzo. His collection included a Livy published in 1469, and now in the British Museum. Ermolao Barbaro and other literary figures greeted his accession as Pontiff with hymns of praise and exultation. And it was true that, despite his absorption in a non-stop round of political activities, he still found the time and means to give striking proof of his concern for humane studies. He encouraged—and subvented—the search for ancient manuscripts. He gave his support to the new, classically inspired, theatre. He honoured men like Pomponio Leto and Fedra Inghirami, and castigated, with bitter disapproval, the frigid conceits of ecclesiastical rhetoric. He furnished the career of Aldus Manutius in a most decisive manner, and contributed to the development of Greek culture by his generous aid to John Lascaris. One person of whom he made a close friend (after having employed him as a major-domo during these years when he was still a car- dinal) was Lorenz Behaim, German by birth, devotee of antiquity, collector of inscriptions, astrologer, man of letters, alchemist, military engineer, a researcher versed in all human knowledge—so much so that Valentino subsequently used him as a kind of walking encyclopaedia.

Robust and muscular, extremely good-looking by the criteria of his age, with a broad, florid face, and gentle, dark (yet very masculine) eyes under fine arching brows, his warmth of utterance as irresistible as his elegant features, Geronimo di Porzio extolled his elegance of manner; Giasone da Milano his serene front and regal glance, his cordial yet majestic expression, his 'genial and heroic' bearing; Gaspare da Verona the gay twinkle in his eye, the ornate smoothness of his discourse, and the extraordinary power of attraction he exerted over women.

This power, it would seem, he exploited somewhat too much. In the late spring of 1459 Pius II dragged his Court off to Mantua, for a congress that was vainly supposed to concert active measures against the Turk. Rodrigo stood out brilliantly amongst those cardinals who—exasperated by the heat of the city and the dullness of life in Lombardy—distracted themselves with boat-excur- sions and gallant adventures, leaving the Pope to break out in bitter complaints about them if he chose. There is a story by Masuccio Salernitano, set precisely in the Mantua of 1459, where reference is made to a handsome cardinal, who carries off the stunningly charming wife of some dim-witted husband. It is a by no means improbable conjecture—based on certain hints and allusions of the writer's—which identifies the seducer as our Spaniard, to whom one Man- tuan chronicler of the period attributed 'the look of a man ready for any kind of mischief'.[1] Nor should we dismiss as pure fantasy the arguments of those who see the seduced woman as Rodrigo Borgia's great love Vannozza Catanei, whom Sanudo and Malipiero appositely refer to as the 'toast of Mantua'. At this point Vannozza was seventeen.

Now we have a change of scene, but the same season of the year: Siena, in the May of 1460. During a baptismal feast held in the house of the wealthy Giovanni de Bichis—the festivities went on for a fortnight, being graced by the presence of some very charming ladies whose husbands and other relatives were rigorously excluded—the cardinal gave proof of such ardent and unruly passions that he became the leading figure in a great scandal. This is the first reliable and historically documented evidence for his anything-but-austere morals. Rumours of his gallantry reached the Pope, who was taking the waters at Petriolo. This time His Holiness, with sober restraint, took pen and paper, and on 11 June sent Rodrigo a reproving letter, full of fatherly affection in form, sorrowful rather than angry, but decidedly pungent as regards its substance, bidding him think of the dishonour he was bringing on an already widely discredited Church, on the much-maligned clergy, and on the memory of his poor uncle, Callistus, 'who, in many people's judgement, did ill to load you with such honours.'

It was all so much wasted effort. Rodrigo apologized, promised to mend his ways, and sought strength to do so: but the flesh is weak, and his life became increasingly bound up in forbidden pleasures, to the dishonour of his dignity as a cardinal-deacon and bishop of the most illustrious Spanish see (though not, as yet, a priest).

Pius II's obsession with the Eastern question had now become a monomania which overstepped the bounds of good sense and carried him away on waves of absurdity. Rodrigo and his colleagues were not sure whether to laugh or weep when they saw him send the Sultan a letter in which he suggested that the latter should embrace Christianity, and offered him the Imperial crown by way of a reward. In point of fact, though this move did have a certain puerile candour about it, one can also see that it implied an extremely cynical opinion of human adaptability.

When the Pontiff subsequently (September 1463) announced his intention of sailing against the Turks in person, Rodrigo was perhaps the first of those cardinals who shook their heads with an ironic and contemptuous smile. He was also a special target for the bitterly sarcastic gibes of the Pope, who knew very well how to read the minds of cardinals of his temperament: 'Let us live amid luxuries, they say; let us pile up wealth, let us pursue luxury, let us ride plump asses and noble destriers, let us trail the hems of our mantles as we go through the city, plump-cheeked under our red hats and wide hoods: let us keep hunting-dogs, and support actors and parasites. . . .'[2]

Pius II was already in the grip of his last fatal illness, but still, with quixotic obstinacy, bent on carrying out his fantastic scheme. A day came when he dragged himself to Ancona, the embarkation-point for an expedition which hoped to sink the Crescent to the bottom of the Aegean. The younger cardinals had no option but to follow him there, with fatalistic resignation. Amongst them, naturally, was Rodrigo, who—anxious not to be outshone by his more zealous and well-endowed colleagues—had equipped a galley at his own expense; but it would be labour lost to seek in him the bold front of the true crusader, eager to conquer or die for the honour of Christ. 'The Vice-Chan-cellor', an envoy of the Marquis of Gonzaga's wrote from Ancona on 10

August 1464, 'is a sick man . . . He has ear-ache, and pain under his right arm-pit . . . The doctor who first examined him holds out little hope for his recovery, *maxime quia paulo ante non solus in lecto dormiverat.*' The prudish circum-locution bears convincing witness to the kind of life the cardinal habitually led.

Yet the suspicion that his disease was venereal in origin could well have been unfounded. Early in April, what with shortage of water, scouring heat, and overcrowding by this malodorous mob of crusaders, plague broke out in Ancona. This alone would suffice to explain Rodrigo's symptoms; alternative theories are unnecessary.

The plague produced near-hysterical chaos amid Pius's rank-and-file, already restless enough from uncertainty as to whether they were coming or going. All this led Rodrigo to toy with the notion of deserting, in search of a more favourable wind. Had it not been for his illness, which immobilized him, he might have been far away when, a few days later, in mid-August, death opportunely claimed the Pope before his lunatic scheme could be im-plemented. The dead Pontiff was taken back to Rome, and everyone else went home.

The conclave which followed was over by 30 August (1464), a rare feat of celerity. Rodrigo Borgia attended it with his head in a bandage, because of his still-purulent ear, which continued to give him pain. The candidate elected was his great friend Pietro Barbo, Eugenius IV's nephew, that smiling gener-ous-hearted man with the ever-open purse and hospitable board; the Venetian who (as the Marquis of Mantua's *oratore* put it) was all 'humanity, love and benevolence'. For the moment, then, Venice was cock-a-hoop. Scarampo, who till the previous day had been confident in his own prospective victory, fumed with jealous rage, while Estouteville, beaten by a short head, sighed regretfully. With Pietro Barbo we enter on the series of 'nepotic Popes' that subsequently produced Alexander VI, Pius III, Julius II, and Clement VII. He was forty-eight years old, and a magnificent physical specimen. Rarely had there been seen a Pope with quite such striking good looks: so much so, in fact, that when he declared his intention of calling himself Formosus II, the cardinals advised him against it, saying that to choose such a name might arouse sus-picions of self-complacent vanity. The handsome Pope-elect gave way on this point; he would, he declared, call himself Mark (Marcus) II. This elicited further objections from the cardinals, on the obvious grounds of opportunism: to say 'Mark' was tantamount to saying 'Venice' and no Pope was permitted any parochial allegiances. However, there were no objections raised when Barbo finally decided on the title of Paul II.

The jubilant Roman populace hurried off to sack his palazzo, after having, with fine impartiality, tried the same trick on the palace of Scarampo, erroneously announced as the conclave's successful candidate. But both Venetians, foreseeing success for themselves, had taken the precaution of bolting and barricading their residences, and of throwing cordons of tough armed thugs around them. The result was that Rome's worthy citizens retired from Scarampo's palazzo empty-handed, and got nothing from Barbo's but a few armfuls of hay. The new Pope consoled them for this humiliating rebuff—after a second assault—by having 1300 ducats distributed amongst them in small change.

The coronation ceremony took place on a dais set up outside St Peter's (16 September). Rodrigo did not attend. It should have been his task, as the senior cardinal-deacon, to place the tiara upon his old friend's head; but continuing illness made this impossible.

The Sacred College assumed that it was now in a dominating position, and could supervene at will. Paul II, though frivolous, worldly, and by no means over-intelligent (he had never managed to learn Latin properly) nevertheless lost no time in stripping away any such illusions. At the beginning of the conclave all the cardinals (except for Scarampo, whose obstinate refusal in this matter may well explain his defeat) subscribed to an agreement, by virtue of which whoever of them was elected Pope bound himself to a series of undertakings which, only implemented, would have made him a puppet in the hands of his cardinals. Among the many obligations enumerated by the convention—crusade, reform, and Ecumenical Council, limitation of the number of cardinals to not more than twenty-four, and dependence on the Sacred College's consent as regards numerous important acts of government—there also figured that of issuing, not more than three days after the coronation ceremony, a Bull confirming the instrument of agreement itself.

But what did the Venetian do? While his most eminent electors pawed the ground in impatient expectation of the Bull, he was busy consulting various legal luminaries. From their pliable wisdom he obtained a response that was in conformity with his desires; and when three days had elapsed he presented to the cardinals a document which, by dint of limitations, corrections, and alterations practically annulled the articles of the agreement. All the cardinals, however, some with a meek smile, others with sighs of resignation, others again with clenched teeth, appended their reverend signatures to this document. Only Carvajal abstained.

On 4 September that young and mildly unsavoury figure Cardinal Gonzaga wrote to his father: 'The man is beginning to put on high-and-mighty airs, and to puff himself up in his own esteem.' This was a justified comment. On the other hand Gonzaga was mistaken in his declared conviction that the Council anticipated by the agreement after a three-year period would have the power to 'make him humble himself' and reduce him to a milder, less extreme position. The agreement wound up in the waste-paper basket, and the Council never met.

Paul II meant to rule the roost; and in reaction to the atmosphere of resent-ment, hostility, and opposition that at once grew up around him, he became increasingly less 'liberal and humane', hardening that handsome, majestic countenance of his into the grim mask of a humourless master. On the neck of any person who gave signs of raising his crest too high there fell a hand which let him feel the harsh authority vested in the Ring of the Fisherman. A touchy person, increasingly conscious of the break between himself and the Curia, ever more reserved and suspicious as time went on, he built up (what with his strictness and his isolation) a peculiarly unfavourable image of himself for posterity—maliciously vindictive and to a great extent undeserved, but not on that account less damaging, even centuries after his death.

In this atmosphere of murky tension, only his friendship with Rodrigo Borgia kept on an even keel. If Rodrigo had not forgotten the courageous solidarity displayed by Barbo during the August of 1458, the Venetian in turn did not forget the action taken by Rodrigo to ensure his triumph in conclave. There is a most apposite comment on this by an envoy named Arrivabene. Writing—before the coronation—to Barbara von Brandenburg, the Marchioness of Gonzaga, he declared: 'Informed opinion predicts that His Reverence Monsignor the Vice-Chancellor will obtain high preferment. . . . His credit is great, and he has certainly earned such favour in that quarter.'

From words to deeds. By early October Rodrigo Borgia had been restored to the full exercise of his office as Vice-Chancellor, which, the previous May, Pius II had cut down to very narrow limits indeed, by reforming the so-called 'College of Abbreviators' auctioning off the posts it contained, and thus flood-ing it with a crowd of Sienese scribblers and men of letters. These fellow-countrymen of the late Pope, now summarily dismissed with a promise of reimbursement for monies expended, gathered at the entrance to the Papal palace, cawing like so many wounded crows, and remained there for twenty days and nights—though not even then did they succeed in winning an audience. The most illustrious member of the group, Bartolomeo Sacchi, known as Il Platina, who once he took pen in hand feared no man alive, now drafted a protest addressed to the Pontiff: a fiery and resounding Latin epistle composed (on the model of Cicero's *Catilinarians*) as an apostrophe, a blazing indictment boiling over with sarcasm, and—like a lion showing its claws—holding out the threat of an appeal to the Council. Fine prose, miraculously, had its due reward. The door that had remained inexorably closed to his companions now opened for him as though at the wave of a magic wand; and immediately afterwards he found himself wafted, with equal ease, into a dungeon under the Castel Sant'Angelo, where his limbs were crushed and racked with torture, and he was then left to meditate on the limitations which prudence dictates where free speech is concerned. There is a tradition that the Pope originally meant to have him beheaded. When four months later, through the intercession of Cardinal Gonzaga, he emerged into the sunlight once more, he was as pallid and emaciated as one returned from the dead, and tottering on his feet like a drunkard.

Thus it was that Rodrigo, through the sacrifice of these Sienese abbreviators, now turned out to starve, once more recovered his full powers: an achievement instrumental in helping him to shake off the depredations of pestilential fever, which had attacked him almost as soon as he had recovered from his other afflictions at Ancona.

Rome seemed under some curse. The plague raged all autumn, and right through the winter and following spring. Then it broke out again. 'Almost every cardinal's house has been turned into a hospital,' Arrivabene wrote. The poor (who were in no position to make hospitals of their homes) died like flies. As a diversion from pestilence, there were earthquakes and hurricanes. During the night of 19–20 January 1465, a thunderbolt struck the Borgia palazzo. But neither celestial portents, nor the miasma of pestilence, nor (as we shall see) shipwreck, attacks by pirates, or the collapse of a ceiling on that great bull-neck of his would have the power to erase the future Alexander VI from the history of Christianity.

Incubi and terrors vanished at a smile from the Venetian Pope, who now spent less and less time in the Vatican, preferring to stay in his brand-new Palace of St Mark, a noble pile that looked like a fortress from the outside and was of sumptuous magnificence within. At the Pontiff's prompting, the Roman carnival season reached unprecedented heights of splendour and gaiety. Even the cardinals were not denied certain modest satisfactions—e.g. the right to wear, at special functions, the most beautiful 'damask mitres, trimmed with pearls', and (as a regular part of their attire) bright red birettas which marked them off from other prelates. It was the Pope himself who thought these up, and personally presented one to each cardinal—a gesture which, in fact, cost him very little. At the same time he ordered for himself a fabulous tiara, sewn with matchless pearls, and valued at no less than sixty thousand ducats, as well as a ceremonial chair (*sedia gestatoria*) which cost more than a grandiose palazzo. He was clearly not disturbed by the fact that his distant predecessors had been told: 'Do not provide gold or silver or copper to fill your purses. . . .'

Grim and quarrelsome though the Pope might be, he still, in his better moments, wanted to see everyone content. He haggled over the subventions to the now elderly Scanderbeg, who in December 1466 reached Rome 'with few horses and in poverty', as Cardinal Gonzaga put it, to entreat the aid that would enable him to go on holding up the Turkish advance; but whenever he moved from the Vatican to the Palace of St Mark, or vice versa, he would solemnly scatter largesse to the multitude all the way.

Throughout the seven years of Paul II's pontificate, Rodrigo's fortunes pros-pered and expanded. In 1468 he was at last ordained a priest, and found him-self assigned the bishopric of Albano, which he held until 1476. Patience, tact, and modesty were his watchwords. He was at great pains to avoid causing offence to anyone, or being involved in a direct clash of opinion, while at the same time building up his credit by favours conferred. His position was being steadily consolidated on a rich foundation of popularity.

Sunstroke, together with indigestion brought on by too much melon (during a lunch eaten, somewhat rashly, in the garden, bareheaded and under a scorching sky) on 26 July 1471 struck Paul II down with apoplexy. His face turned purple and he frothed at the mouth; by the evening of that same day he was dead.

The opening of the conclave found Estouteville and Orsini in the lists; each of them had been more than lavish with his electoral promises. At its close, however, the name which the Vatican sprang on the world was that of Fran-cesco della Rovere, a former Franciscan from Celle Ligure. This effective preacher, learned theologian, and outstanding teacher had been Minister-General of his Order, and—four years previously—a cardinal. He assumed the title of Sixtus IV. Rodrigo played a decisive role in his election, too—meri-torious conduct which the new Pope at once rewarded by granting him the *commenda* of the rich abbey of Subiaco.

From 25 August, the day he received the Papal crown at Rodrigo Borgia's hands, this Franciscan intellectual set himself to rule with an authoritarian manner, a sureness of purpose and a cool lack of scruple which—coming from a man whose past life had been confined to school and monastery—people found as unexpected as they were disconcerting. His pontificate began under two signs: those of cheerful generosity and intrepid nepotism. Our Lady of Poverty's one-time follower, having suddenly come into the possession of

ample riches, celebrated his good fortune with so lavish an outburst of pro-
digality towards the cardinals that it left observers in Rome stunned and
blinking. Twelve days *before* the coronation Arrivabene could declare that
'everyone feels he is seeing the inception of a new world.' In a sprightly aside
he also noted the gradual arrival, from the Ligurian coast, of a voracious horde
of relatives: Della Rovere, Riario and Grosso kinsmen of one sort of another—
brothers, sisters, in-laws, and something like one and a half dozen nephews.
The sheer impact of their descent on Rome, the speed with which they climbed
to the top, and their insolence once they had got there, quite eclipsed that
earlier irruption and seizure of power by the Catalans. The Urbs continued to
look more and more like some rich feeding-trough set aside for the voracious
jaws of each successive Pope's family connections.

   Ligurian winds of change suddenly blew through the Vatican. It was not
long before three of those many nephews stood out unmistakably as standard-
bearers of the clan's bright destiny: Gerolamo Riario on the secular side, and
for ecclesiastical matters his brother Pietro and his cousin Giuliano della
Rovere. No less than four further nephews were appointed cardinals during
the next few years. However, this initial demonstration of nepotism as a considered policy already speaks for itself. It forms an exact repetition of the
scheme inaugurated by Callistus III: the colossus of family power, one foot
rooted in Mother Church, and the other in some allied principality to be
created beside her. A perfect scheme, and one that was to be faithfully adopted
by Rodrigo and Giuliano della Rovere alike. The latter was now a youthful
twenty-eight, his fine athletic figure—till yesterday mortified in a Franciscan
habit—now moving proudly in cardinal's scarlet. During this, his first appearance on the Roman scene, he became a constant companion of his Spanish
colleague, for whose talents and life-style he had the greatest admiration. He
watched Rodrigo's moves, and carefully cultivated his friendship, far from
any presentiment of the bitter enmity that would come between them in future
years.

THE ALLURE OF SPAIN

Sixtus IV, too, inaugurated his reign with a vast crusading project. Still
following in Callistus III's footsteps, at a secret consistory held on 23 December 1471 he appointed five cardinal-legates, whose task it would be to travel
through Europe, organize effective local support, and foster a general military
collaboration for the destruction of the Turkish empire. Amongst them we
find Rodrigo Borgia; the field of operations assigned to him—undoubtedly at
his own request—was Spain.

He reached Ostia and went aboard ship about the middle of May, 1472, accompanied by a train that would not have disgraced a reigning monarch: bishops and other prelates, ambassadors, and similar high dignitaries, gentle men, secretaries and servants. This was his first appearance on the international scene, his first experience of high level diplomacy outside the limits of Vatican routine.

His mission had two objects: to iron out dynastic antagonisms, and to get men, money, and *matériel* from Spain for the crusade. Since only a united nation could make a unanimous effort, the first of these two objectives formed a necessary preliminary to the second; but the internal pacification of Spain must have looked, on the face of it, very much a forlorn hope. That gallant and cultured monarch John II, who fought so determinedly against the Moors of Granada, and gave such impetus to the Spanish literary Renaissance, was in 1454 succeeded on the throne of Castile by his son Henry IV, known—not entirely without reason—as 'the Impotent'. As unlucky on the battlefield as he was in his private domestic life, this colourless monarch also took a severe beating from the Moors, and experienced, in the most bitter fashion imaginable, the ingratitude of his favourite, Beltrán de la Cueva. The harsh lesson provided by his father, who was also betrayed, in an equally vile manner, by *his* favourite, Alvaro de Luna, should have put Henry on guard. The short lived sons whom his wife Joanna of Portugal bore him were said—both privately and in public— to be the fruit of adultery. His surviving daughter, in whom he vested the right of succession, was disdainfully nicknamed 'La Beltraneja', that is, the offspring of Beltrán, his favourite. The nobles, highly restless even under John II's rule, had been in open rebellion against Henry for the past eight years. Beltrán's insolence, resentment of the defeat at the hands of the Moors, and contempt for the blind weakness of their sovereign—these things had opened up what seemed an unbridgeable gulf between the throne and the aristocracy. As if he had not enough crosses to bear already, Henry also possessed an extraordinarily quick witted, daring, energetic sister, from whom his worst mishaps were destined to come: a girl by the name of Isabella, who in 1469 had secretly married, at Valladolid, her cousin Ferdinand, son of King John II of Aragon by his second wife, Joanna Enriquez. The young bride was eighteen, and the bridegroom a year younger when—through the intervention of certain indus trious *conversos*, in particular that immensely wealthy figure Mosén Pedoro de la Caballería—there was tied a matrimonial knot destined to bring into the pages of history the most famous royal couple of modern times. This marriage also eliminated 'Beltraneja' from the scene, besides completing the unification of Spain, and ushering in the most brilliant era the Peninsular Kingdom had ever known, which saw the Moors finally evicted, and the discovery of the New World. Ferdinand and Isabella, as was to be expected, vigorously fanned the flame of sedition which fired the Castilian nobility against their King; Henry reacted, to no useful purpose, by loudly accusing his sister of prodigal luxury and incest, in that she had married her cousin without the necessary Papal dispensation, using a spurious Bull to achieve her ends.

Such was the state of affairs when Rodrigo made his unasked-for interven-tion. He arrived aboard the *Grao*, of Valencia, on a fine, sunny day in June. The descendant of those *caballeros de la Conquista* who in 1238 had wrested the city from Moorish overlordship now made his solemn entry through the Puerta de Serranos (the military North Gate, built on Roman foundations towards the end of the previous century), advancing slowly between two mighty polygonal towers, all hung with bunting, on a thoroughbred horse, bridle-led by a groom. Representatives of the higher nobility had begged the honour of holding the canopy beneath which he proceeded in majesty, eyes sparkling, sensuous lips half parted in a smile. Fanfares, salvoes of musketry and loud cheers welcomed him back to the land of his ancestors. In La Seo—the ex-quisite cathedral which during this period, after two centuries of work, was at last having the final touches put to it—his mellifluous voice made the first public announcement of the crusade. As evidence for this visit of his to the church where his Uncle Alonso first encountered Vincent Ferrer, and where he himself had prayed as a young boy, we have the gifts which he left there, before satisfying his own personal nostalgia (and his importunate relatives) by making a trip to that cradle of memories, Jativa.

Rodrigo stayed in Spain for a good fifteen months, travelling through both Kingdoms, frequenting both Courts, and devoting himself, with incessant zeal, to his role as a peacemaker—which applied as much to the internal affairs of strife-torn Castile as it did to Castile's relations with Aragon: relations that had become strained and angry more because of the bitterness between the two consanguineous ruling families than for any other reason. With the help and advice of Archbishop Pedro Gonzalez de Mendoza, to whom he brought, from the Vatican, the promise of a cardinal's hat (this was in fact conferred upon him on 7 May of the following year) Rodrigo manoeuvred with supreme skill in a situation full of white-hot hatred and resentment. He did in fact manage to achieve a certain easing of tension, inasmuch as during a banquet in Segovia Henry IV and the two young newly-weds were brought together at the same table. It is true that after this meal Henry began to complain of a pain in his side that never left him until the day—not too distant now—of his death (1474); but this may be pure fortuitous coincidence. Rodrigo, using that quick, intuitive mind of his, had already realized that the future lay with these two twenty-year-old cousins, whose union he had supported, and on whom there now fell the benevolent light of his sympathy and approval. That tormented and troublesome figure Henry IV was a ghost from the past: with his disappearance everything would become plain sailing.

The action taken by the cardinal-legate to arouse enthusiasm and collect money for the crusade was likewise appropriately tailored to suit the Spain of his day—a country populated by native-born Catholics, but dominated by newly-converted Jews (their motives often pure opportunism), who had infiltrated every position of influence or authority. The results of his efforts were not outstanding, however, especially in Castile. Spain was weary of crusades after all those she had fought against the Moors, and had still to wage against that Moslem stronghold the Kingdom of Granada; besides, the bulk of the population (those who held by the Old Faith), were ground down as a result of the *conversos'* triumphant prosperity, and had little or no money to spare. Even so, the cardinal's official speeches, sermons by the bishops, the sale of indulgences, and the interested generosity of the great brought a discreet but steady flow of *maravedís* into the coffers of the Vatican's travelling propaganda team.

No criticism, then, could be made of the Papal Legate's diligence, nor of the results brought about by his work, which were exactly what could (with a reasonable dose of optimism) have been foreseen all along. But the Spaniards were not slow to observe that their Italianized fellow-countryman showed rather more of the pride which characterized a high-ranking *parvenu* than he did of that zealous concern proper to God's messengers; that his pleasure in the homage of the great and the cheers of the humble was not without a certain streak of self-complacent vanity; that he cloaked himself with a luxury unbecoming to a man of the Church, and somewhat humiliating in its ill-concealed purpose, this being to give a lesson in elegance and expensive fashion, and to rub home the point that, while Spain might be Spain, Rome was something more. Nor did they take long to realize that, while he certainly did his best to fill the coffers of the crusade, he was by no means averse to bulking out his own purse and weighting down his baggage with various costly gifts. Above all, they became aware that he was far from impervious to the temptations put in his path by hot-blooded feminine Spanish beauty. From now on his wake is littered with malicious accusations, sedulously fostered by the party hostile to his intervention in local antagonisms, and to his obvious sympathy with the young royal couple. Satires and libellous squibs magnified the echoes of such reproof. Ambassadors and prelates began to enumerate them in their dispatches, so that they eventually got as far as Rome. So, after the Pope's famous letter from Corsignano, we have a second batch of evidence concerning Rodrigo's inadequate morals; nor is it any kinder to the janissaries of his suite, who are described as a band of greedy and licentious adventurers.

Towards the end of September 1473 (having first, as an extra precaution, made his will) Rodrigo left the shores of Spain, never to return. He had a calm crossing, with a good following wind. But when they were almost in sight of the Italian coast, the two Venetian vessels on which he and his escort had embarked ran into a violent storm, under dark and hellish clouds, which forced them to alter course. Off Pisa one of them ended its doomed saraband by going to the bottom: about two hundred people, including three bishops, were drowned. Rodrigo, together with his galley, managed to survive; but he was set on by a gang of coastal marauders, who handled him roughly and robbed him of his own private funds, to the tune of some 30,000 new florins. When he reached Pisa, he lost no time in sending an indignant letter to Lorenzo de' Medici: 'Not even among the Moors would there be such cruelty as was shown on this occasion.'

On setting foot in the Vatican once more, the cardinal-legate proudly turned over to the Pontiff the cash gleaned in Spain—which he had somehow kept safe—and acquainted him with the results of all his diplomatic efforts. These results were very much on the positive side: when, soon afterwards, the much-vexed problem of Spanish dissension was at last settled, men had to acknow-ledge the solid benefits which accrued from his work as a peacemaker. He had gauged the terms of the problem with exemplary precision, and given a lead by adumbrating the most feasible solution to it.

At this point the star of Rodrigo Borgia—like those of every other eminent personage in the Roman world—was eclipsed by the dazzling meteors of the Pope's nephews, and in particular by those of Cardinal Pietro Riario and his brother Gerolamo, which were now setting the Rome sky ablaze. (The first was destined to sputter out a few months later, on 5 January 1474, amid the unhealthy exhalations of a madly dissolute life, and the second to be ex-tinguished in a pool of blood before five years had elapsed.) Already Giuliano della Rovere's star was majestically in the ascendant; unlike his cousins, he disciplined his own energies according to a carefully-planned norm. Neverthe-less, he still, on occasion, gave such proof of the stuff he was made of that a penetrating eye would have no trouble in spotting the formidable character hidden within. A spell as legate to the turbulent Ancona Marches, in 1473, had already given people a glimpse of his restless, driving energy.

Until all this robust nepotism should have exhausted its initial vehemence, Rodrigo very prudently remained in the shadows, only emerging, from time to time, for events of particular importance. Thus we find him, on 14 January of the Jubilee Year, 1475, leaving Rome in Giuliano's company to meet that sterling fellow Ferrante, who was making a pilgrimage to the *caput mundi*, his object being not so much to gain indulgences (by which he set very little store), as to work out with the Holy See what policy should be adopted regarding the twenty-five-year defensive alliance recently concluded—at Lorenzo de' Medici's instigation—between Florence, Venice, Milan and Ferrara. Ferrante—a collec-tor of mummies, among other things—had been granted by Pius II the investi-ture which Callistus refused him, and (polite as always) showed his gratitude by punctually dispatching every year the symbolic white horse, though not the tribute. He now embarked on a kind of honeymoon with the Vatican. When at length—after protracted discussions with Sixtus, and his own somewhat per-functory devotions—he set out back for home, it was, once more, Rodrigo and Giuliano who escorted him to the frontier of the Papal States.

We catch another glimpse of Rodrigo Borgia in 1477, wearing the dignified robes of the Papal Legate to Naples, whither he had repaired for the new sovereign's coronation. This act, followed shortly afterwards by the bestowal of a cardinal's hat upon Ferrante's son, John of Aragon, makes it clear that the friendship between Rome and Naples was closer than ever. The truth was that Sixtus needed a good solid alliance to stand on for his duel with Florence.

This duel drew blood in plenty the following year, with the sacrilegious *attentat* of 26 April in Santa Maria del Fiore. The shadow cast by the con-spirators' daggers stretched as far as the Vatican, but did not come anywhere near the vice-chancellor. His non-involvement in the politicking of the Ligu-rian clan—which, under Gerolamo Riario's influence, plunged progressively deeper into a game of chance so hazardous that it brought about Ferrante's withdrawal—grew very noticeable during the years that were left of Sixtus's pontificate.

The period abounded in epoch-changing events. Charles the Bold had his pugnacious life cut tragically short before the walls of Nancy in 1477—a death which removed one whole dynasty from the political map of Europe. That chivalrous figure Maximilian von Habsburg now married the Burgundian's daughter; by so doing he filched a good part of the wily Louis XI's heritage, and precipitated a struggle —for the possession of Flanders—which lasted until the Treaties of Arras and Madrid.[3] On 10 August 1480 the Turks landed at Otranto; but during May 1481 news of Mohammed II's death reached Rome. This was a marvellous stroke of luck, since the dynastic struggle between his two sons—the scowling Bajazet and the romantic Gem—gave Europe a chance to stave off disaster. On the evening of 30 August 1483 death claimed another outstanding victim, in the person of Louis XI; and on 12 August 1484 Sixtus IV likewise passed away.

The cardinals' attendance at his lying-in-state was a quick and perfunctory affair. Not one of all those nephews and other relatives stayed by the body of the man who had—at the expense of the Church's dignity—brought them wealth and power, perhaps paying with pangs of remorse for his impassioned errors. Scarcely had the dead man been removed to the Sala del Pappagallo before his apartment was gone through by extremely thorough looters, who stripped the walls and left the cupboards bare. Burchard and two servants washed Sixtus IV's body; but afterwards the dead Pope lay there, for that first night, un-attended and naked, since no one had even found a shift in which to shroud him.

Cardinals, nephews and other kinsmen had hurried off and shut themselves up in their luxurious houses, all now bristling with men-at-arms. Rodrigo Borgia's palazzo had the protection of some hastily erected barricades, from behind which a number of cannon-muzzles looked out, to discourage any mob violence. All around, Rome roared and exploded like a stormy sea. Gerolamo Riario, hastily abandoning the siege of a Colonna fortress, came back and camped beside the Tiber, but after two days found it advisable to beat a retreat to Isola Farnese. His palazzo in Rome was literally stripped bare by a furious mob. His wife, the twenty-one-year-old Caterina Sforza, lost no time in taking over the command of Castel Sant'Angelo—an early indication of the truly leonine heart which beat in that magnificent body of hers.

After a while, when the rabble had begun to disperse, these most eminent leaders of the Church began to emerge, cautiously, from their houses, to meet one another, to work out agreements and alliances for the forthcoming election; while the great patrician families and the Courts feverishly planned their own pressure-group tactics.

Rodrigo Borgia decided that his hour had come. Throwing off his mask—that of the Curia's humble servant—he launched a most vigorous campaign for his own candidacy, flooding the market with promissory notes in the pro-cess. The office of vice-chancellor, his own palazzo with its priceless furnishings, the *commenda* of the abbey of Subiaco, his episcopal see, endless prebends and benefices—all his sources of revenue, and a great proportion of his liquid capital assets, were available for anyone who enabled him to win St Peter's throne. Since he firmly believed that every man had his price, and also knew that he was in a position to offer more than anyone else, he regarded his victory as a more or less foregone conclusion.

However, he underestimated two factors. There was the disastrous effect of his sudden volte-face in breaking with the Colonnas—the opposition party to which, until now, he had been more or less openly attached—and joining the detested Orsini faction, which he regarded as stronger; and there was also Giuliano della Rovere's remarkable drive and initiative. The trick he played on the Colonna both alienated his friends and provided a splendid weapon for his enemies to employ against him, letting them assert, with some plausibility, that such a man was not to be trusted. At the same time, Giuliano put himself forward as a rival candidate, with a very respectable caucus of cardinals to back him.

Since neither of them could win a clear majority, common sense suggested their combining amicably to secure the election of a *tertius gaudens*—in this case one of the Della Rovere faction, the fifty-two-year-old Giovanni Battista Cibo. The new Pope was a Genoese, of insipid character (not to mention an uncertain number of sons as evidence for a profligate youth), and with all the qualities needed to become a docile puppet in the hands—soft and clever in Rodrigo's case, rough and coarse in that of Giuliano—of either of the two men who had dragged him forth from obscurity. The Pope thus chosen by a combination of opportunistic interests, during the night of 28–29 August, was proclaimed to the world the following morning under the name of Innocent VIII.

This was the time at which Rodrigo 'launched' his first-born, in great style, thus loudly announcing the entry of a new generation of Borgias; and it also marks, for us, an appropriate point at which to discuss his real or presumed sons.

One important warning should be given right at the outset. Concerning their number, and even their genealogical affiliations, there exist various doubts and disagreements; these have called forth whole rivers of ink, and have also been exacerbated, in some cases by lack of evidence, in others by the equivocal or contradictory nature of our sources. It has thus proved possible for certain scholars—some more serious than others, but all with undisguisedly *parti pris* motives—to maintain that what we have here are not sons, but nephews, to attach what commonly passes on the family tree for Rodrigo's progeny, to a phantom brother, and to claim that all of them were born in Spain. It is true that the Bulls of Legitimization—inasmuch as they were dictated by all-too-obvious special interests—do not *per se* constitute absolute and incontrovertible proof of Rodrigo's paternity. Endorsing that paternity, on the other hand, we have the universal acceptance of it by Rodrigo's contemporaries, in all diplomatic circles, and every Court throughout Italy. It is confirmed by historians of the day, and the Pontiff himself never expressly denied it; much later—as the result of a dispatch dated 30 June 1499, from Catanei, the Mantuan *oratore*—he did in fact disclaim paternity as regards Goffredo, but this was no more than an outburst of resentment. Nevertheless, the lack of really clear, positive and incontrovertible documentary evidence does permit a faint shadow of doubt to subsist. Since, moreover, similar uncertainties affect the identity and biographical dating of the women who brought these children into the world, one's best course, clearly, is neither to propose nor to accept some impassioned personal hypothesis, but rather to follow traditional opinion on the subject. At the same time great reservations are desirable, on the grounds—unlikely, but not impossible—that one day some new discovery in the archives may revolutionize the state of our knowledge.

According to the accepted version of events, then, at the beginning of Innocent VIII's pontificate Cardinal Borgia had seven children, all born after his elevation to the purple, and only one before he was ordained priest. Three —Pier Luigi, Jeronima and Isabella, born between 1463 and 1471—are generally attributed to some unknown mother. The other four—Cesare, Giovanni, Lucrezia and Goffredo, born between 1475 and 1481—are all regarded as the children of Vannozza Catanei, by reason of a tradition which has some evidence to support it, in particular the lady's own epitaph. (Her tomb was in Santa Maria del Popolo, and though the epitaph itself is now lost, its text has been preserved in a collection of inscriptions.) This attribution nevertheless remains somewhat dubious as regards Lucrezia, whom the ambassadors of Venice and Mantua describe in certain dispatches as being the child of a different mother.

Some scholars incline to recognize Vannozza as also being the mother of Rodrigo's three eldest children: an attractive conjecture, and one by no means devoid of probability, since it has the advantage of introducing this particular mistress into Rodrigo's life while he was still in the first flower of his youth— which would seem more likely—rather than when he was already turned thirty.

But who was Vannozza?

Few marginal figures in history can have generated so much confusion: the mass of muddled and contradictory evidence concerning her, in one variant version or another, would suffice to extrapolate two or three different Vannozzas. To begin with, nothing precise is known about her birthplace, and even her nationality has been a subject for debate. On the basis of two ancient biographical notices, which survive in manuscript form, the apologists claim that she was Spanish, and (more specifically) a native of Valencia. This, naturally, helps them in their efforts to detach her from Rodrigo, and link her

up with Rodrigo's problematical brother. But other far more reliable documents tell a different story, which leads one rather to suppose that she was in
fact Italian.

Whether or not we are ready to identify her with the lovely Mantuan lady
who was the companion of Cardinal Rodrigo's leisure hours during his 1459
visit to the Gonzagas' city, on some points of her biography there is no room for
doubt. She was born in 1442, and had three remarkably complaisant husbands
—Domenico Giannozzi da Rignano, Antonio da Brescia, and Giorgio della
Croce from Milan—under whose successive aegis she cultivated the fertile
garden of adulterous passion with the cardinal. After their separation he found
her a fourth husband: the Mantuan humanist Carlo Canale, a friend of
Politian's, who dedicated his *Orpheus* to him with a highly ornate epistle
beginning: 'The Lacedaemonians, my most gracious of friends, Messer Carlo,
were wont to. . . .'

From her surviving letters, one gets the impression that she was a far from
uncultivated lady. In those addressed to Alexander VI, she strikes an extremely
obsequious note, which reveals not the faintest hint of even the slightest, most
fleeting, relaxation in tone—let alone of unbecoming familiarity or tenderness
such as in other cases one might expect between two ex-lovers. Her epistolary
language adheres faithfully to the prescribed formulas: '*Beatissime Pater, post
oscula pedum Vestre B.nis*, Vannozza begs humbly at your feet as one who
wishes. . . .' And in conclusion: 'She who day and night prays for Your
Holiness's life, your servant Vannozza de Cathaneis'; or again: 'Your humble
servant and slave Vannozza de Catani.' Even in the letters she sent her children
her language preserved the same tone of courteous deference. 'Your Excellency,'
she wrote to Lucrezia, informing her of the death of Cesare's late secretary,
Agapito Geraldini, 'should bear well in mind the good service which Messer
Agapito de Amelia of blessed memory did for His Excellency our Duke, and
the love and affection which he always had for us especially. . . .' This
rigidly formal court tone was one, moreover, which the young Borgias also
used amongst themselves, as well as towards their father. To all of them, invariably and without any possibility of exception, Alexander VI remained 'His
Holiness', 'the Most blessed Father' whose feet they kissed; there was no instance of one approaching the other with even the slightest falling-off from this
formulaic deference. A stern disciplinary training had accustomed them to
show respect for the accepted forms. The result was that they treated one
another like mutually admiring strangers, or, better, like so many sovereigns
who enjoyed good relations amongst themselves—invariably using the polite
second person plural, and very often flattering titles such as 'Excellence' or

'Your Illustrious Lordship', while not, on occasion, shrinking from the royal 'we'. 'Most illustrious and most excellent Lady, our beloved sister', was how Cesare addressed Lucrezia in a letter dated 20 July 1502, signing it 'Your Most Illustrious Ladyship's brother, who loves Your Ladyship even as himself'.

There is nothing to prevent our supposing that Vannozza was a lady of discreetly elevated sentiments. The long duration of her relationship with Rodrigo (who stayed faithful to her for many years, and even after they parted still continued to give proof of his kindly feelings towards her), the fact that he entrusted his children to her upbringing during their formative years, and the affection with which they always surrounded her—all this leads one to assume that she had something more, and better, than mere physical beauty. She was a first-class administrator and an excellent businesswoman, who by buying and selling houses (coupled with the indirect management of various inns, and a large-scale pawnbroking business) had contrived to accumulate a tidy fortune. At this period she lived on the Piazza Pizzo di Merlo, not far from Rodrigo's palazzo. Later, after her ex-lover had been elected Pope, she moved into a house with a garden and vineyard (still surviving to this day) on the Via Santa Lucia in Selce, not far from the Church of St Peter in Vincoli. The break with Rodrigo presumably took place soon after 1481; coupled with the tragic fate in store for two of her sons it cost her much cruel suffering. This was one of the factors which helped transform her into a devout and charitable lady. Having gone through the classic metamorphosis of the ageing reformed sinner, she passed her declining years in prayer and good works, spending a large proportion of her wealth on charity. She died on 26 November 1518, in her seventy-sixth year. At Leo X's express order a representative of the Papal Court attended her lavish funeral, as did all the more distinguished figures from Rome's official circles—which shows how high Borgia prestige still stood some fifteen years after the 1503 catastrophe. She was buried in Santa Maria del Popolo, her favourite church, where for some years there had lain the knife-torn body of her son Giovanni, the second Duke of Gandia. Her own remains rested there until posthumous moral outrage (which took a singularly embittered stand against the Borgias, even centuries later) saw to it that all trace of her tomb disappeared.

Some have claimed to recognize Vannozza's likeness in the Madonna of Pinturicchio's 'Annunciation', painted between 1493 and 1495 in the Borgia Apartments of the Vatican, and in Girolamo Carpi's 'Portrait of an Unknown Lady', now preserved in the Borghese Gallery. Such attributions are pure fantasy. The one absolutely unchallengeable piece of iconographic testimony is a portrait from the Congregazione di Carità in Rome (faithfully reproduced in a

still-surviving copy to be found at the Congregazione della Santissima Con-
cezione) which shows her already past her prime. This is the face of a sad and
pious lady—almost, one might say, of a penitent—with great dark pensive eyes,
her brow shadowed by a black veil. In her features one seems to recognize those
of Cesare; and her expression, surely, hints at that sense of melancholy which
invaded her later years, when she continued to correspond with Lucrezia from
Rome (yet never brought herself to go and join her in Ferrara), signing her
letters 'The fortunate and unfortunate Vannozza Borgia de Cathaneis'—two
adjectives which summed up her whole extraordinary destiny.

By this time (1484) Rodrigo had already settled his two daughters by—if we
accept the most widely held tradition—some unknown woman. Jeronima, who
had been born in 1470, on 24 January 1482 married a Roman nobleman,
Giovanni Andrea Cesarini; while Isabella—presumably a year younger than
her sister—on 30 April 1483 wed a certain Pietro Giovanni Mattuzzi, a Vatican
official whom Alexander VI subsequently appointed Chancellor of Rome in
Perpetuity. Both matches were honourable, though not outstandingly brilliant;
both were into the circle of the minor nobility gravitating about ecclesiastical
society.

    On the other hand there were fine prospects for Pier Luigi, whose name—
and family plans—both recalled those of Rodrigo's brother, still very much
alive in people's memories. Most authorites date his birth to 1463, though some
place it slightly earlier. On 5 November 1483 Sixtus IV issued a Bull legiti-
mizing this first-born son of Cardinal Rodrigo's, who was then sent off to
Spain. Here, through a combination of his father's money, his own military
skill, and the friendship of Ferdinand of Aragon, he had the chance to make
himself a distinguished career.

    The fascination which his native land had for Rodrigo Borgia—already
obvious from the episode of his legation to Spain in 1472—is not without some
significance, practical no less than psychological. At one level his urge to
publicize, on Spanish soil, the magnitude of his own achievement in the world
sprang from a sentimental impulse akin to that of the emigrant who, having
made a fortune abroad, loves to purchase houses and estates in the land of his
birth. At another, his plan to guarantee his family a large and solid base of
power in Spain sprang from the knowledge that he could not place any long-
term reliance on the prospects available in Italy. Only a few years after his
election as Pope, Rodrigo was to conceive the notion of giving his sons fiefs and
principalities either on Church lands, or else in territory controlled by the
friendly Kingdom of Naples. This notion expanded, with Cesare, into the

dream of a kingdom as such, and it was only through a treacherous stroke of fate that the utopia failed to become reality. For the present, the pole of secular ambitions lay in Spain.

And in Spain, without delay, Pier Luigi began to show his good Borgia blood. As an officer in Ferdinand's army, pledged to the effort to drive the Moors from their last few footholds on Spanish soil, he discharged his military novitiate with outstanding brilliance. In the battle for the storming of Ronda, on 22 May 1485, he was the first to break the Moorish defence line and enter this hilltop Andalusian town. The King rewarded him, together with his brothers Giovanni and Cesare, by conferring upon them, in the field, the title of *egregios*, with its associated prerogatives: one of those honours that thrill the recipient but cost his sovereign nothing. Pier Luigi's accession to the ranks of the Spanish nobility gave him an aura of prestige.

With the backing of his father, who before his departure from Italy had supplied him liberally with funds (we still have the private contract by which, on 3 May 1483, he gave Pier Luigi 50,000 ducats for the acquisition of a fief in Spain) the youthful *egregio* had meanwhile cast his eye on the Duchy of Gandia.

Situated east of Jativa, not far from the Borgias' ancestral eyrie, beside the banks and peaceful waters of the Serpis (or Alcoy), Gandia lies rather less than an hour's walk from the sea: there is a salty, brackish tang in its air, and it has its own fine port down on the coast. An enchanting city, white and gay amid the green of the *huerta* (hence the name: *huerta*–green), it fully deserves its reputation as the 'pearl of Valencia'. It is built to a quadrangular ground plan, and girdled with strong walls; its houses extend along broad, peaceful streets. It has a distinguished history. Like a jewel, it was first removed from the crown of Aragon to be granted as a fief to Admiral Ruggero di Lauria. In 1296 James II transferred its overlordship to Constance of Hohenstaufen, or Swabia, the widowed queen who was destined to end her adventurous life in 1302, among the Poor Clares of Barcelona. After figuring as the apanage of various royal princes, the Duchy was finally sold by King John II, on 4 June 1470, to the city of Valencia.

The negotiations which Cardinal Rodrigo undertook with Ferdinand in due course bore fruit. On 3 December 1485 there was ratified an act by which the King definitively alienated the Duchy in favour of Pier Luigi Borgia, with the right of hereditary transmission, on repayment to Valencia of the sum which that city had disbursed fifteen years previously.

So the cardinal's son became Duke of Gandia; his title might have been acquired by hard cash, but it had also been earnt by the sword, on the field of battle, in accordance with the fine custom observed by the 'knights of antiquity'. By capturing this most illustrious fief, the Borgia family had at one jump reached the highest echelons of the Spanish aristocracy. They continued to hold it until their male line became extinct, in 1740; and it was here, after the col‑ lapse of their ephemeral power in Italy, that the final phase of their history played itself out—a history made illustrious by the cathartic sanctity of Francis, who did not overwhelm his enemies with the weapons of violence and fraud, but through a heroic exercise of abnegation succeeded in conquering himself.

The new Duke's first task was to begin building a bright, elegant palazzo in the Italian fashion, which flanked his gardens on the left bank of the Serpis, and offered a magnificent view, on the far side of the river, across that rich plain stretching away until it met the sea. As a residence it was neither excessively grandiose nor ostentatiously showy, but quite exquisite, displaying a fine patio on which there opened attractively designed mullion windows, with either two or three lights. At the bottom of this patio was the grand stairway, which formed two ramps leading up to the first floor, under a little loggia supported by balusters. Inside, the general impression was of a surprising solemnity, which served to emphasize the Borgias' lofty aspirations: magnificent reception‑halls, a wonderful gallery, a turret looking out over enchanting horizons, and— naturally—some gloomy dungeons.

Another fine palazzo, for use as a town house, was built for Pier Luigi and his descendants in Valencia, on the Plaza San Lorenzo.

All the young Duke now lacked was a high‑born wife; and King Fer‑ dinand, who was still in a mood of cordial generosity, gave his consent for Pier Luigi's betrothal to Maria Enriquez de Luna, the daughter of one of his maternal uncles, though at the time she was only nine years old. Such a match exceeded Rodrigo's most sanguine expectations, since it established a tie of blood between the Borgias and the royal house. The Enriquez family belonged to that aristocratic inner group of *conversos* which (having wormed its way into quite a few royal Spanish beds) was now decidedly eclipsing the old traditional Catholic nobility.

But the pledge of love between Maria Enriquez and the Duke of Gandia had no future. That ill‑luck which dogged all young Borgias now prepared to deliver its second blow. Pier Luigi went on a visit to Italy to see his family, and in the summer of 1488, died there. Gandia, where such felicity awaited him, never saw him alive again.

FROM 1488 TO THE CONCLAVE OF 1492

Gandia, however, did not remain without a duke, nor Maria Enriquez with-out a husband. The young gentleman destined to take Pier Luigi's place was already available from the Borgia reserve in Rome.

For the time being, this young Borgia—his father's last-born and the idol of fashionable Roman society—was a little *too* young: at the time of his brother's death, in fact, Giovanni Borgia was only about twelve years old. His precise age is a matter for dispute: one of those endless chronological problems which bedevil the study of Cardinal Rodrigo's offspring. Scholars are divided on the matter. Some, on the evidence of that not always reliable source Bur-chard, and the authority of a Brief of Dispensation issued by Innocent VIII (August 1488), not to mention Alexander VI's Bull of Legitimization (Sep-tember 1493), regard him as younger than Cesare, and place his birth not earlier than 1476. Others, relying on the very fact that he was chosen as Pier Luigi's successor, are convinced he was older. His future was determined in advance, since the will which the Duke of Gandia drafted on 14 August 1488 —presumably at his father's dictation—named Giovanni as sole residuary legatee, the only other bequest being a sum of 12,000 florins as Lucrezia's dowry.

Cesare, born (possibly at Rignano) on 13 or 14 September 1475, was then thirteen. The stain of his illegitimate origin, which would disqualify him from holding any office or dignity within the Church's sphere of influence, was wiped away on 1 October 1480 by a Bull of Sixtus IV; this gave him dispensa-tion from the need to prove his legitimacy. With so many sons to find places for, Cardinal Rodrigo kept the Vatican Chancellery busy drafting those ingenious documents, and Cesare, too, in due course had a Bull of Legitimization put through on his behalf. Destined for an ecclesiastical career at an age when he was too young either to be consulted or to express an opinion on the matter (one day he was to say of himself: '*Nunca de su voluntad fué clérigo*'), he now found himself well launched on the road that brought in titles and prebends. In March 1482, at the age of six and a half, he became an Apostolic Proto-notary. By July he was a Canon of Valencia Cathedral, and by August Arch-deacon of Jativa and Rector of Gandia. In April 1483 he was made a provost and in September 1484 treasurer of Cartagena Cathedral, subsequently also becoming the holder of a prebend in Majorca, Archdeacon of Tarragona Cathedral, and a Canon of the collegiate church of Lerida. On those slender child's shoulders he bore—proportionately speaking—a load worthy of Atlas.

An agile, quick-witted boy, eyes aglint with energy and intelligence under

his mop of flowing fair hair, he displayed to the world a contemplative temperament beneath which there in fact lurked a violent inner ferment: hard, unremitting thought matched by fiercely simmering instincts. He was passionately
devoted to study, and the acuteness of his mind amazed everyone. At thirteen
he passed for a kind of prodigy. Paolo Pompilio the humanist—the first of many
writers who dedicated their works to him—did not hesitate to offer him his
Syllabica; in a resoundingly rhetorical epistle at the beginning of the book he
extolled Cesare's precocious learning, and predicted—with scant prophetic fore-
sight—that he would become a famous man of letters. His father engaged the
best available tutors for him, of whom the most distinguished was Spannolio
of Majorca.

The adolescent boy moved in a circle of élite minds; it is possible that, in
Spannolio's company, he sometimes lent his fresh grace to the meetings of the
Accademia Romana. About his early youth nothing more is known. A long
sojourn in Spain cannot be ruled out—a hypothesis supported not only by his
perfect mastery of Valencian dialect (which the Borgias habitually employed
amongst themselves), but also by the bulk of his offices and prebends, all linked
with churches in Spanish cities.

And so we come to Lucrezia, who—because of a historiographical tradition
amateurishly reliant on ancient scandal, and adhering to the lust-dagger-poison
trinomial—was to go down to posterity among the famous and ruthless cour-
tesans. Born on 18 April 1480, she was taken from Vannozza's house at a very
early age, and entrusted—as each in turn, were her brothers—to the care of
Adriana del Milá, a young Spanish cousin of Rodrigo's, married to Lodovico
Orsini, Lord of Bassanello. In the Orsini palazzo on Monte Giordano, the
young girl had regular contact with the cream of Rome's nobility, and received
a perfect education in style, manners, culture, religious piety, the whole har-
moniously fused in accordance with the pedagogical concepts of the day. From
this social-cum-intellectual grounding there was to emerge one of the most
fascinating women of the Renaissance: brilliant, capable of sustaining the most
learned discussions, able to converse in French and Spanish as well as Italian, a
discerning connoisseur of Greek and Latin, and a stylishly polished poetess in
all three of the modern languages she possessed.

As for Goffredo, or Jofré, born in 1481, he turned out a mild-mannered,
bashful little boy, so different from his brothers that one is almost tempted to
believe the Mantuan Catanei's testimony, cited earlier, concerning the doubts
expressed by Alexander VI as to his own paternity in this particular case. There
was to be a wild and dissolute period in Goffredo's life, but a brief one, scarcely
more than an isolated episode. Goffredo had the goodness to be found in an

individual made for a life of peace and obscurity. A lamb among young wolves, he moved through events with the distrait, and at times reluctant, air of a man who remains unconvinced by the part he has been given to play, and would much prefer to be somewhere else. On the plane of psychological—if not his‑ torical—truth, there is much to be said for those who see his portrait in the face of the sleeping soldier who, along with two others, is on guard outside Christ's sepulchre in the fresco Pinturicchio painted for the Borgia Apartments, which shows Alexander VI worshipping the Risen Lord. This image of a young man clad in shining armour, yet carelessly fallen asleep before the tomb‑entrance, while his companions are awake and active, offers a most faithful spiritual interpretation of Goffredo's gentle and indolent personality. He drifts across the stage, while the Borgia tragedy unfolds, like some unimportant extra, a pawn in a game that is greater than himself. He died late in 1516, aged thirty‑five, having buried, in silence and obscurity, his memories of that tempestuous era.

The pontificate of Innocent VIII proceeds in a series of violent jerks, under rude pressure from Giuliano della Rovere, *papa et plusquam papa*, who lost no time in putting both hands on the shoulders of his tractable Genoese puppet and, from behind, steering the poor man right, left, or straight forward, as he thought best. To keep an even closer eye on him, and to make it quite clear (for the benefit of anyone who might have doubts about the matter) just who was the master, he himself moved into the Vatican. His relatives, who had trembled on the death of Sixtus IV, now came back out into the bright Roman sunshine, more influential than ever before. Giovanni not only kept his position as City Prefect, but was also appointed the new Captain‑General of the Church.

Endlessly oscillating between sickness and convalescence, and prey to a nervous instability which made him either erupt in outbursts of extremism or retreat in timorous alarm, Giuliano's zombie still proceeded, willy‑nilly, along the programmatic lines which Giuliano had laid down: the first, in order of importance, being the anti‑Aragonese policy inherited from Pope Sixtus.

Beside Ferrante—and no less daunting a figure—there now stood his son Alfonso, Duke of Calabria: a prince who possessed all his father's grim wisdom and treacherous malice, with enough cynicism, in addition, to congratulate himself on the fact. Later, faced with the ordeal of a French invasion, he was to show that, besides the characteristics proper to a suspicious and brutal tyrant, he also had a streak of cowardice in him—which suggested to Commynes the following unchallengeable aphorism: '*Jamais homme cruel ne fut hardi.*' Despiser of every faith and foe to all good principle, Alfonso did not scruple to employ

the most horrendous means; in his struggle against Venice, he went as far as
sending agents to poison the city's wells.

In October 1484 we find him at Rome, dealing with the ever-recurrent
problems that arose between his Kingdom and the Holy See: Ferrante's refusal
to pay tribute, and the Pope's refusal to grant him the investiture. When
Alfonso also brought up the demand for permanent cession of Benevento,
Terracina and Pontecorvo to the Kingdom of Naples, Innocent dug his toes in,
and the Duke of Calabria took himself off, muttering threats. Naples now
refused to send the new Pontiff the usual ritual embassy of submission and
allegiance. In order to obtain this, Giuliano della Rovere clumsily copied the
bad advice which Guido of Montefeltro once gave Pope Boniface VIII:
'Promise much, but perform little.' At his suggestion, the Bulls authorizing the
annexation of these three cities to the Kingdom of Naples were actually pro-
mulgated, but then held back and left in his custody. When put on the spot,
Innocent subsequently was to declare, before a notary—and with the most
shameless candour—that these documents were deliberately concocted in order
to deceive, and that there was no intention of honouring the promises they
embodied.

Faced with so disgusting and childish a fraud, Ferrante and Alfonso naturally lost their tempers; and one morning the Papal State awoke to find Neapolitan troops at its frontier. The situation took a turn for the worse when a
well-timed baronial revolt suggested to the men in the Vatican that a propitious moment had arrived for taking the Aragonese monarch down a peg.
Still at Giuliano's prompting, the Holy See backed this insurrection; and the
result was war.

Right up to the last moment Ferrante did his utmost to avert hostilities, sending his son the cardinal to Rome as a peacemaker. But when this emissary
reached the banks of the Tiber with his olive-branch, he fell sick and died. The
decision was left to force of arms. Supporting the Aragonese (either as co-
belligerents or with moral solidarity) were Milan, Florence, the Orsini faction,
Spain, and the Hungary of Mathias Corvinus. All Innocent could count on
was the backing of Venice, which sent him Roberto di Sanseverino, but did
not abandon its neutrality.

The enemy's mixed forces swept aside any resistance put up by the scattered
Papal troops, and pressed on to the very outskirts of Rome. Here they settled
down to wreak havoc on the capital by means of lightning raids, burning and
pillaging: a many-headed scourge which, combined with famine and internal
disorder, now threatened to sink the city like some old sprung hull. The only
thing that saved Rome was the superhuman energy of Giuliano della Rovere,

who gave a display of tough military discipline and endurance unequalled in his whole fighting career.

Innocent, however, continued to tremble, being well aware that the step from resistance to victory is a long one. He launched desperate appeals to the Emperor, the German princes, and the Swiss. None of them paid any heed. And here there emerges, for the first time, and with clear thematic enunciation, the dominant historical motif of the next few decades, and of Italy's long-lasting period of disasters.

Angle for French intervention by giving fresh encouragement to Angevin claims on Naples, Giuliano kept repeating. Make peace with Ferrante, retorted Rodrigo, who was now acting as spokesman for the aspirations of His Catholic Majesty King Ferdinand (whom he needed for the furtherance of his sons' careers) to intervene in the affairs of the peninsula. France and Spain, thus in-volved in a dispute over Italy, came into sharp collision through the utterances of their respective supporters. Arguments and threats flew to and fro; no one pulled any punches. The consistory of 6 March 1486 degenerated into a mere shouting-match, with the most scabrous insults being freely exchanged before a horror-struck and quaking Innocent VIII.

Seventeen days later, Giuliano embarked at Ostia, on his way to France. He was hoping to return with two distinguished figures in tow: Charles VIII, and René II of Anjou—Duke of Lorraine, and heir to those titles which *le bon roi* left for a luckier and more enterprising man than himself. But at Genoa, where he met the emissaries of the cautious French Duke, discussions rambled on without reaching any firm conclusion. And while he scrabbled on the brink of that deplorable action which, once again under the impetus of hatred for the Borgias, was to be repeated—all too successfully as things turned out—in 1494, various factors (Giuliano's absence from Rome, Rodrigo's shrewd diplomatic finesse, a smoothly elegant intervention by Ferdinand, the swift defeat of the Papal forces, the rebellions which broke out in various parts of the Papal State, his own exhaustion and fear) drove the Pope, in August 1486, to make peace. This peace marked the ascendancy of Rodrigo Borgia, and a triumph for the 'Spanish policy'.

Ferrante showed no sign of resentment. So delighted was he at the way the threatened French invasion had been averted that he agreed to any and every demand, grinning as he signed each article of the treaty. Then, as was his way, he cheerfully proceeded to violate them all. He did not pay the Pope his tribute; he did not give back the cities he had occupied; he dispossessed and dispatched to the next world those barons to whom he should have granted a generous pardon; he dealt more sternly than ever with any uncalled-for ecclesiastical interference. When the Vatican sent a Papal Nuncio, Pietro Menzi, to deliver a very strong protest, Ferrante loaded him with insults and would not listen to a word he said. After this, as a kind of final diabolical flourish, he published a solemn appeal for a Council which would put a little fear of God into the Vatican.

Innocent's heart received some balm for all these wounds from the marriage between his son Franceschetto—one of the most corrupt hedonists in Roman society, a diseased and debt-ridden gambler, a crapulous debauchee of the very worst sort—and the tender young Maddalena de' Medici. Under the astonished eyes of the Papal Court, and to sarcastic comments from the populace—which now, for the first time in history, saw a Pope's son brought noisily and *officially* into the public eye—the wedding was celebrated in the Apostolic Palace, with a solemnity which seemed blithely to ignore the indecorousness of the whole situation. This shameful union had in Maddalena—a candidate for true con-jugal martyrdom—its own pious victim. But Lorenzo the Magnificent, who was not the man to sacrifice his own flesh and blood for nothing (or to make another investment in the political friendship market), afterwards made the Pontiff pay dearly for this pretentious sop to his paternal affections, bullying and on occasion reprimanding him. When, a year before this nuptial bargain was struck, he had emphasized the need to 'get the Pope by the throat', he meant what he said; and in due course, using a variety of methods, he attained his goal. In any case this marriage had, from his point of view, been a good bargain: his daughter's hand in return for a cardinal's hat, to be bestowed upon his second son, the thirteen-year-old Giovanni.

The echoes of these nuptial celebrations had not yet faded when St Peter's territorial heritage began to dance a revolutionary tarantella. In the spring of 1488 there was an orgy of mob violence at Forlí, during which Gerolamo Riario was done to death. Ancona revolted; the city hoisted the Hungarian flag and placed itself under the protection of Mathias Corvinus, Ferrante's son-in-law. There was another fearful outbreak at Faenza, after that dandified figure Galeotto Manfredi (a husband with a frivolous and roving eye) had been murdered at the instigation of his jealous consort, Francesca Bentivoglio. There were bloody clashes in Perugia, part of the chronic struggle between the Oddi and Baglioni families, with a serious danger of the Papal yoke being thrown off and broken. Drawn swords gleamed at Foligno and Spello, over a matter of territorial boundaries. Sparks of revolt were in the air everywhere. And there was Mathias Corvinus, who harassed the Pontiff from the North (just as Ferrante had resumed harrying him from the South); he wanted to get his hands on that much-coveted hostage Gem, and to this end was making play with the threat that he would throw the port of Ancona open to the Turks, and flood all Italy with them.

To lay claim to Gem was aiming a little high. Bajazet's brother had sought refuge with the Knights of Rhodes, who later transferred him to an estate of theirs in Auvergne. Finally he was purchased by Innocent VIII (who in return bestowed a cardinal's hat upon the Grand Master, Pierre d'Aubusson, and a whole clutch of privileges on the Order generally) and then brought out of France, after a costly deal with the Court there. As a hostage he was worth his weight in gold, on at least two counts: the Sultan paid no less than 45,000 ducats annually for his guarding and maintenance, and the possession of his person constituted the best available means of keeping the Great Turk on tenterhooks.

Gem reached Rome on 13 March 1489: he was held in princely captivity, and became a never-failing source of curiosity and amazement. Majestically impassive towards everything going on around him, moderately polite to the Pope, of melancholy temperament (with the occasional furious outburst when he was in a black mood, or drunk), neat and compact in his movements, with one elegant eyebrow slanting obliquely across his forehead and the other dropping over his eye, he ate and drank fantastically, meditated, sat silent, went hunting, played music, wrote poetry. Rome was enchanted by him. Young fops began to adopt Turkish fashions of dress, and artists vied with one another to paint his portrait.

So Mathias would not get Gem. Nevertheless, the pressure which the Hungarian and his father-in-law put on the Papal State became so overwhelming that the most desperate notions began to pullulate in Innocent's brain. He toyed with the idea of excommunicating Ferrante, of bringing the now-reconciled Charles VIII and Maximilian of Austria to Italy and using them to topple him from his throne, of abandoning Rome as altogether too insecure. On the horizon of his shadowy notions there appeared, temptingly, the turreted mass of the Papal Palace in Avignon.

These were agonizing years. Not until the end of 1491 did Ferrante—shrewdly aware of the need not to force the game too hard if France was not to be tempted —lend an encouraging ear to the peace proposals laid before him, on the Pontiff's behalf, by the latter's loyal and capable spokesman, Giovanni Pontano.

Peace was concluded on 27 January 1492. The Duke of Calabria would have his investiture, provided the Aragonese paid the annual levy of 50,000 ducats, and refrained from meddling in ecclesiastical matters. There was to be an amnesty for the surviving barons on the one hand, and a free pardon for the rebellious Roman families on the other. As a pledge of restored concord, a fine match was arranged between Battistina Usodimare, daughter of the Pope's daughter, and the middle-aged Luis of Aragon; while France—having lately ignored her opportunity, a decision she now regretted—was left to complain to her heart's content.

The last years of Innocent VIII's reign brought Rodrigo Borgia some moments well worth the remembering.

In the house of his cousin Adriana del Milá, where Lucrezia and Goffredo were still living, there appeared one day the fabulous Giulia, a picture in ivory, amber and gold, daughter of Pier Luigi Farnese and Giovannia de' Caetani: a legendary beauty thrown up by a mediocre family which, thanks to her and her love-affairs, was to climb high and fast up Fortune's ladder.

As Lucrezia's intimate friend, and the fiancée of Orsino Orsini, Adriana's son, she had moved into a position vis-à-vis the family that was at first hedged about with innocence, but soon—under Cardinal Rodrigo's lustful eye—became smirched and tarnished. With the old Spaniard's appearance on the scene the flower of her prenuptial idyll withered, as though smitten by a blast of tainted air. Round this blonde adolescent child the concupiscent (and all-but-sexagenarian) vice-chancellor of the Church slowly wound his powerful, devious, and blandly caressing tentacles; while she—displaying all the precocious knowledge which characterized young girls in her day—gave him the delectable sight of modesty first trembling, then yielding, and finally melting in passion.

On the evening of 20 May 1489 Giulia crossed the threshold of Rodrigo Borgia's palazzo, accompanied by her fiancé and a small escort of relatives, for the signing of the nuptial contract. This was done in the dazzling Sala delle Stelle, under the benignly smiling eye of the cardinal, as groomsman and patron. The wedding itself, a most magnificent occasion, took place the following day; Only a few days later all Rome was openly talking of Giulia as the vice-chancellor's mistress, and extending to the poor 'cavalier Orsino' those sympathies traditionally reserved for cuckolded husbands. When, three years later, Giulia gave birth to a daughter, Laura, various people in her domestic circle assumed that Rodrigo was the father. (They were probably wrong, since there still exists a notorious letter, dated 22 October 1494, in which Alexander VI accuses Giulia of wanting to go to her husband and get pregnant by him 'a second time'.)

So began a wildly passionate affair, marked by tenderness and jealousy, which can, without fear of contradiction, be defined as the last great 'musical phrase' in Rodrigo's love-life. For the Farnese family it formed the prelude to an upward movement which, less than fifty years later, reached the very pinnacle of fame through Giulia's brother Alexander, who became first cardinal and then Pope.

In 1489 Rodrigo sent Cesare to study at the University of Perugia. Here the young boy went through a stage of religious enthusiasm (probably unique in his history) which was afterwards to leave him with a certain nostalgia for this period of peace and meditation, and to occasion that 'singular benevolence' which he professed to feel for the Umbrian city.[4]

It was in September 1491, while the student was on vacation at Soriano, that Innocent VIII appointed him Bishop of Pamplona, in that same Navarre where, fifteen years later, his star was to fall and be extinguished. To propitiate the pastoral flock entrusted to his theoretical care, the vice-chancellor sent the local authorities a letter fairly dripping with honeyed compliments; and another was drafted (probably at his father's dictation) by the sixteen-year-old prelate himself, in that dynamic, exquisitely elegant hand which is a never-failing joy to the eye, and would seem to indicate an unusual love of penmanship. But Pamplona proved recalcitrant, and it took a stern *monitorium* from the Pope to make the city accept its beardless bishop.

A few weeks later, Cesare transferred to the University of Pisa. This move was decided by Cardinal Rodrigo because Lorenzo the Magnificent's second son, Cardinal Giovanni, had been sent there as a student. Medici friendship was something well worth the winning. During this Pisan period Cesare Borgia reveals a different manner, appearance and way of life from those he had affected while at Perugia. His earlier well-bred restraint acquired overtones of almost barbaric extravagance. Surrounded by a dazzling circle of courtiers, living in a palazzo furnished with something approaching the luxury of a Sardanapalus, owner of a superb stable of thoroughbreds, the cardinal's son quite outshone the limited and restrained dignity of his Florentine friend and coeval—so much so, that the latter found himself at a disadvantage when inviting Cesare to lunch at his house, and had to seek the advice of his family in Florence, by letter, to ensure that he did not make a bad impression. One characteristic feature of Cesare's personality which now became noticeable was the pleasure he took in surrounding himself—he, the well-bred and impeccable gentleman *par excellence*—with a band of swaggering louts, who marched briskly through the streets, taking up the entire sidewalk, and earning covert glances from passers-by. In a way it looks like an artist's whim—the desire to produce a contrast by having a dark penumbra throw his own person into even brighter prominence. In fact it is also a precocious sign of his political flair: the attempt to produce a theatrical impression of formidableness (*terribilità*).

At Giovanni de' Medici's degree examination, on 1 February 1492, Cesare acted as *arguente,* or 'accuser'—which shows that he had terminated his own studies some time before.

Meanwhile, in February 1491, the first aspirant to Lucrezia's hand had appeared, even though she was not yet eleven: Juan Cherubín de Centelles, a young gentleman from the Kingdom of Valencia, related by blood to the very highest Spanish nobility. Clearly Rodrigo was still keeping one eye on the land of his birth, and meant to build his children's future there. Then, two months after this first engagement, there came a second nuptial pact. This time the candidate was Gasparo of Procida, son of the Count of Aversa and Almenara—another Spaniard, but one who had emigrated to Italy.

Rodrigo's election as Pope put paid to both contracts, sweeping away the two fiancés (who were now regarded as expendable) in favour of a more important and useful match. Don Juan Cherubín swallowed this affront with a philosophical shrug of the shoulders; but Don Gasparo, seething with fury, descended on Rome, accompanied by his father, where in indignation over this bare-faced breach of promise, he threatened interventions on his behalf by various highly-placed persons, and only resigned himself to going home after he had pocketed an indemnity of 3000 ducats.

1492 was a memorable year for Spain, Italy and the Borgias. On 2 January Granada fell, and the news—which reached Rome on the night of 1 February, via a personal dispatch from King Ferdinand—set off a wave of jubilation. Rodrigo Borgia, as *de facto* leader of Rome's Spanish community, presented the Roman people with the first *corrida* he had ever sponsored in his life.

On 31 March Their Most Catholic Majesties published an edict presenting the Jews with a brutal choice between conversion and exile. Crowds of refugees choked the main roads out of Spain, trudging away into a future of hardship and misery. *Exitus Israël.* Even Rome, a tolerant city, witnessed the arrival of broken groups from this torn and dispersed people.

On 8 April, there was mourning in Italy. Amid the scents and sounds of spring, when it is saddest to die, Lorenzo the Magnificent breathed his last, in his charming country-house at Careggi. He was only forty-three: the champion of adroit diplomacy, the past-master of compromise, the model of humane tolerance, the brilliant political tightrope-walker, the conjuror with peace, the glory of his era. Cesare Borgia, who had known him and frequented his company (though without finding him a sympathetic character), wrote Piero a letter of condolence, which sought to bring comfort for sorrow in a consideration of the noble virtues of the deceased, who died 'in the odour of Catholic sanctity, leaving glorious and immortal fame behind him'.

On 23 May, in the little Andalusian harbour-town of Palos, a Genoese sailor lately arrived from Granada assembled municipal authorities and citizens in the Church of San Giorgio, where—in the peremptory accents of a man called by God to some high enterprise—he read out a message from Their Majesties, bidding the townspeople furnish him with fully equipped caravels for the crossing of the ocean.

A month later, Innocent VIII collapsed under the weight of that illness which, despite a deceptive improvement at one point, was to prove his last. Its symptoms included agonizing abdominal pains, an old scar in one leg which broke open again, and persistent high fever. The first person to feel the impact of the Pope's sickness was Gem, who found himself subjected to more rigorous surveillance.

Rodrigo Borgia and Giuliano della Rovere snapped and snarled at each other across the dying man's sickbed. The former wanted the Pontiff to turn over Castel Sant'Angelo to the cardinals (at present it was held by Della Rovere); the latter struck like a snake to forestall any such order, reminding the Pope that Rodrigo Borgia was 'a Catalan'.

'If we were not standing in the presence of His Holiness,' Rodrigo snarled, 'I would show you who is vice-chancellor!'

'If we were not here,' Giuliano retorted, '*I* would show *you* that I'm not afraid of you!'

There followed a string of mutual insults fit to make the very scarlet they wore turn a deeper red for shame;[5] and it was war to the knife between them from then on, a war which was to drag itself out (with dramatic consequences for the Church and for Italy) until the older of the two was dead, and Cesare had been eliminated.

The death of Innocent VIII, which took place during the night of 25–26 July 1492, offered Rodrigo Borgia the chance he had missed eight years previously. It was now or, perhaps, never. While the pavements of Rome were reddened with the bloodshed that attended every interregnum, and some 220 corpses awaited burial by pious hands, he set himself—with great decisiveness—to grasp the throne behind which he had stood, as vice-chancellor, for some thirty-five years: half a lifetime, in fact. This time, as before, his campaign was conducted by means of various promises, duly recorded in writing. The weapons at his disposal—the office of vice-chancellor, regarded as 'a second papacy', his grandiose Roman palazzo, with its priceless furnishings, bishoprics in Spain and Italy, abbeys, fortresses, lands, prebends of every kind and size, legateships, piles of chinking gold—formed an unrivalled arsenal, which he had slowly built up, during the reigns of five successive Pontiffs, to meet this supreme final test.

With the conclave about to take place, nevertheless, speculation by no means favoured his chances. The label of 'Catalan', the antipathies which even his polished diplomacy had not succeeded in eradicating, his position at the point of conflict between rival parties and interests, his very status as a personage of high influence—all these things worked to his disadvantage.

He also had what were regarded as two most formidable rivals in the field against him: Giuliano della Rovere and Ascanio Maria Sforza. Giuliano was backed by King Ferrante, who for this occasion had forgotten their recent enmity and (if gossip was to be trusted) had deposited some 200,000 ducats in a certain bank, with which to promote Giuliano's election and hinder that of Rodrigo Borgia. Ascanio could count on the support of those cardinals politically committed to the Duchy of Milan.

There were quite a few observers who held out small hope for any one of these three candidates; Rodrigo, they said, would be defeated because he was Spanish, Giuliano because of his French connections, and Ascanio because he was too young, and brother to that disturbing character Ludovico the Moor. More or less neutral names began to crop up in these people's prognostications: Ardicino della Porta, Giorgio da Costa, Oliviero Carafa, Battista Zeno, Paolo Fregoso, Francesco Piccolomini, and others.

The conclave went into session in the Sistine Chapel on 6 August. Twenty-three cardinals were present. Bernardino López de Carvajal delivered an eloquent speech in which he described the Church's running sores, comparing her to the 'Whore of Babylon', and earnestly besought his colleagues to elect a holy and vigorous shepherd who would implement moral reform, free Christen-dom from the Turkish threat, and (in every sense) open a new era. He also held out for the now customary 'electoral capitulation'. With that, battle was joined.

The first scrutiny was inconclusive, with the Borgia candidate receiving seven votes; so were the second and third, at both of which he raised his support to eight. The third scrutiny took place on the morning of 10 August. During that day the 'guardians' outside sought to extract a decision from the isolated group of cardinals by reducing their meals to a single course. If they still could not reach agreement after that, they would be put on a starvation diet of bread and water.

This, however, did not prove necessary. In a few hours Rodrigo, by playing his strongest cards, had nudged the proceedings towards their end: painful hours, studded with confidential discussions, *ad hominem* haggling, and sudden switches of allegiance. Sforza, Orsini, Colonna, Savelli, Pallavicini, Michiel,

Sclafenati, Sanseverino, Fregoso, Riario, Domenico della Rovere, Giovanni de' Medici, the ninety-five-year-old Maffeo Gherardi—one by one they all fell like rotten-ripe fruit at a touch from the Borgia wand. In the end even that stubborn figure Giuliano followed suit; he was too sensible not to realize that sticking one's toes in at this stage was both obtuse and pointless, and that it would be more sensible to accept the Spaniard's offers. In short, during the course of one exhausting night, the whole anti-Catalan stronghold fell *en bloc*, and harmonious unanimity was achieved. The member of this conclave who carried off the most substantial prize was Cardinal Ascanio, principal author of Rodrigo's success: he got the office of vice-chancellor, the Roman palazzo, the fortress of Nepi, the bishopric of Erlau, and a whole mass of other minor benefices. But those other shrewd gamblers who had bet on a preliminary opposition and a subsequent change of allegiance had no cause for complaint either.

Up to this point in Rodrigo Borgia's election the chief motivation had been *auri sacra fames*; just how far any serious estimate of his experience or abilities was taken into consideration is very hard to say, since one never gets the 'inside' story of a conclave—what was said, argued over, and thought—nor is it possible to penetrate the electors' private consciences. Corruption does not rule out the (admittedly hypothetical) possibility of votes cast for reasons unconnected with personal interests. Such motives, in the Spaniard's case, not only existed, but—on the political plane at least—were superabundant, as his governmental record amply demonstrates.

The morning of 11 August 1492 was stormy and overcast. The crowd that gathered outside the Vatican saw a window open and a cross appear. A prelate leaned out and shouted the tidings of great joy, *gaudium magnum*. Framed above him in the window, hale and majestic, stood the figure of the Pope who, as Alexander VI, was to open a new page of history.

DAWN OF A PONTIFICATE

The unprecedented grandeur of the various acts of homage rendered to the new Pontiff, and the magnificence of the festivities organized for his coronation, on 26 August, provide eloquent testimony regarding the opinion people had of him—and, at the same time, illuminate the view he took of himself, and the tone he meant to give his own reign.

Papal Rome had never seen anything more solemn or fantastical. When Alexander VI emerged from the Vatican, a two-mile stretch of the route along which he would pass was covered with rare carpeting and gay bunting hung from all the adjacent palazzi. At a number of points stood triumphal arches, bearing grossly adulatory inscriptions; there were musicians, singers, and allegorical figures. The guns of Castel Sant'Angelo boomed out in salute; and everywhere one saw the beast from the Borgia blazon, huge and glittering, as though it were some apotheosis of the Apis bull in an ancient Egyptian festival. At dusk the city twinkled with countless celebratory bonfires that reddened the night sky. A fabulous torchlight procession wound its way through the streets like a river of flame, escorting the Pontiff to his Apostolic Palace: 8–10,000 cavaliers, the entire Vatican Court, diplomatic representatives, envoys from the Italian Powers, Rome's guardians and most distinguished citizens, and a really vast crowd following on. In the Lateran basilica, what with the heat and the throng, the Pope fainted. Floramonte Brognolo, the Duke of Mantua's *oratore* described the occasion as stupefying and exhausting: a crazy merry-go-round of dust and sunlight, a congested mass of men and horses, a clamorous saraband that went on from early morning till past nightfall, leaving everyone crushed and gasping.

> *Caesare magna fuit, nunc Roma est maxima: Sextus*
> *regnat Alexander: ille vir, iste deus,*

proclaimed the most pompous of the inscriptions—undoubtedly the high point of Italian flattery during this era.

It was at a consistory held on 31 August, only five days after his coronation, that the first darts were launched from Alexander VI's well-stocked nepotic quiver. His son Cesare got the archbishopric of Valencia, which meant 16,000 ducats a year in revenues, and implicit status as Primate of Spain. His nephew Giovanni Borgia Lanzol (the elder of two homonymous brothers belonging to the same branch of the family, his sister Juana's son and already Archbishop of Monreale) became a cardinal. Goffredo, who was destined for the priesthood, and at the age of eleven was already an Apostolic Notary, received the diocese of Majorca and one or two other prebends.

A new wave of profiteers and fortune-hunters descended on Rome from Spain, preceded by a clutch of the new Pope's relatives, friends of relatives, and friends of the friends. Spaniards wormed their way into every nook and cranny of the Vatican world. They occupied episcopal sees, they penetrated the palazzi and governmental strongholds of the State, they held commands in the armed forces. The Vatican's rich reserve of benefices was thrown open to them; every one of the Pope's sons had places for them in his entourage. By November Giovanni Andrea Boccaccio, the Este family's *oratore*, was already writing in some alarm: 'Ten Papacies would not suffice to satisfy all these relations.'

Though in this case the sheer bare-faced scale of operations caused some alarm, people no longer found such things surprising. Indeed, the Roman people had seen so much of them during the last few decades that they had lost all capacity for astonishment, let alone indignation. The only strong reactions came either from those, like Giuliano della Rovere, who were seething with partisan envy, or else from disgruntled characters who had been done out of the positions they coveted as a result of the 'Catalan triumph'. The populace as a whole, however, merely watched these proceedings with a kind of amused curiosity, laughing derisively and making pointed jokes. Excluded from all the rewards that were handed out with each change of master, squeezed and shorn by every successive government, made sceptical and morally coarse-fibred by dint of watching arrogance and fraud triumph all along the line, lolling idly on the muddy banks of cynicism, and so thick-skinned that he no longer felt the burning touch of scandal, what could the common man do, when faced with the aberrant depravities of the Holy See—already castigated as a 'whore' by Dante—but limit himself to exercising his capricious wit at the whore's expense? This populace had neither ideals nor hope; it respected nothing and nobody. Its natural mode of expression was the pasquinade, and it lost no time in nicknaming Giulia Farnese 'the Bride of Christ'—though this scathingly irreverent appellation provoked no reaction in the lady herself apart from a trill of delighted laughter. The wickedness of the age and the moral decline of society reduced everything to a joke: humanity had become so soiled that it could not take a stand on moral principle.

At this point what most interested everyone was the public image of them-selves that the Borgias were preparing to project: a fascinating spectacle. They were all great natural actors, from whom new and powerful emotions could be expected—not only upon the stage of Roman life, but also, and to an even greater extent, on that of Italian and international politics.

Even in an age when Italian political diplomacy reached exceptional heights of astuteness and cunning, Rodrigo Borgia's abilities were generally regarded as quite outstanding—an estimate which led people to expect some fascinating sport. Though his elevation to the Papal throne aroused some alarm amongst those who could not hope for anything good from a Borgia in power, by and large it was received with satisfaction—even if that notoriously hostile witness Guicciardini, in a much-quoted passage, asserts the contrary. The tears which Ferrante shed on hearing the news do not—given the fibre of the man—sound very credible; and documentary evidence provides direct refutation of the Florentine historian's references to 'terror' and 'horror'. In many people's judge-ment, such moral reservations as they might have were outweighed by technical political considerations; and while qualified neutral observers prepared to follow the Pontiff's every move with close and careful attention, those who wanted to see the Church a strong Power in the material sense were only too glad that the helm of Peter's boat had been taken over by so solid a character, famous for his courage, possessed of a most acute brain, and with the highest ambitions. Nor were there voices lacking, amongst those whose main concern was with spiritual interests, to predict that yesterday's public sinner would become tomorrow's penitent reformer.

And in sober truth, just how lofty an impression the Spaniard was to leave of himself and his pontificate in the minds of men who cannot be suspected of partiality, or a disinclination to pronounce judgement, we can deduce from the fact that—almost a century later—the granite-hard Sixtus V was wont to speak of 'St Peter, Alexander, and Ourselves', thus condensing the Church's history into three names; while that grandiose figure Urban VIII, in the mid-seventeenth century, similarly reduced it to four: 'St Peter, St Sylvester, Alexander and Ourselves'.

Everyone knows, moreover, how Machiavelli dated the beginning of Papal power and prestige at a political level from Rodrigo Borgia's pontificate, giving him the credit for the fact that 'the Church has achieved such greatness in temporal matters; and that whereas before Alexander's time the Italian potentates, *et non solum* those who called themselves potentates, but every baron and gentleman, even the most insignificant, held the Church Temporal in but slight esteem, today a King of France trembles before her.' Then, after noting how, in furtherance of their jealous and suspicious 'balance of power' policy, the four greatest Italian States—the Most Serene Republic [Venice], the Kingdom of Naples, the Duchy of Milan, and the Florentine Republic—used the great Roman families to 'keep the Pope down', thus successfully making him 'weak and powerless', Machiavelli unhesitatingly identified Rodrigo Borgia as the man responsible for upsetting this particular political applecart. 'Then there appeared Alexander VI, who, more than any Pope in history, showed to what extent the Pontiff could mkae his will prevail, using both money and force to this end . . . *And the things he did redounded to the greatness of the Church, which after his death was heir to all his labours.*'[6]

Weighed against our acknowledgement of this fact, and this authority, the conclave's bargains and compromises at once shrink to their proper proportions—a scandalous but ephemeral episode that was no more than incidental to an excellent choice of Pontiff. There are some historians who cannot forgive this mightiest of Popes his mistresses and children, so that their shadow is allowed to darken the writer's mind whenever he has occasion to pronounce judgement on Alexander himself and his achievements. Such *antiborgianesimo* at once deprives the historian's opinion of all critical value, leaving nothing behind but puritanical rhetoric, as laborious as it is peevish.

The new pontificate got away to an excellent start. Alexander's political programme was, naturally, conditioned by the problems that his predecessors had passed on—some still unsolved, others only dealt with in a makeshift fashion: the setting in order of the administration; the repression of anarchy within the State; the search for a vantage-point amid the inter-state rivalries of the New Europe, with particular reference to the struggle between France and Naples, and in the last instance between France and Spain; holding up any further advance by the Turks.

Other equally serious problems loomed ahead in the field of religion and morality: the reformation of the Church, through a radical overhaul of its institutions and customs; the struggle against the various heretical movements, which found a powerful incentive in the disgust provoked by evil examples amongst the hierarchy; the restoration of discipline in the religious Orders, and a better organized programme of activities for them; missionary work in the newly-discovered territories across the ocean, which were enlarging the physical map of the world even as one watched; control of published matter; keeping a close eye on the political affiliations of the Inquisition and, in general, on governmental interference in ecclesiastical matters.

All these problems were faced up to by Alexander VI with resolute mien, considered judgement, and most subtle sagacity—tactical gifts put at the service of indisputable genius, the genius of a statesman used to embracing vast panoramic vistas in his lofty view of things. Not all found a solution, and amongst those destined to remain unsolved were two of the most vexatious: moral reform, and crusading. However, this was not entirely due to lack of good will; in some cases it stemmed from the overriding urgency of situations which demanded an all-out effort by all available means, in others from the weakness of man, whose spirit was willing, but whose flesh was weak. And if, during the second half of his pontificate, his actions laid themselves open to not unjustified criticism, that was through the weakening of a will which, clearly, could not match up to his magnificent intellect: a will which through fatherly affection—and perhaps even through fear—became enslaved to that of Cesare.

These initial measures seemed a prelude to an outstanding pontificate, launched under the sign of that supreme desiderandum for all good government—a preoccupation with justice. The police and the courts were given orders to take most rigorous proceedings against those responsible for the murders perpetrated in Rome during the seventeen days of the interregnum. A long-awaited inspection of prisons, carried out by the members of a specially appointed commission, was the first step towards a more humane organization of the whole prison system. A clearly democratic impulse (within the limitations imposed by the *Zeitgeist*) revealed itself in this Pope at the outset of his pontificate. He appointed four commissioners, whose task it was to collect the various protests, complaints, and requests of the citizen body, with a view to righting every wrong, and gratifying every legitimate aspiration of the community as a whole. He also developed the practice of holding a regular Tuesday audience, at which personal problems liable to benefit from his intervention could be submitted to him. Here we have a generally neglected facet of the man —the supposedly 'diabolical' Alexander VI, welcoming the poor in his palazzo, hearing their petitions with inexhaustible patience, giving each of them prompt justice, and always ready to stretch out a fatherly helping hand at need. But this is a side of him which seems not to interest current Borgia historiography.

Another of Alexander VI's immediate concerns was to reinvigorate finance, which formed the backbone of the State. Here he showed himself a perfect administrator, implementing useful reforms, scrutinizing income and expenditure with the most circumspect strictness, and, above all, imposing a systematic cut-back on expenditure. He himself set the example, by leading an unbelievably frugal life, stripped of all superfluities. His meals comprised one course only, with the result that anyone who could kept well away from his table. Household expenses, during this initial phase of his pontificate, did not exceed 700 ducats a month: a derisory figure, when compared with the 8000 which his future successor Julius II managed to get through. The benefits conferred by his administration—the latter being sustained by a financial ability which shone out at every moment and in all circumstances—made themselves felt throughout the economic life of the State, bringing its subjects the highest standard of living they had ever enjoyed within people's memory. Indeed, when the Borgias disappeared from the scene, it was not long before the populace bitterly regretted their going.

Diplomats close to Alexander VI during this early period were pleasantly impressed by the admirable way he went about his affairs. He put out peace feelers in all directions; he spoke of reforming the Papal Court; he seemed determined to keep his sons outside Vatican circles. Cesare, in fact, who, on receipt of the conclave's decision had left Siena, where he had a horse entered for the races, and at once set off for Rome, received an order *en route* telling him to stop at Spoleto. There he was obliged to spend several months, kicking his heels in furious impatience.

With impressive—and cumulative—speed, the unanimity finally achieved by the conclave revealed its temporary and artificial character. Under the pressure of events, and of divergent interests, cards were flung down on the table in the most wildly reckless fashion. The false smiles vanished, faces grew hard and unyielding. On one side there stood Alexander VI, with his vice-chancellor Ascanio Sforza; on the other, Giuliano della Rovere, with the militant hard core of the opposition party. These two men stood at the centre of two con-flicting power blocs, with various Italian and foreign Powers behind them, and the seeds of disaster contained within their hostility.

The first skirmishes took place over the unwitting person of the twelve-year-old Lucrezia, when Cardinal Ascanio—a scarlet-clad marriage broker—sought to arrange for her betrothal to a forty-six-year-old cousin of his, Giovanni Sforza, Count of Cotignola and Lord of Pesaro.

Such a match could not fail to raise Ferrante's hackles, inasmuch as it would inevitably strengthen the position of Ludovico the Moor, now bent on usurping the Duchy of Milan from his unwarlike nephew Gian Galeazzo by force of arms. This could not leave him indifferent for the young Duke's wife was his niece Isabella of Aragon, and the Moor had embarked on a treacherous course of intrigue with France.

There was also the marriage between King Ladislaw of Hungary and the sterile Beatrice of Aragon, Ferrante's daughter and the widow of Mathias Corvinus. Ferrante's animosity was sharpened still further by the fact that, during this same period, Alexander—again, under pressure from the Moor—had come around to the idea of declaring this union invalid and thus enabling Ladislaw to marry Bianca Maria Sforza. The struggle that went on in the Vatican over Beatrice's fate (with complicated interventions by Budapest, Milan and Naples) was dictated solely, in the coldest, most calculating way imaginable, by reasons of State.

A third incident aggravated the tension still further: Franceschetto Cibo's sale, to Virginio Orsini, of his fiefs at Cerveteri and Anguillara, both within Church territory. It did not require exceptional discernment to guess that the 40,000 ducats for the purchase of these lands had been disbursed by Ferrante, who was using Orsini as his agent to 'put a bone in the Pope's throat' (the phrase is Guicciardini's). Nor was Alexander slow to sense behind this astute transaction, the industrious presence of Giuliano della Rovere, still flying an Aragonese banner. There followed—in full consistory—one of those crudely vulgar clashes between them which from now on set the tone for their relation-ship. Towards the end of the year the Ligurian found it desirable to shake Rome's perfidious dust off his feet, and retire to his cardinal's seat at Ostia, where he took up residence in a stupendous (and assault-proof) stronghold built for him by Baccio Pontelli. This fortress became a focal-point for the opposition.

By the beginning of 1493, then, the situation was clear, and both sides' positions plainly defined.

Ferrante took certain precautions at a military level, putting troops on the alert for a possible intervention in defence of the threatened Orsini clan; he also worked hard in the diplomatic sphere, sending the King and Queen of Spain a malicious pamphlet directed against the Pope, crammed with every sort of accusation, moral and political alike. This was the first *parti pris* slander-campaign directed against Rodrigo Borgia; it was accompanied by a fusillade of letters in Spain, with the object of damaging his reputation in just those circles where he meant to let the tree of his family ambitions put out fresh leaves.

It was not long before a letter reached the Vatican from the Western shores of the Mediterranean, bearing the signature of Don Enrique Enriquez, King Ferdinand's uncle, and the father of Pier Luigi's ex-fiancée, now promised to Giovanni: a bitter letter, which referred, in tones of heartfelt anxiety, to the unpleasant gossip then circulating in Spain at the Borgias' expense. On 23 March 1493 a long reply was dispatched from Rome—its signatory being the datary Juan López, Bishop of Perugia, though Cesare was in all likelihood responsible for drafting it—which not only furnished a point-by-point rebuttal of all *sinistra informacion* put into circulation by the enemies of *Su Beatitud*, but then passed from apologia to extolment, enthusiastically describing the Pope's kindness, justice, and mercy, his religious devoutness, his liberality, his large-scale projects for the embellishment of Rome, the peace and security which flourished under his aegis.

Meanwhile a rumour spread concerning a possible alliance between Milan, Venice, and the Holy See. In the face of so alarming a threat, Ferrante found it expedient to resurrect his complaisance once more. The affair of Cerveteri and Anguillara, he informed the Pope, could be smoothed over. And since it was rumoured that Cesare meant to renounce his ecclesiastical career ('People are saying that the Bishop of Valencia is about to doff his habit,' the Mantuan *oratore* Floramonte Brognolo wrote on 19 March 1493), why not marry him off to a princess from the House of Aragon, and use this union to cement their ancient friendship?

The proposal came to nothing. Though Cesare had in fact reached Rome some while before, after his period of quarantine at Spoleto, and had moved into Domenico della Rovere's palazzo (where he was now leading a most enjoyable existence), the time was not yet ripe for him to change his career. In

1. *Urban VI, from a fifteenth-century wood-cut.*

2. *Saint Peter's and the Vatican from a fifteenth-century engraving.*

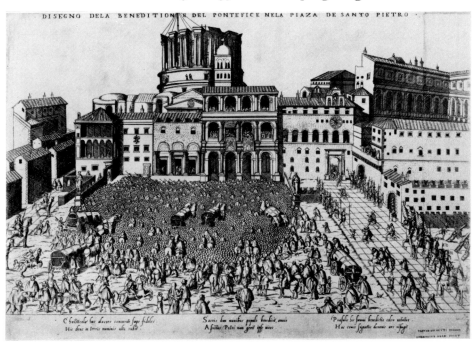

DISEGNO DELA BENEDITIONE DEL PONTEFICE NELA PIAZA DE SANTO PIETRO·

3. *Callistus III by Sano di Pietro.*

4. *Eugenius IV by Salviati.* ▶

5. *Cesare Borgia as a young boy by Pinturicchio.*

6. *Alfonso of Aragon, medal by Francesco di Giorgio.*

7. *The bulls, emblem of the Borgias, and a portrait of Alexander VI.*

9. *Giulia Farnese, detail from the* Transfiguration *by Raphael.* ▶

8. *Alexander VI, portrait bust by Pasquale da Caravaggio.*

10. *Charles VIII of France by Jean Perréal.*

11. *The Duke of Gandia, detail from the* Disputation of Saint Catherine *by
Pinturicchio.*

12. *The Castello Estense, Ferrara.*

13. *Lucrezia Borgia, detail from the* Disputation of Saint Catherine *by* ▶
    Pinturicchio.

14. *Alfonso d'Este by Dosso Dossi.*

15. *Goffredo Borgia and Sancia d'Aragona, detail from the* Disputation of Saint Catherine *by Pinturicchio.*

16. *Castel Sant' Angelo, Rome. Anonymous pen and ink drawing about 1540.*

17. *View of Rome, wood-cut 1486. From Jacopo Fillippo Foresti da Bergamo,* Supplementum Chronicarum, *Venice 1486.*

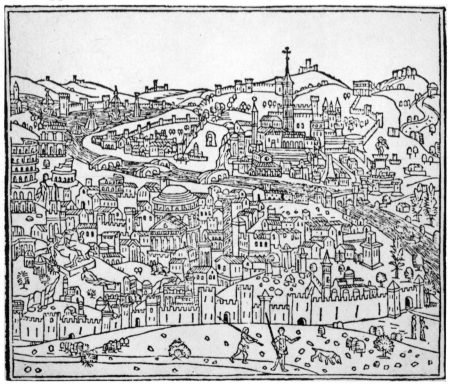

18. *Presumed portrait of Cesare Borgia by an unknown painter (formerly attributed to Leonardo da Vinci).*

19. *Niccolò Machiavelli, terracotta bust of the fifteenth century.*

any case, even with the one to which he was at present committed, he still found, and harvested, all the pleasures that his youth could desire. As everyone observed, he did not attach much importance to the small tonsure under his fashionable velvet bonnet. With his extraordinary good looks, unmatchable elegance, and nobly courteous demeanour, he charmed ladies and their cavaliers alike. Every day he added some new touch to his incipient legend, dazzling the Urbs with the splendour of his person and the luxurious life he led. He was already very much the fashionable man of the moment—and, as yet, still more loved than feared. Embroidered on the breast of his cope were two interwoven initials, his own and that of some mysterious lady; and a Spanish poet had made flattering allusion to this in his verses.

Ferrante's attempt to achieve a *rapprochement* could not avert the eventuality he most feared. On 25 April 1493 the conclusion of an alliance between Milan, Venice, and the Holy See, with Mantua, Ferrara and Siena as member States, was officially announced in Rome. The wind blowing against the Orsini family now developed into a regular tempest, and the King of Naples found himself faced with an unwelcome choice of alternatives: he must either abandon them to their fate, or else embark on a war that fairly teemed with hazardous unknown factors. If he had, in fact, felt real grief when informed of Rodrigo Borgia's election, he must now feel that his tears were justified.

During the breathing-space which Alexander VI meanwhile gave his enemies—allowing time for them to reflect and for allied reinforcements to reach the Papal State—there took place the wedding of Lucrezia and Giovanni Sforza. The marriage contract was signed on 2 February; amongst other clauses, it laid down that the union should not be physically consummated for another year, and fixed Lucrezia's dowry at 31,000 ducats. Lucrezia herself was now living in the palazzo of Santa Maria in Portico, built ten years previously by Cardinal Zeno, and situated in the immediate vicinity of the Vatican. With her were Adriana del Milá and Giulia Farnese, the latter more lovely than ever after giving birth to a daughter, Laura (who in 1505 was to marry Niccolò della Rovere, Julius II's nephew and brother to Cardinal Galeotto). Giulia had reached that full, mature beauty which shines out in the kneeling woman of Raphael's 'Transfiguration', and the statue of 'Justice' sculpted by Guglielmo della Porta for the sepulchral monument of the Farnese Pope: marvellous images in which, according to one tradition, we can recognize Giulia's own likeness.

Lucrezia, Adriana, and Giulia: a seemingly indissoluble feminine trio. Many great persons who were visiting Rome came to pay homage to the young

Borgia girl in the palazzo of Santa Maria in Portico; and in November of the previous year she had had her first meeting with the sixteen-year-old Alfonso d'Este, already married to Anna Sforza, Galeazzo Maria's sister, and destined, less than nine years later, to become her own second husband.

That middle-aged illegitimate widower the Lord of Pesaro, into whose lap Lucrezia's virgin beauty had been tossed as a matter of policy, reached Rome on 9 June. He was welcomed, at the Porta del Popolo, by his fiancée's brothers, together with various dignitaries from the Curia, and ambassadors accredited to the Holy See. He was a handsome bearded man, with a smooth brow and flowing wavy hair.

The wedding was celebrated three days later in magnificent style, with the whole of official Rome present. It was followed by an evening banquet in the Vatican gardens. We have one convincing account of this occasion from the pen of the Este family's *oratore*, Giovanni Andrea Boccaccio, and another (somewhat more acid) from that of the libellous Infessura. The guests included a number of very cheerful cardinals, Giulia Farnese and Adriana del Milá, distinguished civic dignitaries, and ladies whose beauty was as rare and special as their pedigrees. The Pope, surrounded by his household, was over-flowing with joy. There were gifts to be offered to the bridal couple, theatrical interludes, musical performances, women dancing (a special aesthetic passion of Rodrigo Borgia's); between them these items kept the party going all night.

Sforza, in his capacity as a captain of militia (paid jointly by the Duke of Milan and the Vatican), stayed on in Rome, under the auspices of the recently concluded treaty. Lucrezia, however—leaving her husband to sigh in frustra-tion, and perhaps with a sigh or two of her own—went back to the palazzo of Santa Maria in Portico, where she resumed her hothouse gynaeceum existence.

A few days later there reached Rome an ambassador from the King of Spain, one Diego López de Haro, who had come to make the ritual 'act of obedience' in the name of his sovereigns, but he also profited by his audience with Alexan-der VI (19 June) to make it clear that Ferdinand had the interests of the House of Aragon at heart, and to urge the Pope to accept a friendly settlement of their differences.

All of which clearly signified that Ferrante had made his decision: he was ready to yield all along the line, provided there no longer hung over his King-dom the threat of a French expedition promoted by the new alliance.

However, like the crafty gambler he was, before offering peace and concord he made one last attempt, during the second half of June, at intimidation. He ordered his eldest son Alfonso to lead an army to the frontiers of the Papal State, and sent his next-eldest son, Federico, to Rome, to try and scare the Pope into a formal promise that he would not grant the investiture of Naples to the French King.

This gambit misfired pathetically; whereupon Federico took himself off to the great opposition leader in Ostia, hoping to reach some agreement with him and his friends. But here there reached him a curt order from his father: he was to go back to Rome, and offer the Pope a complete surrender, with the re-iterated suggestion of a marriage between some girl of royal Aragonese blood and Cesare or Goffredo. Not wholly unconnected with this sudden submission was the fact that an envoy from the French King, Peron de Basche, was even then on his way to Rome.

Complete agreement was reached: Virginio Orsini would pay the Pope 35,000 ducats, in return for the regular assignment of those fiefs he had bought under the counter from Cibo; the Aragonese would disgorge their annual tribute in future without any fuss, as a *quid pro quo* for the investiture. Ferrante would henceforth abstain from supporting the dissident group at Ostia, and would provide one of his nieces—Sancia, the Duke of Calabria's natural daughter—as a bride for Goffredo Borgia, at the same time creating the latter Prince of Squillace and Count of Cariati, as well as logothete and proto-notary of the Kingdom this side of Capo Faro.

The satisfaction of peace regained reached its climax when the ambassador, Diego López de Haro, delighted by the outcome of his mission, produced the surprise he had been holding back as a reward—the full assent of the Spanish King and Queen to Giovanni Borgia's match with Maria Enriquez (though in fact Queen Isabella had been reluctant to approve it, and had only done so after much persuasion). Thus in Italy with Lucrezia and Goffredo, and in Spain with Giovanni, the House of the Grazing Ox was making its way into the family trees of princes and sovereigns.

The roaring secessionist in his Ostian fortress was left to draw the obvious conclusion from all this, which he duly did: by 24 July we find him in Rome, fraternally seated at table with the Pope and Virginio Orsini. The gay cor-diality displayed by Rodrigo Borgia, a man of peace if ever there was one, sounds genuine enough; but the heart of the Ligurian lion, like that of the Roman 'bear' (Orsini), was seething with anger, hatred, and the lust for revenge.

The rest was a succession of acts agreeable to all parties. On 1 August, the treaty between Naples and the Vatican was signed. Three days later Giovanni Borgia —laden with cash, gifts, and wise parental advice—left for Spain. On 6 August a Bull of Acknowledgement was issued declaring Goffredo, *domicello romano*, to be the Pope's son, begotten when the latter was 'Bishop of Oporto and Vice-Chancellor of the Holy Roman Church, on a widowed lady'.

Then, by way of an interlude, came the arrival of the French ambassador, the firm rejection of his proposals, and his departure homewards empty-handed. On 17 August Orsini was formally invested with Cerveteri and Anguillara. By the end of the month it was clear that one consequence of the Pope's reconciliation with Ferrante, and the resultant tension between him and Ludovico the Moor, had been the discrediting of Cardinal Ascanio. Giuliano della Rovere now supplanted his adversary, and had the pleasure of seeing him evicted from his apartment in the Vatican.

The friendship between Giuliano and Rodrigo did not, however, survive until the autumn. Alexander VI set about appointing a whole batch of new cardinals. He had two good reasons for doing this. In the first place, he needed extra funds for the Papal Treasury; and many prelates were willing to pay an appropriately high fee in return for a cardinal's hat. More important, he wanted to ensure the docility of the Sacred College by packing it with his own sup-porters. The anti-Borgia faction seethed with fury, being well aware of the object of such a move. When they learnt that Cesare was to be one of those elevated to the scarlet, a howl of protest went up, above which the high and strident voice of Giuliano made itself heard in no uncertain terms, swearing, by all that was holy, that he did not mean to let him 'dishonour and profane' the Sacred College in such a fashion. But Alexander VI, realizing in advance that the opposition was bound to seize on the canonical impediment of illegi-timacy, had with some forethought set up a commission of cardinals to investigate Cesare's allegedly improper origins. The results of this enquiry were all that he could wish, and formed the basis for two Bulls which neatly disposed of the problem. The first of these—designed for public consumption, and a tissue of lies—proclaimed to the world that Cesare was the legitimate son of Domenico Giannozzi of Rignano and his consort Vannozza Catanei; the second, drafted on the same date, but approved in secret, made a quite different claim, namely that Cesare was Alexander's son by 'a married lady'.

On 20 September, in defiance of Giuliano and the whole anti-Borgia faction, the Bishop of Valencia was raised to the rank of cardinal. Nor was this all. Another candidate for the scarlet at the same time was none other than Alexander Farnese, brother to the 'Bride of Christ', a handsome young man of twenty-five, already an Apostolic Protonotary, and Treasurer-General.

This dealt the opposition a well-nigh mortal blow. Giuliano della Rovere scornfully shook the dust of Rome from his heels and took the road back to

Ostia, where he fell ill from sheer fury. Ferrante gnawed his lips, while Ascanio once more raised his head.

Since an epidemic was raging in Rome, Alexander and Cesare allowed themselves a spell away from the city—perhaps the most peaceful interlude in their action-crammed lives, and beyond doubt the occasion of a closer personal *rapprochement* between them. On 23 October they left the Urbs and set out for Viterbo, a traditional holiday resort for the Papal Court. Then they moved on towards Orvieto with a stop at Capodimonte, which was to set malicious pens using up quite a deal of ink since the party awaiting the Pope in the Farnese family's castle, at the edge of the blue Lago di Bolsena, included Giulia—the 'Bride of Christ' in person. It was not until 23 November that Alexander tore himself away from this species of enchanted island, and moved across to the red-walled Etruscan city. He made a splendid entry into Bolsena, escorted by sixteen cardinals, ambassadors from the various Italian powers, Lucrezia's patient husband, and Giulia's no less accommodating consort. On the summit of a column, in the fabulous glory of that bright autumnal day, there shone the Borgia bull, in gold. During the receptions and religious functions which continued throughout their stay at Orvieto (and spun it out to a fortnight) Cesare appeared taciturn to the point of boredom, brooding over his own private and impenetrable thoughts. Perhaps he was meditating on the lesson to be learnt from recent events, and had already drawn from them the conclusions that were to inspire his own inexorable future course of action. Or perhaps the constant reminder of his brother in Spain, launched on a brilliant cloak-and-sword career, had already sparked off in him that hidden fury which was eventually to make him change his career. *Clérigo* by no choice of his own, he only recovered from this bout of introspective apathy when the Pontiff announced his intention of turning Orvieto into a key stronghold of the Papal State, and of making Cesare its governor. This proposal was implemented in less than a year.

Meanwhile a busy correspondence was going to and fro between Orvieto and Spain. The four majestic galleys which bore the second Duke of Gandia thither landed without mishap at Barcelona, where the Court was in residence. (This was not, in all likelihood, the first time that Giovanni Borgia had set foot in Spain: documents exist which suggest that he may well have made a lengthy visit to the land of his ancestors between 1488 and 1492, for the conclusion of the marriage contract.) His wedding to Maria Enriquez was celebrated late that August, under the benevolent eye of Ferdinand, and the somewhat forced smile which Isabella put on for the occasion.

During the autumn, however, disturbing letters concerning his son's

behaviour began to reach the Pope at Orvieto. Giovanni had, apparently, forgotten not only the minutely detailed advice which his father had written down
and given him on departure, as a kind of viaticum, but also his youthful bride.
The poor girl was regularly left tossing in her bed, waiting for her husband's
return: it turned out that the young libertine—he was only seventeen—spent his
nights wandering through the most *louche* districts of the city, hunting adventurous cats and cutting the throats of stray dogs. He had gathered together a
gang of other daredevils like himself. He was associating with girls of dubious
reputation and losing fantastic sums at gambling. Worst of all, he had not even
attempted to consummate his marriage, clearly finding more to attract him in the
nocturnal temptations of this Mediterranean city than in his bride's yearning
virginity.

From Orvieto, and afterwards from Rome, letter after letter was sent off to
him. The remonstrances, reproofs, and threats of his father (who nevertheless
could not conceal his affection, calling him 'our most beloved Duke', and sending him endless gifts of money) were reinforced by Cesare's earnest exhortations.
He made it clear to his 'most illustrious Lord and dearest brother' how much
the Pontiff had been saddened by the information reaching him on the subject
of Giovanni's 'evil conduct'. He urged his brother to behave more circum-
spectly, and, above all, to achieve the consummation of his marriage, a most
pressing duty. It was as though he were discussing some unpleasant task that
had to be discharged once and for all. His epistolary prose style, in Valencian
dialect, here and there even takes on a tone of pathos: 'If you feel any compassion
for me, please alleviate my worries. . . .'

Giovanni, meanwhile, had moved—together with his wife—to the white
eyrie of Gandia. From here he replied that all these charges were the most
infamous calumnies, written by people 'with little brain or in a state of drunken-
ness'. He protested that, for their own malicious purposes, they had taken his
innocent strolls along the seashore in the company of honest gentlemen and
irreproachable cousins, and turned them into fictional nights of debauchery. He
swore he had never omitted to perform his marital duties, a claim he backed by
listing the precise time on each day at which he had slept with his wife.

Proof positive of his attentions was forthcoming twice in succession during
the period of residence at Gandia, with the birth, first of Isabel, and then of
Juan II. Two children in under two years of marriage: what more could
anyone want?

THE FRENCH INVASION

Sine luce, sine cruce, sine Deo, on 25 January 1494 Ferrante's withered soul fled this world. Naples and France once more flung themselves on the Vatican, the one to obtain, the other to block the confirmation of that investiture which had already been formally guaranteed by Innocent III to the son of the deceased. Naples offered loyalty and homage, the punctual payment of feudal tribute, and highly advantageous prospects for the young Borgia's advancement; France threatened the Pope with invasion and a Council in the event of her claims on the Kingdom being rejected.

Alexander accepted the Neapolitan proposals, under the impression that he could free himself from this irksome buzz of intimidation by the French with one wave of his ringed hand, writing Charles VIII a letter in which he expressed sorrow and amazement at the King's behaviour, while exhorting him, as a friend, to rechannel his warlike fury against the Turks. Then, by way of appeasement, he sent Charles the Golden Rose, and the promise of a cardinal's hat for his favourite Briçonnet, Bishop of Saint-Malo—a favour which the King had already solicited in a personal letter to Cesare Borgia.[7]

During a consistory held on 22 March, while the Golden Rose was *en route* for France, Alexander VI had a Bull read out by which—in agreement with that noble principle binding one to a proper observance of sworn treaties—he confirmed that the investiture was granted to Alfonso of Aragon.

And at another consistory, that of 18 April, after a bitter debate lasting for over eight hours, he finally broke the opposition, giving his nephew, Cardinal Giovanni Borgia Lanzol, the task of going to Naples and there crowning the new sovereign. On the same day Cesare, just back from taking the waters at Stigliano (where he had gone to cure himself of a slight indisposition), wrote ths Duke of Gandia an affectionate letter, informing him of the negotiations which he and Virginio Orsini had been conducting on the Pope's behalf with the Aragonese claimant, and which had now reached a satisfactory conclusion. Amongst the various results achieved, there was one which could not leave him indifferent: 'His Holiness, who loves you dearly and thinks only of making you as great as may be, has obtained for Your Lordship from the King's Majesty the very finest State in his Kingdom, *videlicet*, the principality of Tricarico and the counties of Carinola and Claramonte, with twelve thousand ducats' annual revenue.' By way of comment he added: 'We have good reason, brother, ever to kiss the ground on which His Holiness walks.' This use of the plural was justified, since he, too, had acquired substantial benefits from the conclusion of the pact.

On 8 May came Alfonso's coronation. Three days later, in the Castel

Nuovo chapel, Goffredo, now Prince of Squillace, was married to Sancia of Aragon.[8] That night there was a celebratory banquet which went on till three in the morning. Afterwards the young bridal couple—scarcely more than children—were escorted to their palazzo, accompanied into the very bridal chamber, undressed by the bridesmaids, and put to bed, naked. Here, as Bur chard tells us, they set about 'kissing each other without shame or restraint', under the indulgent gaze of the King, the Papal Legate, his retinue, and the bridesmaids, until—after half an hour or so—they all took their leave. Goffredo was to remain in the Kingdom for the time being, dividing his honeymoon be tween the Court and his feudal estate. He was a shy boy of thirteen, thrown into matrimony with a girl two years his senior who had highly precocious instincts and the temperament of a whore.

The die was now cast, and—with equal resolution—the opposition, too, pro ceeded to make its throw. Giuliano della Rovere reappeared in Rome on 26 March, and went back to his stronghold at Ostia on 18 April. On the night of 23 April he embarked, clandestinely, for France, leaving the strongly defended fortress in the hands of his brother Giovanni, Lord of Senigallia and *praefectus Urbis*.

French ambassadors who reached Rome in May faced the Pontiff with a renewed request for recognition of Angevin claims. When they got an evasive response from him, they secretly hired the Colonna and other noble Roman families as *condottieri*, ready for the day when diplomacy would be replaced by the sword.

Ludovico the Moor was weaving the web of his pro French policy, his object being to ensure a successful usurpation for himself at his nephew's ex pense by protecting it against any possible Neapolitan reaction. Every day he became more swollen with self complacency, optimism and arrogance. He was playing a game which would lead to the ruin of the Italian peninsula (and would, eventually, destroy him as well); yet he was so infatuated with his own performance that he believed the King of France and the Emperor Maximilian of Austria (who had married Bianca Maria Sforza, *en secondes noces*, in Novem ber of the previous year) were passively subject to his will, regarding the first as an imbecile and the second as a tractable puppet. 'The King of France and the King of the Romans', he remarked conceitedly to an emissary from his brother the cardinal, 'have promised me they will summon a Council any time I want.'[9] He even earmarked for Ascanio the Papal Tiara which this Council would tear from the head of Alexander VI; if the dithering Ascanio did not, in the event, want to be made Pope, so much the worse for him: 'The loss will be his, we can always elect someone else.' All this braggadocio revealed him for the man he really was: astute in the highest degree over details, but superficial when it came to the overall assessment of situations and their potential lines of development.

Venice, while hypocritically masking her face behind the domino of a feigned neutrality, was keeping her diplomatic representatives busy whispering persuasive words of encouragement for the undertaking in Charles VIII's ear. Meanwhile in Florence there was the bony figure of Savonarola, prophet of apocalyptic doom and the Messiah of harsh theocratic government, thundering from his pulpit against the immorality of Florence and the putrid corruption of Babylon-by-the-Tiber; he saw the King of France as a new Cyrus, sent by God to castigate sinners and cleanse the deep-bemired Church of its filth.

The eloquence of Giuliano della Rovere, Ludovico the Moor's scheming and financial support, much flattery from Venice, and echoes of the oratorical campaign launched by the Dominican Prior of San Marco in Florence—these alone would certainly not suffice to swing France's vast military potential into action, and fling it headlong down the peninsula. However, in so far as they found a most fertile breeding-ground in the monarch's limitless ambitions, they did to some extent succeed in precipitating matters. Here they joined forces with various other factors: the pressure put on him by some of his advisers, the assurances of Neapolitan refugees who had escaped Ferrante's 'purges', the burning urgency behind certain long-standing but much-frustrated dreams of revenge, national resentment against the Aragonese, dissatisfaction at Alexander VI's repeated refusals, the uncontrollable desire for expansion felt by a country which knew itself the strongest in Europe, the aggressive nature of an army that was eager for adventure, and the knowledge that to acquire an international supremacy which would supplant the authority of the Empire meant forestalling Spain in external conquests.

Charles VIII enunciated his programme, which was to occupy the Kingdom of Naples, and thereafter sail on a crusade against the Turk. As a by-product of this plan (only the first half of it really interested him), he from time to time let drop suggestions for reforming the Church through the convocation of a Council, designed to depose this Spanish reprobate from the Papal throne which he had so insecurely conquered.

There is, according to Shakespeare, no tragedy in the world which does not contain elements of comedy, or at certain moments does not take a plunge into pure farce. Even the heroes of the most dramatic situations will succumb—right in the middle of the events highlighting their stature—to those miseries which are inseparable from the human condition.

A group of letters, for long centuries buried in the obscurity of the Vatican's Secret Archive, and brought into the light of day by Ludwig von Pastor, reveals an Alexander VI who is no woolly-minded rhetorician, but a sharply-etched living character, baring his heart before our very eyes. We have seen the Pope who grieved and waxed indignant and was moved almost to tears, with Collenuccio, over the vileness of Italy. We have seen the Pontiff who, in full consistory, declared himself ready to lose 'his mitre, his State, and his life' could he but avoid becoming a King's slave, and who, with the French already at the gates of Rome, cried out to the Prince of Anhalt that not even if they held a knife to his throat would he bow the knee before mere arrogant power. Beside such portraits we can now glimpse another Rodrigo Borgia, at once humbler and more interesting: exposed to our scrutiny first in his carnal tenderness, then in a mood of wounded and burning passion.

Of the forty-four letters published by Pastor, and covering a period from 20 November 1493 to the end of December the following year, some are exclusively political in character, shedding light on events during the period from the first development of tension with France to the occupation of Rome: they contain the signatures of such persons as Charles VIII, Cardinal Ascanio, Giovanni Sforza, and the Duke of Gandia. Others (sixteen in all) are written by Lucrezia Borgia, Giulia Farnese and Adriana del Milá to Alexander VI, or by him to the three women, and provide invaluable evidence as to the nature of their relationships one with another.

Early in June 1494 the inseparable feminine trio, entrusted to the discreet charge of a Toledan named Francisco Gaçet, or Gasset, the Pope's right-hand man, and also accompanied by Giovanni Sforza, left Rome and moved to Pesaro. Here, on 8 June, amid pelting rain, Lucrezia celebrated her first appearance as a wife and *signora*, which at once triggered off an exchange of letters characterized, on both sides, by intense nostalgia: obsequious, and a little exaggerated, on the lady's part, smiling and already impatient, on that of the Pope.

On 10 June all three members of the trio took up their pens to send Alexander VI an enthusiastic description of the reception they had been given, and the festivities they had enjoyed—not without a touch of melancholy because he himself, the summit and plenitude of every blessing, was so far distant from them.

Adriana del Milá wrote: 'Signor Johanni (Giovanni) is as kind to us, in every possible way, as could well be desired; yet I am filled with continual longing, and think of nothing, save to be near Your Holiness and live in Your Holiness's shadow; being here, far from Your Beatitude, I seem to stand at the world's end. . . .'

Lucrezia wrote: 'Let Your Holiness be assured that I shall never be happy save when I have frequent news of Your Beatitude. . . .'

Giulia wrote: 'And since perchance Your Holiness may believe, reading the above-mentioned things, that we are in great joy and happiness, we do certify this as a great error, since being absent from Your Holiness, and all my happiness and well-being depending thereupon, I cannot taste such delights with any satisfaction . . . Wheresoever my treasure is, there shall my heart be also . . . And he who says the contrary is right foolish; so we beseech Your Holiness, do not forget us, having confined us here, and if Your Holiness please to remember us, bring us back soon to kiss the feet we miss and long for. . . .' On the back of the sheet, by way of address, we read: 'To my one and only lord.'

A fortnight later, the piece of news on which we find the three ladies embroidering their comments—I have made some slight corrections to their rather wild orthography—is the arrival in Pesaro of Caterina Gonzaga. Giulia, with the generosity typical of all really beautiful women, depicts her as in the bloom of loveliness; Lucrezia, with rather more objectivity, praises her stature ('she is six inches taller than Madame Julia'), her pale complexion, her hands and her figure, while at the same time not glossing over the coarseness of her mouth and teeth and hair, her 'huge white' eyes, her nose, her over-long and too-masculine face. Nor (being a perfect, enchanting, and tireless dancer herself) is she satisfied with Caterina's qualities as a ballerina. All in all, she concludes, *praesentia minuit famam.*

So convincingly do the Pope's replies emphasize one aspect of his character that I feel the episode is worth dwelling on for this reason alone. What emerges from them, with the most vivid clarity, is Rodrigo Borgia's capacity to remove himself from the drama going on around him, his readiness to escape, briefly, from anxiety, his gift for keeping calm when at the centre of a raging hurricane.

Burchard was afterwards to write, in a diary entry for 4 and 5 September 1502, how on their way back from Piombino, aboard two small galleys, Alexander VI and Cesare were caught in so terrifying a storm that the cardinals of their retinue began to weep, and Duke Valentino—who can scarcely be accused of having an over-impressionable nature—got into a boat and had himself rowed back to dry land. But Alexander VI would do nothing of the sort: he stayed with his ship, sitting on the poop while members of the crew, almost out of their minds with fear, lay prone on the deck. Firm and impassive, at each especially violent assault of the waves he made the sign of the cross, and pronounced the name of Jesus; and from time to time he would urge the sailors to light the galley stove and fry up some fish.

Such, to the last detail, is the picture he presents of himself, amid the pressure of catastrophic events, in these letters to Lucrezia and Giulia. They are cheerful letters, as though nothing was going on around him, and all the more cheerful in that during the previous few days a rumour had got round Rome which threw him into great consternation, and then fortunately turned out to be false: Lucrezia, it alleged, was very seriously ill (some even spoke of her death). He wrote to his daughter as though nothing but this rediscovered happiness in her health meant anything to him. Charles VIII and his advancing army, the peril closing in on Rome, all became things which for a brief moment ceased even to exist, let alone to matter: 'Donna Lucrecia, our dearest daughter, truly you have given us four or five days of great sorrow and anxiety, by reason of the dreadful and bitter rumour which spread throughout Rome, that you were either dead or truly so sick that your life was despaired of. You may guess what agony our mind sustained, by reason of that warm and boundless love we bear you, as much as any person in this world . . . We give thanks to God and Our Lady in Her glory that you escaped all danger; and be assured, we shall not rest content until we have seen you in person. . . .' To Giulia, who had praised Caterina Gonzaga's beauty somewhat too generously, he wrote: 'We know well that your expatiating and dilating on the beauty of this person, who is not worthy so much as to untie your shoes, is due to the great modesty you affect, in this as in all other matters. We are well aware, too, why you acted thus; so that, you being informed that all who wrote us said that beside you she seemed but a lantern held against the sun, we might the more appreciate your beauty, of which, to tell the truth, we never doubted. And we would wish, that just as we know this clearly, so you for your part were wholly destined and made over, with no reserves, to that person who loves you more than anything else in the world'.

An extraordinary madrigal to intone in the midst of such events. Note, too, how the wily Pope gives the faintest hint of a malicious smile as he extracts, from the hyperbolic praises set down by Giulia's pen, the kernel of astute calculation hidden behind them; note with how smooth a transition, despite his involuted sentence structure, this consummate seducer slips from mere gallantry to the invocation of a love as total ('with no reserves') as it is exclusive.

However, the music was very soon to change its tune.

Before Madame Adriana left, Alexander VI had told her that she was to be back in Rome by the beginning of July. Now, in a long letter written on the 8th, he ordered her to delay no longer; and at the same time—while describing the details of a military situation which was to involve Giovanni Sforza very closely, and fill Pesaro with armed troops destined for the defence of the Romagna—he made it quite clear that he wanted both Lucrezia and Giulia to come back with her, the former, for preference, without her husband.

At this point, however, a breathless courier arrived in Pesaro, with a message for Giulia from Cardinal Farnese: their brother Angelo was dying at Capodimonte. Both Giulia and her mother-in-law Adriana, after some hesitation because of the fear of doing anything which might displease the Pope, resolved to leave, there and then, for the castle on the shores of Lake Bolsena. Giovanni Sforza informed Alexander VI of their decision, without concealing his own vexation; he knew the Pope's touchy and suspicious susceptibilities all too well. 'God knows,' he wrote, 'how strongly I dissuaded them, and how much I regretted that they went without the knowledge or permission of Your Holiness . . . They were determined to act thus out of duty to a blood-relative, and obedience to the Most Reverend Monsignor, but what they did was not to my liking.'

It was not to the Pope's liking, either. He at once sent Lucrezia a very brisk reproof for not having prevented this departure. Lucrezia replied with a letter which, while justifying herself and her husband ('my lord and master') with an account of their vain attempts to dissuade the two women, also attempted to mitigate the gravity of their arbitrary act by emphasizing the state of mind they were in at the time.

As always, it did not take long for the wrath of the Vatican's *grande impulsivo* to be placated—so much so, indeed, that he merely sent Giulia a letter advising her to 'watch her virtue'. Just how sure she felt of his unshakeable good will can be seen from her reply. A rumour (false as it turned out) was in the air to the effect that the Bishop of Rimini had been murdered. Giulia immediately wrote back on the evening of 14 August—from Gradoli, on the north-west shore of the lake—requesting this bishopric for her brother ('my cardinal', as she termed him). In a postscript she added: 'Since Your Holiness writes exhorting me strongly to act as befits me, to watch my virtue, in these matters I can at once set Your Holiness' mind at rest. Be assured that day and night I have no other thought in my mind—both for my own honour and for love of Your Holiness— than to show myself another St Catherine.' On this point she invoked the testimony of Madame Adriana and Messer Gaçet, who were always at her side.

But things now became further complicated by the appearance on the scene of Giulia's husband. From Bassanello, where he had been relieving his vexed mind by means of hunting expeditions, he began loudly demanding Giulia's return to his side, while the Pope, with equal insistence, wanted her near *him*.

A peremptory pontifical veto stopped the young lady from moving any further than the threshold of Capodimonte Castle. By now Alexander VI was exceedingly angry. Madame Adriana, urgently summoned to Rome, was told to secure the intervention of Cardinal Farnese (himself on holiday by Lake

Bolsena) with a view to making the frenzied Orsino submit to the Vatican's wishes, and at all costs to prevent him and Giulia from meeting. But the car-dinal, faced with a mission of this sort, became elusive and recalcitrant, feeling it to be dishonourable as well as irksome. He lacked the courage to 'make so open a break with Orsino, and on such grounds'; besides, he was too well ac-quainted with 'the way Orsino's mind worked; he was sure to fill everyone up with a mass of slanderous lies.' Such was the story which Adriana, now back in Capodimonte, dispatched to the Pope on 15 October, and which finds con-firmation in another letter, of the same date, written by Francisco Gaçet.[10] Both, in conclusion, beg the Pope to make his own decision known, and humbly express the opinion that it might be as well to summon Giulia's husband to Rome—along with Virginio, head of the Orsini clan—in order to 'prevent this thing'.

What thing? We cannot be certain. The fact that during this period the con-duct of some of the Orsini was beginning to arouse suspicion, taken with the strained interpretation of a reference by Alexander VI, in a letter I quote below in full, to 'matters concerning our state', has led to the supposition that in this stormy episode there was some problem of a political nature. What remains quite certain, however, is that any such dubious and hypothetical reason of State was overlaid in Rodrigo Borgia's mind by furious jealousy, which his remoteness from Giulia merely served to exacerbate.

On 18 October a disturbing message reached Capodimonte from Bassanello, the sender being a friar, Teseo Seripando, whose habit could often be heard rustling through the rooms of the Orsini castle. Orsino, he wrote, was beside himself with rage, 'fulminating and behaving in the most unusual fashion', swearing that 'even at the sacrifice of a thousand lives, if he had them, and all his worldly goods', he would not let Giulia go to Rome.

The Capodimonte group felt the water lapping round its chin. Madame Adriana, in despair, sent the Pope a few anxious lines by courier saying: 'We no longer have any excuse to find for Orsino.' The courier returned from Rome at breakneck speed with three letters, all dated 22 October—one for her, one for Cardinal Farnese, and one for Giulia—in which every word hisses with fury, and every phrase is like a blow.

To Adriana he wrote: 'At last you have revealed all the evil and malice in your heart . . . Rest assured that you will suffer most condign punishment for your deceit.' And meanwhile, woe to her if she stirred from Capodimonte: ex-communication, eternal malediction, and confiscation of all her goods.

'You know well', he reminded Cardinal Farnese, 'how much we have done for you, and with how much love; never would we have believed how swiftly

you were to forget our favours, and to set Ursino above ourselves. *Iterum* we beseech and exhort you not to repay us in such coin, since thus you do not satisfy
those promises you so often gave us, much less your own honour and welfare.'

To Giulia, lastly, he sent the following message—countersigned at the head of
the page with the Greek initials of Jesus Christ—which might well figure as a
masterpiece of brutality in any anthology of love-letters:

Ungrateful and perfidious Julia. We have received a letter of yours, by
Navarico's hand, in which you signify and declare that your intention is not
to come here unless Ursino so wills it; and though hitherto we understood
well enough both your wicked inclinations, and from whom you sought
advice, nevertheless in consideration of your feigned and pretended assurances,
we could not wholly persuade ourselves that you were capable of treating us
with such ingratitude and disloyalty (having so often sworn and given your
word to us that you were at our command, and would not keep company
with Ursino) as now to do the contrary and go to Bassanello, at open peril of
your life; nor can I believe that you are acting thus except to get yourself pregnant a second time by that *equia* of Bassanello. And we hope that very soon
both you and Madame Adriana, most ungrateful of women, will acknowledge your fault and suffer condign punishment for it. And moreover, as regarding the present we command you, on pain of excommunication *latae
sententiae* and eternal malediction, that you do not stir forth from Capo de
Monte (or de Marta), much less go to Bassanello for matters concerning our
state.

Those who conjecture that the episode had some sort of political foundation rest
their argument mainly on the last five words of this letter (which are in Rodrigo's
own minute handwriting, with nervous marginal and interlinear glosses). But
a careful and unprejudiced reading of the text suggests a more delicate and subtle
explanation, of a quite different sort. Giulia was determined, by hook or crook,
to rejoin her husband. After conferring with her mother-in-law and her brother
the cardinal, she obviously tried to make her design acceptable to the Pontiff by
presenting it as a useful political move. Alexander VI did not rise to the bait.
Convinced that her only reason for hurrying off to Bassanello when the young
and lusty 'equia' demanded her presence there was to 'get pregnant' for a second
time in his conjugal embrace, Rodrigo forbade her to go there on any excuse
whatever, putative reasons of State included. The extreme clarity of the text
admits no other interpretation.

Giulia had no option but to obey. Towards the end of November she was
still at Capodimonte. When she finally made up her mind to return to Rome,

together with her mother-in-law and her sister Jeronima (Girolama), the party
ran into a detachment of the French advance guard on the Viterbo road. (This
group, under the command of Ives d'Allègre, had already made a number of
incursions into the territories of the Papal State.) All three ladies were taken
prisoner, and escorted to Montefiascone. The news left all Italy convulsed with
laughter, except for the Pope, who was horrified, and hastily sent off Cardinal
Ascanio, accompanied by Galeazzo Sanseverino, to intercede with the King for
the release of the three women. Their request was granted immediately. A guard
of honour, composed of gallant French cavaliers, escorted them as far as the
gates of Rome, where a much-relieved—and indeed jubilant—Alexander VI
did not scruple to go out and meet them himself in the costume of a Spanish
gentleman: a black brocade-striped topcoat, a baldric with sword and dagger,
velvet-trimmed boots and bonnet.

'So it was', Machiavelli wrote in Chapter XII of *The Prince*, 'that Charles, King
of France, was able to conquer Italy *col gesso*'—with a billeting-officer's chalk.
This scornful phrase is also to be found in the *Mémoires* of Philippe de Commynes. Few people realize that it first issued from the lips of Alexander VI.

At the moment when the beautiful Giulia waved her escort a smiling farewell, and once more placed herself under the Pope's impassioned aegis, the
situation reached its most fiercely critical point. All that these months had
brought was a jumble of failed attempts and an overshadowing, unstoppable
series of threats which grew steadily nearer and greater, till now they seemed on
the point of laying siege to the man in the Vatican, to Rome, to the State itself.

The sudden wreck of all military plans that followed the naval defeat and
Caterina Sforza's volte-face; the collapse of Naples' forces; the uselessness of all
appeals to those beyond the confines of the peninsula, as of every effort made to
put pressure on the nationalist sentiments of an Italy which in fact did not exist;
the defection of the cardinals; the latent hostility and subsequent open rebellion
of the Roman nobility—this constant progression of failures and disasters had
reduced Alexander VI to the condition of a man who is left, virtually on his
own, to face the onrush of an avalanche. There was no one on whom he could
completely rely, or whose word he could trust, save Cesare, who during these
months had worked like a demon at his side.

It is easy, and obvious, and (for that matter) objectively justified to say that
Rodrigo Borgia put up this remarkable resistance to defend his threatened tiara,
and the advantages—now at hazard—which his sons enjoyed as a result of the
Aragonese alliance. But it is likewise only fair to recognize that he was, at the
same time, defending the dignity of the Apostolic See, which had been attacked

by an arrogant, puffed-up King and betrayed by a junta of treacherous cardinals. It is also fair to admit that he set an example of political honesty by faithfully observing a pact for which his predecessor had been responsible, and expos- ing himself to disaster in the process. Above all, it is only right and proper to recognize that the fearless stand he took did much to redeem the low, self- seeking, opportunistic attitude of the Italian States. Only the most tendentious sort of historiography can persistently ignore the lesson in pride they got from this Spaniard, who was the sole person, at the time, to talk about the honour of Italy, the only man to stand firm against the invader, or to denounce the shame- ful conduct of those who smilingly opened the door to the aggressor; the only person, in short, who spoke and acted *as an Italian* (this point was made, after a memorable discussion with him, by the Este ambassador, Pandolfo Collenuc- cio); a man of lofty purpose, a poet of powerful utterance, who within ten years was to pay with his life for the crime of having believed in that great dream of *italianità*—betrayed and crippled by events—which formed the mainspring of Borgia policy.

Behind this indomitable resistance we must undoubtedly acknowledge one major factor—the galvanic presence of Cesare, who from now on worms him- self arrogantly into the Pope's very spirit and mind. At nineteen, this *monstrum* of energy—who nine years later was suddenly to end his stunningly precocious career as a man of action, and who remained unique, down the vista of the centuries, for sureness of inspiration and rigour of method—was now at the very height of his inner powers. And up to this 'year before the years of misery', as Guicciardini terms 1494, we must picture him constantly at Alexander's side: first implementing his father's shrewd policies, then inspiring bold decisions and instigating acts of ruthless cruelty, and finally as the terrible master of an irre- vocably subjugated will.

The French banner now flew over the stronghold of Ostia. Cesare surrendered himself as a hostage into the hands of the Colonna family—a precaution de- manded by that wavering turncoat Ascanio, before he came to Rome and risked a last attempt at breaking the Pope's resistance by means of intimidatory arguments.

Invaded from the north, blockaded at the mouth of the Tiber by the French fleet, its most vital strategic points occupied by the Colonna and Savelli families' levies, the Papal State resembled a piece of flotsam blown hither and thither by a hurricane.

When Alexander VI complained about the irruption of French troops into Papal territory, and the depredations they had wrought there, Charles VIII replied by sending Cardinal Jean Villiers de la Groslaye to remind the Pope that if the mercenaries of this expeditionary force—though admittedly under orders to march on Rome *par le grant chemin*—had commandeered supplies in the Papal State, His Holiness had no cause for complaint: '*Ils y peuvent aussi bien passer que ceulx du roy Alfonse d'Aragon, lequel ni ses prédécesseurs ne firent jamais si grans services au Saint Siège Apostolique que les très chrestiens roys nos prédécesseurs.*'

In his efforts to halt the King on the road to invasion, Alexander VI had recourse to an extreme makeshift expedient, declaring himself willing to meet with Charles for the purpose of jointly planning the much-publicized crusade. Charles, protesting that he was unworthy of such an honour, mockingly reiterated his offer to come and pay homage to the Pontiff in his own palace.

The Moor's brother reappeared in Rome on 2 December. He found the city feverish and on the brink of insurrection, with Alexander busy organizing defence works. A series of discussions took place between Cardinals Ascanio Sforza, Federico Sanseverino and Bernardino Lunati on the one hand, and the Papal Secretary, Juan López, on the other. The Pope himself—whom the three hoped to talk into surrendering—scornfully held aloof. On 9 December a rumour circulated that agreement had been reached, and that Rodrigo Borgia was willing to capitulate. At this point, however, an enlightening little *coup de théâtre* took place. While Ascanio Sforza, together with Prospero Colonna, was making ready for departure to bring these glad tidings to the King at French headquarters, Alexander VI threw both of them into prison, and Sanseverino and Lunati as well. The noise of the keys turning in the locks of their four cells in Castel Sant'Angelo, put an abrupt end to this period of diplomatic negotiation, and announced a policy of vigorous resistance. The arrival of a small Neapolitan army, jointly led by Frederick of Aragon, Giulio Orsini and the Count of Pitigliano, was enough to stifle any remaining hesitations.

But ten days later, with the approach of the invaders, everything collapsed. On 18 December—by which time the defection of the Orsini clan had destroyed any last faint possibility of military resistance—it looked as though Alexander, at the urging of the Duke of Calabria, meant to flee to Naples.

He stayed put.

The next morning, from a window in the Vatican, he saw a troop of French cavalry galloping through the meadows by the river-bank. Ives d'Allègre and Ligny, with the advance guard, were on the brow of Monte Mario. A deputy of Roman citizens, spokesmen for the unrest caused by fear and famine, now arrived bearing an ultimatum. Alexander had two days in which to reach an accommodation with the King of France. Failing this, the populace would open the gates to the invader.

An armistice was arranged. The Duke of Calabria, provided with a safe-conduct by Charles VIII, proceeded to evacuate Rome. On 27 December French troops began to enter the city. They had the thrust and momentum of a tidal wave. Alexander VI, who had something like a thousand armed men at his disposal, and during these last few days, realizing the impossibility of ever prodding the corpse-like Roman citizenry into action, had even tried to play on the warlike instincts of the city's German colony, now shut himself up in the Vatican with his Spanish bodyguard. Cesare, who had been released by the Colonna in return for Cardinal Ascanio, was once more at his side.

Charles VIII entered Rome on the evening of 31 December, and took up residence in the splendid Palace of St Mark. Within a few days—while his troops, meanwhile, taught Rome's population just what it meant to be occupied by a foreign army—he and his gentlemanly retinue transformed the palace into a fair approximation to the Augean Stables.

Negotiations were carried out in frantic haste, against a background of daily looting and burning, murder, arrogant violence, extortion and rape. Cesare acted as principal spokesman for the Vatican. Charles VIII was determined to get two things at all costs: the surrender of Castel Sant'Angelo, and the investiture of the Kingdom of Naples. At the same time, Giuliano della Rovere and those cardinals supporting him subjected the King to a tireless battery of pressurizing and propaganda in favour of summoning a Council that would declare the Pontiff deposed. A point came at which the clash between the King's claims and the Borgia party's stubborn refusal to budge assumed violent overtones, so that Alexander deemed it prudent for him and Cesare to seek refuge in Castel Sant'Angelo.

Thereupon the King trained his artillery on the fortress, and twice seemed on the point of ordering his gunners to fire. Alexander VI declared that at the very first shot he would take up his position on the ramparts, with the triple crown on his head, and holding the monstrance. The cannons remained silent. However, during the night of 10 January 1495, a stretch of wall collapsed, thus making any defence against an eventual attack impossible. He therefore agreed to resume negotiations, and these resulted in the agreement reached on the 15th.

The King of France obtained a good deal. He got Cesare Borgia, for a start, officially as a legate, but in fact as a hostage. He also got Gem, in anticipation of the crusade which was to follow the conquest of Naples (but not, however, the annual sum which the Sultan still disbursed with regal punctuality, for Gem's maintenance). The cardinals of the opposition party were granted immunity, and his own troops given free passage through Papal territory. He also obtained the fortress of Civitavecchia, and various other concessions of minor importance.

A good deal, then—but neither the investiture of Naples nor the surrender of Castel Sant'Angelo, the two things he really had set his heart on obtaining. What was more, he paid for this satisfaction with a full acknowledgement of the Pope's authority, both spiritual and temporal, formally pledging himself to ren der him obedience, not to cause him any molestation, and indeed to defend him from those who planned such molestation themselves. *Desinit in piscem.* . . .

To all appearances victorious, but in fact substantially worsted, he left Rome on 28 January, taking his somewhat dubious trophies with him: the Bull con cerning free passage through the Papal State, Gem (together with his retinue of bearded Turkish servants), and Cesare, riding on a black mule, with a princely baggage train of no less than nineteen waggons, each draped in a cloth bearing his coat of arms. At a short distance from the Urbs, two of these carts unobtru sively left the convoy and returned the way they had come. They were the only ones carrying full trunks; the other seventeen were loaded with empty boxes.

At Velletri, Charles VIII found the Spanish ambassador Antonio de Fonseca awaiting him. Taking certain clauses in the Treaty of Barcelona as his text, this envoy proceeded to unload on Charles all the indignation his sover eigns felt for Charles's villainous treatment of the Pope. He ordered him to release Cesare Borgia, and registered a protest, in very round terms, against his attack on the Kingdom of Naples. Finally, making a great show of anger, he tore the treaty itself into pieces, which he then threw, insultingly, at Charles's feet. The King was still seething with fury at this affront when Cesare accom panied him to his private apartments and—after amiably exhorting him to calm himself—wished him a very good night. Next morning, Charles VIII was abruptly woken with the news that Cesare had disappeared, leaving nothing behind save one mocking memento—his cardinal's robe, flung across the bed, empty and crumpled.

During the night the Pope's son had stolen out of the palace disguised as a stable boy. Hurrying through the darkness, he had crossed the city and left by the Porta Napoletana; half a mile beyond the walls he had found his equerry Francesco dello Scacco waiting for him, with a horse capable of travelling far and fast. Displaying that remarkable physical dexterity for which he was al ready famous, he placed one hand on his mount's back and vaulted straight into the saddle, galloping off with a flash of white teeth in the darkness and the echo of a ferocious laugh lost in the wind behind him. When dawn broke he was already in Rome, at the house of Francesco Flores. Then, abruptly, he disap peared once more. He was glimpsed at Rignano and, later, at Spoleto. For a while he became an impalpable and elusive ghost, whom someone claimed to have seen 'with only three horses', dashing through the countryside, 'now here, now there'.

The King of France made furious remonstrances: had it not been for the inter-vention of Giuliano della Rovere, he would have hanged the Mayor of Velletri, and burned down the city. In answer to his complaints, Alexander merely said that he was very sorry, but he knew nothing about the matter. On 5 February, every attempt to find the fugitive having failed, Charles VIII decided to press on for Naples. Cesare reappeared in Rome towards the end of March. On 1 April, in the square facing the Basilica of St Peter's, a group of Spaniards fell on a detachment of Swiss mercenaries from the French army who were preparing to return to their own country, killing sixteen, wounding many more, robbing and manhandling the rest. Many people at once detected Cesare's hand in this vio-lent episode—and others perpetrated against French officials passing through Rome—as a personal *quid pro quo* for the looting and ransacking by the invaders, on 8 January, of one of his mother Vannozza's houses.

Meanwhile Charles reached Naples without encountering any opposition worthy of mention, and there proceeded to give himself over in the most abandoned fashion to Mediterranean pleasures. His henchmen followed his example. The magic of a Neapolitan spring made the sap rise in their veins, and they duly turned the city into one great sweaty brothel, a single gigantic bed damp with endless intercourse.

The party was a delirious one, but of brief duration. On 25 February, only three days after the occupation of Naples, Gem died: not of delayed-action poison administered by the Borgias, as legend had it, but from his own excesses. The King sent his body to Constantinople, and stopped talking about a crusade. Dark clouds were gathering in the north, where good work by Vatican diplomats and the fear of an over-strong France led Rome, Milan, Venice, Spain and the Emperor to form a fraternal alliance, the so-called 'Holy League'. Its apparent object was to wage war against the Turk, but in fact it aimed to cut the ground from under the feet of an invader who had advanced too far and too fast for comfort. Then came a devastating epidemic of syphilis, referred to by the French as the 'Neapolitan disease', and by the Neapolitans as the 'French disease'. The excitement and triumph of victory, having degenerated into a Bacchanalian route, now expired amid the lamentations of pustular troops, and the ominous muttering of an exasperated populace.

On 12 May Charles VIII crowned his Italian adventure with a grandiose theatrical gesture. Robed in imperial majesty, a diadem on his large head, holding the sceptre in his right hand and the orb in his left, he made his way in procession to the Cathedral. Eight days later, with half his army, he set out on the homeward journey. In the meantime he had sent an embassy of prelates and great lords to Alexander VI, soliciting a meeting, and as one last attempt to extract the concession of the investiture from him. With this in mind, he offered the Pope an annual tribute of 50,000 ducats, and the payment of two yearly in- stalments not yet disbursed by the Aragonese. The Pontiff gave a faint smile, shrugged his shoulders, and took off, strongly escorted, for Orvieto.

There he heard that the King, on reaching Rome, had stayed for no more than two days—just long enough to reiterate his devout loyalty as a good Christian— before setting forth again, in the direction of Bracciano, whence he was now putting out fresh feelers for a discussion.

Alexander VI thereupon withdrew to Perugia. At this point the conqueror, finally convinced that the Pope was not exactly on fire to meet him again, re- signed himself to more direct action. Ahead of him there lay the ambuscade of Fornovo, where, in an atmosphere akin to the fifth act of a tragedy, he was to lose everything except his life.

With Charles VIII on his way back to France, the Pope in Rome more firmly established than ever, and the Aragonese—aided by Gonzalo Fernandez de Cordoba and his Spaniards—well on the road to recovery, the flood-waters were sinking back into their normal channel. The shock had set irresistible forces in motion, but now it looked as though everything was more or less back to the *status quo*.

By the courage he had shown under threat of invasion, by his continued loyalty to the Aragonese, and, not least, by the humiliating defeat he had in- flicted on the reformers who wanted to see him deposed from his pontificate, Alexander had set his signature to one of the finest political achievements of the period. One scarcely knows which to admire more: his determination, his honesty or his astuteness.

THE ACHIEVEMENTS AND DEATH OF THE
DUKE OF GANDIA

The hurricane of this 'barbarian' invasion had shaken people's minds—all the more profoundly in that it had also disrupted the stable order of things. For the common man, the Middle Ages had not ended. The conscience of the masses— still Christian, despite the paganizing trend of the humanists, and still super- stitious, despite the rationalism which typified this new age—interpreted events in basically religious terms. Under the impetus of that irrepressible sense of guilt which has dogged human history, it saw in the French invasion the first announcement of a new deluge, decreed by God to punish and sweep away the corruption of this world.

In the confusion of the times, the utterances of St Brigid of Sweden and Gioacchino da Fiore once more gained widespread currency, with their pre-dictions of Rome's fourth destruction and the engulfment of the present de-generate Church, to be followed by a renewal of Christianity through the pure light of the Spirit. Apocalypse, in other words, was to be the prelude to rebirth. This was just the interpretation of the recent disaster which—lifting his head beneath a Biblically dark and lurid sky—was given by Savonarola: 'Just as the world was renewed by the Flood, so God now sends these tribulations to renew His Church.'

Over Rome, in particular, more than any other city in Italy (as though it were Babylon, threatened by Divine Wrath) there now hung a heavy cloud of terror, in which all the exhalations of sin, every breath of shame, each sigh of remorse seemed to have been distilled. In December of that year (1495) the Tiber over-flowed its banks, turning Rome into a kind of muddy lagoon. After thirty-six hours the waters subsided, leaving the streets thick with the corpses of men and animals. The city presented a picture of nightmare desolation. Houses had collapsed, and bridges were swept away. Every edifice was thick with mud. The inundation was soon followed by famine and pestilence. In this cataclysm everyone saw proof that God's wrathful hand was once more at work; the God who, at moments of supreme human depravity, would strike down the Sodoms and Gomorrahs of this world. A month later, terror was heightened by reports of supernatural happenings. Various individuals, pale as death, their hair standing on end and their eyes bolting out of their heads, babbled of seeing some kind of monster on the Tiber's still-muddy banks. The Venetian *oratori* passed on a diligent description of this creature to the Most Serene Republic, so that the chronicler Domenico Malipiero, *decano di mare* and author of the highly valuable *Annals* (1457–1500), was able to compose a detailed portrait of it: an ass's head on the body of a woman; one human arm, the other resembling a proboscis; the bearded face of an old man on its back; a tail resembling a neck, which ended in a snake's head, jaws agape; scaly limbs, with one foot resembling that of an ox, and the other an eagle's talon. Not even Dante, in the most horrific depths of his Inferno, encountered anything worse than this.

On 27 June Alexander and Cesare returned from their diplomatic excursion to Perugia, and in the shady quiet of the Vatican studied the situation created by the departure—one might almost say flight—of Charles VIII. Perils a good deal more tangible than any threatened by prophets of divine vengeance, or feared by those who went hunting for supernatural portents, revealed themselves clearly to the two men's keen scrutiny. There was the continued presence of considerable French forces, not only in the Kingdom of Naples itself, but also in various Florentine strongholds dominating the key mountain passes of the Apennines, with a steady influx of support and reinforcements from France. There was Charles VIII himself, who, first from Asti, and afterwards from the far side of the Alps, spoke of his return to the Italian peninsula as something certain and inevitable, occasionally larding his remarks with allusions, open or hidden, to his plans for Church reform and the convocation of a Council. There was the obstinately pro-French policy of Florence, where Savonarola lost no opportunity to whip up people's continuing faith in the spiritual mission of the 'new Cyrus', while pouring forth on the Roman Curia a torrential flow of rhetoric, seething with insults, sarcastic asides, and sinister prophecies. Another serious cause for preoccupation was the intervention of Spain in Italian affairs— very useful for the moment, but foreseeably destined, within a very short space of time, to become a serious and unpredictable hazard. Finally, in a more immediate and more urgent sphere of interests, there were two other bones of contention which made the Borgias hoarse with fury: Ostia, over which the French flag still flew, and the Orsini clan, who had not only collaborated with the advancing enemy during the autumn of the previous year, but since then—in open defiance of the Church—had continued to give the invaders military support.

Against all these threats Alexander VI reacted with characteristic vigour. In Savonarola's case, so long as the friar had been content to aim shafts at his private life, and to inveigh against *tempora* and *mores*, he had given ample proof of his tolerance (not unmixed with good-natured contempt). But now that Savonarola was openly urging Charles VIII to rebel against Rome's spiritual authority, and doing all he could to obstruct the anti-French *entente* by stopping Florence from joining it, the Pope decided it was time to act, and his elegant hand descended firmly on the agitator's cowl. In a Brief dated 21 July 1495 (which also, however, contained flattering references to Savonarola's work for the salvation of men's souls) he ordered the preacher to come to Rome, for the purpose of clarifying his alleged prophetic gifts, and the private motives which led him to express himself as a direct and personal spokesman of the Almighty. Then, as the Dominican found various excuses for refusing this invitation, he issued a second Brief. This, dated 8 September, was addressed to the friars of Santa Croce—lifelong enemies of those in San Marco—and not only ordered the so-called prophet to abstain from preaching, but also placed his monastery under the jurisdiction of the Lombard Congregation: both perfectly legitimate decisions. However, in a letter dated 29 September, Savonarola tried to extricate both himself and his religious house from the necessity of obeying them. He emphasized his own submission to the Church's jurisdiction, denying that he had proclaimed himself a prophet, but at the same time adding that to do so would not constitute a heresy, since some of his predictions had already come true, and others would be fulfilled in the future. He also objected that referring his case to the Lombard Congregation meant, in effect, handing it over to the jurisdiction and verdict of a known adversary. As a good jurist, Alexander VI admitted the validity of this objection, and revoked his decree regarding the monastery—but not the ban on Savonarola's preaching. This ban the friar promptly contravened, by delivering three sermons the following month, followed, during the Lent of 1496, by a formidable summing-up of his views which touched heights of unheard-of violence, and was delivered in coarsely graphic common speech, verging on the scandalous as regards both the realism of its terms and the audacity of its imagery. All this gave people grounds for suspecting him of some paranoid obsession, steeped in hatred and tinged with a Messianic complex. The sermon he delivered on the 'cowards of Rome', taking his text from a passage by the prophet Amos, was so shatteringly virulent that it terrified the congregation, and caused people to claim that certain passages could never be repeated.

In point of fact, Savonarola was a perfect example of the Christian who, in an age of opportunistic Christianity comfortably established on a basis of compromise, and contaminated by wealth, sophistication, power and hypocrisy, still retained his intransigence and his integrity. He was a Christian who held by the radicalism of the Gospels, in an epoch when the Church—now degenerated into a State, and wholly oblivious of the precept which set it against the 'spirit of this world'—by betraying its original vocation had fallen into a corruption far worse than that which now drove him to such furious invective. Afire with the illusion that the *civitas Dei* could be realized here on earth, yet lucidly aware of the superhuman difficulties inherent in his campaign against forces that were both stronger and more subtle than he was, he found, in the depths of his mystically-orientated soul, a desire for martyrdom which—in sudden flashes—revealed his presentiment of failure: 'O Lord, *da mihi hoc martyrium*! I see the knife already sharpened for me. . . .'

It would seem that Alexander VI, in a characteristically Borgia-like attempt to make him more tractable, sent Cesare to him with the offer of a cardinal's hat. This move makes it quite clear that the Pope underrated his opponent. In his *XIXth Oration, on Ruth and Michea*, Savonarola stated: 'I do not want these hats, nor any mitre, great or small. The only thing I want is what Thou hast given to Thy saints: death. A red hat, a hat of blood, this I desire. . . .'

By now the time for blandishments was past and the span of Alexander's patience was—even more precipitately—approaching its end. Considerations of religious discipline and political interest, solicitations from the Roman Curia and pressure from the League (in the face of the scandal which this friar's preaching aroused, not only in Florence, not only even in Italy, together with the danger it represented for the survival of the anti-French front) made it abundantly clear that the day of rigorous reprisal was at hand.

In the South, the League's forces, under Gonzalo Fernandez de Cordoba and that youthful *condottiere* Guidobaldo da Montefeltro, were drawing their lives ever closer about the few troops Charles VIII had left behind to guard his ephemeral conquests. From here, late in the afternoon of Friday, 20 May 1946, there reached Rome Goffredo and Sancia, now Prince and Princess of Squillace. Lucrezia (accompanied by twelve maids of honour), the ambassadors of the Italian and foreign Powers, Rome's civic authorities, the nobility, and repre-sentatives from the tiny Cardinals' Courts, all streamed out to meet the couple at the Porta del Laterano. After a pause in the basilica, the procession made its way across the Urbs in the mild yet still-warm evening air: the princely couple seemed to embody a 'triumph of youth'. Goffredo rode a superb bay horse. Tawny lights glinted in his long, rippling hair; the face it framed was alive and laughing. Sancia's dark southern beauty was thrown into even sharper promin-ence by juxtaposition with Lucrezia's blonde prettiness. Her horse's trappings were of black silk, and she rode it easily, matching its movements with the har-monious sway of her lithe, full-bosomed body, and darting bright, almost insolently cheerful glances around from those beguiling, mischievous eyes of hers. Their meeting with the Pope, who had been peering through the half-open shutters of a window in the Vatican, waiting for the procession to arrive, half out of his mind with impatience and delight, before he finally went down into the hall where his cardinals were assembled, was a scene of most tender and melting affection.

The Prince and Princess of Squillace took up residence in the palazzo of Cardinal Ardicino della Porta, not far from Castel Sant'Angelo. Two days later, during a service in St Peter's (it was the Sunday of Pentecost) Sancia and Lucrezia aroused the indignation of Burchard, the master of ceremonies, by their unseemly behaviour. Perched on the marble stand used for the reading of the Epistle and the Gospel, they spent the whole of an admittedly interminable sermon whispering and giggling to one another. (In fact the Pope himself, who had little time for prolix oratory, likewise lost patience with the preacher on this occasion.) Sancia was a bubbling fountain of gaiety; and through contact with her the gentle Lucrezia found a new joy in living.

The presence of Goffredo and these two young ladies soothed the Pontiff's mind, after the period of tension he had been through, and even struck a spark of jollity from the youthful, yet meditative and enigmatic, personality of Cesare. Now the family was almost completely reunited, the only still-absent member being Giovanni. But Alexander VI (who, had it not been for King Ferdinand's opposition, would have long since brought Giovanni back to Rome) had already taken steps for his recall from Spain, where—surrounded by his wife, his two young children Juan and Isabel, and a court of 135 *caballeros*—he led the life of a most distinguished *grand seigneur*, dividing his time between Gandia and Valencia, between the King's service and the chase, as bored as any decadent monarch.

So the Vatican and its immediate environments enjoyed a pleasant summer. In July there came the news of Atella's capitulation, which marked the final collapse of French resistance in the realm. Amongst the prisoners taken were Virginio Orsini and his son Giovanni Giordano. Alexander solicitously sent word to the Gran Capitano, bidding him keep them in close custody—a fiat which procured the family's two most formidable members a good long spell of cenobitic life within the walls of the Castel dell'Ovo.

By the end of February the Pope had declared them rebels, with all the consequences ensuing from such a decision; and on 1 June he delivered a fulminating broadside of censure and punitive measures against the entire Orsini clan, which included a decree confiscating all their property. He was only waiting for the arrival of the Duke of Gandia from Spain before launching a military campaign against the Orsini, this being regarded as a prelude to the Church's repayment for all the arrogance and treachery she had borne at the hands of Rome's great noble families. Resentment of their behaviour both during and after the French invasion was reinforced by the never-to-be-forgotten memory of the summer of 1458, when, on Callistus III's death, they rose against Pedro Luís. The Borgias had long memories, and knew how to bide their time. Cesare too, when betrayed by his *condottieri*, would one day say of himself: 'I am awaiting my opportunity.'

The League's star was now in the ascendant. On 18 July England joined it, which accentuated its European character. A month later, the Emperor Maximilian risked marching into Italy—a gesture of force to which he had been put up by Ludovico the Moor. He had three objectives in view: to wrest from the French the key city of Asti (the most important link in their communications system, and the strategic base for their Italian operations) and place it under the Moor's control; to force Savoy and Monferrato into the League; and to teach the Florentines a sharp lesson, by depriving them of Leghorn and giving Pisa her permanent freedom—moves which would, it was hoped, shift Florence away from the French alliance. However, to conquer cities, impose one's wishes on other states, and teach governments a lesson are projects which call for ade quate forces; and Maximilian's were so small as to be ridiculous. What was more his allies in the League—holy by name but ultra treacherous by nature— took great care not to support this venture. As a result, the ingenuous Maxi milian made a bigger fool of himself than on any other occasion in his entire life, and went cursing back northwards to the Tyrol.

The history of the Borgias is not just a web of crimes and moral delinquency, as many slanderers alleged in their own day, and countless more have repeated for the benefit of posterity. Nor, on the other hand, does it consist only of those lofty designs and brilliant *coups de théâtre* which cluster so thickly around their political activities. Another part of the tapestry is their penchant for splendid processions, among the finest and most memorable of a luxurious era which in such parades provided one of the most characteristic manifestations of its culture.

That which accompanied the Duke of Gandia's entry into Rome on 10 August 1496 left a dazzling memory in various Renaissance chronicles, and provided inspiration for the poet, Bernardino Corso, whose modest lyrical imagination was balanced by a painstaking accuracy over detail. In a *sonetto caudato* [that is, a 'tailed sonnet' with an additional tercet, or more, after the normal fourteen lines] he set down a minute description of the Duke's apparel, the colour and trappings of his horse, the livery worn by his Spanish footman and Moorish groom, not forgetting even the pages and jesters:

> His surcoat was of velvet brown, its breast
> And sleeves embroidered with so many jewels
> That all stared awestruck at him as he passed . . .

This passion for fine clothes and jewellery, pushed to the limits of almost inso lent ostentatiousness, was to remain one of the most striking and characteristic features of this pleasure loving youth.

He was twenty years old, and Alexander VI had summoned him to Rome as prospective commander of the campaign against the Orsini. For such a task he was wholly lacking in preparatory experience; yet he faced up to it with that ready and cheerful self assurance which sprang naturally from a temperament ever eager for the unexpected. Just to be on the safe side, however, the Pontiff, who despite his lofty conception of the Borgias' innate *virtus* never failed to comply with the dictates of prudence, gave him Guidobaldo da Montefeltro as a lieutenant. Though scarcely four years Giovanni's senior, Guidobaldo could already call himself a seasoned veteran of the battlefield.

On 26 October the Duke of Gandia received his insignia as Gonfalonier and Captain-General of the Church, and the following day he set out with his troops. Galloping over hill and dale, from one fortress to the next, as though borne on by some irresistible wind of victory, and laughing as he went in that arrogant, insolent way he had, Giovanni stripped the Orsini faction of their city and almost all their fortified strongholds. But it was at Bracciano, on the western shore of the lake of that name, that the really decisive test awaited him. Here his opponents, encouraged by the water protecting their rear, had dug themselves in for a resistance *à outrance*. In that massive fortress, its flanks as strong as the sides of a mountain, and the standard of France flying over its five battlemented round-towers, Bartolomeo d'Alviano and his wife (Virginio Orsini's sister) were organizing the defences in a most resolute and energetic fashion. On the northern side of the same lake lay Trevignano: this meant that the attackers were compelled to divide their forces.

One assault followed another. Trevignano fell, but Bracciano repelled all attempts to storm it. Guidobaldo was wounded, and the Duke of Gandia had to bear the full weight of command alone. The siege threatened to drag on for ever; and meanwhile the persistent winter rains turned the camp into a waste of clinging mud, where the soldiers felt that they were slowly putrefying in their sodden, rotting tents. A number of small boats were hastily built at Rome and sent off to the besiegers by armed convoy, so that they could invest the fortress from the lakeward side. The convoy, however, was intercepted and captured by a band of Orsini supporters. Those under siege made continual sorties, darting out now here, now there, conducting non-stop nuisance raids against the Papal troops, scattering their reinforcements, and even, on occasion, pushing on as far as Rome. Eventually Giovanni Borgia tried to provoke desertions among the defenders by promising them higher pay if they came over to his side. That same day a donkey was seen to emerge from the walls of Bracciano, and come trotting towards the Gonfalonier's lines. It bore a placard hanging from its neck, inscribed with a verse distich. If the metre was somewhat lame, the *vis* remained undeniably effective:

> Let me come through, in me you see a
> Ambassador to the Duke of Gandia.

'And behind its tail,' Sanudo relates, 'there was a letter addressed to the said Duke with much ill matter therein.'

The situation suddenly took a critical turn when two sizeable groups of rein-forcements took the road to help the Orsini—one from Città di Castello, under Vitellozzo Vitelli, and the other, commanded by the Baglioni, from

Perugia. Both forces had been raised with cash subventions supplied by Charles VIII. The Papal army found itself forced to raise the siege in some haste to avoid being caught between two fires, and now moved off northwards. Some where near Sutri, on 27 January 1497, it was caught by surprise and attacked on the march; and though its troops fought with extraordinary valour they suffered a disastrous defeat. Eight hundred men were left dead on the field of battle, Guidobaldo was taken prisoner, while the Duke of Gandia himself was wounded, and only managed to get to safety by precipitate flight.

The Orsini faction's forces were now at the very gates of Rome; and Alexan der VI was obliged, with more haste than dignity, to sue for peace. In return for 50,000 gold ducats, he restored to the Orsini all those strongholds they had lost, except Cerveteri and Anguillara, the two cities which, in 1493, Virginio had improperly acquired from Franceschetto Cibo with funds supplied by the King of Naples—subsequently being invested in possession of them by Alexander VI himself, whose compelling motive at the time was fear of the French. The Pontifical Treasury did not stretch to ransoming Guidobaldo, who could only free himself by literally scraping up every last penny he had—something he was never to forget. Of the 50,000 ducats paid over by the Orsini, the Pope gave some 40,000 to the Duke of Gandia by way of a consolation prize for his failure.

A fortnight after peace had been concluded, Gonzalo de Cordoba arrived in Rome, to assume command—again, in conjunction with Giovanni Borgia— of the operation against Ostia. The harbour city had to be cleared of a respected Navarrese pirate named Menaldo Guerra, who, together with a French garri son, now occupied the fortress (inseparably bound up with memories of Giuli ano della Rovere) and controlled a good stretch of the coast of Latium into the bargain. For the Gran Capitano, this business was the merest trifle. He left Rome on 22 February, and was back again by 8 March, with the pirate in chains and a large string of prisoners. The Duke of Gandia shared the honour of a triumphal entry with him.

Now the Borgias could breathe again. The young King Ferrandino, Alfonso II's son, had died without issue, and the Aragonese restoration had brought to the throne of Naples his paternal uncle, Frederick. In point of fact, Alexander VI had hesitated some time before granting him the investiture, wondering whether to reserve this throne as a future gift for the Duke of Gandia. Finally, however, he let it go, haggling over the concession, and obtaining the dukedom of Benevento for his son by way of compensation. To this he added a couple of cities which were detached from the Church's territorial patrimony, and pre sented the whole lot—with the docile assent of the Sacred College, obtained at a consistory held on 7 June—to the Captain-General of the Papal militia. Duke of Gandia, Prince of Tricarico, Count of Carinola and Claramonte, Duke of Benevento, Terracina and Pontecorvo, Gonfalonier of the Church—by now Giovanni Borgia had revenues at his disposal worthy of a minor sovereign, and could reasonably entertain the most highflown ambitions for the future.

Cesare's mood, on the other hand, seemed to have taken a turn for the worse. He was irate and taciturn, shut in on himself. He seldom wore his scarlet robe. As soon as he could, he would change into riding-clothes, leap on a horse, and set off on one of those long, exhausting hunting expeditions he so enjoyed, as though to dispel some hidden rage by violent motion and breathe the air of the wide open spaces. Late in the previous autumn a rumour had spread that he was having an affair with Sancia, who found him infinitely more attractive than the immature Goffredo—though she did not, it would seem, keep her favours for him alone. She had grown up in a licentious Court, and took her pleasure where she found it, with a hand as firm as it was capricious. Volatile, highly intelligent, an untameable wild filly, she held her own even with the Pontiff, who more than once was obliged to threaten to send her straight home to Squillace. After the Duke of Gandia's return from the Ostia expedition, she showed signs of preferring his cheerful exuberance to the cool impenetrability of that gloomy introvert, the twenty-two-year-old cardinal.

The day after the announcement of the bestowal of this new dukedom on Giovanni Borgia, Cesare—who the previous year had been appointed governor and castellan, in perpetuity, of Orvieto—was given the title of Papal Legate, and chosen to perform the coronation ceremony for Frederick of Aragon. Both brothers now began to make preparations for travelling South. Only one of them, however, was destined to leave. For the other, there lay in store a journey from which no return was possible.

On Wednesday 14 June a rumour went round Rome that strange sounds had been heard in St Peter's basilica, while torches, propelled by no human agency, danced in the air. That evening the Duke of Gandia, Cesare, Goffredo, Sancia, and the young Giovanni, all dined together under the tender gaze of Vannozza, in the gardened house she owned near San Pietro in Vincoli, among the ruins and verdure of the Esquiline. During the course of this convivial evening a masked man was shown in, whispered something in the Duke's ear, and left. No one found this remarkable, either because they knew the young warrior's adventurous habits, or else because the mysterious visitor had recently become something akin to his shadow.

At nightfall, the party took horse and rode in the direction of Trastevere. The

man with the mask was there, going on in front with the grooms. Outside the
Palazzo Cesarini, where Cardinal Ascanio Sforza lived, the Duke parted
company with the others (who were going on towards the suburbs) without
saying where he himself was bound. At their suggestion that he should provide
himself with an escort, he merely shrugged, smiled, and waved his hand in farewell. He told his groom to go to his palazzo and collect certain arms, and then
to wait for him in the Piazza Giudea. If he had not showed up there within an
hour, the groom was to go home. Then he took the masked man on to his own
horse, and rode away into the darkness.

From that moment, nothing more was seen or heard of him. His disappearance filled the Pope with consternation, and terrified the Roman populace,
which now had the alarming sight of Spanish patrols, grimly menacing, working their way through every last alley and corner of the city. They found the
groom, who was on the point of death, and past giving them any information.
They found Giovanni's horse, the stirrups of which showed signs of a furious
struggle. Nothing else.

Somewhat later, a Dalmatian boatman testified that during the night of
Wednesday to Thursday he had seen some people throw a body into the Tiber,
but had not paid much attention to the incident, since on countless other
occasions he had witnessed similar nocturnal scenes. Three hundred men now
feverishly set about dragging the river. It was the net of a fisherman named
Battistino da Taglia which, shortly after midday on Friday 16 June, drew the
Duke's body up out of the water. It had nine knife-wounds in it, the throat had
been cut, both hands were tied together, and a stone was attached to the neck.
A pair of gloves still hung from the Duke's belt, his dagger was at his side, and
his purse, with thirty ducats in it, remained untouched. The point at which the
body had been discovered was roughly level with Santa Maria del Popolo,
opposite the garden (which sloped down to the river bank) of a small villa
belonging to Cardinal Ascanio.

The bloodless corpse was borne to Castel Sant'Angelo, washed, and attired
in the uniform of a Gonfalonier of the Church. In the calmness of death it regained its earlier beauty. We have testimony to this transfiguration in the dead
Duke's body from witnesses who actually saw him. Some afterwards claimed to
recognize his idealized features in the Christ of Michelangelo's 'Pietà'. The
artist reached Rome a few days after the tragedy, and found the whole city still
buzzing with it. Legend perhaps; but a significant and enticing one, by no
means without a faint element of plausibility, since the young sculptor was
given this commission by Cardinal Jean Villiers de la Groslaye, a close friend
of the Borgia family.

That evening the funeral cortege emerged from Castel Sant'Angelo and made its way towards Santa Maria del Popolo. On the river-bank, at the point where the body had been fished up, the Borgia men-at-arms unsheathed their swords in the gleam of the torchlight and swore a vendetta. The Duke of Gandia, in his brocade-covered coffin, was laid to his last rest in the Chapel of Santa Lucia, on the right of the high altar, where his mother had prepared a sepulchre for him and his children.

Pedro Luís in 1458, Pierluigi in 1488, now Giovanni in 1497 (and, though no one knew it then, in 1507 it would be Cesare's turn): destiny had successively struck down the finest and most exuberant flowers on the Borgia stem. What was more, it attacked precisely those splendid young men on whom the ambitions of two Pontiffs had chosen to build—with wealth culpably abstracted from the Church—the family's secular fortunes.

Alexander VI was too genuine a believer not to see in this misfortune the admonitory and punitive hand of God. For three days he lay shut in his room, not touching food, prostrate with agony, till he had no tears left to shed. Then, at last, he emerged, calmly determined to repent and mend his ways. He set himself to change his whole way of life. At a consistory held on 19 June he pronounced these words: 'A harder blow could not have been dealt us, since we loved the Duke of Gandia above all other things in the world. To restore him to life, we would gladly give seven tiaras. It is because of our sins that God has sent this sore trial upon us, since the Duke of Gandia did not deserve so terrible a death ... May God forgive whoever committed the crime. We, however, are determined from henceforth to see to our own reform, and that of the Church ... We wish to renounce nepotism, and to begin this reform with ourselves, proceeding thence to the other members of the Church, and bringing our enterprise to a successful conclusion.' He set up a commission of six cardinals and two auditors of the Rota, with the task of proceeding to an accurate examination of evils and abuses, and of formulating detailed proposals regarding the provisions to be adopted for their elimination. On 7 August, as a first step in the implementation of his anti-nepotism campaign, he sent Goffredo and Sancia back to Squillace. He declared it to be his wish that Lucrezia should go and live in Spain. He had, he said, decided gradually to eliminate the presence around him of all his relatives. While the commission went briskly about its work, he arranged a series of consultations with the whole Sacred College, beginning in early November, to discuss its deliberations concerning reform. Various documents still survive as evidence for this period of lofty intentions: draft proposals, with detailed additions and emendations, various decrees, a

Papal Bull, a highly circumstantial scheme of statutes touching on all sore points in the Church's structure, spiritual no less than administrative. All these afford ample authority for the claim that, if Alexander VI had had the strength to hold by the inspiration which came to fruition in him while he was absorbed by grief, the Church would undoubtedly have been spared another half century of scandals—not to mention the lacerating (and seemingly incurable) wound dealt her by the Protestant Reformation.

But that strength he lacked. The cumulative pressure of various factors which—day by day and ever more ineluctably—came to frustrate his original emergent impulse was simply too great. On the one hand he found himself assailed by the force of political circumstance, and various situations dependent on the existing context of events; on the other he had to reckon with his own incurable weakness of will, the boundless love he bore his children, his in-grained inconstancy, the ease with which he could forget anguish, the terrible attraction pleasures held for him, and—this above all—the frightful stranglehold which Cesare now had on him. All these factors militated against his redemp-tion.

No later than February of the following year the Venetian ambassador could write: 'The Pontiff is doing all he can—indeed, he thinks of nothing else—to promote the interests of his sons, *videlicet* him they call Valenza, and Don Jufredo.' The assertion was all too true.

As for the power which 'Valenza' had acquired over him, from the moment he replaced his murdered brother as head of the family, evidence can be found in abundance. The Pope felt Cesare's demoniac will and energy hanging over him like an incubus—against which he from time to time rebelled, though only in private, with a flash of uneasiness and fear. When in the autumn of 1499 Cesare set off to seek his fortune in France, Alexander VI was heard to say: 'I would give the fourth part of my papacy for that man not to come back.'[11]

The masked man vanished without trace. No one knew his name, or could recognize his face. It was never determined just what role he played in the affair. Was he a go-between used by Giovanni for his dangerous amorous adventures? Was he a stalking-horse, a decoy in someone's pay? Was he the actual author of the crime? All these hypotheses had a certain plausibility.

Police investigation, though carried out with extreme diligence, came to nothing. All the interrogations—most often accompanied by torture—produced not the vaguest hint to suggest what direction enquiries should take. All the houses along the Tiber as far as Santa Maria del Popolo, not excluding the palazzo of Cardinal Ascanio, were subjected to a thorough search, without result. Nothing that could be regarded as a clue was found among the Duke's papers, except for certain letters from Fabrizio Colonna which begged him to be on his guard against 'a Roman' in whom he put absolute trust.

It was a perfect crime, an enigma which has remained unsolved until the present day. Its reverberations were enormous. Suspicions, whispered rumours, various conjectures culled from diplomatic reports flew abroad in all directions.

Starting, first of all, from the hypothesis of an abortive erotic adventure, the rumour-mongers brought up the names of two particular women: a certain Madame Damiata, the Duke's acknowledged mistress, and the Countess della Mirandola, to whom he was known to have been strongly attracted. The police concentrated particularly on the latter, since she lived near the Tiber, in the area where the body was discovered, and Giovanni's mount had been found in the immediate vicinity of her house. But both women were able to prove, in the most conclusive manner, that they had nothing whatsoever to do with the mystery.

Every rumour which gained currency was brought to the attention of the Pontiff. Like will-o'-the-wisps, the whispered accusations danced in the air, pointing now at this person, now at that. One of the first to be victimized by them was the innocuous sixteen-year-old Goffredo, on the grounds of his alleged fury and exasperation at Sancia's liaison with the Duke. However, at a consistory held on 19 June Alexander VI firmly dismissed this libel: 'Concerning the Prince of Squillace,' he declared, '*minime.*'

Could it have been, as some thought, a vendetta conducted by Guidobaldo da Montefeltro, because of the subordinate role which the Borgias assigned to him during the campaign against the Orsini, coupled with their refusal to ransom him when he was taken prisoner? Here again the Pontiff ruled out any possibility of guilt: 'Concerning the Duke of Urbino we have no doubts.'

Another candidate was Giovanni Sforza, long detested by the Borgias as a spy of the Moor's who had insinuated himself into their family circle, and who therefore knew his days were numbered, not only as Lucrezia's husband, but also—if he stayed on in Rome—as an inhabitant of this vale of tears. He had, in fact, cleared out during the spring, and gone to ground in his retreat at Pesaro. However, gossip asserted that he had slipped back to the Urbs in secret to commit the crime. A certain recent episode lent some plausibility to this suggestion. Giovanni Sforza had had a Spanish friend of the Duke's killed, in the house of a courtesan; and the Duke had retorted by hanging some of Sforza's grooms from the battlements of the Tor di Nona. Sforza was quite capable of perpetrating such a crime, through the agency of hired killers if not in person. The hatred which seethed within him as a result of his ignominious ejection from Lucrezia's bed had reached such heights of violence as to suggest the possibility of some such action. However, in his case also the Pontiff pronounced what amounted to full absolution: 'It has been suggested that the Lord of Pesaro had him murdered; we are quite certain this is not true.'

Suspicion fell with particular insistence on Cardinal Ascanio, because of a number of motives which, when put together, were pretty convincing. There was his inveterate political hostility to the Borgias, which reached an almost convulsive pitch during Charles VIII's invasion. There was a quarrel which had broken out a few days earlier in his house, during a banquet, between him and the Duke of Gandia, with an exchange of the most sanguinary insults. There was his kinship with young Sforza, and the fact that the body had been found opposite the garden of his villa. So fiercely peremptory was the accusing voice of public opinion that he fled from his own palazzo, leaving it to be invaded and ransacked by the Borgias' supporters, and took up residence in the vice-chancellor's quarters. Here, quaking, he barricaded himself in, his heart in his mouth, feverishly dictating coded letters to be sent to his brother, the Moor. He did not put in an appearance at the consistory held on 19 June, but left the Spanish ambassador to make his excuses, begging the Pontiff, through his representative, not to heed the rumours that were circulating about him. Alexander sent him reassurances and invitations: 'God forbid,' he declared, 'that I should have so terrible a suspicion where the Cardinal is concerned! I have always regarded him as a brother, and if he came here he would be most welcome.' Despite all this, Ascanio would only agree to meet him with a large escort of diplomatic representatives, who accompanied him to the very doorway. During their discussion, which lasted for five hours, Alexander declared himself wholly convinced of the cardinal's innocence. Afterwards, however, he appeared to have changed his mind on this score, while the cardinal—still terrified of reprisals by the Duke's closest and most loyal friends—hurriedly left the dangerous vicinity of Rome. Suspicion obstinately clung to him: in August the Venetian *oratore* reported that very many people were convinced of his guilt, and a year later, on 14 June 1498, wrote that Alexander VI possessed incontrovertible proof of it.

So we come to the most obvious target for such conjectures: the Orsini clan. Being involved in a struggle to the death with the Borgias, and certain of a swift resumption of hostilities, they were more directly interested than anyone else in the elimination of the Gonfalonier of the Church—not foreseeing (how could they?) that this office would be taken over by Cesare, a much more formidable figure. The mysterious circumstances surrounding the death of their clan-leader Virginio—this had taken place during April, in the Castel dell'Ovo, where he was held prisoner at the behest of the Pope and the Spanish lobby—could have put the final edge on their determination to conduct a vendetta. On various occasions Alexander VI let it be known that he was convinced of their guilt. Whether this assertion was based on hard evidence, or should be taken as pure political opportunism, one cannot tell. It is true that he exculpated all other suspects, but not them. And this silence on his part, whether backed by proof or not, whether based on a mere hunch or inspired by political calculation, is the one feeble ray of light (or what looks like light) that history can find in the otherwise impenetrable darkness which clings around the tragedy.

Eight months later the crime was held to be fratricide; the guilty party's name was Cesare Borgia. 'I understand that the Duke of Gandia's death was procured by his brother the Cardinal.' This apodictic assertion, set down on 22 February 1498 by the goose-quill of Alberto della Pigna, the Ferrarese *oratore*, originated in Venice. Taken up by a hundred other pens, repeated by voices which speedily became a loud chorus, it spread the world over and endured for centuries. Even today, though ever more rarely, it is still sometimes heard.

No one bothered to ask what supporting evidence there was for this revelation. No one investigated its origins. No one connected the Ferrarese *oratore*'s phrase 'I understand' with the presence in Venice of Giovanni Sforza and a number of Orsini fugitives from Rome, all full of furious spite against the Borgias, bubbling with poisonous slander and only too eager to squirt it out.

Of all the explanations that have been excogitated *a posteriori* to provide a reason and a motive for this act of fratricide, and of all the attendant circumstances adduced in order to provide this gratuitous hypothesis with some basis in solid fact, there is not one which can stand up to hostile critical scrutiny. However, since so slanderous a version of events has now been abandoned by virtually all serious students of the period, I refrain from refuting it yet again in these pages. The problem should now be regarded as closed.[12]

I may add that the ground in which the conviction of fratricide took root most vigorously—not at once, but with the passage of time—was Gandia. It seems that Maria Enriquez became openly convinced of Cesare's guilt, even though, with Alexander VI's consent, she had appointed him guardian of her children and fiduciary trustee for the administration of their property in Italy; and after his fall, it was rumoured that her religious piety and pursuit of holiness did not stop her doing everything she could to blacken his name with Their Most Catholic Majesties. On this point firm information is lacking. One fact, however, is significant. A few years after Duke Valentino's death, a member of Gandia's ducal house—Cristóbal Hernández del Castillo, Gentleman of the

Bedchamber to the murdered man's son—while giving evidence at a trial declared that he had not known Giovanni Borgia, '*a quíen mató su hermano, el duque de Valentinois.*'

LUCREZIA AND THE ROMAN INFANTE

At Capua, on 10 August 1497, Cesare duly saw Frederick of Aragon crowned. Then he accompanied the Court to Naples where he and the King thrashed out the problems concerning young Juan's succession to the deceased Duke of Gandia's Neapolitan fiefs. He felt out the ground for Lucrezia's projected marriage to a prince from the House of Aragon; he purchased the favours of Countess Maria Díaz Garlón, and plunged into a number of casual love affairs. Frederick had been obliged to pay him at least 12,000 ducats as an advance on his travelling expenses; and to maintain him and his retinue of three hundred knights in the style to which they were accustomed had almost bled the poor man dry. No one can have been more relieved than Frederick when Cesare took his departure once more.

He returned to Rome accompanied by a most attractive Sicilian girl, and with *treponema pallidum* circulating in his blood. This did not disturb him: he applied to Gaspare Torella, the Pope's physician (and a bishop to boot), who knew all there was to be known concerning the 'French disease' (to which he gave the delightful appellation of *pudendagra*) and set about curing Cesare with a most remarkable course of therapy. His colleagues might prescribe preparations of mercury, but such things were not for him. He preferred certain ointments of a quite different sort, together with various decoctions and inhalants. He expounded his revolutionary theories in a pamphlet which he dedicated to Cesare —glad and proud to give publicity, at one and the same time, to the cardinal's glorious misadventure and his own therapeutic methods. After a lengthy course of treatment Cesare was still in full possession of his *pudendagra*, and carried decorative signs of it around with him in the shape of persistent pustular eruptions, which disfigured his countenance and added to his *terribilità* and mystery by leading him, as time went by, to appear ever more frequently behind a mask of black silk.

Less fortuitous than might appear at first sight, perhaps, is the clear and well-documented connection between the symptoms of this illness and a marked increase of harshness in Cesare's disposition. It was, precisely, during this period that he began to harden into a savage predator, without pity or remorse. The watershed between the old Cesare—that mild, cheerful figure—and the new, steely Cesare who marches across the page of history, like some evil genius of violence, must indubitably be associated with the murder of the Duke of Gandia, after which he laughed seldom, and unpleasantly when he did. At the same time, syphilis also possibly played some part in the remarkable hardening of his character. The first victim to experience this incipient *terribilità* of his was probably a Spanish gentleman in the Papal Court, Pedro Calderon, known as Perotto, who was guilty of having cast his eyes (if not his hands) on the all-too-willing Lucrezia.

It was in Holy Week, 1497, that Giovanni Sforza suddenly fled from the dangerous air of Rome, and shortly afterwards Lucrezia, too, left the city, seeking refuge in the San Sisto Convent on the Via Appia. World-weariness? The need to escape the storm that was breaking around her? Orders from her father? Or simply the need to hide somewhere? On 8 June the *oratore* Donato Aretino wrote to Cardinal Ippolito d'Este as follows: 'Madame Lucrezia, the Pope's daughter and wife to the Lord of Pesaro, has vanished secretly from her palazzo and gone to a nunnery known as San Sisto, where she still remains; some say she wishes to become a nun herself, while others report various different allegations *quae non sunt credenda litteris*.'

The 'various allegations' which, according to the cautious Este diplomat, were not the kind one could set down in a letter, others did not hesitate to reveal, some vaguely, some in more specific detail. When Giovanni Sforza disappeared from Rome, the *oratore* of Milan had attributed his abrupt departure to resentment at Lucrezia's reprehensible behaviour: 'I rather fancy that some motive not unconnected with his wife's virtue led him, first to entertain grave suspicions concerning her, and then to make a departure of this sort.'

In fact it all too soon became apparent just what kind of misdemeanours the fugitive was imputing to his consort. Rejected by the Borgias, who realized that they had undervalued Lucrezia by bestowing her on so paltry a backwoods squire, and wanted to use her as a means of gaining admission to that redoubtable stronghold the House of Aragon, Giovanni Sforza was forced to fight his battle, somewhat desperately, with the weapons of defamation, accusing his wife of incestuous relationships with her father and brothers. These harebrained tactics compromised him dangerously in public opinion, arousing the suspicion that he had either murdered the Duke of Gandia himself, or else arranged for his removal, as part of a vendetta in which he figured as the betrayed husband. At the same time, with breathtaking illogicality, he kept insisting, from Pesaro, that he wanted Lucrezia back. Above all, he obstinately refused to give the Borgias that declaration of 'non-consummated union' which was indispensable if the Pope was to annul his marriage.

Among the motives 'not unconnected with his wife's virtue' was there anything more tangible than his *parti pris* fantasies about incest? Could he have had information concerning the romance which existed (or so Roman gossip alleged) between Lucrezia and Don Pedro? We cannot tell.

For a good six months, anyhow, he played his part in a contest which—for sheer grotesque comedy, if for no other reason—would have sufficed to keep the Borgias in the forefront of the news, even without the other devilries by which they managed to make themselves a more or less daily talking-point. There they were, with imperturbable demureness, claiming that the girl was *incorrupta*, or still wholly virginal—a state of affairs they blamed on her husband's impotence —and demanding that this impotence of his should be acknowledged in writing, by means of a document fortified with all the sanctions of legal bureaucracy. Ranged against them was the husband himself, seething with fury, calling on all the saints to bear him witness when he swore that he 'had known her carnally on countless occasions'—though naturally he could not offer proof of this—and making desperate, almost lunatic efforts to recover the wife whom they had sent to a nunnery.

Late that spring he travelled, in disguise, to Milan, where, putting on the appearance of a poor relation soliciting aid, he duly presented himself to the Moor. Ludovico listened patiently to his complaints, and—though well aware there was nothing to be done about the matter—offered him some kind of satis-faction by writing to Cardinal Ascanio. The cardinal had a word with the Pope, and on 19 June sent his answer. The Pope was very sorry, he 'would have liked this marriage to be a lasting one', but since 'it had remained unconsum-mated as a result of impotence', he felt himself obliged to annul it, and insisted on having the by now famous declaration. Keeping a straight face—though his eyes were glinting with mischief under the dense fringe of his hair, cut level with his eyebrows—the Moor shrugged, and told his long-suffering petitioner that one possibility still remained. It was, moreover, something simple and indeed pleasant. Giovanni must 'give proof of himself with women' by displaying his virility in the presence of the Papal Legate and other reliable witnesses. Giovanni Sforza refused. Then the Moor changed his tone. He made it very clear that neither he nor Cardinal Ascanio, as vice-chancellor of the Church, had any desire to fall out with the Borgias over Giovanni's matrimonial wrangles. First with exhortations, then with steadily decreasing friendliness, and finally with the peremptory insistence of someone thoroughly annoyed, he made it clear that nothing but surrender would serve. For six long months Sforza dragged out his stubborn and entrenched resistance, however, now seasoning it with complaints, now with viperish variations on the triple-incest theme. For six months he continued to plug the theme of his virility and the innumerable occasions of which he had had 'knowledge' of Lucrezia. Quite apart from the humiliation he felt, he was tormented by the fear of having to restore Lucrezia's dowry: 31,000 ducats, no less. On this score, however, he soon won official reassurance. The Pope would not only allow him to retain it, but (accord⁄ ing to the Mantuan envoy in Rome) was even prepared to 'let him have something in addition', provided he lost no time in releasing that all⁄important disclaimer.

In December, with a pen that scorched his fingers, Giovanni Sforza signed the declaration in which he solemnly proclaimed his own impotence and the non⁄ consummation of his marriage.

Lucrezia was still in the Convent of San Sisto, whither she had either fled of her own accord, or been forced to flee, in order to avoid the loud and scandalous repercussions of this affair, and to restore her virginal image a little (if we may so put it) in preparation for yet another marriage. The new husband selected for her was Alfonso of Calabria, an illegitimate son of the monarch of that name, and nephew to the present sovereign, Frederick.

The holy ladies of the nunnery had shown themselves deplorably susceptible to the wind of fashion and high society that had blown into their lives with Lucrezia's appearance in their midst. Indeed, such gusto did they display in abandoning the old austerity of their regime, that after their fair⁄haired guest's departure sweeping reforms were necessary to bring them back to the sublime joys of self⁄mortification, and to exorcize the atmosphere—a mixture of the drawing⁄room and some sophisticated Arcadia—which had grown up inside those pious walls.

Towards the end of February 1498 a piece of news broke which deserved to make the front page everywhere. Lucrezia was pregnant. She herself laid the blame (or the merit, according to one's point of view) for her imminent motherhood at the door of that enterprising character Don Pedro, *alias* Perotto. From that moment he dropped out of sight, and no one had any idea what became of him. We know, now, that he was languishing in a prison cell, morti⁄ fying himself with memories of what Dante calls 'the time of sweet desires'. On 2 March Cristoforo Poggio, secretary of the Bentivoglio family, wrote to the Marquis of Gonzaga from Bologna: 'As for this fellow Perotto, His Holiness's first gentleman of the bedchamber—you will recall his sudden disappearance— I now gather that he is in prison for having got His Holiness's daughter Madame Lucrezia with child.'

Thirteen days later Lucrezia gave birth to a boy. This information stems from an agent of the Este in Venice. Two reports circulated, then, based on unspecified Roman sources, and composed by clerks in notably peripheral Chancelleries—with a total absence of Roman documentary evidence either confirming or denying them.

This leads one to formulate two open questions:

(1) Did Lucrezia really have this child?

(2) If she did, is it to be identified with the famous 'Roman Infante', born precisely during this period?

The most plausible answer to the first question is 'No', which renders super-fluous any need for an answer to the second. If Lucrezia had really given birth in the waiting-period between two marriages, such an event would hardly have passed unobserved, leaving no trace in the correspondence of the various *oratori* accredited to the Vatican; nor could a child of the Borgias have escaped being identified and catalogued. We may, furthermore, assume that the Borgias would most certainly have avoided proclaiming Lucrezia's virginity to the four winds, if while—to Giovanni Sforza's shame and the delight of the Aragonese prince—they were so proudly advertising it, she had turned out to be pregnant all the time. Her adventure with Perotto certainly never reached this particular point of no return.

As for the Roman Infante, all history can do is to accept his existence without pressing too hard for evidence concerning his origin—and, above all, without attempting to ascertain the name of his mother. He was given the baptismal name of Giovanni; in September 1501, at the age of three, he was to be invested with the Duchy of Nepi (including Palestrina, Olevano, Frascati, and other towns); he grew up at Lucrezia's side, always being referred to by her as 'brother', and so described in the documents concerning him. On 8 July 1519, when the news of her death reached him in France, he wrote to the Duke Alfonso d'Este that no loss in the whole world could cause him more sorrow than that *'de la señora duquesa mi hermana'*. No one—except those who still raved about incest—ever, then or later, called the brother–sister relationship in question. That stern figure Alfonso d'Este (who never allowed Lucrezia to bring her legitimate son by her second marriage to Court at Ferrara, or even to receive him while there) would certainly not have given her permission to send for the young Duke of Nepi if she had been his mother, and had conceived him by a lover, out of wedlock.

Whose son, then, *was* this Giovanni Borgia? Various suggestions have been made, all sedulously picked up and repeated by the gossip-mongers. Putative parents for the child include Alexander VI and Lucrezia, Cesare and Lu-crezia, Perotto and Lucrezia, or Alexander VI and Giulia Farnese. Side by side with all these variant combinations we must consider two baffling Bulls issued by the Pope on the same day (1 September 1501). In the first, the Roman Infante is described as the son of Cesare Borgia and a 'marriageable woman'; in the second, as the son of Alexander VI and the same woman ('. . . *non de praefato duce, sed de nobis et de dicta muliere*').

Various hypotheses have been put forward to explain the simultaneous promulgation of two contradictory Bulls. According to some, the first was an 'official version', dictated by motives of expediency, while the second was left in reserve, a secret weapon only to be produced in case of real need, if, for example, the young Duke's claim was seriously challenged. According to others, *both* Bulls were fabrications, cooked up by some unscrupulous lawyer at a time when the Infante, now grown-up, had to defend his rights to the Duchy of Nepi. Since each document cancels out the other, they were not taken into consideration.

The Roman Infante, then, was not born of an incestuous union; nor can Perotto be claimed as his father. All we can say is that he was the late offspring of a man who still retained his hot and passionate instincts.

But as far as Perotto was concerned it sufficed for Cesare that he had desperately wanted to court his sister, thus exposing her to the slanderous gossip which inevitably circulated about the Borgias—and this at the precise moment when they were going to so much trouble to get the House of Aragon interested in her. 'Valenza' disliked and resented a bad press. When, on 2 March 1498, the ill-informed Cristoforo Poggio wrote that Perotto had been put in prison 'for having got His Holiness's daughter with child', the wretched man had already been out of jail—and enjoying eternal repose—for a good three weeks.

Even as regards the nature of his death accounts differ. According to the grim narrative of the Venetian *oratore* Paolo Cappello, Cesare stabbed him under the mantle of the Pontiff himself, whither he had fled to seek sanctuary— a melodramatic episode which the diplomat heightened with one really virtuoso touch, specifying that the blood of the victim spurted up into the Pope's face.

Burchard, more credibly, informs us that on Thursday 8 February Don Pedro fell, *non libenter* (that is, not of his own free will) into the waters of the Tiber, from which he was not fished out again until the 14th. That *non libenter* is a touch of sophisticated humour which makes one forget how crustily pedantic this German master of ceremonies was in the ordinary way.

A comparison of dates can sometimes reveal some very odd coincidences, which raise considerations worth dwelling on at some length. It is hard to repress a feeling of sorrow—and a temptation to cynicism—when one notes the exact simultaneity of the Pope's senile adventure and the final phase in the tragedy of Savonarola.

On the news of the Duke of Gandia's assassination, the friar of San Marco had written Alexander VI a letter warm with affectionate sentiments. On 22 May 1497 he sent him another, which opened with the following words: 'Why is my lord so incensed against his servant?' But it was already nine days since the drafting, in the Vatican Chancellery, of that Brief of Excommunication which cast him forth from the Church's fellowship. This document was deliberately scornful in tone; it dealt with a person of major importance in the life of contemporary Europe as though he were some obscure nobody: 'From many reliable sources we hear that a certain friar, Gerolamo Savonarola, at present said to be vicar of San Marco in Florence. . . .'

On 11 February 1498, the excommunicated friar reascended the pulpit of the Duomo in Florence, and gave vent to all his exasperation in words that were burning with scorn, defiance, and a readiness to embrace martyrdom in defence of truth. He impugned and challenged the validity of the censure passed upon him by a Pope who was now a 'broken dagger'; and in sermon after sermon on the Sundays that followed he poured forth his nauseated fury on Rome, the Curia, and the clergy both high and low, with their concubines and publicly acknowledged offspring. 'Come hither, O degenerate Church,' he cried. 'I gave you fine raiment, saith the Lord, and you have made it into an idol. Your vessels you turn to pride, and your sacraments to simony; in lasciviousness you have become a shameless whore. You are worse than the beasts, you are a monster and an abomination. Time was when you felt shame for your sins, but no longer. You have built a house of public ill-fame, a common brothel . . .' And again, of priests: 'They sell benefices, they sell the sacraments, they sell nuptial Masses, they sell everything. And then they are frightened of excommunication! When evening comes, one will betake himself to the gambling-table, another to his concubine . . . This poison has reached such heights in Rome that France, Germany, the whole world are sickened by it. Things have come to such a pass that we must counsel all men to keep clear of Rome, and say: Do you want to ruin your young son? Then make a priest of him. . . .'

These were the times in which the Roman Infante was born; and round the name of Lucrezia—drawing closer and closer until they had caught it in a net of opprobrium—the rumours of incest continued to circulate. 'The time is drawing near,' Savonarola one day exclaimed, 'when we will turn the stopcock and open the jakes, and then such stinking filth and fetid matter will issue from the city of Rome as will spread throughout the length and breadth of Christendom.'

The now irretrievable breakdown of the situation found him ready for his final duel with the 'atheist' in the Vatican. On 13 March he fired off a challenging letter to the Pope; then he issued an impassioned invitation to the sovereigns of Europe to press for the convocation of a Council. 'I assure you *in verbo Domini,*' he wrote, 'that this Alexander is no Pope, nor can he be considered as such. Leaving aside the fact that he purchased his pontifical throne with simony, and that he daily assigns ecclesiastical benefices to those who pay highest for them; and leaving aside also his other vices, well known to all men, I assert that he is no Christian, and does not believe in God's existence. . . .'

Alexander VI picked up the gauntlet. Calmly and resolutely, he made ready for battle. On 23 May 1498 the failed reformer's emaciated corpse, strangled and garrotted, hung dangling in the Piazza della Signoria, licked by voracious flames; and with a brief sigh Alexander VI turned back to his own affairs. He had tried every method he knew to bring Savonarola to his right mind, to restore his sense of discipline and obedience, and to lead him back into the paths of wisdom. He would even have been prepared to pay the man to keep quiet. He detested violence. But when a man becomes dangerous, and will not listen to reason, then stern measures become necessary.

In mid-June 1498 the prince destined to replace Giovanni Sforza (now removed from that office) as Lucrezia's husband paid a visit to Rome, in a strictly private capacity. He was escorted as far as Marino by about fifty horsemen, but from there on pursued his journey with no more than half a dozen companions. This was the Pope's idea. The whole affair had already provoked far too much comment, most of it very far from favourable. He had no wish for it to attract any superfluous publicity at this delicate stage in the negotiation. Even so, the news was all round the Urbs in a flash.

Alexander VI greeted the visitor with every sign of warm affection; the next day Cesare received him in his own apartments and overwhelmed him with courtesies. 'Yesterday,' Ascanio wrote to the Moor, 'the cardinal of Valencia bore him off from the company to his own quarters, and (as I am informed) loaded him with every imaginable sign of respect and friendship.' Two years later to the day, exactly on the second anniversary of his arrival in Rome, the boy was to learn just how much reliance could be placed on Cesare's 'endearments'.

His first meeting with Lucrezia took place in the Pontiff's presence. They were both eighteen years old; and the good looks of Alfonso, which had dazzled all who beheld him, seemed designed and preordained *ab aeterno* to stand beside those of the young Borgia girl. It suddenly became clear to everyone that though this union had in fact been determined by the coldest political motives in the world, it was also going to turn out a love-match.

Six days after the arrival of Alfonso—on whom his uncle Frederick had

recently bestowed the overlordship of Bisceglie, together with the title of Duke—
the wedding took place, very quietly. Though the actual ceremony was intimate and private, after a reasonable time celebrations inevitably followed:
'parties, banquets and every sort of junketing', as the Mantuan *oratore* reported
on 8 August, though there were no public figures or diplomatic representatives
among the guests. In fact, just before dinner Cesare's gentlemen, upon a disagreement with those of Sancia, drew their swords in the Pope's presence, and
all but came to blows, leaving the guests to serve their own refreshments and
sweetmeats. The banquet lasted till dawn, with intervals for dancing and a
theatrical performance, in which Cesare enjoyed parading himself as the
Unicorn.

Among the various clauses in the marriage contract was one requiring the
Duke of Bisceglie to remain with his wife in Rome for a year, before carrying
her off to his remote feudal domain beside the sea.

CESARE: FROM THE SCARLET TO THE SWORD

The removal of the Duke of Gandia, mailed fist of the Church and chief representative of the family's secular ambitions, upset all the Borgias' carefully constructed plans. His post could not be left vacant. And in the tense political
situation of the day, the need for a replacement made itself felt with especial
urgency.

Was it to be Cesare or Goffredo? The choice of the second would indubitably
facilitate matters; but there were two considerations which militated against it—
the boy's lack of years (at the time of his brother's murder he was barely sixteen),
and doubts as to whether he possessed a sufficiently aggressive temperament.
Ergo, there was nothing for it but to appoint Cesare.

This came as an unwelcome necessity, and one not without difficulties for the
Pontiff, since the metamorphosis of a cardinal could not be carried through
without considerable scandal and strong opposition. There were, in point of
fact, clear indications of both from the moment when (in August 1497) word
began to spread around that Alexander VI, in Machiavelli's phrase, 'had it in
mind to remove Duke Valentino's habit and give him secular status'.

The decision was duly taken. However, as his office required, the Pope simu-
lated a certain perplexity and reluctance in the matter. Though these deceived
no one at the time, they have made a great impression on some historians. He
assumed the mask of a thwarted man; sighing heavily, he confided his problem
to Ascanio, the vice-chancellor, and to one or two other cardinals. He made it
clear that he could not fail to recognize—though it went against his heart to do

so—the validity of the reasons which Cesare adduced for his return to 'the world': his now amply confirmed lack of a vocation, his consciousness of his own unworthiness, his fear of damning his soul, and finally (if we can trust the author of the *Anales de la Corona de Aragón*) the fact of having discovered the illegitimacy of his own birth. (His acceptance of a cardinal's hat had been made in the belief that he was the legitimate son of Domenico Giannozzi da Rignano.) In short, Borgia guile invented a drama of conscience to camouflage a move dictated solely by considerations of political advantage and private ambition.

Luckily, Cesare was only a cardinal sub-deacon; that is, he still occupied the lowest of the three ranks in the so-called major Orders. The rumour of his imminent return to layman's status was promptly capped by that of a very cool exchange of functions inside the family circle: Cesare would pass on his cardinal's hat to Goffredo, who in return would give up his wife, Sancia, the latter (as Cardinal Ascanio wrote on 20 August 1497) being still 'carnally intact'.

In actual fact Cesare was on the point of renouncing a position which brought him in an annual income of 35,000 ducats, and of abandoning a career which might well culminate in the Papal tiara. With such a change of life and occupation in view, he hoped to secure a springboard which would allow him to create himself a prestigious principate, and possibly even to lay hands on a throne.

From the Vatican, he and Alexander cast their gaze over the entire peninsula, seeking the most vulnerable spot. Siena, Pisa, Imola, Forlí and other cities of the Romagna shuddered as they felt that searching scrutiny dwell on them in turn.

There was no hesitation over the choice of a bride: Carlotta of Aragon, King Frederick's daughter. Considering the present extreme weakness of the Kingdom of Naples, dynastically tottering and constantly afflicted by baronial intransigence, Carlotta's hand meant a real and personal mortgage on the crown. Lucrezia's marriage to Sancia's brother constituted a necessary preliminary to this second union: as the Borgias planned it, she provided a kind of *quid pro quo*.

However, when the matter was sounded out, Carlotta of Aragon withdrew her hand in some disdain, as though that of Cesare repelled her, while her father clearly found this Borgia proposal an unwelcome embarrassment, the sort of vexatious claim made by people 'who were never satisfied with what they had'. As Carlotta was then living at the French Court, Alexander sent Charles VIII a request to put the required pressure on her. Charles promised to do so; but immediately afterwards he had the unfortunate idea of dying from an apoplectic stroke, at Amboise. This was on 7 April 1498: the same day which, in Florence,

witnessed the barbarous ordeal by fire designed to ascertain God's will concerning Savonarola, who had threatened the 'new Cyrus' with Heaven's
wrath for failing to undertake the reform of the Church. Charles left no direct
heir. He was succeeded by his cousin, Louis d'Orléans, a man of thirty-six,
visibly weighed down by his adventurous and exhausting past, and whose
early wild excesses had now given way to a cold and cunning astuteness.

At Rome, meanwhile, the situation deteriorated, with a resurgence of pure
anarchy. So long as Alexander VI managed to keep up the engrained hostility
between the Colonna and Orsini factions—who for a number of months kept
snarling at each other both in the Urbs and around their respective strongholds—
everything went comparatively smoothly. But when the two quarrelling
families realized what he was up to, and made a private pact to deal with him,
things took on a very different complexion. Their provocative, challenging
attitude reached the Borgias even inside the walls of the Vatican. One morning
the Pontiff found pinned to the door of his library (or, according to other
sources, on a column, in his palazzo) a composition in verse inciting the two
great Roman families to attack him: it ended with a couplet which, by reason of
the allusion it contained, was not only savage, but cruel:

> Merge, Tiber, vitulos animosas ultor in undas:
> bos cadat inferno victima magna Iovi.[13]

Cesare fretted with anger and impatience. Things really had to be speeded
up; the Papal State could not allow itself much more time without anyone to
wield the sword on its behalf. And since Naples was hostile to any attempt at a
rapprochement, one had to find, and use, some point d'appui capable of breaking
down her stubborn resistance.

In this resentful atmosphere, and impelled by the desire to secure Carlotta's
hand at all costs, Vatican policy took a new turning. Old grudges were buried
and the Pope began to look towards France. At the first indication of this
change in course, the Italian Powers turned pale with alarm: the Vatican's
volte-face left the anti-French League of 1495 a dead letter. The Aragonese
trembled; so, to an equal extent, did Ludovico the Moor, since Louis XII, over
and above the title of King of France, Jerusalem and the Two Sicilies, had also
assumed that of Duke of Milan. The ghost of his grandmother Valentina—a
legitimate daughter of the Visconti, not a bastard, like the present Lord of
Milan's mother—was there to recall his weakened (but by no means extinct)
claims on the dukedom.

Through a cordial and solicitous exchange of embassies—led by Georges
d'Amboise, Archbishop of Rouen, the King's most trusted adviser, and Giuli-

ano della Rovere, Legate of Avignon, who showed himself only too happy to support this new Borgia policy—agreement was rapidly reached.

Louis XII had three aims in view: to detach the Vatican from any solidarity with the Moor and the Aragonese, because of his plans to conquer Lombardy and (in the second place) the Kingdom of Naples; to obtain an annulment of his marriage to his cousin Jeanne de Berry, daughter of Louis XI, so that he could then contract a new match with Charles VIII's widow, Anne of Brittany, and thus obtain possession of her vast duchy; and to get Georges d'Amboise a cardinal's hat.

In return for Alexander's undertaking to back him over the first and third points, while doing all he could (within the limits imposed by canon law) to give him satisfaction on the second also, Louis promised the Pope the following concessions on Cesare's behalf: personal support for his prospective marriage; the dukedom of Valence, the county of Diois and the overlordship of Issoudun; one hundred armed cavalrymen, payed for by the royal exchequer (four hun/dred, in the event of war in Italy); a life/pension, the collar of the Order of St Michael, and a position of the highest dignity at his Court. He would also send the Pope—to guarantee peace and order in the Papal State during Cesare's absence—a thousand of his own men, to be paid for with secret funds. By means of letters patent to the members of the League, he would pledge himself to de/fend Alexander against any attempt at molestation. He would consult the Pope in advance over any plans regarding the Kingdom of Naples, and undertook to take no action in that quarter without him. Lastly, there was the matter of Cardinals Giuliano della Rovere and Raimondo Peraudi, ringleaders of the anti/Borgia faction. At the Pope's request, Louis agreed to return both of them to Rome at any given moment, though recommending them to Alexander's well/known kindliness.

The terms of this agreement show just how handsome a *quid pro quo* the Borgias contrived to extract—in an area where their family ambitions were in/volved—for a political manoeuvre which (provoked by so seemingly futile a reason as one minor princess's refusal of a marriage/offer) was to change the whole future of Italy. It shattered those precarious conditions governing the balance of power in the peninsula; and by unleashing the imperialistic ambitions of France and Spain it ushered in a period of violent change and upheaval in the affairs of Europe. Thus it was that Cesare Borgia became, in sober fact, one of those key figures who rise like columns at each new turning/point of history.

The legal commission which Alexander VI set up to examine Louis XII's request for an annulment of his marriage went about its task with great dispatch, poring for hours, in the sultry summer heat, over the documents which reached them from the French Court. Jeanne de Berry at last resigned herself to drinking the bitter cup of repudiation. She agreed to sign a document declaring that the marriage had never been consummated because of a congenital physical malformation on her part. This done, the whole matter was settled in no time at all. The ecclesiastical tribunal was ready; the Pope had no reason to reproach himself; and the King of France, rejoicing, did all he could to stifle his own pangs of conscience, and turn a deaf ear to protests raised by indignant theologians in the Sorbonne. Jeanne broke the lute with which she had hitherto consoled her hours of sadness, vowed herself to God, and departed to her native Bourges, where she shut herself up in a convent which she had founded for women suffering—like herself—from weariness of the world. She was thirty-four years old. During the seven years which remained to her, she was often to be visited by another disappointed woman: Cesare Borgia's wife. Silently removed from the history of France, she now made a brilliant entry into that of the Church, as founder of the Order of the Annunciation. On 28 May 1950 she was proclaimed a saint.

At a secret consistory held on 17 August 1498, Alexander VI proposed, and the cardinals meekly approved, Cesare's return to lay status: a decision which subsequently led Sanudo to make some sour comments on the function of the Sacred College. Cardinal Ardicino della Porta had been refused, by a majority of his colleagues, permission to relinquish the scarlet in order to take vows as a friar; yet Cesare, by unanimous vote, was now allowed to jettison his cardinal's hat so that he could go to France, take a wife there, and get up to God knows what dirty games into the bargain. 'Everything in God's Church is going to rack and ruin,' the Vatican diarist commented.

That same day there arrived in Rome the French ambassador Louis de Villeneuve, whose task it was to bring the ex-cardinal his letters patent as Duke of Valence, and to accompany him to France.

Cesare's preparations for this journey were those of some satrap, going to show himself to the world in all his dazzling splendour. The entire peninsula was laid under contribution for the very best that its warehouses, jewellers' shops, craftsmen's booths and thoroughbred stud-farms could supply. Fabulous sums were spent on the preparation of baggage, clothes, and escort for this herald of Italian civilization, who was setting forth—as though into some barbarian country—to sweep a still half-medieval France with the mighty wind of the Renaissance in all its joy and self-confident pride. The Church's coffers released torrents of gold; Alexander's imaginative resourcefulness found some highly ingenious ways (including the confiscation of the Bishop of Calahorra's goods, after he had been charged with heresy) of quickly boosting his revenues: 100,000 ducats were laid out on preparations for the journey; 200,000 went into Cesare's purse as a viaticum.

It was on the morning of 1 October that the new Duke of Valence (who had celebrated his twenty-third birthday a few days earlier), wearing a doublet of white damask with gold stripes, and a mantle and cap of black velvet, left Rome and rode towards the sea. His retinue included thirty gentlemen, a good hundred servants, pages, musicians and grooms, several dozen thoroughbred horses, his majordomo Ramiro de Lorca, his secretary Agapito Geraldini, and his physician Gaspare Torella (still committed to keeping an eye on his *puden-dagra*). It took twelve waggons and seventy mules to carry all his baggage. The six French galleys awaiting him at Civitavecchia were by no means too many.

They set sail on 3 October, with Cesare aboard the *Louise*. It was a bright morning, and he stayed on deck. From Marseilles they made their way to Avignon, where Cesare was met by Giuliano della Rovere, and thence to Valence, the capital of his Duchy. Next stop on the journey was Lyons; and then, in mild and pleasant autumn weather, they traversed the Bourbonnais, Berry, and Touraine. During this period the kings of France seldom resided in Paris. (Their main successive establishments there were the royal palace of the Île de la Cité, built by St Louis and enlarged by Philip the Fair; the old Louvre and the Palais de St Paul, chosen as his residence by Charles V; and the Palais des Tournelles, acquired by the Crown in 1407, where in 1514 Louis XII was to die.) They much preferred their châteaux on the Loire, amid the peace of the countryside.

On this occasion the King was awaiting his young Italian guest in the Great Keep of that extraordinary architectural complex the Castle of Chinon, sacred to the memory of Joan of Arc's first meeting with the Dauphin, and now re-duced to a picturesque maze of ruins. Cesare's progress through France had left behind it a trail of stunned amazement, destined to fill the chronicles of the period and to echo on down the centuries. When his retinue came within sight of the castle, Louis XII and his courtiers fairly had their breath taken away. In vain did they try, with some *mot d'esprit*, to shake off the dazzling spell that was now cast over them. The spectacle unfolding before their eyes was in fact a supreme example of Renaissance splendour.

At the King's Court, Cesare Borgia made it quite clear, from the very first moment, and throughout his lengthy sojourn there, exactly what notion he had of himself and his destiny. He gave a superb performance of himself (if one may put it that way). All attempts at irony or familiarity froze at one glance from those steely eyes. Anybody who expected to see him in the role of intimidated petitioner was very quickly disillusioned. In the most peremptory and resolute manner, he presented himself as the representative of a great foreign power— more than foreign, universal—which had three most valuable favours to bestow: support for the Milan venture, a dispensation for the annulment of Louis's marriage, and a cardinal's hat for Amboise. Above all, he was a creditor, now presenting for repayment a promissory note which bore the King's signature.

Yet even though the entire Court adjudged him 'the handsomest man of his age' (a description duly recorded in the pages of a contemporary French chronicler), Carlotta of Aragon did not go back on her refusal. Being in love with an undistinguished French nobleman, Nicholas de Laval, and duly en-couraged to stand firm by her father, she went on shaking her head. One day she remarked that she did not fancy the prospect of being known as 'madama la cardinalessa'. The King did all he could to convince Cesare that he was putting pressure on her, that his patience was becoming exhausted; he even went so far as to threaten Carlotta with expulsion from his Court. But in his heart of hearts he cannot have been all that sorry that Carlotta kept the door of the House of Aragon closed against this formidable aspirant, since he too had his eye on the Kingdom of Naples. On 24 February 1499 two Neapolitan am-bassadors presented themselves before the King. Rhetorically offering him, in the name of their master, 'his person and his realm', they tried to sound out Louis's own intentions; at the same time they stated in round terms, that King Frederick would never give his daughter to the Pope's bastard. Louis XII promptly showed them the door. Cesare was duly given a detailed account of the interview, and went as pale as marble. In a cutting voice he listed the various bastards of the Aragonese dynasty, and added—with a sinister glint in his eye— that they would talk of this matter again when the time was ripe. His patience was rapidly becoming exhausted; and with increasing frequency he threatened to bring the entire project crashing down in ruins.

Back in Rome, the Pope (who made no bones about accusing Louis XII of double-dealing and trickery) was even more impatient than Cesare. The rap-prochement with France, and the blow which this struck at the League, had brought down a storm of recrimination on the Vatican, in particular from Naples, Spain, and Ludovico the Moor, with whom the Colonna faction was now making common cause.

The diplomatic counter-offensive began with the arrival of ambassadors from Portugal, a carefully-deployed advance guard acting for Their Most Catholic Majesties and the Emperor Maximilian. They were received by Alexander VI on 27 November 1498, and proceeded to make deprecatory comments on his nepotism, his simoniac practices, and his political treachery. They did not rule out the unhappy possibility that his conduct might force Christendom to move towards the convocation of a Council.

At a consistory held a few days later, Ascanio delivered a sharp broadside against the Pope. In scorching terms he stigmatized Alexander's volte-face, by which—merely in order to advance Cesare's career—he would bring down ruin on all Italy from beyond the Alps. The Pope's reply was curt and biting: 'Are you not aware, Monsignor, that it was your brother who invited the French into Italy?'[14]

On 22 December the Spanish ambassadors arrived. Solemn, compassionate and lugubrious, they poured out a series of heartfelt reproaches. But the moment they alluded to the steps he had taken to obtain the tiara, Alexander cut them short, retorting that he had been elected Pope by unanimous vote, and had every right to the throne he occupied, whereas *their* sovereigns had stolen the kingdom, and kept possession of it in shameless violation of every common law, and against all conscience, as mere usurpers. And when (at the most heated moment of a diatribe that went far beyond the normal bounds of propriety) the ambassadors cast the miserable death of the Duke of Gandia in his teeth, as a proof of divine wrath, Alexander countered this blow with an equally insidious comment. 'Your King and Queen,' he said, 'have suffered still more sorely from the hand of God, who has destroyed their issue and posterity as a punishment for meddling in matters that concern the Church alone!'[15]

There followed further confrontations and angry exchanges, until January brought a concerted attack by Spaniards and Portuguese together. The discussion took place in the presence of the senior cardinals, and was extremely violent. One ambassador, at a certain point, so far forgot the normal rules governing diplomatic language as to query Alexander's status as legitimate Head of the Church. The Pontiff who, at the age of twelve had allegedly disembowelled a schoolfellow for 'saying some indecent words to him', was now overcome by that blinding fury which formed part of his Borgia heritage. In a voice hoarse with rage he threatened to have this insolent fellow thrown into the Tiber; after which he let fly on the Queen of Spain's private life, at one stroke tearing the veil of her respectability from top to bottom, and then proceeded with harsh vehemence, to castigate Their Most Catholic Majesties' persistent interference in the affairs of the Church.

His courage did not fail him; but courage is the dissimulation and repression of a fear which exists, even if it does not let itself be seen. And this man of sixty-eight was afraid. Alone amid a storm of hostility, confined to his palace by the turbulence of a nobility which had already scented Cesare's aggressive plans for the future, forced to fill the Vatican with guards and to surround himself with a massive escort when he carried out his religious functions in Rome's basilicas, he fairly shook with terror. He drafted a scheme for the establishment of a militia to maintain public order and keep a check on the nobility, something along the lines of the Spanish *hermandad*. The interminable delay in reaching a solution to Cesare's matrimonial problem, and the consequent prolongation of all those uncertainties connected with it, produced a state of suspension which simply intensified anxiety.

It was not only the grim shadow of danger which concerned Alexander; he also had serious doubts regarding the timeliness of this switch in alliances which he had let himself be dragged into by his son. The thought of invasion, the knowledge of his own responsibility for it, and the consequences he foresaw if and when it took place, became more oppressive and intolerable as the days went by. He could not find any adequate answer to the remonstrances flung at him by the Powers he had betrayed, nor did he manage to repress in himself his longstanding and engrained animosity against France.

He tried to play for time. He sought makeshift solutions. He had a heartfelt and unhappy discussion with Cardinal Ascanio, begging him, for the general good and, in the first instance, for the benefit of his brother the Moor, to persuade the King of Naples to agree to this union. 'Impossible,' the vicechancellor replied coldly.

On 9 February 1499 Venice signed a pact with France, promising acquiescence in the invasion; this undercover agreement procured her the acquisition of Cremona and Ghiara d'Adda. Alexander VI was immediately informed of this development by Giuliano della Rovere, who also passed on an invitation from Louis XII to join the alliance. The news threw the Pope into consternation. On 12 March the Venetian *oratore* wrote (with good reason) that if Cesare had not been in France, the Pontiff would have aligned himself with Milan in the hope of averting or repelling the attack when it came. It is also of some significance that Cesare—thus exposing himself, with impressive temerity, to a risk which could well cost him dear—maintained a secret correspondence, while at Louis XII's Court, with the Duke of Milan, who was bound to him by certain rather mysterious connivances. This is made quite clear in a letter he wrote the Moor from Lyons as late as 5 August, when the French troops under Trivulzio's command had already crossed the Alps.

To sum up, then, there exists a whole mass of evidence which leads one to suspect that, during the summer of 1498, the Borgias had planned a daring— too daring—masterpiece of deviousness and bad faith, turning *pro tempore* to the

King of France for the sole purpose of effecting a quick exchange of favours: quick enough, that is, to let them pull out of this alliance, hands full, in good time for a *rapprochement* with the League, a restoration of the 1495 line-up, and a move to block the expedition against Milan.

Now they found themselves defeated by time. Carlotta's resistance had en-sured the failure of their gambit; and the stone they had set rolling, blithely confident of their ability to halt it on the edge of the abyss, was now plunging downwards with irresistible momentum.

Events moved on implacably, with unrest at home and foreign intimidation abroad continuing unchecked. Rebellion was brewing at various points in the Papal State; Spain and France both threatened to withdraw from their oath of obedience to Rome. Fear pricked Alexander's body like a hair-shirt. Terrifying visions suddenly flashed before his eyes under the vaults of St Peter's Basilica. To hold Spain at bay he decided to take back the dukedom of Benevento from the Duke of Gandia's young son, and reabsorb it into the territory of the Church. He made over a large proportion of Cesare's Spanish benefices to prelates who were in Ferdinand's good books. He closed first one eye, and then both, to the improper interference by these *Reyes Católicos* in Church affairs, against which he had recently inveighed so vehemently. He promised to send his sons and relatives miles away from Rome, and undertook to carry out various radical reforms.

Then suddenly, about mid-May, his whole bearing changed: he became assured, not to say jubilant. His fear had vanished, and with it the need to simulate crises of conscience and plans for mending his ways. He emphatically confirmed his adherence to the French cause, and was heard to declare that the Milanese dynasty must be eliminated from the scene.

What had happened? Dispatches from France had brought news of Cesare's wedding, already an accomplished fact. As a replacement for the unassailable Neapolitan princess, Louis had finally played the card he was holding in reserve: another Carlotta (or Charlotte), another King's daughter, another flower from that *verger d'honneur*, Anne of Brittany's Court, sixteen years old, and the most beautiful of all those beautiful young girls who moved in the Queen's circle. Politically speaking, it certainly could not be said that this Charlotte was worth as much as her predecessor; but her good looks, her royal blood, and her ties of kinship with the French dynasty all made her an ex-tremely valuable catch. Her full name was Charlotte d'Albret; her father, Alain Le Grand, held patriarchal court in his mighty castle at Nérac. One of her brothers, John, was King of Navarre, while another, Amanieu, had embarked on an ecclesiastical career, and hoped to win a cardinal's hat (which, thanks to this marriage, he did on 28 September the following year).

Negotiations for the match were long-drawn-out and exhausting, mostly because of the ever-increasing demands made by Alain, who brought to bear the sly and surly tactics of a typical cunning peasant. Finally, however, on 10 May 1499, agreement was reached, and the marriage contract drawn up, in Blois Castle. This prolix and detailed document (executed in the presence of the sovereigns) brought the marriage into the context of the current political situation, and—in a lengthy preamble—virtually made it conditional upon the reliance the King placed on the aid of that *hault et puissant prince don Caesar de Bourga*, not to mention his 'relations, friends and allies', in the campaign for the conquest of 'his' dukedom of Milan and 'his' Kingdom of Naples. The wedding itself took place that very day, in the same castle, with Cardinal d'Amboise officiating. On 23 May a courier brought Alexander VI the news that Cesare, now at last married, had consummated the match, with some gusto, on Sunday the 12th, giving proof of his virility to his bride (as Burchard diligently noted) no less than *octo vices successive*. This detail is confirmed by a personal letter to Alexander from the King, who apparently had a competition with the new bridegroom, and was forced to confess, in all humility, that he could not match such an achievement. The marriage did undoubtedly provide, not only the students of Paris, but also gentlemen at Court, with ample material for skits and lampoons, in which they reviled and ridiculed the Pope; but these were negligible side-effects. A hundred casks of vintage Burgundy, sent by Louis XII to his friend in the Vatican, formed the hymn of joy which concluded a long period of tribulation. 'We are his,' Alexander exclaimed then, 'because of the love he bears our Duke!'[16]

On 19 May, before the King and his entire Court, Cesare received the insignia of the Order of St Michael. There then took place the act of adoption, by virtue of which the Duke of Valence (or Valentino, as Italians were not slow to style him) became Cesare of France, a kinsman of the King's, and acquired the right to add the prestigious lilies to the Borgia ox on his coat of arms.

Everything was now accomplished, and Cesare accompanied the King to Lyons to busy himself with the preparations for the expedition. Even during this period—at Romorantin Castle, on his estate at Issoudun, and during a final return visit to Blois—he spent most of his time with Charlotte. On 14 May he had given her full authority to administer his possessions on French soil; to assist her, as procurator or attorney, he left her his lieutenant Charles Seytre, Lord of Noveysan. Early in September he set out from Lyons, and reached Grenoble by the ninth. Charlotte (who by now was pregnant) never saw him again.

Rome had an eventful summer. During the night of 13–14 July Cardinal Ascanio secretly slipped away to join his brother in Milan, and be near the gathering storm. Alexander VI sent him orders to return, under pain of losing his office and benefices, but to no avail. Seals were placed on the doors of the Chancellery. Two other cardinals, Colonna and Sanseverino, disappeared in a similar fashion. But the most talked-of flight was that of Alfonso of Bisceglie, which took place just before dawn on 2 August. It became known almost immediately that he was at Genazzano, under the fierce protection of the Colonna faction. A letter in which he begged his wife to join him was intercepted, and found its way into the Pontiff's hands. Alexander first assailed Lucrezia with accusations and reproaches, then made her write to the fugitive in an effort to get him back, and finally, moved to pity (a Venetian *oratore* noted that she was six months pregnant and always in tears), sent her out to be governor of Spoleto, a post normally held by a cardinal-legate. Her escort included Goffredo, still in pain from a wound in the thigh inflicted on 30 June by a quarrel from some unknown person's crossbow 'while he was pleasuring himself', to borrow the phrase of the Mantuan *oratore*. It was the low ways into which he had fallen —copying the late Duke of Gandia—that were to blame for his predicament. The Pope, who already looked on him with something less than enthusiasm, was extremely displeased by the incident ('not because the boy is his own son,' the *oratore* made clear, 'but as a matter of honour') and flew into a tremendous rage. During the quarrel harsh words were exchanged between him and Sancia, who had lately returned from her brief exile.

Lucrezia now settled down in the large and powerful fortress of Spoleto (built during the second half of the fourteenth century by a Spanish cardinal, Egidio Albornoz, as a combined bulwark of defence and majestic residence). She may have been tempted to rejoin her husband: the Neapolitan frontier was less than two hours away at a hard gallop. But she preferred to follow the Pope's commands, and beg him to come to her—which the wretched Alfonso in due course did.

On 25 September a meeting was held at Nepi; those present included Alfonso and Lucrezia, Alexander VI, Goffredo, and four cardinals. This city, until recently part of Cardinal Ascanio's domains, was to become Lucrezia's place of residence. Delighted at having restored domestic harmony, the Pontiff was bubbling over with the ambitious plans he cherished on Cesare's behalf.

Back in Rome, he received the news of Louis XII's triumphant entry into Milan, and his eyes glowed with pride when he learnt that Valentino had out-shone everyone else during that memorable parade of 6 October, in which there took part the very cream of Italy's turncoats, opportunists, and lickspittles:

Francesco Gonzaga, self-styled 'victor' of Fornovo; the Duke of Savoy, who had sold his own neutrality, and freedom of passage, to both Ludovico and the French; Ercole d'Este, father-in-law to the dispossessed Lord of Milan; and various others. The Moor—after entrusting the custody and defence of his castle to the faithful Bernardino da Corte, who lost no time in opening it to Trivulzio for an agreed sum—had sought refuge with Maximilian in the Tyrol. So had Ascanio.

The Pontiff celebrated this French triumph, the prelude to Cesare's ascent, by dealing a shrewd blow at the Caetani. It made no difference that they were relatives of Giulia Farnese. One member of the family, an Apostolic Proto-notary, was accused of *lèse-majesté* and imprisoned in Castel Sant'Angelo, where with quite stunning rapidity he left the land of the living. Another was killed by Valentino's mercenaries, while a third, miraculously, only saved his life by taking off for Mantua, as fast as his horse would carry him. The family's possessions were then sold, for 80,000 ducats, to Lucrezia.

Meanwhile Lucrezia herself had returned to Rome for her *accouchement*. On 1 November she gave birth to a boy, who was baptized in the Sistine Chapel, being given the Pontiff's name, Rodrigo. Everything was going marvellously. The ambassadors stationed in Rome were able to report that the Pope had re-turned to his 'customary solaces'—not excluding evening parties in the company of ladies. 'In this palace at the present time,' wrote Antonio Giustinian, a Venetian, 'no feast or other entertainment takes place without them.' Another observer reported, on 14 August: 'Madame Julia has returned to His Holiness our lord and master.' A masterfully concise comment, but one that said all that was necessary.

THE CONQUEST OF THE ROMAGNA

Through the emblematic figures and mottoes on his ceremonial sword—en-graved for him by the goldsmith Ercole de' Fedeli, probably to Pinturicchio's designs—Cesare Borgia revealed his ambitions and aims as a conqueror. This weapon (which after the fall, or perhaps after the death, of Valentino passed mysteriously into Spain, and then came back to Italy two centuries later) is unanimously acknowledged to be the most beautiful sword in the world, the very *'regina delle spade'*.[17] It also constitutes the most genuine and direct piece of evidence for Cesare's personality: it is the mirror of his ideals, a psychological revelation of the man himself, a conceptual illustration of the *ordo novus* which he tried to impose on the strife-torn Italy of his day.

On one side of the blade, among other lesser figurations, we have the Crossing of the Rubicon, a Cupid, armed and blindfolded, and two mottoes (CUM NUMINE CAESARIS OMEN and IACTA EST ALEA), which proclaim the exalta'tion of calculated risk in warfare, and of the battle of love. On the other, we find a Triumph of Caesar, the figure of Fides enthroned, a terrestrial globe set on a broken column, with an eagle above it, wings outspread, a hind stretched out among figures celebrating the restoration of peace with dancing and music, and the motto FIDES PRAEVALET ARMIS. All this reveals a sure confidence in victory, and the determination to create a harmonious coexistence after the con'quest—a civic structure upheld by force, but founded on loyalty, peace, and concord.

Of Cesare's faithful adherence to the first part of this programme for life and conduct, dominated by pride in the great name he bore, and inspired by the example of the Borgias' alleged ancestor, there can be no doubt: his whole brief career as a soldier and man of action bears ample witness to it. As for the zeal he brought to implementing the Roman concepts and ideals inherent in the second part, and the highly valuable results he here achieved, we have evidence for this not only from admirers such as Machiavelli, but also from hostile witnesses like Guicciardini.

Cesare's programme of action, which he put into operation during the autumn of 1499, proceeded in two directions. He was determined to eliminate those country landowners who had moved away from their original feudal role as deputies responsible for the government of Church lands, and were now petty tyrants, refusing to acknowledge any central authority, ruthless with their subjects, given to savage internecine feuding, and bound by no dictates save those of violence and fraud. He also meant to stamp out that anarchy which had become endemic among the great Roman patrician families, a sword of Damo'cles perpetually suspended over every Pope's head.

The object of the first campaign was to recover the Romagna and the Marches. The political map of the Romagna presented the following centres of resistance: Imola and Forlí, in the domains of Caterina Sforza, who ruled on behalf of her son Ottaviano; Faenza, held by Astorre III Manfredi; Ravenna and Cervia, which had passed under the control of Venice; Rimini, now in the hands of Pandolfo Malatesta, and covered by the protective shadow of the Lion of St Mark. Only Cesena, among the sizeable cities of the Romagna, was more or less unprotestingly obedient to Papal authority. In the Marches, there were three *signorie* which would have to be neutralized: that of Giovanni Sforza at Pesaro, that of Guidobaldo da Montefeltro at Urbino, and that of Giulio Cesare da Varano at Camerino. After that it would be the turn of Umbria and Bologna.

It goes without saying that of the territories brought back under the Church's direct dominion, a reasonable proportion would be assigned to Cesare, to create a State in the peninsula. It would then be up to him to enlarge this at the expense of other States: above all, Tuscany, which the Borgias kept under constant scrutiny, in search of a weak point.

Cesare was aiming higher, and further, than anyone imagined. In his mind the final goal was a Kingdom: the nucleus of a Kingdom of Italy.

On 9 November 1499 he finally set out. He was twenty-four years old. His army consisted of 300 French knights, under the red-bearded Ives d'Allègre, as gay and lighthearted a boon companion as his name suggests; 4,000 Gascons and Swiss, commanded by the Bailiff of Dijon; a handful of troops recruited at Cesena by Achille Tiberti and Ercole Bentivoglio; and a contingent of Italo-Spanish soldiers who had arrived from the Papal States, under Vitellozzo Vitelli, the man who had already inflicted a defeat on the late Duke of Gandia— in all, a round total of some 15,000 men.

At Modena, on 17 November, Cesare abruptly left his troops and galloped at breakneck speed to Rome. By the 21st he was back again. No one ever knew the reason for this sudden diversion. It is supposed that it had some connection with an attempt, engineered by Caterina Sforza, to poison the Pope by sending him a letter which had been for some while in close contact with the corpse of a plague victim: a method in fact consonant with the practice (then fairly widespread) of eliminating tiresome characters by impregnating their clothes, arms, or other possessions, with some poisonous substance. The use of a letter formed a variant not without a certain originality; various sources allude to this attempt of Caterina's, adding that the bearers of the lethal document were discovered and imprisoned on 18 November, and (after making a full confession) were removed from prison to the stake. But the connection between Cesare's ride to Rome and the attempt instigated by the 'daughter of iniquity' (as Alexander VI referred to her in the circumstances) remains purely conjectural.

The march was resumed. On 25 November the gates of Imola opened at his soldiers' breath: all it took was a command to surrender, shouted out (between two trumpet blasts) by a herald with a troop of horsemen to escort him. Its fortress, on the other hand, put up a tough resistance, being defended by a first-class garrison, under the command of Dionigi di Naldo. Nevertheless, a rigorous siege, protracted bombardments, and the non-appearance of a relief column forced the defenders, on 12 December, to capitulate. Next day, Cardinal Giovanni Borgia *junior*, who was following his cousin's army in the capacity of

Papal Legate, received the city's oath of loyalty. Lesser strongholds in the surrounding countryside now lowered their drawbridges.

At Forlí, in the fortress of Ravaldino—garrisoned by 2,000 men, and provided with arms, munitions and victuals in abundance—was Caterina Sforza, the 'virago', the 'first lady of Italy', the toughest, bravest, most splendid female figure (I would maintain) in all history: the fierce heart of a lioness in a magnificent Amazon's body. She had lived her whole life with the scent of blood in her nostrils. When she was thirteen they had murdered her father; her first husband, Gerolamo Riario, had been killed by an angry mob and flung out of a window of his own palazzo, while her second, Giacomo Feo, was assassinated while she looked on. Conflict and danger she breathed as though they were her natural element. No adversity could put her down, no enemy make her afraid, no peril dismay her.

> I filled my stout fortress
> With victuals and guns
> And many a man and muckle riches:
> And castellan there was none
> Other than my own person . . .

These lines are from *Caterina's Lament*, which the people still sang centuries afterwards, in memory of that legendary siege.

At the news of Imola's surrender, she ordered those Imolese hostages she held in the fortress to be beheaded. When the citizens of Forlí surrendered themselves —'like whores', as Sanudo puts it—to Valentino's authority, she gave a fierce shout of joy on learning of the sack with which the Bailiff of Dijon's French and Swiss troops repaid their compliance, and wished the city a happy Christmas by bombarding its town-hall, and the houses of those who had advocated capitu-lation.

On St Stephen's Day Valentino appeared beneath the walls of the Ravaldino fortress on horseback, 'like a paladin', and through the agency of a trumpeter asked to parley 'with the lady in charge'. She appeared on the bastions, and, having heard his request for an honourable surrender, invited him to meet her later for a second parley, before the castle moat. In due course he appeared at the rendezvous, and dismounted. Caterina came out of the castle and they began their discussion. Keeping up a non-stop flow of talk, Caterina slowly coaxed him towards the drawbridge. Only a swift acrobatic leap prevented him being whipped aloft and taken prisoner.

For a fortnight thereafter Cesare bombarded the defences with furious inten-sity. He promised 10,000 ducats—an impressive sum—to anyone who brought him Caterina alive. On the morning of 12 January 1500 he ordered a direct assault on the now breached and shattered stronghold. The battle raged on till evening. Hundreds of corpses lay in the ditches, on the battlements, round the courtyards: it was an inferno. Caterina herself fought side by side with her men, sword in hand, a howling beast dealing out lethal blows all round her. When dusk fell, Cesare had a herald call her from below the walls, and ordered her to surrender, to put a stop to the slaughter which had all but annihilated her garrison.

'My lord Duke,' she replied, 'I am with you.' But at this point the hand of a Gascon captain fell on her shoulder. 'My lady,' he told her, 'you are the Bailiff of Dijon's prisoner.'[18]

Because of the derisory ease with which she had been captured, Cesare reduced his reward to 4,000 ducats. A violent argument ensued between him and the Bailiff, in a devastated courtyard of the castle, over who should have possession of the prisoner. Finally, Cesare took swift, authoritative action, and bore her off, by torchlight, to a mansion in the city of Forlí. It was whispered that he used violence on her and 'pleasured himself' at her expense. But no one actually saw anything happen, and Caterina never claimed to have been subjected to outrage.

If the warrior had given good proof of himself, the administrator now stepped into the limelight, with that energetic shrewdness he possessed in full measure, to deal with the settlement of the conquered territories. He entrusted the various strongholds to new castellans, making arrangements for their immediate restoration. He nominated mayors and municipal councillors for each city and borough. He reduced taxes. As governor of the little state he appointed Ramiro de Lorca, making him responsible for the enforcement of all his, Cesare's, dispositions. Though at the same time still caught up in all the cares and duties of a military campaign, he got through a prodigious quantity of business. In the administrative sphere no less than the military, he seemed to have an innate touch of genius to help and inspire him.

After this enthusiastic beginning, there followed a series of setbacks. On the morning of 14 January he learnt that Cardinal Giovanni *junior* had breathed his last at Fossombrone, while on his way from Urbino to congratulate Cesare for having successfully stormed the fortress of Forlí. The cardinal's death was ascribed to poison, administered at Cesare's request—though in fact Cesare had close ties of affection with his cousin, and wept for him like a brother.

Valentino was now making ready for a move against Pesaro. At the last moment, however, the enraged Bailiff of Dijon found occasion, on 20 January, to let mutiny break out amongst his mercenaries. The public excuse was dissatisfaction with their pay; but a far more compelling motive was provided by Cesare's rigorous clamp-down on their looting activities. The Bailiff profited by the atmosphere he had himself stirred up to seize the prisoner. Valentino's reaction was typical. He ordered a review-parade of his troops to be held in the main square of Forlí, and drew them up in such a fashion that the mutineers found themselves boxed in between the fiercely loyal Spaniards who formed his personal guard, Ives d'Allègre's French knights, the regiments of Vitellozzo Vitelli, and the reinforcements Achille Tiberti had brought in from Cesena. They were also threatened by his cannon, which had been carefully trained on them. Cesare now rode up, drew rein in front of this rebellious group, and harangued them with icy violence, refusing them any increase in pay, threatening them with savage reprisals, and stigmatizing their shameful acts of rapine in contemptuous terms. The mutiny collapsed, and the Bailiff returned the prisoner. As Cesare passed slowly along the ranks, he got an ovation not only from his own troops, but also from the citizens who crowded the sides of the piazza, in recognition of a victory that was the most convincing apotheosis of his conqueror's temperament.

He was already on the march again with his troops, and scarcely a day's journey from Pesaro, when a courier from Trivulzio met him at Montefiore. The dispatch he brought bade Cesare send back the King's troops at once to block the advance of Ludovico the Moor, who had swooped down to the rescue from the Alps, with a force of Swiss and German mercenaries, and had already recaptured Como. Trivulzio was abandoning Milan in order to concentrate his forces beyond the Ticino. In the face of such a situation, to dislodge Giovanni Sforza from his stronghold on the Adriatic became a matter of purely secondary importance.

Cesare had no option but to obey. On 5 February—while he was despondently making his way to Rome, by way of Urbino, Spoleto, and Civitacastellana—the Moor re-entered Milan.

'He laughed and wept at once,' Sanudo said of Alexander VI, describing the frenzied joy which seized the Pope on hearing of Cesare's approach. The two words give a wonderfully vivid impression of what was referred to as the Pontiffs' *carnalità*, the boundless affection he lavished on his children.

It was a Jubilee year; but this was no reason for neglecting the Carnival. Indeed, Alexander anticipated its beginning.

Cesare made his triumphal entry into the Urbs on the evening of 26 February. He rode between Cardinals Farnese and Orsini, preceded by Goffredo, Lucrezia's husband, and his own troops. According to some chroniclers, the procession included Caterina Sforza, dressed all in black, her wrists bound with gold fetters. Next day, eleven allegorical floats, inspired by the achieve ments of Julius Caesar, filed into the Piazza Navona, and from there made their way through the streets of the city, to celebrate—not without a touch of ridicu lous hyperbole—the returning hero's modest conquests. On 9 March Cesare received the vicariate of all territories he had occupied, with the right of heredi tary succession in perpetuity. Twenty days later, in the brightly-lit Basilica of St Peter's, to a background of music, he was presented with the Golden Rose and the insignia of Gonfalonier and Captain-General of the Church.

Yet such honours and triumphs could not dispel the shadow which in these days weighed on his mind. He had presentiments of an early and violent death, which he confided to his friends: 'I know that at the age of twenty-six I stand in danger of ending my life under arms, and by the sword.' The Mantuan *oratore*, when passing this piece of information on to the Gonzaga Court, added: 'And for this reason he does no business, but devotes himself to good living and enjoyment.'

There were balls and love-affairs, hunting expeditions and bull-fights. Cesare astonished Rome with his skill as a *torero*.[19] He was stupefied by the endless round of festivities and began to suffer from melancholia; his life was dominated by a kind of *carpe diem* fatalism. Two pieces of news, however, con trived to jerk him out of his torpor. The first came from the field of battle at Novara: on 10 April the Moor had suffered a disastrous defeat, and had fallen into the hands of the French, who were now preparing to carry him captive beyond the Alps. The second was from France: Charlotte had given birth to a daughter, who was named Luisa.

The dispossessed mistress of Forlí continued intractable. She refused to sign a formal act renouncing the *signoria* that had been wrested from her. Nor would she underwrite the expenses of the campaign against her. After an unsuccessful attempt to escape, she was confined, fuming, to a dungeon in Castel Sant' Angelo—where she had given early proof of her intrepidity on the death of Sixtus IV. Subjected to a non-stop barrage of blandishments and threats, she yielded neither to pressure from the Borgias, nor to the urging of her sons, who made common cause with the Borgias to wear down her indomitable resistance. More than a year was to pass before, in the summer of 1501, as the result of determined representations by Ives d'Allègre, she recovered a somewhat pre carious freedom, and took herself off to Florence.

While Alexander VI was about to hold audience one day, the ceiling of the audience-chamber collapsed (such a storm was raging outside that the roof overhead had been stripped bare), leaving the Pontiff buried under a heap of

VIRTVTVM
OMNIVM
VAS

VITIA VIR
VTI SVBI
CEBIE

A
ES
HI
EG
RIS
AV
TE
LV
I

20. *Lorenzo de Medici by Vasari.*

HIERONYMI·FERRARIENSIS·A·DEO
MISSI·PROPHETÆ·EFFIGIES

22. *Savonarola by Fra Bartolomeo.*

◀ 21. *Alexander VI, detail from the* Resurrection *by Pinturicchio.*

23. *Guidobaldo I, Duke of Urbino, bas-relief of the fifteenth century.*

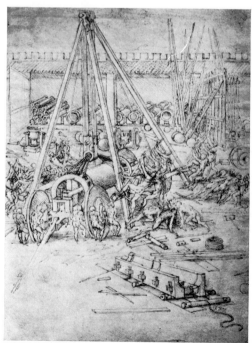

24. *Mounting a gun, drawing by Leonardo da Vinci.*

25. *Julius II by Raphael.*

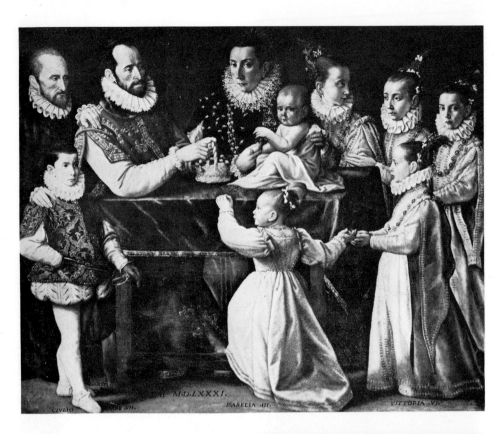

26. *The Colonna family by Scipione Pulzone.*

27. *Louis XII of France, attributed to Jean Perréal.*

28. The Virgen de Los Caballeros *by Paolo de San Leocadio. Giovanni Borgia,*
Duke of Gandia, is kneeling on the right and on the left are Cesare and Goffredo.

29. *Palazzo of Sforza Cesarini, Rome.*

masonry. It seemed to be significant that the incident had happened on 30 June, the feast-day of SS Peter and Paul: it thus assumed the nature of an admonition or punishment on the part of the two Apostles, who were presumably annoyed with him for some reason. On several previous occasions the hoary old sinner had had a dangerously close brush with death—from the collapse of a lightning-struck wall, from the attentions of a maddened deer, from the fall of a huge candelabra. Now, he was dragged out of the ruins, battered, bloody and un-conscious. People thought he was dead. Yet within a very few days he was brisker, sprightlier and more lighthearted than ever. He discharged his debt to Heaven by re-establishing the Angelus (instituted earlier at Callistus III's behest but now fallen into disuse), which was once more rung morning and evening. He declared that he was entering the ninth year of his pontificate with certainty of having a further nine years ahead of him; such was the pronounce-ment of an infallible astrologer, who had foreseen his own Papal tiara, while also predicting that Cesare would be crowned King of Italy. He set about elaborating his various projects with renewed energy. According to the am-bassadors he got younger every day. Each morning he shook off the previous night's worries, and proceeded to enjoy himself with tremendous gusto. The Venetian *oratore* Paolo Cappello, who on 3 July paid him a visit to congratulate him on the danger he had escaped found him with Lucrezia, the Duke of Bisceglie, and a 'damsel' who at this period was 'the Pope's favourite'.

On this occasion Cappello also had an interesting exchange with Cesare, urging him to secure the goodwill of Venice, so that he might induce her to wink at his forthcoming campaign of aggression. Duke Valentino related his reply to the accident which had befallen the Pope. 'Ambassador,' he said, 'I have seen the danger in which I stand. I no longer want to depend on words, nor indeed on the Pope's grace. I mean to apply myself to establishing this *signoria* of mine.' To which the Venetian replied: 'You are very sensible. Without the Pope, you and your prospects wouldn't last more than four days.'[20]

Three years later, this prophecy was fulfilled.

On the evening of 15 July the Duke of Bisceglie walked out of the Vatican. In St Peter's Square, just under the Loggia delle Benedizioni (the balcony from which the Popes bestow their blessing on the crowd), he was assailed by masked cut-throats. Defending himself with all the vigour of his twenty years, he tried to get away to safety. But other members of the gang cut off his line of retreat, felling him to the ground. The shouts of his two companions brought out the Papal Guard. The Duke's assailants, who had been dragging him off to where a large group of their accomplices stood waiting, with horses (their task probably being to whisk him away and dump him in the river) now took to their heels.

The wretched youth was carried into the Vatican, his skull split open by a sword-stroke, one gash in his arm, another in his thigh, and recovered consciousness just as a prelate was giving him absolution *in articulo mortis*. Lucrezia and Sancia came hurrying round, and from that moment never left his bedside. The Pope himself kept watch at the door of the sick-room. King Frederick, who was at once informed, sent his best physician. After a week the patient began to mend. Cesare too paid him a visit, in the Pope's company. On going out afterwards he is said to have muttered: 'What is not done at lunch can be done at dinner.'[21]

The lightning-swift disappearance of those who carried out the attack, and a certain slackness and negligence in the subsequent investigations—promptly noted by the ambassadors—prevented any certain identification of the person, or persons, responsible. But from the very beginning one fearful name was, privately, on all men's lips: that of Cesare. Various motives for the crime were attributed to him: resentment at Carlotta's refusal of his suit; an attempt to bind the Pope still more closely to the French by eliminating from the family this surviving link with Aragon; the convenience of making Lucrezia available for some new political-cum-matrimonial manoeuvre; and, inevitably, jealousy, fermented in the foul precipitate of his incestuous passions. However, now as previously, weighty presumptive factors made suspicions converge on the Orsini, who were convinced (not without reason) that the Duke of Bisceglie had been working against them. He had, it was said, reached a secret understanding with the Colonna clan now allied to the King of Naples, and was aiding them to the detriment of the Orsini.

Nevertheless, the young Duke himself was convinced of Cesare's guilt; he now—a decision he announced through clenched teeth—made up his mind to carry out a vendetta. Both Lucrezia and Sancia did all they could to dissuade him from his purpose, but in vain. The Pontiff had guards posted all round the convalescent's bedchamber—an equally useless precaution, as it turned out. On 18 August Alfonso looked through his window, and saw Cesare strolling in the garden below. He promptly grabbed his bow, and loosed off an arrow at him, which missed its target. Cesare's counterblow came before the day was out. Accounts of it vary over matters of detail, but are in substantial agreement as to the main course of events. Cesare entered the Duke's room with a few members of his bodyguard, sent out all those present, and called upon that sinister figure Don Miguel de Corella, known as Micheletto, to carry out his part of the business (he being a professional garrotter).

The Neapolitan ambassador sought refuge in the palazzo of his Spanish colleague. An attempt was made to force some Neapolitan servants of the Duke's to confess to a plot against Cesare's life, though it did not succeed. During a discussion with the diplomatic representative of Venice, on 23 August, the Pontiff said that Alfonso had made an attempt on Duke Valentino's life: the only reference he ever made to this sanguinary tragedy. A rumour circulated that, when Cesare's men burst in, Alfonso had fallen out of bed and banged his head on the stone floor, dying instantaneously, as the Florentine ambassador wrote, 'of fright and pain'. It is hard to say whether this version was derisive, or merely naive. An impenetrable cloak of silence descended on the murder. Lucrezia fell ill: she felt she was dying of grief, but still held her tongue. On 30 August, pale and thin, she set out for Nepi with an escort of six hundred cavaliers. There she remained, with her accustomed docility, a weak, resigned creature, until her father and brother should dispose of her once more.

After this forced interruption, Cesare made preparations to resume his campaign in the autumn. All through the sultry summer months Vatican officials continued to work at high pressure, accumulating essential funds, raising fresh regiments, and—since both Rimini and Faenza figured among his objectives—softening up Venetian resistance.

Alexander went about the task of restocking his Treasury (in order to finance this expedition) by a number of ingenious devices. Conspicuous among them was the simultaneous appointment of no less than twelve cardinals, eleven of whom (the twelfth being one of the two Borgias included in the batch) were required to disburse, in return for the much-coveted red hat, sums ranging from a minimum of 10,000 to a maximum of 25,000 gold ducats.

The problem of manpower was somewhat more difficult. The French troops stationed in Italy—without whom nothing could be done—were at present committed to the perennial Florentine border campaign against Pisa. It was a piece of good luck that at this point the Pisans gave them a sharp drubbing and forced them to raise the siege, thus rendering them available once more. Meanwhile Valentino was making a most valiant effort to improve things on his own account, augmenting and training his personal troops—the nucleus of what was soon to become the finest army in Italy—and enrolling a number of distinguished *condottieri* under his banner: Vitellozzo Vitelli, Gian Paolo Baglioni, Ercole Bentivoglio, Alexander Farnese, Achille Tiberti, and other warrior-scions of the Roman nobility.

Venice's scowling hostility was softened by a most provident recrudescence of the Turkish threat, which now drew so alarmingly close to the Serene Republic that it had her on her knees before the Vatican. The islands and commercial colonies of the Levant fell, one by one, into the hands of the infidels, who plundered their wealth and impaled their inhabitants. The Aegean and the Adriatic were both dominated by the Crescent; Moslem hordes reached Bosnia, and thrust on in a series of lightning raids that brought them as far as Taglia-mento and, finally, to the walls of Vicenza. What did the Venetians want? European backing for the crusade, and the collection of funds—through the normal method of tithes and special levies—to finance a war of liberation. Alexander VI, though still faced with the same kind of reluctance on the part of the Western powers as had all but martyred Callistus III, now at last girded himself for the struggle against these Moslem barbarians. He promised vigorous action by the Vatican, and was in fact as good as his word, undertaking an in-tense diplomatic campaign to arouse Europe, and providing generous support for Venice's endeavours. His tone, however, began to change. The ingratiating amiability which till lately had characterized it was now reinforced by the stern note of a man who is in a position to deliver reproofs and assert his claims. He had the whip-hand. The Venetian Senate not only pledged itself to abandon Rimini and Faenza to their fate, but appointed Cesare Captain of the Republic, conferred the title of 'Venetian gentleman' upon him, and presented him with a palazzo in case he might ever make a stay on the lagoon.

Before the campaign opened, there came the bloodless capture of Cesena, effected through an astute exploitation of the internecine quarrels between the Martinelli and Tiberti families. On 2 August of that year (1500) the city fell into the hands of the pro-Borgia faction after a tiny *coup d'état*. Faced with the Vatican's threat of harsh reprisals if the opposition group made the slightest move, Cesena surrendered to Duke Valentino. Bertinoro and Savignano followed its example. The Borgias showed themselves equally adroit at this type of conquest, which, in political terminology, is normally referred to as 'peaceful penetration'.

After the astrologers had given it as their opinion that 1 October was indica-ted as the most propitious day for the inception of his undertaking, Cesare put an end to this Roman interlude. On 30 September he held a review of his troops: not less than 12,000 men in all, including the 300 knights and 2,000 mercenaries given him by Louis XII, the bands which the various *condottieri* brought with them, and some recently recruited soldiers of fortune. But the pearl and flower of the army about to take the field was his Spanish-Italian militia, amongst whom the hardy inhabitants of the Romagna were very soon to show themselves pre-eminent. This highly trained and disciplined body of men had superb *esprit de corps* and was fanatically devoted to him. Its members were equipped with splendid uniforms, weapons, and armour: steel helmets, spears and swords, yellow-and-red jerkins with Cesare's coat of arms on the breast. His heart beat proudly at the sight of them, and with good reason.

Valentino marched out on 1 October, accompanied by a princely staff, well furnished with cash, and followed by an artillery-train which had no equal throughout the peninsula, and played a noteworthy part in making him so formidable an opponent. (Too late did Italy realize, in this confrontation with France and Spain, that her wealth and culture could only be protected behind bristling rows of cannon.) No one knew where he was making for, whether Pesaro, Rimini, or Faenza. He vanished into the Umbrian valleys. Torrential and incessant rain forced him to call a halt at Deruta.

He had been there four days when news reached him that Pandolfo Malatesta, the brutal and rapacious Lord of Rimini—preferring the sweet tinkle of ducats to the cannons' ponderous measure as background music for his surrender— had on 10 October come to terms with Giovanni Olivieri, the Duke's lieu tenant-general at Cesena. After handing over his entire domain *en bloc*, Mala testa had taken ship for Cervia.

That same day, in Pesaro, the populace gathered below Giovanni Sforza's fortress, and staged a pseudo-demonstration of pretended loyalty and enthusiasm, their object being to lure him out and get their hands on him. Lucrezia's ex husband smelt a rat, and set out his brother Galeazzo instead, who came back jubilant and deeply touched. The next day another identical demonstration took place; once again this astute *seigneur* sent his brother, who, this time, did not return. Under cover of darkness Sforza fled like a hunted criminal, without 'so much as a change of shirt'. He boarded a 'light bark'—by now he carried precious little weight himself—and prayed for a wind that would blow him swiftly to Venice.

The ignominious collapse of these two fiefs showed not only that they were rotten, and surrounded by the hatred of their subjects, but that reports of the good government set up by Valentino in those areas so far conquered had already begun to produce excellent propaganda effects on the populace at large.

Cesare entered Pesaro on the evening of 27 October, wearing black velvet over his chain-mail, and steel-gauntleted, riding a dapple-grey horse. He had come from Fano. In pelting rain, he passed between two packed ranks of cheering onlookers. Before him went a thousand cavalry, a thousand foot soldiers, and the athletic members of his personal bodyguard, each wearing a black velvet doublet and mantle, with a scaled bandolier in the form of a hydra, and a dagger at his side. Behind him came a hundred halberdiers, in pink-and black cloth uniforms. He entered the fugitive's palazzo, which still contained numerous traces of Lucrezia's sojourn, and—since he was making only a very brief stop here—at once set to work. That distinguished citizen of Pesaro Pandolfo Collenuccio, back home again for the first time after long years of exile, had a long discussion with Cesare in his capacity as ambassador from Ercole I d'Este, and was quite won over by the Duke's charm and energy, the vast scope of his ideas. From one of Collenuccio's letters we learn that on this occasion Valentino went to bed shortly before dawn, but a few brief hours later was up again and as active as ever.

On 30 October Cesare entered Rimini, and at once set preparations afoot for the conquest of Faenza. He knew the city would put up a stubborn resistance, and that he woud have to 'attack it fiercely'.[22] Its overlord was the fifteen-year-old Astorre III Manfredi, a svelte and proud adolescent who had grown up in the shadow of a domestic tragedy. He was only three when his mother— Francesca Bentivoglio, daughter of the so-called 'tyrant' of Bologna—murdered her husband in their bedchamber, with the aid of some hired assassins. Her motive was conjugal jealousy, diabolically encouraged by her relatives, who wanted Faenza under their control. Immediately afterwards the citizens, seeing in this child the guarantee of their independence, proclaimed him their overlord, and pressed round him with near-idolatrous devotion.

Now, on Valentino's approach, they cut down all trees in the surrounding countryside, shut themselves up within the walls, and prepared to resist. One by one the strongholds round about fell to Valentino's assaults, but Faenza itself proved firm and solid as any rock. Neither the close siege maintained by the assailants, nor the fierce bombardments (which continued for days on end), nor the assaults, nor the attempts to corrupt and infiltrate the garrison for purposes of betrayal, sufficed to crack it open.

With late November came heavy snowstorms, which forced Cesare to raise the siege. He wintered at Cesena, with brief visits to Forlí and Rimini, busying himself with the administrative organization of his domains, and, above all, finding relief for his fretting impatience in a wild round of entertainment: all-night balls, banquets, hunting-parties, love-affairs, bull-fights, rustic festivals, and trials of strength at which he put down the local country Samsons. It would seem that during this interlude his character revealed itself in a new light. A gay and simple exuberance, limpid as spring-water, broke through the crust of calculation and cracked the mask of toughness. His repressed childhood, characteristic of a man who grew up in an atmosphere of unremitting discipline, had a late resurgence. Even the famous abduction of Dorotea Caracciolo can be fitted, as a sort of light-hearted prank, into the overall mood of this period. (The lady in question was one of the most beautiful creatures in all Italy, the daughter of Roberto Malatesta, and married to a Neapolitan *condottiere* in the service of the Most Serene Republic. She was captured by Cesare—very gallantly—while travelling between Urbino and Venice. Despite the uproar this incident produced in the Courts of half Europe, it was not until December 1503 that she was able to rejoin her husband, after spending almost three years at Cesare's side.)

The siege of Faenza was resumed, with extreme violence, when winter was over, and culminated in three successive general assaults between 16 and 21 April. A traitor who climbed down from the walls to reveal the desperate plight of the besieged, and indicate the weakest points in the defences, was promptly hanged by Cesare, who felt unbounded admiration for Faenza's citizens, and said that with troops of their calibre he would quickly conquer all Italy. On 25 April the city at last surrendered, gasping, and bleeding from countless wounds. It received the honourable and generous terms which its heroism deserved: *inter alia*, a guarantee that Astorre and his relatives would be at full liberty to go whithersoever they pleased, without let and hindrance, keeping their estates intact. But when the young dispossessed sovereign and his natural brother Giovanni Evangelista met Cesare, they were so spellbound by his charm, and so dazzled by the prospect of living in the radiance of his glory, that they accepted an invitation to stay with him.

They had no idea they were putting themselves in the destructive hands— always to be feared, but most of all when they caressed one—of a man con/ strained by no rules save those of coldly logical reasons of State. They were equally unaware that in certain situations reasons of State could call for the suppression of dispossessed sovereigns in order to forestall the possibility of any attempts at restoration.

From that moment we have only fragmentary evidence for their activities. But on 20 June 1501, less than two months after Faenza fell, they were locked away in Castel Sant'Angelo; and on 9 June the following year they were fished out of the Tiber with stones tied round their necks.

Astorre, too, was long remembered in popular ballads:

> Weep, you of Faenza who have lost so true
> A lord, so noble and fine was he.
> Weep, and let all the world weep too.
>
> With Valentino I go on alone
> Since fortune wills things thus . . .

BORGIA AND ESTE

Cesare did not delay for one moment. From the very outset of his conquest, in the clear-sighted knowledge that he must act fast, before Louis XII took back his troops and mobilized them for his own imminent attack on Naples, he deliberately forced the pace. From Rome, where Alexander VI had now proclaimed him Duke of the Romagna, he caught echoes of the triumphant outburst provoked by his occupation of Faenza. Meanwhile he was on the march again.

His first objective was Castel Bolognese; it would have been Bologna itself, had it not been for the French veto, which placed this city off limits for him. Employing the excuse of the aid which Giovanni Bentivoglio had offered the defenders of Faenza (aid which in fact they had scornfully refused), he ordered him to hand the place over. Then, with a quick series of raids on various towns, and a threatening advance, he put himself in a strong position to dictate terms. He was at Villa Fontana when two ambassadors arrived from Bologna, at a breakneck gallop, to tell him that their master accepted his request without cavil. But Valentino was no longer content with Castel Bolognese. As a price for restoring the territories he had occupied, and for once more coming to the assistance of the Bentivoglio family, he asked that the citizens of Bologna should for three years furnish him with a hundred men-at-arms and three hundred horses; that they should pay an allowance for their maintenance; and that they should pledge themselves to send a son of the Bentivoglio family to fight beneath his banner, together with 3,000 men.

Then he burst into Tuscany. This was the booty which lay closest to his covetous heart; but it, too, was debarred from his eager talons by Louis XII, who had begun to observe his movements with uneasy suspicion. Florence, exhausted by her Pisan war, suspected the worst—all the more so since in the shadow of the Borgia banner stood the irresistible Giuliano de' Medici, and with him there came the threat of a possible *coup* by the still very active Medici faction. A peremptory Brief from the Pope, prompted by dictates of caution, forbade Cesare to launch any offensive in the Republic, and intimated that he should return to Rome at once. This was at a time when the Orsini (themselves kinsmen of the Medici) were persistently badgering him for action against Florence, while the ferocious Vitellozzo Vitelli (whose brother the Florentines had murdered) prostrated himself at his feet in floods of tears, begging to be given a free hand for a vendetta.

Valentino's goal was Piombino, *signoria* of the Appiano family: a prize of minor importance, but secure, and set for good measure on the flank of Tuscany. Paying no heed to his father's command, he asked Florence for free passage through her territories. Florence agreed to grant this, on four conditions: that his troops advanced by separate isolated units, that they took different roads, that they did not enter any fortified cities, and that they did not bring with them either Vitellozzo, or the Orsini, or any Florentine exiles (amongst whom was Giuliano). Cesare came back with four insolent and exorbitant demands of his own, made solely for purposes of intimidation. The Signoria was to appoint him its *condottiere*; it was to abstain from helping the Lord of Piombino in any way whatsoever; it was to hand over certain hostages, selected by Vitellozzo; and it was either to accept the return of the Medici, or else to set up some government which it would be possible to trust. Then he pressed ahead, ignoring a second Brief from the Pope. With his present line of behaviour, his cool audacity reached a point not far from madness. Every further step he took was a challenge that bore the risk of disaster.

This daring psychological manoeuvre gave the Signoria something of a nervous shock. An agreement was concluded on 15 May at Campi Bisenzio. Camouflaging their humiliation behind a mask of amiability, the Florentines granted Cesare, for three years, a *condotta* of three hundred menatarms, together with an annual allowance of 36,000 ducats, not to mention free passage through their territory, and their own undertaking not to give the Lord of Piombino any kind of support. With a further blackmailing demand for 9,000 ducats in advance, and a generous supply of artillery—a demand which, as he was well aware, could not possibly be accepted—he extracted the refusal which he needed. This would be his excuse for giving Vitellozzo the satisfaction of pursuing a vendetta, perpetrated over a vast area, with every kind of violence and devastation.

The territory behind Piombino, together with the islands of Elba and Pianosa, fell in a flash before Valentino's determined assault. The Pope, meanwhile, had sent him a fleet of fifteen warships. Jacopo IV Appiano, leaving his brother Gherardo in command, slipped through the enemy's guardposts and went off to offer the Genoese a chance of acquiring his State. Despite the extreme modesty of the price he asked, they shook their heads. Then he tried to carry his case to Louis XII, but was turned back at the French frontier.

Leaving Vitellozzo, together with Giulio and Paolo Orsini, to storm Jacopo's little capital (an aim which they only achieved three months later, by starving the defenders out), Cesare hurried off to Rome, whence he and the French would soon embark on the campaign against Naples.

From Naples, in September, he came back to the shady haven of the Vatican,

with 20,000 ducats paid him by France, 20,000 more from Spain, the credit
for the seizure of Capua—an episode which clinched the whole campaign—
and a dark stain on his reputation because of the sack and other crimes which
followed the city's capture: amongst the most infamous incidents in the whole
history of warfare.

With the Pope's blessing, and behind the hypocritical camouflage of an
undertaking destined to guarantee bases suitable for a decisive crusade, in
November 1500 the two signatories of the dubious Treaty of Granada divided
up the Kingdom between them. While the Spanish Gran Capitano and the
French marshal Béraud Stuart d'Aubigny—in conformity with the secret instructions of their respective sovereigns—both warily kept on the alert for that
not far distant moment when each of the two aggressors would try to eliminate
the other, the last King of the Aragonese dynasty was on his way to France,
accompanied by Sannazzaro and a few faithful friends.

The Borgia vendetta had run its course. But they, who never loved the French,
now had ample cause to ask themselves whether, by encouraging the enslave-
ment of Italy to Louis XII, and by aiding him to establish himself on the frontiers of the Papal State, they had not paid too high a price for the furtherance of
Cesare's career.

A picture of Rome during this period (in somewhat heightened colours) is
given by Agostino Vespucci, clerk to the Florentine Chancellery, writing in
that coarse, humorous style they both affected to his friend Niccolò Machiavelli:
'The Pope, it seems to me, is being given furiously to think by this Turkish
rumour, which already is much noised abroad; he is beginning to sigh and say:
Heu, quae me tellus, quae me aequora possunt accipere? He doubles the palace guards
day and night, *praebet se quibuscumque difficillimum, et tamen animus eius sullaturit et
proscripturit in dies magis*, so that, *omnibus videntibus*, he strips this man of his
possessions and that of his life, some he sends into exile, others to the galley-
bench; in another case again he will confiscate a man's house and put some
marrano [recently converted Jew or Moor] into it: *et haec nulla aut levi de causa.*
Further, he lets the said *marrani* commit many outrages upon the barons and
their friends, laying hands on their possessions, stripping their warehouses and
huiusmodi mille.' It was, in fact a period during which, because of the Aragonese
decline, the Borgia big stick began to fall on those Roman families which had
used Aragon's support to harass the Pontiff, put pressure on the Borgia clan,
and keep the whole Papal State in confusion. The previous year the Caetani
had been bullied into submission; now it was the turn of the Colonna and the
Savelli. Excommunicated, and in great consternation, they saw all their finest

possessions—Castelgandolfo, Rocca di Papa, Sermoneta, Genazzano, and others—confiscated and occupied. None of them could escape.

Vespucci went on: 'There is a better market for those benefices which have cost nothing but a titular offering in kind. The Rota has ceased to function, since *omne ius stat in armis*, and in these *Marrani, adeo*, to such an extent, that the Turk appears a necessity, since Christians take no step to extirpate this carrion of mankind: *ita omnes qui bene sentiunt, uno ore locuntur.*' And he concluded: 'It remains for me to say that (as observers have noted) apart from the Pope, who has his illicit flock with him permanently, every evening twenty-five or more women, between the time of the Ave and one o'clock, are brought to the Palace on somebody's crupper, *adeo*, to such an extent that the whole Palace has openly become a brothel, stained with filthiness of every sort.'

As a contrast to the Florentine's lethal epistolary prose style there was the clumsy Latin of Burchard, who in his house on the Via del Sudario—a meeting-place for Rome's German colony—filled pages of his *Diary* with episodes such as that of Alexander VI and Lucrezia looking on, with great enjoyment, at a furious coupling of stallions and female donkeys, or that of the banquet which Cesare gave for the Pontiff and his sister during the evening of 30 October 1501, at which there appeared fifty 'honest whores', first as fellow-guests, then as naked dancers, and finally as animals involved in various games and competitions which only a perverted imagination could have dreamed up.

The improbability of this picture is so manifest that we can safely number it among those other lewd fabrications which hate-inspired and slanderous malice accumulated round the Borgias, in a dense cloud of poisonous and lubricious whispering. Even if we make every allowance, for the *mores* of the day and the profligate inclinations of the characters involved, to the full extent authorized by our most reliable evidence, the very idea that Valentino could lay on so monstrous an evening's entertainment for his father and sister still remains, quite literally, inconceivable. Against such a possibility there stand, not only the nature of their known relations one with the other, which is far removed from the familiarity of tavern-libertines, but also Cesare's own character. To anyone who has seriously studied the facts of his life, and the revealing details of his psychological make-up, this picture of a vulgar Trimalchio is wholly unacceptable. Cesare was young and hot-blooded, it is true. The list of women whom he courted, ravished, loved, bought and bent, willy-nilly, to his desires goes on for ever. Some have a permanent niche in history as a kind of constellation round his name, from that 'honest courtesan' of Florence, Fiammetta Micheli, whose house can still be seen in Rome, to Countess Maria Díaz

Garlón; from Dorotea Caracciolo to Pantasilea Baglioni, wife of Bartolomeo d'Alviano; from Lucrezia's maid of honour Drusilla, by whom he probably had his two illegitimate children Camilla Lucrezia and Gerolamo, to an un-known mistress who, in the summer of 1504, voluntarily shared his imprison-ment. But in addition to his passionate senses the man had a lofty mind. Into these love-affairs he somehow contrived to inject a note of wistful sentimentality, mid-way between the Petrarchan and the romantic, which reflected the secret hue of his inner life—a life in which reckless self-confidence was sometimes assailed by a presentiment of imminent death, and a fatalism which took its temper from certain profound and mysterious voices. His favourite love-song— so much his favourite that it was handed down, in one sixteenth-century manu-script, as 'Duke Valentino's choice'—harped on the themes of separation and distance:

> Your sweet features will always
> Stay in my memory . . .

And on an exquisite medallion (undoubtedly commissioned by him as a love-token) we find two lines of verse which strikingly evoke the picture of a Cesare very different from that suggested in the pages of Burchard:

> Bend your eyes in pity to my lament
> Since Fortune wills you not to yield consent

At the same time it was serious, and to some extent symptomatic, that rumours such as those picked up by the German master of ceremonies should in fact circulate concerning the Borgias.

A month and a half after the episode of this alleged banquet, there issued from the Spanish encampment at Taranto that anonymous pamphlet (in all likelihood written by some member of the Colonna faction) which goes under the name of the *Letter to Savelli*: a compendium, one might almost say a direc-tory, of Borgia infamy. It listed every crime attributed to the various members of the family—simoniac double-dealing, wantonness, cruelty, treachery, malversa-tion, rapine, incest and murder. The echoes which this document has aroused down the ages, and the degree of credence given to it, have amply avenged the Roman nobility for the spoliations they underwent.

Alexander VI roared with laughter as he read this effusion, whereas Cesare became furiously angry. He was, in fact, still smarting from its impact when, on 5 December 1501, he made an example of a certain Neapolitan who (while strolling through the suburbs, masked for Carnival) had made it clear that the contents of the pamphlet were familiar to him. A spy informed Cesare, who at once had the man arrested and brought before the Curia of Santa Croce. Not long afterwards, people saw one of this careless talker's hands, neatly severed, hung out from a window in the same building, with his tongue attached to the little finger. For two days it continued to adorn the grille—a persuasive invitation to silence.

Even during this period of waiting, which (with a few brief interruptions) lasted from September 1501 until the June of 1502, Valentino led the capricious and unpredictable existence which he found congenial in a pause between two campaigns.

If it was true, as Vespucci wrote, that the Pope made himself difficult of access, Cesare was downright elusive. Foreign ambassadors were forced to kick their heels for days at a time in his ante-chambers, or left to tramp the sidewalks of Rome until they got so exasperated that they gave up and went home. Even the envoys from the Este, who had come on a matter of such high interest as Lucrezia's marriage, were subjected to the same treatment. Twice in succession Valentino—indolently lolling in bed—received them, with his famous spell-binding charm and amiability; but after that, they never again managed to cross his threshold. They went and complained to the Pontiff, who met their remon-strances, and their pleas for his good offices on their behalf, with polite sighs of regret. He was very sorry, he said, but the Duke had his own somewhat idio-syncratic way of life, turning day into night and *vice versa*; and he consoled them with the story of certain gentlemen from Rimini, who had been waiting for over two months in the hope of getting a personal interview with him.

At the same time, Valentino's secretaries and servants could have added that there were certain individuals who fell into a quite different category. The mo-ment they set foot in Rome, they needed only to whisper their name, and they would be received at once, whatever the hour. In carefully-protected seclusion, Valentino was busy, weaving and interlacing the threads of secret agreements with various traitors, lodged in the palazzi of his designated victims, to prepare the ground for the campaign of aggression he now had in mind.

From melancholy Nepi, Lucrezia had, some while since, returned to Rome, ready for whatever new political use her family might make of her. Widowed through Cesare's action, she now awaited the decision—by him and the Pope—which would put an end to her widowhood. The eyes of her two provident relatives had already fallen on the Duke of Ferrara's son—another Alfonso, so that the lucky girl would not even be called upon to make an effort when getting used (in moments of intimacy) to substituting her third husband's name for that of her second.

Negotiations for this match went on for months and proceeded with laborious slowness. The Borgias regarded such a marriage as in the highest degree advantageous. The family had a European reputation; and the geographical location of the Duchy of Este, on the borders of the Venetian Republic and the Romagna—not to mention the military weight it carried in the lineup of the peninsula's various forces—carried certain obvious political and strategic advantages. The Este themselves had no less strong and open an interest in such a marriage. Their *signoria* was an ancient ecclesiastical fief, exposed to the danger of intervention by armed force. This match, they hoped (perhaps illusorily), might act as a kind of lightningconductor. No one can say for certain what the Borgias had in mind when they passed Lucrezia on to the Este. Did they mean to exclude the Duchy from their programme of conquest, contenting themselves with this guarantee of its alliance? Or were they placing their valuable (if docile) pawn there with some more insidious ploy in view? At all events, without the catastrophe of 1503, it is hard to believe that Ferrara would have long been able to save itself from the expansion of Cesare's 'Kingdom'.

At first, it seems, Alfonso d'Este proved somewhat squeamish, and showed a certain reluctance to take into his bed a lady with quite so stormy a past behind her. In actual fact, the Este were in no position to cast the first stone against the Borgias. Though culturally remarkable, their past history had more than one scabrous or bloodbespattered page in it—most notoriously, the episode of Parisina.[23] The events connected with the various successions formed a whole sequence of gory episodes, crammed with conspiracies, struggles between the few legitimate sons and the innumerable bastards (or bastard's bastards), and various throatslittings, poisonings, or beheadings of kinsmen by kinsmen. The prospective bridegroom's father—not to look too far back in the pages of these domestic annals—had shown a quite remarkable lack of emotion when it proved necessary to decapitate his nephew Niccolò, who had been found guilty of attempted usurpation. It was not to be wondered at that he should now make so many demands over the matter of the dowry. An immensely rich man, he was at the same time both ruthlessly grasping and quite shamefully mean. In 1473 he had thought up the custom of going out, as he called it 'for a little adventure': this meant issuing forth from his palazzo towards nightfall, on certain days of the year, and pressurizing citizens who were more welltodo than he was into giving him presents, either cash or kind. For this marriage, he wanted the Pope to bestow upon Lucrezia 200,000 gold ducats, guaranteed by the Borgia estates in the Romagna, plus the cities of Cento and Pieve, together with the harbour of Cesenatico; he also asked that the feudal dues which Ferrara was obliged to pay the Church each year should be cut by fourfifths. It was during the course of these exhausting negotiations that Valentino refused to give any further audiences to the Este emissaries; as for Alexander VI, he was heard to remark, with a grimace of disgust, that Ercole 'went about his business like a huckster'. They settled on 100,000 ducats, cash down; but this sum was augmented by over 200,000 more in jewellery, works of art, rare furniture, clothes and linen, and horses (complete with trappings and saddle-cloths). To give some idea of Lucrezia's fabulous trousseau, one need only point out that it included two hundred chemises, each of them valued at a hundred ducats, while the trimming for one dress alone cost fifteen, each sleeve thirty, a dress 20,000, and a hat more than 10,000. Translated into present-day values, these figures would leave one absolutely flabbergasted. And on top of all this, the gift of the two localities asked for—with not the reduction, but the abolition, of the tribute. The Borgias had numerous sins on their conscience, but no one could accuse them of niggardliness. Faced with such generosity even Isabella (the bridegroom's sister, and married to the hero of Fornovo, she had watched the bargaining, from Mantua, with a very puritanical twist to her mouth) found her objections beginning to crumble.

After a fortnight's travelling, the party coming to fetch away the bride reached Rome two days before Christmas: a cavalcade of 500 persons, prominent among them the cream of the aristocracy from Ferrara and the other cities of the Duchy, together with Cardinal Ippolito and other members of the Duke's family. Cesare, in French costume, with pages, 100 gentlemen on horseback, and 200 Swiss halberdiers (to which must be added the 2,000 troops accompanying Rome's civic authorities) went out to meet his guests at the Porta del Popolo. The splendid parade—the most memorable one of Alexander VI's entire pontificate—set off amid trumpet-blasts and peals of ordnance from the ramparts of Castel Sant'Angelo. After a visit of homage to the Pope, the delegation then called upon the bride, who was awaiting them in a white dress woven with gold thread, a Spanish tunic trimmed and lined with sable, rich brocade sleeves, and a green veiled bonnet which bore strips of beaten gold, and was decorated with pearls. She stood there, leaning on the arm of an elderly Italian gentleman dressed in black velvet, with a gold collar, and curtseyed as she greeted her visitors. Her gracefulness enchanted them.

From that moment, Borgia Rome was caught up by a giddy whirlwind, in which, for the next thirteen days, Lucrezia and Cesare could be seen spinning, like figures transformed into bright revolving meteors. Everyone else seemed reduced to the status of spectators. Receptions, mock sea-fights, *corridas*, recitals, and spectacular Moorish balls followed one another without a break, against a background of Roman Carnival, and in an extraordinary atmosphere which left the guests from Ferrara dazed and breathless. But the image which remained most firmly impressed on everyone, from those fabulous, crazy days of colour and music, was that of Cesare and Lucrezia, turning and twisting to the fiery rhythms of a Spanish dance, laughing, lost to the world, with the air of people bidding farewell to their youth.

On 6 January (1502) the new Duchess of Ferrara took her leave of the Pope. It was a long discussion, full of injunctions and advice. Then Cesare appeared in the doorway, ready to take her away. With sad eyes Alexander watched the departure of this daughter who resembled him so closely, not only by reason of her mild and amiable disposition, but also (to judge from the most reliable iconographic evidence) as regards her actual features. He was still calling after her as she went, telling her to keep cheerful, and to rely on him completely if there was anything she needed. He was never to set eyes on her again.

Something still harder for her to bear was separation from her little son Rodrigo and young Giovanni (the Roman Infante). She left them both in Cesare's tender care and already assured of ample and solid guarantees for a future of the very first rank. Alexander VI had made two Duchies out of the rich lands he took from the Caetani, the Savelli and the Colonna, conferring them on Lucrezia's two boys, Rodrigo getting the Duchy of Sermoneta, and Giovanni that of Nepi.

Lucrezia set off, with the large party from Ferrara, at three o'clock in the afternoon. She wore a gown of gold thread covered with crimson brocade stripes and lined with ermine; the white mule she rode had saddle-cloth and trappings of beaten silver, gold-fringed. The whole procession numbered over a thousand persons. Cesare, who at his own expense had raised an escort of honour—two hundred cavaliers from the most illustrious patrician families, with musicians and singers and clowns to lighten her journey—rode beside her for a long stretch of the road outside Rome. His melancholy, when he came back, dissolved into a smile at the thought of the pleasant surprises he had arranged for her benefit—with timely organization and a munificence worthy of the man he was—in the various cities she would stop at during her long trip: princely receptions, feasts, spectacles, presents. This was why he had wanted her itinerary to diverge from the shortest, most direct route, by way of Pesaro and the Romagna. It was not until 2 February that Lucrezia finally reached Ferrara, and began a new life, her second, under the auspices of virtue and culture.

As though to shake off the sadness induced by this separation, the Pope and Duke Valentino embarked at Civitavecchia, and went on a visit to Piombino and the island of Elba. It was a pleasant trip, of which Cesare took advantage to study existing fortifications and plan new ones. On their return journey they were surprised, and badly shaken, by the storm already mentioned above, which, though violent enough, was still not quite so lethal as many people in Italy could have hoped.

Early that spring, in Rome, Cesare Borgia was approached by Leonardo da Vinci—just then emerging from the long period of hand-to-mouth existence which followed that shipwreck of his prospects brought about by the Moor's fall in fortune. The Lord of Milan had been ambitious, intelligent, and most fortunate in his choice of artists; at his Court Leonardo had spent the seventeen happiest and most creative years of his entire life. But for the last two and a half years he had lived in a sad state of uncertainty. Neither at Mantua, with the Gonzagas, nor in Venice (where he had done research on certain diabolical bomb-like devices which, it was hoped, would blow the Turkish fleet out of the water), nor in Florence (where he had felt *dépaysé*, isolated, and eclipsed in the city's eyes by the bursting revelation of Michelangelo), had he found his true haven. Now he had come to offer his services to Duke Valentino: not as an artist, since at this period he was sick of painting, but as a military engineer, architect, and inventor.

A thrilling moment in history, this meeting between two men who both (though in very different ways) were such extraordinary figures: the one a youthful genius of action and living, who daily created the premises for the 'New Age' he dreamed of, and with matchless enthusiasm moulded the master-piece that was his own existence into the image of his intense and urgent spirit; the other, the greatest genius of the day in the field of art, scientific speculation and thought, already at the noon-day peak of his maturity.

Leonardo, then, came to Cesare with an offer of personal collaboration, for motives which his biographers by and large have failed to understand. They thus remain condemned to a state of perplexity when studying the close companion-ship which developed between the mild, abstracted, 'secretive' notary's son from Vinci and the formidable son of the Pope. The motives were many, and all strong ones. Leonardo knew that in Valentino he would find a patron with sufficient acumen and intellectual curiosity to give due credit to his astonishing claims as an inventor, which neither Ludovico nor the Venetians had taken seriously. He also trusted his generosity, for the costly backing of research and experiments. He admired Cesare's temperament, his brilliance, that moral in-dependence which left him free from all prejudice, and the interest which exceptional men aroused in him. There was, lastly, their identity of political and social outlook, abundantly and convincingly documented from Leon-ardo's own writings, where in scathing aphorisms he proclaims his contempt for the common herd, the need to neutralize 'magnates', or petty local tyrants, the place which force, strictness, and authority have in human government. One such phrase must suffice: 'Anything to root out a villain.' It could have been Cesare Borgia's motto. And who can say whether it, and others like it, may not have sprung from a contemplation of his career?

From the very first moment Valentino appreciated the greatness of the man facing him. We may well ask just what Leonardo's destiny might have been, and how many great pages this friendship might have written in the annals of history, had not Cesare's career been broken off little more than a year after they first met. Certainly Leonardo would have been spared a sad and declining old age, compounded from disappointments, weariness, exile and despair.

The first job Cesare gave him was to visit Piombino and conduct surveys for new fortification projects. At Urbino, Pesaro, Rimini, Cesena, and Imola— not to mention Rome itself—we catch rare but enlightening glimpses of this tireless genius (appointed the Borgia's architect and inspector of works by letters patent dated 18 August 1502 from Pavia), either at Cesare's side or else close on his heels, in the act of writing up his notes (to the accompaniment of marvellous little sketches) on the pages of a parchment-bound pocket-book which hung from his belt by a tiny chain. At the young Duke's behest, he was to carry out projects for military works, undertake and supervise construction jobs, and prepare siege-engines and other special machines for the difficult assault on Ceri; draw up proper plans for the scheme of the canal, harbour and fortifications at Cesenatico; and construct a meticulously accurate map of Imola (where he also may have built the villa, now destroyed, which was to be known as La Valentina).

The spare time he had left from his activities on Cesare's behalf he devoted to his own observations, scientific investigations, and studies. His patron not only left him ample leisure, but followed his enquiries with considerable interest, always showing himself eager to facilitate them in any way he could, and to get him the books he wanted. Evidence for this is provided by a note dated 1502, preserved in the minuscule *Manuscript L* now held by the Institut de France: 'Borgia will get you the Bishop of Padua's Archimedes, and Vitellozzo that belonging to the faubourg of San Sepolcro.'

The concentrated attention which he devoted to Piombino that spring made it clear that Cesare was taking a renewed interest in Tuscany. In May, Pisa re-peated its offer of voluntary surrender first made as far back as 1499. Alexander VI, who up to this point had hesitated and temporized for fear of complications, decided that the moment had come, that it was 'now or never'. Louis XII would not listen to protests from Florence while he was preparing for a fresh descent into Italy to confront the Spaniards, and he stood equally in need of the Papal State's friendship and Cesare's military collaboration. Venice had too much trouble on her hands from the Turks to think about anything else. The ever-impecunious Maximilian (to whom Alexander sent a messenger provided with what amounted to a sort of blank cheque) would presumably be all too willing to sell his consent at a high price.

Thanks to the work that had been carried out behind the scenes by the Vatican, the leak in the Tuscan dyke suddenly grew larger. There was a Medici-inspired revolt at Arezzo, which opened its gates to a prompt irruption of Borgia troops under Vitellozzo, Gian Paolo Baglioni, and Bishop Giulio Vitelli. The entire Vale of Chiana passed into the hands of the *valentineschi*, as Duke Valentino's supporters were known. Cesare's banner flew over the walls of Pisa. The Borgias were clearly surprised by the rapid progress of events. The situation was developing faster than their plans had anticipated, and threatened to throw out the whole timing of their programme. It was only by a kind of miracle, and through their own frantic efforts, that they managed to keep a restraining hand on Vitellozzo, who was raging like a madman to hurl his forces against Florence.

Meanwhile Cesare had girt on his sword and taken the field for his third campaign.

THE PLOT OF THE CONDOTTIERI

On the evening of 20 June 1502 the thirty-year-old Guidobaldo da Montefeltro was dining in the cool of the countryside, at the Zoccolanti, not far from Urbino. He was heard to express some words of pity for the wretched Varano family, overlords of Camerino, against whom this new thrust of Valentino's was said to be aimed. In the middle of his remarks three couriers galloped up, one after the other, panting for breath, with news that bade fair to ruin his di-gestion. Cesare, said the first, had been seen leaving the Camerino road, and moving towards the Montefeltro's city. Cesare, gasped the second, was already at Cagli. Cesare's troops, the third cried hoarsely, had already cut off and en-circled Urbino itself.

Guidobaldo sprang to horse, rode back into the panic-stricken city, and hurried to his palazzo. By candlelight, and surrounded by anxious faces, he held one of the quickest and most desperate councils known to history. Sur-prise ruled out all possibility of resistance. Nothing remained but to attempt flight. Even this was risky enough. He took with him his nephew Francesco

Maria della Rovere, and surrounded by a small escort of archers, sallied forth into the countryside. Luckily his wife, Elisabetta Gonzaga, was at Mantua; so to Mantua he too made his way, travelling by night. He finally got there, aided by some lucky star, after seven days of difficult cross-country peregrinations during which—miraculously—he passed through the enemy's lines and the treacherous lands of the Romagna. The only possessions he brought to safety were the sum-mer clothes he stood up in.

Cesare entered Urbino, lance on thigh, at first dawn on the morning of the 21st. He received formal submission from the Mayor and other representatives of the people, assigned the various civic offices to new men, and had three individuals beheaded, amongst them Dolce de' Dotti, Guidobaldo's secretary: three traitors, it was whispered, who had undertaken to deliver their master into Cesare's hands, but instead had let him escape. He issued a proclamation in-viting the citizens to continue peacefully about their affairs. Finally, he lost him-self in rapturous contemplation of the Montefeltro palace, Luciano Laurana's masterpiece and 'the most beautiful royal residence in Italy'. He inspected its magnificent treasures, which could easily stand comparison with the collections in the Vatican: works by Giusto di Gand, Paolo Uccello, Piero della Fran-cesca, Pedro Berruguete and Melozzo da Forlí; statues and busts, medallions and miniatures, virtuoso jewellery and Flemish tapestries, and a priceless library crammed with works in Italian, Greek, Latin and Hebrew, with precious bindings and amazing ornamentation, chosen for the most part by that prince of bibliographers, Vespasiano da Bisticci. Too many possessions, pronounced Cesare, whose rapacity was stimulated by a fine aesthetic taste; and he displayed a remarkable connoisseur's flair when it came to stripping the various rooms, picking furniture, works of art, books and hangings to send to Cesena for the embellishment of his own palazzo—not to mention the consignment he dis-patched to the Vatican, to make the Pope forgive him for the real or imaginary crime of having carried out this manoeuvre without consulting him first.

In point of fact, such a piece of aggression did not figure in the original pro-gramme at all—or perhaps the idea was to make it appear unpremeditated. Guidobaldo was a friend, an ally, a meek and respectful 'vicar' of the Church, who paid his tribute regularly, never failed to send congratulations on the Duke's successes, and when asked for any service, performed it with exemplary conscientiousness. As recently as the previous year, Cesare had sent him a choice gift of oysters from Cesenatico, and since then, within the last few months, had let him know that he 'had no other brother in Italy save him'.

In the palace of the Este (who were related to Guidobaldo's wife) Lucrezia could no longer look anyone in the face without blushing for shame.

By way of reply to the murmur of indignation that had arisen from every part of the terrified peninsula, Cesare, in a letter to the Pope dated 21 June, explained that during the march on Camerino he had come upon proof positive that Guidobaldo had been supplying aid to the Varano family. Such treachery could not go unpunished.

The conquest went on, under the direction of his lieutenants, while he him-self delayed at Urbino for urgent discussions with two delegates from the Florentine Signoria. He had asked for this meeting himself, and was now expecting the Florentine envoys daily, for a clarification of mutual policy. They arrived on the 24th: Francesco Soderini, Bishop of Volterra, and his secretary Niccolò Machiavelli. He received them that same evening, in the silent palace of Montefeltro, where he now resided, surrounded by his numerous scowling bodyguards. This was the first occasion on which Machiavelli—the most acute and impassioned political observer of all time, the most enthusiastic and effect-ive future exegete of Cesare's personality, methods, and ideals, and of his achievement as a rationally perfect 'prince'—had come into contact with him; and his passionate curiosity beat its wings like a moth about the light which bewitches it, twitching its antennae.[24]

Valentino, in a lordly fashion, led off at once with the tone of a man who has suffered wrong. He harshly accused the Signoria of having violated the agree-ment concluded in May the previous year, of not having 'good intentions' towards him and of 'slandering him as a murderer'. He let fall a declaration which startled his two interlocutors: 'This government of yours is not to my liking, you will have to change it.' Then came the curt, snarling threat: 'Other-wise, you will very soon realize that I do not wish to live in this fashion; and if you do not find me a friend, you will experience my enmity.'

When the two envoys finally managed to interrupt this crackling indictment, they deprecated what had happened at Pisa and Arezzo, and conveyed the Signoria's desire that he should recall 'his man' Vitellozzo, the cross and incu-bus of Florence, from Tuscany. At this he struck like a snake.

'Do not look to me to do you this favour! . . . It is true that Vitellozzo is my man, but I swear to you that I never knew anything about the Treaty of Arezzo . . . I am by no means displeased by what you have lost; on the contrary, it has given me much enjoyment. . . .' Every phrase was a whiplash. Then, speaking of himself, he enunciated a plea in self-justification which burnt itself into Machiavelli's brain like a brand, and echoed in his memory for years, even after Cesare's fall and death: 'My task is not to tyrannize, but to destroy tyrants.'

Nothing could be truer—even though in destroying them he proceeded, of necessity, with their own methods, the only possible or valid ones for the age in which he lived, trampling down piety, loyalty, and every other standard.

The first discussion concluded with an injunction that they should make up their minds promptly. 'Between you and me,' he said, 'there can be no half-way measures. You must either be my friends or my enemies.' The second, the following day wound up with an ultimatum: the Signoria had four days in which to debate a reply on which the issue of peace or war would depend.

What was it that Valentino demanded? Confirmation of the *condotta* granted him a year earlier, with an annual stipend of 36,000 ducats. As a guarantee that the agreement would be observed, he wanted to reserve the right to dispose of the goods and persons of those Florentines resident in the Papal State and the Duchy of Romagna. Only on these conditions would he recall Vitellozzo. Otherwise, like Brennus the Gaul, he would throw his sword into the scales.

The duel between Cesare and Florence was in fact dominated by one factor which determined both the relentless threats of the one and the temporizing pro-crastination of the other: Louis XII's invasion. For Cesare this meant the end of all pressure on Tuscany; for the Signoria, freedom from his molestations. Hence the frantic haste of the one and the delaying tactics of the other.

It was because of this ultimatum that Machiavelli found himself galloping post-haste to Florence, while Soderini undertook the task of gathering all pos-sible clues as to Valentino's real intentions. This was a hopeless project, since Valentino never gave any such clues away. A master of silence no less than of the spoken word, he trusted no man in the world, and kept his lips hermetically sealed regarding his own decisions. He had so perfectly trained an army that he could strike camp and be on the march inside an hour—and when he set off, no one save he knew where they were going.

To gain precious time, the Signoria spread itself in assurances of friendship and—though accepting the Duke's requests in broad outline—haggled over the exact amount of the stipend, or insisted that the troops of the *condotta* should remain in Florentine territory. Meanwhile, Louis XII crossed the Alps. Cesare did not budge one inch from his position: it was all or nothing, he said, and he supported his reasons with such a wealth of argument that Soderini could scarcely keep in countenance. 'His brilliance and eloquence,' he wrote after-wards, 'know no limits.'

But Louis XII was now in Italy, and Cesare realized that he had lost the hand. He still tried to give Soderini pause for thought, saying that even if the French *were* in Italy, they would not be there for ever, and the problem was bound to come to the surface again. Then he said he would rather refer the question to the King of France and the Pope, declining all responsibility for what they might decide between them. Finally, he made yet another bid to extract a *quid pro quo* for something that had now become inevitable—the recall of Vitellozzo—showing himself generously prepared to make do with the confirmation of the *condotta* and 18,000 ducats on account. Deadline, 20 July.

But on the 19th Soderini left him high and dry, clambering on his mule and returning whence he had come. A French advance guard was sweeping through the Vale of Chiana, and there were hopes that it might dislodge Vitellozzo gratis. For once, with fortune's aid, the great gambler had had the tables turned on him.

While Cesare was busy with his own *coup de main* at Urbino, his troops had been working much the same trick on the little republic of San Marino, whither he subsequently dispatched the 'cruel and efficient' Ramiro de Lorca to arrange matters according to the by now well-known Borgia formula. The following day they burst into Camerino. Of the four sons of old Giulio Cesare da Varano (a petty tyrant of the type then in fashion, a fratricide when occasion demanded, and a tortuous intriguer and ruthless despot whose hobby happened to be art-patronage) only three were there with him; the fourth had gone off on a quick trip to Venice, in search of assistance. He had occasion to thank the gods for this decision, even if his journey proved useless, since his father, now blockaded in the stronghold of Pergola, was strangled there during October, while his three brothers—the youngest only seventeen—died shortly afterwards. These 'special jobs', were the work of Don Miguel de Corella, the Duke of Romagna's strong right arm: an arm incomparably expert in the use of the garrotte. It is, furthermore, of interest to note that Don Miguel was not, in fact, some crude, uneducated butcher, but a gentleman who lived daily in the company of Cesare, with whom he would appear to have been a student at the University of Pisa, and whose friendship he enjoyed. If he was prepared to present himself to the world behind the terrifying mask of a common executioner, that was due solely to his fanatical devotion. No one, not even after Valentino's fall, ever got him to break the silence which hid—beneath its deep and impenetrable waters—the explanation of so many enigmas in the history of the Borgias.

The trick played on Guidobaldo, and the fate which befell the Varano family, terrified those members of the squirearchy who had still survived unscathed; they now began to look around and tell tales among themselves like survivors from some multi-stage hurricane. The uncrowned, the despoiled, the fugitives and the exiles, having escaped Don Miguel's noose, began to hope that the brigand had filled his cup to overflowing with these latest exploits, and in so doing had signed his own death-warrant.

When Louis XII reached Milan, everyone hurried there with gifts and com-plaints: Giovanni Sforza, Guidobaldo, Francesco Gonzaga, a nephew of Varano's, two sons of Bentivoglio, delegates from Venice, envoys from Florence. It looked like a plenary assembly of the anti-Borgia liberation-front. The bearded Marquis of Mantua proclaimed himself ready to draw the sword of Fornovo once more and to assume command of a League war against the usurper.

Louis XII accepted the gifts benignly; but just how seriously he took the complaints became clear on the morning of 5 August, when news got out that he had left town, accompanied by a small escort, and gone to attend a meeting with Cesare. What had happened?

After the departure of Soderini, there reached the palace of Urbino one Francisco Troches, a fine humanist and Cesare's personal private secretary, now back from a mission to the King of France. As a result of the discussion he had with him, Valentino sent Vitellozzo an order to surrender Arezzo, and clear out of the place double-quick, unless he wanted Cesare to march on Città di Castello. Then, garbed as a Knight of Jerusalem, and with four officials only by way of escort, he sprang on his horse and rode away. He made a short stop at Ferrara to see Lucrezia again, who, with her husband, had settled in the gran-diose medieval Castel Vecchio, and at the time had just had a miscarriage. And now, he was here, with Louis.

On the unlikely chance that there was anyone to whom the King's act of extreme deference in meeting Valentino had not yet conveyed its clear and very simple message, the news that hourly leaked out from the castle soon blew away any last lingering shreds of illusion. Louis XII had insisted on his 'cousin' being his guest; he had provided him with clothes from his personal wardrobe; during the evening he had bustled about on foot at Cesare's dinner, ordering him the choicest delicacies; and before retiring for the night he had paid a visit, in his shirtsleeves, to the Duke's bedchamber.

One by one those who had come with their tales of woe went back home. The last to leave was the Marquis of Mantua, *condottiere*-designate of the defunct (and now buried) League. He had a proposal to make to Cesare. Two years before there had been talk of betrothing his son Federico to the daughter Duke Valentino had in France, Luisa. Well, why not resume negotiations? He would be only too happy to do so.

Cesare remained at the King's side throughout his stay in Italy. Their dis-cussions gave rise to a new agreement. While Cesare pledged himself to take part personally, with 10,000 men, in the forthcoming operations against the Spaniards for exclusive control of the Kingdom of Naples, Louis XII guaran-teed him three hundred knights and full liberty of action against the Bentivoglio of Bologna, the Baglioni of Perugia, and the Vitelli of Città di Castello. Naturally, appearances must be preserved, since he had furnished the Bentivoglio with a still-valid guarantee of protection. It was true that in the agreement such a guarantee was explicitly subordinated to the condition that the Church's own rights were not prejudiced—an escape clause which made it possible for him to shrug his shoulders while those entitled to his protection went under.

Cesare accompanied the King to Pavia, Genoa, and, on his homeward journey, as far as Asti. Then he wished him *bon voyage*, and galloped off at breakneck speed towards the Romagna, with the air of one who had lost too much time already, and felt the earth scorching the soles of his feet.

When he reached Imola he established himself in its great fortress, and with feverish energy began to organize the expedition against Bologna—an undertaking which called for the greatest sustained effort of his entire life, and had, moreover, to be carried through very fast, before Louis XII sent him off on campaign against the Gran Capitano. On every count—the city's military potential, the ability of the Bentivoglio family, and the predictable stubbornness with which their proudly loyal subjects would resist Cesare's unprovoked aggression—this looked like being an extremely tough ordeal. But so glittering was the prize that he had made up his mind to spare neither efforts nor means. Alexander VI had already justified the attack in advance, by accusing the Bentivoglio clan of misgovernment and of lending support to the rebels, for which he summoned them to appear before him in Rome. It is very likely that both Borgias, exulting in the freedom of action they had finally won from the French King, had a private and dazzling vision of Bologna as the future capital of the Duchy of Romagna. It was in fact the richest, most beautiful, and largest city in the whole Papal State. Its name alone shed glory on it.

Everything around Cesare functioned with perfect efficiency; but his secret intelligence service was something quite out of the ordinary. Suddenly, right in the middle of the preparations which he was making, with the assistance of his closest collaborators (including Leonardo), he seemed to stop short, like an animal that scents danger.

Five of his *condottieri* met in Todi, and held a discussion at which they decided to abstain from participation in the campaign against the Bentivoglio, and to take joint action to prevent any further territorial expansion of Duke Valentino's dominion.

The five included Vitellozzo Vitelli, Lord of Città di Castello, whom Cesare summed up to a nicety for Machiavelli's benefit: 'I cannot say I have

ever seen him perform a warm-hearted act, for which he makes the French
disease his excuse; all he is good for is to despoil defenceless countries, to rob
men who are afraid to face him, and to gain his ends through base treachery.'
There was Gian Paolo Baglioni, Lord of Perugia, fierce and intrepid, a brilliant
soldier, toughened by those savage internecine conflicts which perennially
bloodied his city; there was Oliverotto, Lord of Fermo, risen to power through
the murder of his maternal uncle, who had brought him up with such loving
and fatherly care; there were Paolo Orsini, Lord of Palombara, and Francesco
Orsini, Duke of Gravina, representatives of a family which, though it might
hitherto have saved itself by collaborating with the Borgias, could not forget
the campaign of 1496–7, or delude itself as to the fate it would suffer, all too
soon, through one of Alexander's notorious decretals.

Early in October the five *condottieri* gathered at La Magione, an Orsini-held
castle situated a few miles from the eastern shore of Lake Trasimeno. The
honours of the house were in the hands of Cardinal Battista Orsini, bowed down
with years and almost blind, but still enthusiastically attached to the realities of
this world, and with scant concern for the next one, a stout trencherman and
obsessional gambler. The gang was now increased by four new members, who
came in the guise of representatives: Ermete Bentivoglio, on behalf of his family;
Ottaviano Fregoso, representing his uncle, Guidobaldo da Montefeltro;
Antonio da Venafro and Guido Pecci, for Pandolfo Petrucci, Lord of Siena.

Here, in a freedom-loving and heroical atmosphere re-echoing with much
windy braggadocio, it was easy enough to proclaim that the tyrant must at all
costs be halted in his present positions, stripped of the spoils with which he had
grown great at other men's expense, and eliminated from the political scene in
Italy. Vitellozzo, between the fits of venereal convulsions which had forced him
to arrive for the meeting in a litter, did not hesitate to bind himself to a specific
deadline: within a year, they could rest assured, he would either have driven
Valentino out, or else hold him captive.

What was it drove these men, so full of rancour and terror, to engage on so
deadly a game, from which—as they very well knew—their opponent would
not suffer them to withdraw until he had played his very last card? Fear of being
struck down by his strong right hand; resentment at the inevitable admission of
this fear; the hatred and envy they felt for this priest's son whose career advanced
with such irresistible impetus, wiping out, from the stock of Italy's great potentates, whole families haloed in illustrious tradition. Experience, moreover, made
it plain that Cesare's cards were invariably winners. Only momentary annoy-
ance and the euphoric intoxication of that collective fantasy induced by highflown words ('cross the Rubicon under arms', 'all for one and one for all', 'to

die in this endeavour') could sustain them in such illusory arrogance. An interval of silence, after those first loud and confident proclamations, would suffice to deflate their heroics, and sink them in a bottomless pit of discourage-ment.

The military strategy which these confederates worked out was an excellent one: to put in the field, between them, 8,000 foot-soldiers and 600 men-at-arms ('in round numbers', they hastily specified); to launch an attack from Bologna in the direction of Imola, and at the same time to invade the Duchy of Urbino, where their operations would gain support from the anti-Borgia insurrection already in progress; and from the Duchy of Urbino to go back up the Adriatic coast, cut off Cesare's retreat, and catch him between two fires.

In the light of what followed, it became clear that this enterprise was like a worm-ridden apple. A number of maggots were busily tunnelling away in its substance: the lack of a leader they were all prepared to obey; individual greed, which devoted its energies (with hidden calculations on everyone's part) to swallowing up the biggest and best mouthfuls of the projected booty; and, above all, the progressive collapse of that lion-like extremism which had marked the venture at its outset. Some began to 'have second thoughts' on this topic; and all of them, one after the other, secretly took the prudent course of hedging their bets on both sides, and (whether sincerely or out of mere hypocrisy) seeking a reconciliation. In this way they all walked into the net which Valentino so affectionately held out for them.

The conspiracy of La Magione at once became public knowledge through-out the length and breadth of Italy. The news produced one effect of notable importance: it encouraged the rebels in the Duchy of Urbino. Having, by a neat stratagem, won control of the fortress of San Leo, they overwhelmed the Borgia garrisons, successfully promoted a general revolt in the name of freedom, and recalled Guidobaldo from Venice, whither his kinsman Francesco Gonzaga had sent him to await better times.

Cesare, Machiavelli was to affirm in his famous *Description of the means em-ployed by Duke Valentino for the destruction of Vitellozzo Vitelli, Oliverotto da Fermo, Signor Pagolo and the Duke of Gravina Orsini,* a work composed, for blatantly literary purposes, when the affair was over, 'found himself much affrighted at Imola. . . .' This is a wholly false assertion dictated by purely artistic considerations. Its aim was to produce a gloomy background at the start, to throw into even brighter prominence the courage shown by Cesare during the subsequent course of events and the decisive phase of his reaction to the danger. The Machiavelli of the *Description* is in fact given the lie by the

Machiavelli of the *Legation*—that is to say, the fifty-two letters which he himself, as a direct observer of the way the situation developed, and the Duke's conduct in it, sent day by day to the Dieci di Balía (the Florentine War Magistracy).

If Cesare *was* afraid, he gave not the least sign of it. He did not conceal his angry disappointment at this defection, which, by robbing him of a good proportion of his troops and forcing him to defend himself, cut short his preparations for the assault upon Bologna. Even less did he bother to hide the indignation which this act of betrayal aroused in him. Yet from the very first moment he appeared confident in himself, in his own superiority, in the success of his reprisals. His rage seethed with contempt.

His immediate reactions proceeded along three lines, each chosen with an infallible instinct. First, to gain time, and sow perplexity and dissension in the conspirators' ranks, he sent an emissary to La Magione—Roberto Orsini, known as 'the Ursino cavalier'—with the task of working on the five rebel leaders separately. He was to assure each of them in turn of Cesare's continued benevolence, and invite them to return to his allegiance, offering them pay increases and extra lands.

Secondly, to prevent the Florentine Signoria from aligning itself with the *condottieri* (who were in fact trying to exploit its resentments and obtain its military collaboration) he offered Florence a treaty of alliance, and invited the Signoria to send a delegate with whom he could discuss terms. The delegate chosen was none other than Machiavelli, who arrived on 7 October 1502, and hung around until 22 January 1503.

Thirdly, Cesare reinforced his position in such a way as to discourage any further aggression, arming and consolidating the strongholds of the Romagna, strengthening the garrisons, getting French troops sent to him from Lombardy, frantically recruiting troops both in the Duchy and in Tuscany, and hiring a strong phalanx of Swiss mercenaries.

The Duchy of Urbino was temporarily lost; the Republic of San Marino had likewise thrown off its yoke; Venice was watchful, ready to pounce on him at the first sign of weakness; his scattered troops outside the Romagna were, at his orders, beating a hasty retreat, scattering destruction and death as they went. But his superb self-confidence never cracked. During those nightly discussions he had with Machiavelli, after an exhausting day's work, he was for ever emphasizing it. Tall and pale in his black velvet costume, a shadowy, feline figure, he would pace from corner to corner of the room in the flickering candlelight, fingers clasping the scent-bottle from which he was never separated, the smile playing about his lips now contemptuous, now coldly cruel.

The conspirators of La Magione? 'A bunch of failures.'

The confederate forces? 'They do well to talk of *men-at-arms in round numbers*—which means precisely nothing.'

His enemies? 'I have no wish to boast, but I am happy to let events show the mettle of which they, and we, are made. And I esteem them the less in that I know them, and their people, all too well.'

The upshot of the conflict? 'This year the stars are running against all who rebel . . . Peradventure my enemies will have leisure to repent of the treachery they have shown me.'

As for the Florentine alliance, while making it plain that he wanted this, he concealed his desperate need for support. And indeed, on 7 October, after their first discussion, the Signoria's representative had most opportunely emphasized the Duke's imperturbability in the face of all the conspirators' efforts, writing that he 'adjudged them more insensate than he could well imagine, in that they had lacked the wit to hit on the best time to attack him.' They were, he said, truly lacking in finesse; instead of holding their hand until the French were gone, or the Pope dead, they wanted to sink their fangs into him now, 'while the King of France is in Italy, and His Holiness yet lives; the which things kindled so hot a fire beneath them that it called for more water than they could come by to put it out.'

It says much for the Duke's self-assurance, for the shrewdness of his manoeuvres and his overwhelming military superiority (including artillery better than any in the entire peninsula) that Machiavelli, in the dispatches he sent to the Signoria, predicted victory for him, with a confidence that can hardly have been at all welcome in Florence. Indeed, it induced the good *frater Blasius*—in other words, his most faithful friend and colleague, Biagio Buonaccorsi—to suggest, confidentially, in a letter dated 28 October, that he should abstain from 'over-bold conclusions' and too-peremptory predictions concerning the ultimate success of 'that gentleman of yours', since in Florence people were still banking on a confederate victory.

The confederates themselves, however, banked on it less and less. Assailed by ever more urgent second thoughts concerning the enterprise they had undertaken, they now hastened to protest themselves faithful 'soldiers of the Church', sending Valentino furtive embassies to assure him of their loyalty and devotion, and humbly asking for an opportunity to redeem themselves. All, that is, except Oliverotto da Fermo.

Cesare's hypocritical manoeuvres had called out a similar response from his opponents: attempts to lull his suspicions, to catch him with his guard down, tricks, over which he and Machiavelli had a good laugh together: 'Look at the way they go about their business. They stick to a policy of conciliation, they write me friendly letters ... Meanwhile I temporize, listen to all they tell me, and await my opportunity.'

A catalyzing element in this situation was the vain, garrulous, and meddlesome Lord of Palombara, Paolo Orsini—'Madonna Paola', as his rude fellow-conspirators called him. On 25 October he arrived in Imola and expressed humble regrets on behalf of the rebel group, after which he mooted the proposal of a treaty of reconciliation. Valentino now felt he had the lot of them in the hollow of his hand. Convinced of their bad faith, and knowing only too well just how much importance either he or they would attach to such an agree-ment, he obligingly had the worthless document drawn up, and let Madonna Paola go off with it.

Because of one particular clause, which did not at all please the ex-conspira-tors—in that it made the implementation of the pact conditional on the approval of the French King and the Holy See, thus for all practical purposes rendering it inoperative—the 'scrap of paper' kept going backwards and forwards between Imola and the *condottieri*, growing ever thicker with emendations. Meanwhile Vitellozzo, Oliverotto and Baglioni went coolly on with the war, liberating Camerino, besieging Pesaro, marching in the direction of Rimini. But men of good will always prevail in the end; and on 26 November 'Signor Pagolo' was able to bring the treaty back to Valentino in its final form, duly signed by every member of the company. The wrongs done on both sides were to be forgiven and forgotten. There was to be a renewal of alliance 'in perpetuity' between the Duke and the *condottieri*, with a reciprocal defence clause by which each party undertook to defend the other against any attack, and to recover the *signorie* of Urbino and Camerino on Cesare's behalf. The dispute with Bologna was to be settled by arbitration. There were unanimous threats of ruin and extermination against any who violated this pact of friendship.

All this caused much amusement in the stronghold of Imola—as doubtless it also did in the camp of the confederates, who were convinced that they now had the arch-trickster in the bag.

On 2 December Cesare signed a secret agreement with the Bentivoglio clan, after negotiations conducted in Rome between Alexander VI and plenipotenti-aries from Bologna. This was a treaty of friendship—likewise 'in perpetuity'—by virtue of which the Bentivoglio purchased themselves a somewhat precarious immunity, undertaking to provide Valentino with a hundred men-at-arms and two hundred horses, besides confirming, for eight years, the *condotta* they had voted him in the spring of 1501, with an annual stipend of 12,000 ducats.

Guidobaldo's brief restoration was now over, and he once more took the road into exile, with that stoic resignation which typified his character. Gian Maria Varano also left town, though rather less stoically, slipping away at dead of night. Meanwhile Cesare set off from Imola, taking Dorotea Caracciolo with him: he could never quite bring himself to restore her to her husband.

At Cesena he found raging famine, caused by the protracted billeting of troops in the town. He poured out vast sums and adopted a number of emer-gency measures to rectify this situation and by so doing earned the blessings of the entire citizen body. Since there were murmurings that this shortage of pro-visions had been due to the malversations of Ramiro de Lorca, the minister whom he had made Governor of the Romagna, with the task of crushing all further resistance, he had him thrown into prison. Found guilty at his trial of 'corruption, extortion, and rapine', Ramiro was discovered, on Christmas morning, in the main square of Cesena, beheaded and quartered in the tradi-tional manner. This act of Cesare's sent Machiavelli into raptures, as a trans-cendental lesson in political virtuosity. Without bothering to enquire whether the imputations were well-founded, the Florentine saw in Cesare's gesture only the keen astuteness of the 'prince' who, after making use of a minister to pacify a region by dint of cruelty, then rewards him for such service by sacrificing him to the hatred of the populace.

Three days before Christmas the bulk of the French knights left Cesare, and took the road back into Lombardy. The most varied conjectures have been made as to the motives for their departure; Machiavelli claims that it was Cesare himself who dismissed them (keeping a hundred or so under the command of his kinsman Jean de Foix, Anne d'Albret's husband) in order to reassure the seemingly repentant conspirators. Again, to 'avoid arousing suspicion' he had so arranged matters that it was they who proposed the time and place for a meeting. To begin with, they announced themselves willing to march at his side for the conquest of Tuscany; then, when he refused to wage war against the Florentines, they invited him to lead them on an expedition against the strong-hold of Senigallia, whose defender, Andrea Doria, was anxious—or so they said—to surrender to Cesare in person.

This is where the hypothesis of the *condottieri*'s sincerity or good faith com-pletely falls to the ground. The fact that, without being asked, they took the initiative to lure him away from the impregnable Romagna, 'encouraging him to come and join them', at once reveals their treacherous intentions. So, with equal clarity, does the fact that all of them (with the exception of Petrucci, who had stayed in Perugia on the grounds of indisposition) were holding themselves in readiness to welcome him.

Valentino knew very well the risk he was running; and the conspirators were equally well aware of the danger to which *they* would be exposed. The morality and customs of the day left no scope for illusion. After the offence—even after the reconciliation—there came, inevitably, the vendetta. Besides, Valentino was known to all as a man who never forgave. A *coup de main*, in the fashion of the times, was bound to settle this dispute sooner or later; it only remained to be seen who would plan and execute it with greater expertise.

The dispatches which make up Machiavelli's *Legation*—an on-the-spot recording of events, not an *a posteriori* reworking of the record—leave no doubts on this score. Cesare 'had sensed in advance that these reconciled enemies of his were trying, under the pretence of acquiring Sinigaglia in his name, to lay hands on him and secure his person . . . Wherefore he sought to prevent them.' The Signoria's representative is careful not to assert that treachery was, in fact, what the *condottieri* had in mind (how could he have known such a thing?); but he does make it clear that this was what Cesare himself firmly believed. In letters written after the tragedy, indeed, the Duke was to express his conviction very roundly: 'Because of the sport which these Frenchmen made of me by withdrawing to Lombardy, they (the conspirators) believed they too could fool me in their way, and give effect to their first intentions; for this reason they flocked to support my enterprise against Sinigaglia with all their forces and, under the colour and semblance of support, planned that against me which, having foreseen and discovered it betimes, I was able to prevent.'[25]

So off Cesare marched to storm the stronghold of Senigallia. He left Cesena on 26 December, and by the 29th was at Fano. From the Malatestas' palazzo he sent the four *condottieri* orders to pull their troops out of the city (which had already been occupied), to close all the gates save that by which he himself would enter, and to await him outside it. The two Orsini promptly obeyed; Vitellozzo obeyed as well, though with extreme reluctance, being now filled with the blackest forebodings. On the other hand, Oliverotto, who had always shown himself restive as regards the reconciliation, refused: he remained in the city, and his soldiers with him.

That evening Cesare summoned Don Miguel de Corella, Francisco Loris (his cousin, Papal Treasurer and Bishop of Perpignon), and six other faithful friends. Having outlined his plan, he divided them into four pairs, and made each couple responsible for keeping one of the traitors between them.

He left Fano at dawn on 31 December, a Saturday. He passed Metauro, and sent his 15,000 men on ahead of him, after giving very precise instructions to their officers. Outside Senigallia the cavalry opened ranks to let the foot-soldiers pass through. They crossed the Ponte della Misa, and entered the city. Then

Valentino advanced in his turn, slowly, and paused between the two wings of the cavalry. Here he was in due course joined by the two Orsini, and then by Vitellozzo, who cuts a far less noble and dignified figure in the dispatch from the *Legation* than in the pages of the *Description*: 'Vitellozzo appeared riding on a small mule, with a black threadbare gown wrapped round his shoulders, and over it a loose black cloak lined with green; no one who saw him could have guessed that this was the man who twice that year, under the Duke's patronage, had sought to drive the French King out of Italy. His face was pallid and amazed, the which made plain, to all who beheld it, that his death was at hand.'

Cesare greeted his three friends—lost, and now recovered—with a smiling countenance, while the six guards stationed themselves solicitously beside them. At a nod from him, Don Miguel de Corella hurried off in search of Oliverotto, who—not for nothing, as it turned out—had kept his distance. He found him surrounded by his troops, who were drawn up as though for a drill exercise; and with a sterling display of light-hearted camaraderie induced him to dismiss them to their lodgings, after which the two of them went back to the bridge. Valentino's face under the stinging gusts of a December wind, shone with gaiety: the cheerfulness of a good shepherd who has got back his straying sheep.

The entire company now passed through the gate into the city. Cesare dismounted outside the house which had been put at his disposal, and invited the four *condottieri* to come in and spend a little time with him. He went ahead of them into the entrance-court, crossed it, climbed the first steps of a staircase, and then abruptly turned round. Having checked that all the four were there, he raised his eyes to heaven. This was the signal. His men at once seized them, telling them they were prisoners. Indifferent to the howl of furious desperation that went up from Paolo Orsini's throat, Valentino hurried up the rest of the stairway, opened a door, and disappeared from view.

Oliverotto's men saw the Duke come thundering down on them at the head of his cavalry, in a ferocious charge. Then it was the turn of Vitellozzo's and Orsini's troops, quartered in the suburbs beyond the walls. Finally, when he got back, his own infantry, who had been looting and plundering, were given a taste of his cold fury: a few on-the-spot executions soon restored order, and a sinister silence fell over those blood-bespattered streets.

Cesare spent the rest of that day making his dispositions and dictating letters. His tense, expressionless face was like the mask of some terrible god. When evening came, he dismissed all his staff, and remained alone for long hours, shut up in his work-closet. When the night was half through, he had Vitellozzo and Oliverotto brought up to one of the main rooms for summary trial. With the help of torture, a full confession of treachery was wrung from both the accused, who now assailed each other in turn with angry and tearful recriminations. Then sentence was pronounced on them. Vitellozzo asked for the comforts of religion, and, says Machiavelli, 'prayed that he might beg the Pope to grant him plenary indulgence for his sins.' Oliverotto, on the other hand, as one Urbino chronicler attests, 'did not wish to make his confession'. They were seated back to back on a bench, with one length of cord fastened round both their necks. Then the *torcolo*, the garrotter's bar, was inserted through the cord, and twisted round and round, so that the two of them were strangled simultaneously, uttering the death-rattle together in a kind of ghastly comradeship. This job was carried out either by Master Micheletto, or else (accounts differ) by a certain Giannetto Borgia, a distant relation of Valentino's. The two corpses were dragged out to a public square, where they remained for three days. Only after the Duke had left the city (which was destined to acquire the most widespread fame as a result of this incident) did anyone dare to give them burial, in the Church of Santa Maria della Misericordia.

For the two Orsini the moment was not yet ripe; but under their feet, too, a great gulf had opened up.

Cesare sent official notification of his exploit to the various Courts and governments, presenting it as an act of legitimate self-defence, and expressing the conviction that 'the whole world' had good cause to rejoice at its outcome, 'and *maxime* Italy', as the beneficial extirpation of a 'public and calamitous plague affecting all peoples'.[26]

Congratulations and plaudits reached him from every part of the peninsula. Not even Venice or Florence wanted their voice to be lacking from this united chorus of admiration. 'A rare and wonderful exploit,' said Machiavelli. An episode 'worthy of ancient Rome', was Louis XII's verdict. 'A most exquisite deception', Paolo Giovio later wrote, as though describing some consummate work of art.

AUGUST 1503

The marvellous skill and sovereign precision with which everything had been planned in Alexander VI's mind became obvious almost the moment Valentino departed from Senigallia, taking his two doomed captives with him. On 2 January 1503 the old, blind Cardinal Orsini, who had been the conspirators' tutelary deity, was arrested in the Vatican by the Papal police, and thrown into prison like any common malefactor—an act which formed the New Year's main course, as it were, with the rounding up of many well-known figures from among the cardinal's friends and relatives thrown in as a side-dish.

This was the flourish of the baton with which Alexander VI initiated a general attack on the family. The undertaking had long been envisaged in his carefully planned programme, but had been put off until it could be carried out in the most advantageous conditions, from strength. It would form the cul-minating phase of his campaign for the internal consolidation of the Papal State. The stranglehold of the Colonna, Savelli, and Caetani families had al-ready been broken. With the Orsini clan similarly weakened, the Church could breathe freely once more.

A gale of terror swept through Rome; more and more people fled the city. To stop this centrifugal movement Alexander VI made emphatically reassur-ing pronouncements: the guilty had all been seized, no one was any longer in danger, they could all relax and enjoy the Carnival. He then set a personal example of how such enjoyment might best be attained.

Cesare and his cavalry swept through central Italy. The mere noise of his approach, breathing threats, laying down terms, and on occasion letting his fierce troops off the leash for a spell of devastation, was enough to make Giulio Vitelli abandon Città di Castello, Gian Paolo Baglioni Perugia, and Pandolfo Petrucci Siena. Meanwhile a Papal army assailed the Orsini's strongholds one after another, reducing their territories *en route*. The commander of this task-force was Goffredo, who showed a cool competence, revealing unsuspected talents as a *condottiere*. From October of the previous year his wife had been living in the seclusion of Castel Sant'Angelo, whither the Pope had relegated her to atone for the latest offences in her adventurous life.

On 18 January, at Castel della Pieve, Cesare had his two prisoners strangled. Cardinal Orsini, with only the rats and spiders of Castel Sant'Angelo for company, lay racked by spasms of hunger. Immediately after his arrest the Pope had confiscated all his possessions. A woman who had been a close friend of the prisoner's went, masked, to the Vatican, and by offering a pearl of inestim-able value managed to get his detention made less rigorous.

The Orsini clan rallied to the rescue. They launched a counter-attack which, sustained by the fury of despair, took them to the very walls of Rome. They stormed the Ponte Nomentano and marched on the Vatican. The surviving forces of the other great families fought at their side. The attack was driven off; but Alexander had had a bad fright, and peremptorily recalled Duke Valentino from Tuscany.

And now we have the strange spectacle of the Pope, first with impatience, then in mounting fury, and finally with the grimmest threats of punishments, trying to dislodge the Gonfalonier of the Church from his position near Siena, while the latter ignored his commands and made it all too clear that he had not

the slightest intention of budging. Alexander got to the point of loading
Cesare with the most opprobrious epithets, and complaining bitterly of his
conduct in full consistory, adding: 'We will carry out this expedition.' It looked
as though he was doing all he could to give maximum publicity to the clash
between them: the Duke's obstinate reluctance, and the tenacity with which he
was trying to force his will. In other words, it might be said that he wanted all
responsibility for the campaign against the Orsini to devolve on *his* head, so as
to exculpate Cesare in advance.

This in fact was no more than the truth. Of the two motives which could pro-
long Valentino's absence—the advantageous possibilities that were opening up
in Tuscany, with a new offer of surrender on Pisa's part, and the hesitation to
go beyond certain limits in dealing with the Roman family—the second was
presumably the more compelling. Over the Orsini, in fact, there were spread
the friendly and protective wings of the French King, to whom Cesare was
still bound by ties of allegiance, while the Pope had already begun to break
away from him. Moreover, of the two leaders of that proudly fierce resistance
which the family was now opposing to the Church's armed assault—Giovanni
Giordano, Lord of Bracciano, and Niccolò, Count of Pitigliano—the one was
his colleague in the knightly French Order of St Michael, and therefore, as far
as he was concerned, inviolable, while the other had the solid support of the
Most Serene Republic behind him.

Eventually, however, Cesare showed that he was prepared—very much
against the grain—to obey the Pope's commands, and on 28 January he set
forth. He dragged out the journey as long as he could, allowing himself frequent
halts; but when he debouched from Umbria and flung himself against the
Orsini fortresses, the campaign began to go badly for the Roman family. Only
two strongholds—Bracciano and Cere (Cerveteri)—were still holding out
when word of his arrival got round Rome. Few people, in point of fact, had
actually seen his face, since (in accordance with what was now a regular
practice) he always wore a mask. The Venetian ambassador, describing an
audience he had had with Alexander VI, mentioned that he pretended not to
have heard the news of the Duke's arrival, since the Pontiff himself did not say
a word about it.

The war went on. Cesare made it his business to arrange a meeting with a
confidential agent of Giovanni Giordano Orsini (later to marry Pope Julius
II's daughter), and to show him—with the sadness of a man whose will and
feelings alike have been outraged—a fearful Papal Bull of 1 February, which
enjoined him to 'march against the whole House of Orsini and seize all he
could of them, sparing neither women nor children'. At the same time he

showed himself willing to assume custody of all his adversary's possessions, pending arbitration by the King of France, with full assurance that they would not be touched meanwhile.

After massive bombardments, and with the assistance of certain siege/ engines invented by Leonardo, he successfully stormed Cere, treating his opponents with great consideration when they yielded. However, he abstained from any serious effort against Bracciano, where Giovanni Giordano had gone to ground, even though Alexander VI was threatening it with excommunica/ tion and plundering. On 8 April he signed an armistice. Then, with the Pope's consent, Giovanni Giordano set out for France to solicit the mediation, and favour, of Louis XII.

At this moment the Borgias had attained the very highest peak of their success. All their enemies, it could be said, were now eliminated. Those anarchic and destructive forces which for so long had gnawed, like ulcers, at the structure of the Papal State, and rendered the Popes' temporal power more or less derisory, had been (with a few unimportant exceptions) destroyed. The Duchy of Romagna, with its wise ordinances, its well/disciplined civic life, and the exem/ plary functioning of its courts of justice, was a model state. The army—the first national army of Italy—with its Romagna/recruited soldiers in helmet and cuirass, wearing elegant uniforms in Valentino's colours (a surcoat quartered in yellow and red, with the name *Cesar* on breast and back), and animated by a remarkable *esprit de corps*, formed a secure guarantee of defence against any attack. And all this had come about in little more than three years, from the day when Cesare, lately returned from France, had embarked on his first campaign. Nothing seemed able to resist him. The exceptional gifts which sustained him, and the unheard/of good fortune which accompanied all his exploits, gave him the fearful quality of a man who seemed to identify himself with destiny. On the day—still more or less distant, but seemingly inevitable—when he at last succeeded in incorporating Tuscany in his domains, he would dominate the entire peninsula. No one dared hazard a guess as to his final destination.

But in the spring of 1503 fear and hatred fermented around the Borgias, acrid and oppressive as the miasma from a swamp. On 22 February, Cardinal Orsini died in Castel Sant'Angelo. 'Not wanting to know more than is necessary,' Burchard noted in his *Diary*, 'I did not attend the funeral, and have not inter/ vened in any way.' But many people were murmuring that Orsini had 'drunk the cup prepared at the Pope's orders'.

Poison was also mentioned—this time, perhaps, with greater plausibility— when during the night of 10-11 April the Venetian cardinal Giovanni

Michiel, Paul II's nephew, died miserably after two days of violent vomiting. He left vast riches, valued at 150,000 ducats, which duly found their way to the Vatican. Public rumour accused Cesare of direct responsibility for this profitable liquidation, and held Alexander guilty of connivance, through fear of his terrible son. As with every other crime of this sort ascribed to the Borgias, here too there is no secure and incontrovertible proof. It is, however, true that the cardinal's majordomo, Asquinio da Colloredo, arrested by Julius II on 17 December 1503, afterwards confessed that he had administered poison to his master on behalf of the Pope and the Duke of Romagna, receiving one thousand ducats as a reward. The trial, however, was set up by Julius II primarily to create a climate of public opinion hostile to Valentino, and to initiate the moral demolition of the Borgias. It took place in a heated, troubled atmosphere, so that no one dared to speak of their legitimate suspicions; and in the second place, the confession was obtained by means of bestial torture.

Other sour comments on the methods used by the Borgias to obtain the money they needed for their costly policies were lent some plausibility by an auction of new clerkships in the Curia, which netted 64,000 ducats, and yet another batch of cardinals, created on 31 May: nine appointments, all most handsomely paid for, so that the operation brought in between 120 and 130,000 ducats.

One highly significant fact about this election, held under Cesare's auspices, was that no less than five Spaniards became cardinals, flanked by a small group consisting of three Italians and one German. Five Spaniards—but not a single Frenchman. All of which goes to show that Valentino agreed with those views which had lately been maturing in the Pope's mind, and that the Borgias' political bark was little by little preparing to change course, and once more follow in the wake of the strongest, whoever could best reward their friendship. From Louis XII they had already obtained all they could hope for. What was more, his troops had been ill-advised enough to get themselves beaten. It was not hard to predict that the moment was now close at hand when they would have to take the bitter return road to their own country, and the Papal State would find itself with the Spaniards on its southern frontier. The game had seemed to favour the French so long as Gonzalo de Cordoba had remained be-sieged within the walls of Barletta (a town commemorated by one of those rare and tiny episodes of gallant pride in the vast sea of Italian humiliation which marks the period as a whole); but when, later, the Gran Capitano broke the siege-lines, the whole balance of fortune was turned upside-down. In two battles, at Seminara and Cerignola, the French lost both their supremacy and their leaders. During the first the Maréchal d'Aubigny was taken prisoner, and during the second, Louis d'Armagnac, Duke of Nemours. Two weeks later, on 14 May, the Spaniards entered Naples.

There was no longer even any reason to mention Cesare Borgia's intervention in a war which had been so swiftly and irrevocably decided. Vatican diplomacy, guided as always by that opportunism which is the most common helm in politics, began with a cunning hand to plot the curve of that fine reversal of direction which would carry it towards Spain: a wide and gentle curve, to be sure, since the French had not yet been ejected from the northern part of the realm.

This volte-face was to be the Borgias' final political undertaking, embarked on but never concluded. Their dominant idea, in the short space of time left to them before the abyss swallowed them up, was a new bloc comprising Spain, Venice, and the Church. With one foot in a Spanish stirrup, and the other in a Venetian, they would continue their ride with distinguished success.

The manoeuvring for a *rapprochement* was conducted with their accustomed delicacy. But Venice refused to be hypnotized by the golden warblings of these two nightingales; and Alexander VI—who saw in this much-cherished alliance, *inter alia*, the promise of a truly 'Italian' policy, such as he had shown himself anxious to implement in the time of Charles VIII—was bitterly dashed down by the refusal. He told the ambassador who informed him of it: 'We are disappointed of a great hope which we had in that most illustrious Signoria, since we hoped that together we might redress the fortunes of this wretched, war-torn land that is Italy.'

It is in the context of this final political move by the Borgias that there also occurred the last of those ruthless punishments they meted out. They did not have a monopoly of such behaviour, which was then general; but in their case more than others the act of punishment does seem to have been exploited as a means of impressing on people's minds the image of a sinister *terribilità*.

One of the men who had most enjoyed the friendship, confidence, and generosity both of the Pope and of the Duke, Francisco Troches, on 19 May fled from Rome and took ship at Civitavecchia for France. The motives for his flight are uncertain. It seems that he was vexed at not having been included in the list of forthcoming cardinals (compiled by Cesare), and perhaps let slip some over-acid complaint about his omission—or passed on information to Louis XII concerning the Borgias' volte-face. Valentino's diplomatic wrath pursued him implacably. The Genoese police authorities were alerted; they picked Troches up in Corsica, and sent him back home. On 8 June Cesare had him tried and condemned. According to a dispatch by the Este ambassador, he secretly watched the execution, from a hidden vantage-point.

Alexander VI had entered his seventy-second year with a fair following wind, and was now ploughing his way through the waters in majestic bliss. He had good health, an iron constitution, unquenchable optimism and astonishing cheerfulness of mood. Time might have made his body heavy, but not his spirit. Fate was smiling on his affairs and on his children.

It would not be long now before Cesare laid hands on Tuscany. Negotia-tions (conducted to a background tinkle of ducats) with the Emperor Maxi-milian for the investiture of Pisa, Siena and Lucca were proceeding as well as could be desired. In Rome, the expeditionary force was being mustered with brisk dispatch. Already, both in the Vatican and at the various Courts of the peninsula, the present Duke of Romagna was being spoken of as a future king. People even ventured conjectures as to the name of his realm. The Kingdom of Adria, some said.

Lucrezia, concerning whom the Pope kept himself informed with affection-ate assiduity, was leading a peaceful, and, in so far as her mild disposition allowed, a happy existence in the great castle of Ferrara. Madame Adriana del Milá was still her inseparable companion, and she also now had what she referred to as her 'four Caterinas'—the Valencian, the Neapolitan, the Moor (whom she loved loading with jewels and elegant dresses, to enjoy the effect they made against her dark skin), and that feather-brained little goose whom she had nicknamed Deda. Whatever Lucrezia was saying or doing, the Pope knew all about it. He knew that Lucrezia's new environment had given her a sympa-thetic welcome, and that Lucrezia in turn had fascinated Ferrara with her demure and modest grace. He also knew that Alfonso left her alone during the day-time while he sallied forth 'to seek his pleasure in divers places', but that at night he never omitted to sleep with her. So you see, he explained to the Ferrarese ambassador with a smile, there's nothing to worry about. The fact that Alfonso went 'to seek his pleasure' was not only right and natural, given his age, but also constituted a good sign of virility. The important thing was that he should treat his wife properly and give her children—as this nocturnal assiduity of his led one to hope that he would.

Finally there was Goffredo, the pale and foolish Goffredo: even he had given some cause for satisfaction during the initial phase of that campaign against the Orsini. So everything was going à merveille; and the hope of still having a few years of his pontificate left to him, enough time in which to consolidate the Church's temporal authority, Cesare's power, and the fortunes of his blood-relatives, was one he never abandoned.

But with the coming and the advance of summer his exuberance began to droop like the leaves of a sick plant. His mood became strangely gloomy. The stifling heat made people predict an epidemic of malarial-type fever, and this prophecy very soon came true. Suddenly Alexander VI seemed to feel the weight of his years, of his exertions and pleasures, passions and anxieties: the whole cumulative burden of a long life, in which there had been not one idle hour, now bore down on that massive body of his, once agile and athletic, but now fallen into flabby and panting obesity. His thoughts beat unquiet wings against walls of terror. Presentiments of death treacherously assailed him.

The epidemic broke out in August. 'Many are sick,' wrote the Catanei's *oratore*. 'It is not the plague, but *solum* fevers, which kill quickly.' One person they speedily killed was Cardinal Giovanni Borgia Lanzol, Archbishop of Monreale, then aged fifty. While the usual lunatic exponents of dark theories began murmuring their inevitable refrain about poisoning, the Pope succumbed to genuine distress over his nephew's death. As he watched the passing of the funeral cortege from a window of the Apostolic Palace, he expressed gloomy forebodings, saying that the month of August was fatal for obese persons. An owl brushed against him, an intrusive black omen, and fell dead at his feet. Deathly pale, shaking his head and shuffling as he walked, he withdrew to his bedchamber.

The eleventh anniversary of his election as Pope fell on 11 August. Ambassadors who were present at the Mass he celebrated noted the heavy shadow of sadness and physical suffering on his face. In a discussion with the Venetian *oratore* he observed that his ill health was due to disappointment at the failure to conclude an agreement with the Most Serene Republic. Next day he was forced to take to his bed with fever and vomiting, which went on all afternoon and right through the night.

Then Rome received a violent shock, which rocked the city to its foundations. Despite all the precautions taken to prevent the facts becoming known, news did somehow leak out of the Vatican, and spread abroad, that Cesare too was seriously ill. He had been seized and struck down by sickness when on the point of setting forth to conquer Tuscany: forcibly plucked back from the threshold of his enterprise, as it were, even as he was putting one foot forward to cross it.

He was suffering from a malignant tertian fever, not—as the sillier rumours had it—from poisoning. (The story went that Alexander and Cesare had both been guests at dinner in Cardinal Adriano da Corneto's country house, where through an error, or deliberate manipulation, on the part of the majordomo they themselves drank the wine which they had prepared to poison their fellow-guests.) From that moment everything happened with disastrous speed. Under the terrified gaze of the two invalids in the Vatican, one on the point of death, and the other immobilized at the only moment in his whole life when inertia spelt ruin, the landslide got under way, and began its unstoppable downward movement.

Around the Vatican all was confusion; while the various ambassadors dashed off feverish dispatches, Rome and Italy held their breath and waited. For a week, while periods of deceptive recovery alternated with fresh onsets of fever and vomiting, the Pope's tough constitution fought its ultimate battle. On the morning of the 18th, after an agonized night, he had the Bishop of Carinola brought in to confess him, celebrate Mass at his bedside, and give him Communion and Extreme Unction. Towards nightfall, the windows were thrown open to the brightness and breeze of a late Roman sunset. Alexander VI was dead—of apoplexy.

Under the supervision of Burchard, the master of ceremonies, the body was washed, dressed, and carried to the Sala del Pappagallo, where the Pontiff normally robed himself for High Mass and formal audiences. He was laid out on a table, between two torches, and left there. No one kept vigil by him through the night. Not a single cardinal bothered to come and see him next morning, when he was moved across to St Peter's—first behind the High Altar, then at the entrance to the choir, with an iron grille by way of protection, there being reason to fear that the hand of an enemy might do him some mischief. The corpse presented a terrifying spectacle, being swollen and black, with its tongue filling the entire mouth, which was wide open. Even in these few short hours after death it had already begun to give off the stink of putrefaction. When dusk fell, six porters and two carpenters came to dispose of it. Joking and laughing, they roughly shoved it into a too-narrow coffin, forcing it down by brute force. Then they put in the mitre, leaving it all askew on the dead man's head, and closed the lid. All this took place in the dark, empty church.

Alexander VI's remains were laid to rest in that same 'Rotunda' of Santa Maria delle Febbri where he had built a grandiose sepulchral monument to his uncle Callistus III. Here they remained—in a sarcophagus which afterwards disappeared, but is described in the *Vitae et res gestae romanorum pontificum* by the Spanish Dominican Ciaconio—until 1586, when both chapel and monuments (save for a few fragments) were destroyed to make room for the erection of the obelisk in St Peter's Square. The bones of the two Pontiffs were then transferred to the new Basilica of St Peter. From here they were removed in 1610 for re-burial, at the Spaniards' request, in their church of Santa Maria di Monserrato. Enclosed in a single wooden casket, they found a resting-place in the sacristy linen-cupboard. On the casket was pinned a sheet of paper bearing the legend: '*Los huesos de dos Papas están en esta caseta, y son Calisto y Alexandro VI, y eran españoles.*' It would be hard to conceive any more ignoble or irreverent treatment of a man's remains.

Not until 21 August 1889, through the piety of Pope Leo XIII, were these poor bones granted a modest sarcophagus, with the inscription: 'CALIXTUS III, ALEXANDER VI, PP. MM.' '*En esta vida no le queda sino muecha infamia, y en la otra es de creer que mucha pena, si Nuestro Señor no usó con él de grandísima misericordia,*' Ferdinand of Spain wrote to his ambassador Rojas, in response to the letter informing him of the death of a Pope to whom he owed not a little. The presumptuous self-righteousness of this judgement—enunciated by a sovereign who would have been better employed looking to his own vices—was by no means isolated. An upsurge of partisan hatred produced endless cruel epitaphs and mocking epigrams, legends which spoke of infernal pacts and devils carrying off the soul of the great sinner.

Sinner he undoubtedly was, like all men. Perhaps a greater sinner than most, too, given the exceptionally powerful nature of his instincts, the influence of a highly corrupt age, and the weakness which ever sapped his will. Yet he was well aware of his own weakness and unworthiness (which indeed he confessed from the height of his own Papal throne), and in that better than the men who pronounced sentence on him.

Both for sovereign breadth of intelligence and generosity of temperament he can justly be termed a great man, among the most outstanding figures of his age. But he was also a great ruler of the Papal State, as for some while now scholars have begun to understand and admit, after centuries of ill-founded evaluation, in thrall to ancient derogatory propaganda and shot through with puritan prejudice.

A target for contemporary calumny and destined to be long misjudged by a historiographical tradition based upon those calumnies, the man who now lay in the chapel of Santa Maria delle Febbri was to become—and this is surely the most significant paradox of his life—one of history's most privileged characters, who had witnessed, or been involved in (whether as minor character or protagonist), some of the world's most memorable events: the unification of Spain, the discovery of America, the sub-division of the new continent (which he carried out in 1493) between Spain and Portugal, the arrival of Christian missions in these still barely-civilized lands, the first development of the printing-press, the dawn of the High Renaissance, the explosion of new artistic and architectural splendours in Rome. The transformation of the Città Leonina (the Trastevere quarter, including the Vatican), the opening up of the Via Alessandrina, the grandiose building projects which drove new roads through the quarters around the Vatican, the repairs to Castel Sant'Angelo carried out

by Antonio da Sangallo, the strengthening of the Torre di Nona, the archae-
ologically perfect restoration of the Porta Settimiana, the embellishments added
to the Apostolic Palace, the Torre Borgia, the two national German churches
built in Rome during this period, Trinità dei Monti, Santa Maria di Monserrato, the Chancellery Palace, Bramante's chapel, and, above all, the Borgia
Apartments with their Pinturicchio frescoes—incomparably valuable evidence
not only for the iconography of the Borgias, but also for the reconstruction of
their day-to-day environment and their inner life—this whole complex of
achievements goes back to Alexander's period, and proclaims the vast scope and
vision of his pontificate.

'PLEUREZ, VAILLANTS HOMMES DE GUERRE'

Cesare's fate now plunged into the depths. The rest of his history was the fight—
as useless as it was heroic—of a man who, struck down by a quirk of fortune,
struggled back to his feet and seemed, for a while, once more to control his
destiny, but with two throws of the dice, two decisions that went wrong through
over-audacity, contrived to give himself the *coup de grâce*.

His first decision, when someone came to his bedside and informed him that
the Pontiff had expired, was to forestall the plundering of the Vatican by
sending Miguel de Corella, with a determined band of picked men, to seize
the entire contents of the Papal Treasury—money, jewellery, silver plate, everything. The job was flawlessly carried out; the cardinal in charge, with a
dagger pointing at his throat, proved most co-operative: 300,000 ducats, in
money and *objets d'art*, were deposited by Cesare in the strongrooms of Castel
Sant'Angelo.

In Rome some thought he was dead. The quarrels between the various
factions, the return of the exiles (who at once launched their own vendettas),
the rioting and criminal excesses of the mob, the approach of French troops on
their way out and Spanish troops hot in pursuit of them—all this produced an
atmosphere of terror and panic throughout the city. The old anti-Catalan fury
had a violent resurgence. Houses and shops in the Spanish quarter of Banchi
were set on fire. One of Paolo Orsini's sons, Fabio, bathed his face and hands
in the blood of a Borgia he had murdered. The whole clan now attempted a
coup; but Goffredo and Don Miguel, at the head of their fellow-countrymen,
quelled this rising with extreme severity, and burnt down the palazzo of Monte
Giordano.

Only an exceptionally robust constitution made it possible for Cesare to survive the violence of his tertian fever—not to mention the 'cure' prescribed by one

doctor, who made him lie down, naked, in the hot belly of a freshly-disem-bowelled mule, and then plunge into a tub of icy water.

Confined to bed and reduced to a pale ghost of his former self, surrounded by waves of hostile reaction and beset by perils of every sort, he now summoned up all his indomitable inner energy, all his boundless courage. The wealth of the Vatican, the hundreds of thousands of ducats he had deposited with banks and invested in the business houses of Genoa, Venice, and Florence, the unswerv-ingly loyal friends who surrounded him, the army he had at his command, his office as Gonfalonier and Captain-General of the Church, the backing he could count on among the cardinals, above all his own reputation—all of these left him, still, a most powerful and formidable figure. The Sacred College would inevitably have to reckon with him.

He now laid down the main lines of his strategy. These included a deal with the Colonna family (to whom he restored their confiscated possessions), as a means of clamping down on the aggressive activities of the Orsini; negotiations with the cardinals to obtain confirmation of his office, with full responsibility on his part for the maintenance of public order; and an immediate transfer of Romagna troops from the Duchy to Orvieto, a move that should encourage proper respect in friend and foe alike.

With the conclave now imminent, the Sacred College carefully warned all *condottieri* and armed forces to keep their distance from Rome. This order also applied to Cesare, who, pleading the excuse of illness, put up a spirited resist-ance to it, with the object of gaining time. He profited by this respite to play a diplomatic double game designed—with the situation so uncertain and fluid from one moment to the next—to leave every loophole open to him. While, on the one hand, he professed ardently pro-Spanish feelings to that Spanish-oriented character Prospero Colonna (who had come to Rome and started an affair with Sancia), on the other he made fresh approaches to Louis XII's ambassador, and renewed his promise of military collaboration for the recon-quest of Naples.

At the end of August he finally had to make up his mind to sign the agree-ment between himself and the cardinals, obliging him to leave Rome within three days. The Sacred College, for its part, offered him a formal guarantee of security, which extended to his relatives and the Spanish prelates; it declared itself ready to warn Venice against touching lands which belonged to the Duchy of Romagna (the nibbling process had in fact already begun), and to exhort the Duke's subjects to remain loyal; and it authorized him to take his artillery with him when he went.

On 1 September, in his obsessional concern with safeguarding the Romagna, his personal fief, he abruptly threw off the mask of Spanish solidarity, and signed a mutual-aid pact with France, which—through Lombardy—was in a better position to help him preserve the Duchy. Louis XII, in fact, at once publicly proclaimed the territorial integrity of the Romagna.

Next day Cesare left Rome, in a litter borne by halberdiers and deferentially escorted for a part of the way by the ambassadors of France, Spain and Germany. To Prospero Colonna, as to everyone else, he had declared that his destination was Tivoli; and thither the Roman *condottieri* had already preceded him, with the artillery. But Valentino now unexpectedly changed his itinerary *en route*, turning off towards Nepi, where the French troops lay. Prospero Colonna had never in his life had so cool a trick played on him; and as a final insult he found himself also left in the lurch by the Borgia artillery-train, which went off by another road to rejoin its commander. Colonna relieved his wounded feelings by going off to Naples with Sancia; he never forgot this underhand deception. Cesare, meanwhile, accompanied by Vannozza and Goffredo, arrived in Nepi.

From the castle where Lucrezia had spent the most miserable days of her life, Cesare now followed, hour by hour, and with impotent rage, the course of events in Rome and the swift disintegration of his most recent conquests. At Urbino, Piombino, Perugia, Camerino, Città di Castello, Pesaro and Rimini, the surviving overlords of yesterday—or their heirs—came flocking back to re-occupy the palazzi whence, a year earlier, they had fled in fear and trembling. Amid this succession of calamities, only the Duchy of Romagna continued to hold out, with rock-like solidity.

Meanwhile, within the bosom of the conclave, the interests of the Great Powers were at joust in lists where three main rival candidates now con-fronted one another: Amboise for France, Carvajal for Spain, and Giuliano della Rovere for Venice. The balance of power between these three factions was such as to make a compromise solution inevitable. As a result the electors' votes all went to a mild and tremulous old man named Francesco Piccolomini Todeschini, who in homage to the memory of his uncle, Pius II, decided to call himself Pius III.

However, he was not to have time in which to become accustomed to his change of name. Brought into the history of the Popes on 22 September through the door of a makeshift compromise, he departed from it again on 18 October through that of death. His twenty-six-day pontificate, unimportant in many re-spects, had proved very useful to Cesare, against whom the Orsini and Colonna families were now turning—their differences forgotten—with unbridled fury, while Gian Paolo Baglioni also joined in the chase, and two cuckolded husbands, Caracciolo and Alviano, charged at him, heads down, from opposite directions.

Cesare returned to Rome, with his mother and brother, on 3 October, and took up residence in the palazzo of Domenico della Rovere. He found himself surrounded by enemies who were only waiting for his appearance to spring on him and pull him down. The tender and pathetic protection of the old dotard in the Vatican (who in large measure owed the fleeting honour of his tiara to Cesare) did not suffice to break the ring of hatred with which he was surrounded. Indeed, this same Pius III, on being upbraided by the anti-Borgia cardinals for extending his protection to Cesare at all (though it remained a matter of words rather than deeds), made a senile and whimpering apology, saying he had been bamboozled by the Spanish cardinals, and promising to exert himself no longer on the Duke's behalf.

Cesare's manner remained high-handed to the point of arrogance; but his position was steadily deteriorating. When Gonzalo de Cordoba debarred Spanish officers from taking service under his banner, desertions made catastrophic inroads amongst his troops. One most bitter pill for him to swallow was the departure of Ugo de Moncada, one of his most brilliant captains, and his companion in a number of unforgettable exploits.

Deprived of a safe retreat, subject to strange fluctuations of mood and thought, he gave the impression of being a mere pawn at the mercy of circumstances. His intimate friends found it hard to recognize him. Under his assumption of confidence they began to descry hints of bewilderment.

He employed makeshift expedients, plain lies, moves that were too blatantly devious. He attempted a reconciliation with the Orsini, which—incredibly—came off, only to founder again twenty-four hours later. He thought of seeking refuge in the Romagna, where the people loved him and his military resources were strong; but he had, in the end, to acknowledge the impossibility of his ever getting there. He attempted a sortie from Rome, but an attack by the Orsini and Alviano forced him to beat a precipitate retreat, and it was only with difficulty that he escaped by seeking refuge in the Vatican. Finding even this a somewhat insecure hide-out, he hurried through the covered passageway leading to Castel Sant'Angelo. With him he took two young boys: Lucrezia's son Rodrigo, and Giovanni, the Roman Infante. Two more children very soon joined him: Gerolamo and Camilla, his offspring by some unknown woman, and still of very tender years.

At once refuge and cage, the fortress by the river-bank offered no more than a brief respite in the destiny of the conqueror who, as Machiavelli afterwards wrote, 'being thus reproved by fortune, was now slipping towards his grave'.

But he fought that descent all the way, clawing wildly, scrabbling for every foothold, changing his plans and tactics with each change of circumstances. The man who had always given the impression of not knowing what it meant to hesitate, and who at every juncture was seen to make a quick, clear, trenchant decision, now wavered to and fro like a crazy compass-needle. What was more, his ever-changing alignments—now with the Colonna family and Spain, now with France and the Orsini—had aggravated his own position, since neither one side nor the other could forgive his treacherous shifts of alliance, or fully credit his good faith when he patched the relationship up again.

Faced with this new Cesare Borgia, the protagonist of the last act in the drama —that is, the period between the Pope's death and the night of Viana—we can-not avoid a feeling of perplexity, so clear-cut and incontrovertible seems the break, in his personality and actions alike. Even making due allowance for the mental confusion caused by illness, there can be one explanation only for his sudden fall: the loss of that matchless guide and mentor, his father. In the light of those negative proofs now furnished by Valentino, it becomes very clear just how large a proportion of his success must be ascribed to the Pope's shrewd and experienced political insight. His defects become apparent, the delineation of his features emerges in more exact proportions. When we separate out what properly belongs to Alexander and to Cesare respectively, we find ourselves faced with an undeniably exceptional man of action, who was, however, accustomed to steer a course which another hand, not his, had set: a superb executive officer, formidable when it came to detached and, as it were, episodic exploits, but too rash and impetuous, too confident in himself and his own good fortune, too much (in one sense) a gambler and adventurer for that patient pro-cess of co-ordination which forms the framework of all major strategic and political planning.

The disappearance of Pius III, and the consequent interregnum, rendered in-operative that *noli tangere* with which the twenty-six-day Pope had sought to safeguard Cesare's dukedom. They also, because of this, led to further restora-tions, in the very heart of the Romagna itself: the Manfredi returned to Faenza, while the Ordelaffi, stealing a march on Caterina Sforza, took possession of Forlí. However, the best strongholds still remained in the hands of Duke Valentino's supporters.

The most outstanding candidate at the forthcoming conclave was Giuliano della Rovere, the cardinal who for several decades had been battling against the Borgias, whom he detested with all the bitterness of his naturally bilious temperament. He was sixty years old, and his ambitions to become Pope had been thwarted too often already. He regarded this conclave as his last chance.

Cesare's support would bring in a good third of the votes in the Sacred College. At a discussion between the two men which took place on 29 October, in one of the Vatican's audience-chambers, the Ligurian staked all his chances on a reconciliation, pegging this to a series of pledges which he undertook with the firm intention of breaking every last one of them. Until a very few days before he had tried to ruin Cesare in any way he could, stirring up his enemies, asking Pius III for freedom of action against him, angrily pressing for his expulsion from Rome, and threatening a mass rising of anti-Borgia elements. Now he guaranteed Cesare, in writing, confirmation in his office as Gonfalonier and Captain-General of the Church, the survival of his dukedom, unconditional collaboration for the recovery of those cities he had lost, and compensation for the Spanish cardinals. Then, gently bending his bow to the cord of friendship, he proposed a match between Cesare's daughter Luisa and his own nephew Francesco Maria della Rovere.

The Ligurian had a European reputation for sincerity; but Cesare was not unaware that a lifetime's loyalty could—when the importance of the appoint-ment merited it—constitute the guarantee for a well-placed lie. He set little store by their past enmity, knowing that, in politics, the mutual advantages of an agreement can cancel out all personal resentments. In the case of Giuliano della Rovere, however, mortified by decades of rancour, this rule did not apply.

There was only one reason for Cesare's taking the bait which Giuliano offered him. With bad faith of the sort practised by the man now sitting opposite him, he relied on getting the upper hand by his own astuteness, beating Giuliano when the time came, and using his now-confirmed official position to get him-self back to the Romagna, reconquer the territories he had lost, and consolidate his own power in complete independence of the Church. Against this calcula-tion there stood that of his adversary. Giuliano planned to use his support to squeeze a majority vote out of the conclave; after that he meant to smash him, bringing back under the Church's direct control all those territories which the Borgias had torn from the grasp of tyrants.

Cesare had made a truly gigantic blunder. He could have sold the dozen or so votes he controlled to any other candidate, for the same price and at far less risk. Banking on the superiority of his own cunning in any show-down with Giuliano, and not attaching due weight to the latter's capacity for spiteful resentment, he made the worst choice available, and in so doing put his own neck into the noose.

The following six months saw a hard-fought duel—at first hypocritically glossed over with cordiality, then ever tenser, ruder, and more blatant—between Cesare's determination to hold what he had, and the Pope's plans for getting it back. While the latter continued to lavish promises on his powerless Gon- falonier, he spoke out very roundly to others: 'It is our wish that the States may return to the Church . . . It is not our desire that the Duke should persuade himself that we wish to favour him, or that a single rogue should be left in the Romagna.'[27]

Valentino instantly penetrated the deception, but found no way of getting round it. That frenzied indecisiveness to which his illness seemed to have re- duced him now proceeded to entangle him in its toils. He lived in a kind of gloomy daze. 'He has no idea where he should be or go,' Machiavelli wrote of him. 'He seems out of his mind,' said Cardinal Vera de Ercilla, his former tutor. His disease tormented him. His face 'marred and pitted', his eyes like hot coals in their dark, hollow sockets, and with that cruel mouth of his, he horri- fied all who met him. The realization of this fact would make him burst out in strident peals of laughter.

He did his best to break the invisible bonds which held him captive. He told Julius II that he would gladly mount an expedition on the Church's behalf for the reconquest of those territories in the Romagna which had been annexed by Venice, or re-occupied by the country gentry. Having obtained the necessary permission from the Pope, he worked out his plans and set preparations afoot. Once more he seemed to have become the old Valentino, the man of crisp decisions, confident action, and perfect, ultra-swift organization. From all this it became convincingly clear that he was made for a military career, and that only in the field of action could he be fully himself.

He set out on 19 November. At Ostia a flotilla of galleons was awaiting him, together with five hundred foot-soldiers. They were to disembark at Leghorn, and from there join up with the forces led through Tuscany by Miguel de Corella and Taddeo della Volpe.

But scarcely had he left Rome before Julius II issued an order to the civic authorities and population of the Romagna telling them to regard themselves as subjects of the Church, and not of Cesare. And scarcely had he reached Ostia when Cardinal Soderini appeared and asked him, in the Pope's name, for the proper 'passwords' that would open the gates of the Romagna fortresses, and induce their castellans to hand them over. His response was a flat refusal. At this point he found himself escorted back to Rome under arrest, where it was not long before he learnt that his troops in Tuscany had been attacked and routed by the Florentines. Both Miguel de Corella and Taddeo della Volpe were prisoners.

There now began that acute phase of hostility between him and the Pope which may fairly be termed the 'war of the passwords': a war conducted, by Julius II, with a range of tactics which varied from blandishments to threats, from promises of freedom to intensification of surveillance; and on Cesare's part with persistent and unshakeable obstinacy. He would not supply the informa- tion, and that was that. A third party to the contest now appeared in the person of Guidobaldo da Montefeltro, who at this time was a guest of the Vatican. At a meeting with his victim of the previous year, on 2 December, Valentino played the part of the repentant sinner, imploring pardon and cursing his father's memory; but he did not let slip this opportunity of insisting on the lofti- ness of the motives which had impelled him, and the valuable results he had achieved: 'Under my rule the cities of the Romagna have begun to enjoy that peace and tranquillity which hitherto they had never so much as dreamed of, let alone enjoyed!'[28]

On the evening of 3 December he threw in the sponge and gave Guido- baldo the passwords, so that he could pass them on to the Pope. This was the price of his freedom. Julius II now pledged himself to let him depart for what- soever destination he pleased, together with his household and his possessions. However, the castellans of the Romagna fortresses still refused to open their gates to the Papal commissioners, saying that the passwords had been extorted from their Duke by force, and that they would only hand over the fortresses when he had been set at liberty. One of the commissioners never got back at all: this was Pedro de Oviedo, a former officer of Cesare's, whom the castellan of Cesena had had hanged from his battlements as a traitor. About the same time, in Tuscany, Miguel de Corella was enduring, in stoically intrepid silence, the tortures with which his Florentine captors were vainly trying to make him reveal various alleged crimes by the Borgias; while Taddeo della Volpe, on being offered the chance of taking service as a *condottiere* under the Signoria, replied that he would prefer imprisonment.

Their loyalty was a comfort; but the Duke paid for it. He was now isolated in the Torre Borgia, which had been built by his father. According to the testi- mony of the Mantuan ambassador, he was seen to weep while they were taking him thither. A wave of terror struck his friends and relatives. Two Spanish cardinals fled to Naples, taking with them Lucrezia's young son and the Roman Infante. Vannozza made ready to disappear at a moment's notice, as did all the prisoner's other relatives. Baggage waggons laden with Cesare's riches were dispatched from Rome and Cesena to Cardinal Ippolito d'Este at Ferrara, but fell into the hands of the Florentines and the Bentivoglio *en route*. By now Cesare had recovered from his brief spell of dejection. Still weakened

by his illness, but morally strong, he presented a proud, scornful, yet fatalisti-
cally serene front to the world. 'When I am in the direst adversity,' he said one
day, 'it is then I most fortify my spirit.' Elegant as ever, he would talk or play
chess with those whom the Pope allowed to come and keep him company.
Among his visitors was Machiavelli, who now, in his letters and dispatches,
took pleasure in spitefully trampling on his fallen idol, substituting mockery for
admiration.

The year 1504 opened under the auspices of Spain's power triumphant: on 1
January the Gran Capitano's troops entered Gaeta. France disappeared from
the long-contested realm; and Julius II, the passionate Francophile of yesterday
and all time, found himself suddenly attracted by Spain. It was with the
Spanish that he now began to negotiate an agreement: sooner or later he would
have to release his prisoner, and what he was now doing would render Cesare
harmless.

On 28 January a definite bargain was struck. Cesare would be transferred to
Ostia or Civitavecchia, in the custody of Cardinal Carvajal, and given forty
days to see that the fortresses of the Romagna were handed over to the Pope's
commissioners. If he managed this, he would be free to leave for France; otherwise he would be brought back to Rome as a prisoner.

On 14 February the two adversaries dined together, in an atmosphere of
great mutual amiability. The following morning Valentino embarked on the
Tiber, and left behind him, for ever, the city of his triumphs and his humilia-
tions.

It was not until the night of 19-20 April, thanks to the kindly accommodation of his warder, that he managed to get away from Ostia. The castellans of
the Romagna were still refusing to surrender their fortresses while the Duke
lacked complete freedom; he himself protested to Julius II at his forced delay 'in
this place, where, it seemed to him, he was worse off than in prison'. And it
became necessary to modify the clauses of the previous agreement with a new
convention, dated 10 March.

It was not to France that Valentino turned his steps, but to Naples. This was
his second mistaken decision: wrongheaded to the point of foolhardiness. He
could have approached Louis XII, who had little to complain of in his conduct, since by and large he had remained faithful throughout; instead, he was
going to entrust himself to Ferdinand, who notoriously—and for very good
reasons—hated him just as he had hated his father; to Isabella, who nursed a
genuine loathing for him; to men such as Gonzalo de Cordoba and Prospero
Colonna and the Duke of Bisceglie's relatives, who could scarcely wait to

get their hands on him. He turned his back on the calculating but secure pro￼tection of France—where he had his wife and daughter, relatives at the Albret Court, companions-in-arms who were close to the King, not to mention castles and lands of his own—to throw himself on the mercy of Spain, where he had nothing but enemies. Once again the gambler assumed he could break the bank with an unexpected card, and reverse his luck with an act of crazy audacity. The card he took along was an offer of conquests in Tuscany for Spain.

From Gaeta he sent a messenger to his captains and supporters in Rome, with the secret news of his destination, and of the imminent expedition. A flock of faithful stalwarts now took the road southward. In the Vatican they still had no notion where he had got to.

At Naples he was received by the Gran Capitano and all the more important members of the Spanish government, as though his power were still that which he had wielded a year before. He proceeded to outline his two-part programme: he offered to put himself at the service of Their Most Catholic Majesties; he also offered, on Spain's behalf, to undertake the occupation of Piombino and Pisa, as bases for operations against Florence, now allied with the French. He asked for men and supplies.

Having obtained Gonzalo's consent, he set about the realization of the pro￼ject with furious energy. He arranged for money to be forwarded (though lately, in Rome, he had affected to be a poor man, the banker Alessandro Franci alone held some 300,000 ducats on deposit from him) and began recruiting men for the expedition, unaware of the pact that had been concluded—behind his back—between Julius II and the King and Queen of Spain. He also knew nothing of certain orders issued by the Gran Capitano.

By 25 May everything was ready, and his departure fixed for dawn the following morning. That evening Cesare went to say goodbye to Gonzalo, who embraced him and wished him good luck. He went home with the famous captain Pedro Navarro, spent a little more time talking to him, and then suggested that he retire, since there were not many hours left for sleep. The captain shook his head; he had orders to stay beside him, he told Cesare, and to keep awake at all times.

Cesare's face blanched. 'Santa Maria!' he cried, 'I am betrayed!'[29] Betrayed on the King's orders, by a gentleman, a soldier like Gonzalo, who, having furnished him with a safe-conduct, then found the means to get it back and destroy it.

There followed three months of imprisonment: mild at first, but then solitary confinement. His gaoler—invisible but all too real—was the Pope himself, furious because the castellan of Forlì had not yet handed over his fortress, then switching from threats to blandishments, and promising him his freedom once the handover was complete. Eventually Cesare yielded, and wrote to the castellan exhorting him to desist from a futile resistance to fortune, which was now 'too angry' with him. But his promised freedom turned out to be removal from prison to a galley which sailed from Naples on 20 August 1504, taking him 'under close surveillance' to Spain, in the custody of Ettore Fieramosca and Prospero Colonna.

Cesare was taken ashore at Alicante, and from there escorted to Valencia. He must have felt his pulse quicken as he traversed the ancient pastures of the Borgia ox, the land of his ancestors. They passed very close to Gandia, where his brother's widow pricked up her ears at the news of his coming.

Spain had made ready a fine castle for him, set on a sharp spur some six hundred feet high, rising wedge-like above the boundless and solitary plain, motionless as a great ship becalmed in some petrified sea. Numerous ring-walls and keeps, one above the other, surrounded the actual fortress, its great tower rising high above a scene of glaring desolation which stretched as far as the eye could see. At the foot of the castle rock were a number of cave-dwellings. Here, in the custody of the giant Gabriel de Guzmán, Cesare was to remain for many a long month, watching the seasons come and go, while throughout France and Italy and Spain the wildest rumours and counter-rumours spread and inter-wove themselves on his account. Never before had the name of Cesare Borgia been so continually on men's lips. It was said that Maria Enriquez wanted to have him brought to trial for the murder of the Duke of Gandia. It was said that King Ferdinand, yielding to urgent petitions which reached him from all quarters, meant to set him at liberty. It was said that he would shortly return to Italy at the head of an expeditionary force. And so it went on: rumours, tremors of joy, shudders of fear. The man who still dominated Europe's atten-tion knew nothing of all this; he remained there on his rock, remote from the living world.

The summer of 1505 found him shut up in another tower, that of the castle of Mota at Medina del Campo, a vast fortress—whether more imposing or terrifying it would be hard to say—which formed a residence for the sovereigns of Castile. Behind these walls, on 26 November the previous year, there had died Queen Isabella, Cesare's most relentless enemy, whose removal opened up the thorny problem of the Spanish succession. The heir to the throne of Castile was her daughter Joanna, a half-witted creature who spent her days at the kitchen range in the castle of Mota. Ferdinand had had himself proclaimed Regent; but the mad girl's husband, Philip the Fair, did not accept the decision of the

Cortes, and came hurrying out of Flanders into Spain to assert his rights. The situation was a tense one; and Valentino, unexpectedly, became a bone of contention between the two antagonists. Ferdinand, hoping to employ him as a military commander on the expedition he planned to make into Italy, with the object of cutting that over-ambitious character Gonzalo de Cordoba down to size, asked his son-in-law to release him. Philip, who also had it in mind to make use of Cesare's services if the situation between his father-in-law and him-self ever came to a show-down, flatly refused his request.

On 25 September 1506 Philip the Fair died, eighteen days after Ferdinand set out for Italy. Cesare had now been confined in the top of that Cyclopean tower for over a year. He escaped on the evening of 25 October, letting him-self down into the dizzy void on a rope. His guards spotted what he was at, and cut the rope, so that he plummeted down to the ground, a horrifying fall which left him broken, bloody, and almost unconscious. Accomplices hoisted him on to a horse and galloped away, with their pursuers hot on their heels. In the end they managed to shake them off. Their first stop was at Villalon, fief of the Count of Benavente, who led the anti-Ferdinand party in Castile. From here—in a fraught odyssey of peril and ambush, through November's rains and snows—Cesare finally made his way to the north coast, on the Atlantic. His goal was Pamplona, the capital of his kinsman Jean d'Albret, King of Navarre. He arrived there on 3 December, and burst into the royal palace with a smile of demoniacal triumph on his face.

His first concern was to notify the King of France, the Courts in Italy, and likewise his many friends there, that he had regained his freedom. (He must have conveyed the news to his wife and Lucrezia somewhat earlier: the Duchess of Ferrara had it by 26 November.) These letters were couched in courtly official language. Their tone looked back to the past; it was as though the events of August 1503 had never happened. They were the proclamations of a sovereign. In Italy the enthusiasm of those with a taste for nostalgia flared up like a forest fire.

Jean d'Albret was tied up in a civil war which could well lose him his throne; Cesare could hardly have arrived at a more opportune moment. It was vital to quell the revolt, led by Louis de Beaumont, leader of the party which wanted to hand over Navarre to Ferdinand. For almost two years now the rebel had been holding out in the fortified town of Viana, an impregnable retreat, its lofty grey walls dominating a rough, wooded countryside, and making mock of all attempts to take them by storm. From here Beaumont carried out devastating raids, and was steadily extending his dominion, with the lightning tactics that mark a first-class guerrilla leader.

As soon as the weather permitted, Cesare marched against Viana, and camped beneath its walls with his army: 5,000 foot-soldiers, about 1,000 cavalry, 200 knights and 130 men-at-arms. The city was successfully stormed, and Valentino then prepared for an assault on the castle, where Beaumont and his men had gone to ground.

On the night of 11 March, taking advantage of a storm, which forced Cesare's troops to take shelter, the besieged poured out of the castle and pre-pared for a raid. They managed to get some provision-convoys through the enemy lines, and then, emboldened, attacked one of Cesare's outposts. When the alarm was given, Cesare, in haste and fury, donned his armour, leapt into the saddle, and charged to the attack. His horse stumbled, throwing him. He got up, cursing, clambered on to his mount again, and galloped off, sword in hand, to join the pursuit. He found himself on his own. Formidable as never in his life before, he thundered down on the enemy, laying three of them low. But Beaumont, who had spotted this yelling horseman from some way off, though without recognizing him, urged his troops on against him. They ringed him round, feinting, circling, gradually luring him into a steep gorge. Convul-sively whirling about, this way and that, on his rearing horse, dealing out frenzied blows on all sides, Cesare spent his last moments exhibiting that courage, that fury, which formed the dominant leitmotif of his entire existence. Pitched out of the saddle by a lance-thrust which pierced his armpit, he still fought on, until his knees gave under him, and the savaged body lay still.

Jean d'Albret, coming up with his officers and men, found Cesare slumped beside his dead horse: naked, since the enemy had stripped him of everything. On that pale and bloodless body were the reddened gashes of no less than twenty-three wounds.

In Navarre, for many years to come, they sang a ditty which, if it was not in fact written with Cesare in mind, could have fitted no other person better.

> *Pleurez, vaillants hommes de guerre,*
> *pleurez, Navarrais au grand coeur.*
> *Un crêpe s'étend sur votre terre:*
> *il n'est plus, l'illustre vainqueur . . .*

He was buried at Viana, in the huge and majestic church of Santa Maria. That same year, Jean d'Albret of Navarre had a sarcophagus constructed for him, with a marble urn on which as we read in the *Anales del Reino di Navarra* by José Moret, 'were portrayed, in relief, the Kings of Holy Writ, in postures of mourning for such a death'.

By command of a late seventeenth-century Bishop of Calahorra, the sarcophagus was destroyed, and the remains of Alexander VI's son buried under the public highway, before the front steps of the church. Rediscovered through the efforts of the historian Charles Yriarte—the skeleton was intact, but crumbled into dust as soon as it was touched—Cesare's remains were gathered up and laid to rest once more.

His cracked tombstone, its fragments carefully put together again, now lies on the ground to the right of the church. Those who follow the trail of the Borgias through Spain till they come, finally, to Viana, can read the following inscription, cut in most beautiful lettering:

CESAR BORGIA
GENERALISIMO DE LOS EJERCITOS
DE NAVARRA Y PONTIFICIOS
MUERTO EN CAMPOS DE VIANO
EL XI DE MARZO DE MDVII.

THE DECLINE
OF THE FAMILY

*T*HE collapse of Borgia power in Italy reduced the personal destinies of the survivors to a channel of respectable normality. The clamour and scandal, the terror and hatred which had hitherto surrounded their name were now gradually replaced by the deference one accords to the colour-less heirs of an uproarious past age.

The only person who continued to live very much in the here-and-now of the century's opening decades was Lucrezia. The spotlight of curiosity (which had been trained with such insistence on the entire family) still picked her out. Her important position—combined with the monstrously romanticized story of her life (half slander, half fantasy) which was already in circulation—is enough to explain this persistent interest. It must also have found some incentive in the lavish tributes paid to her beauty, her intellectual gifts, and her personal quali-ties by the poets and men of letters attached to the Court of the Este. Amongst these servants of the Muses there were two in particular who helped to establish what we may term the 'second image' of Lucrezia Borgia, superimposing one legend on another, and obliterating (as though on a palimpsest) the obscene caricature-portrait of a Roman Thais with their own idealized picture of the supremely virtuous Duchess of Ferrara. And both poets, quite apart from their writings, saw to it that she continued to be talked about, for reasons of a some-what different nature.

That irresistible figure Pietro Bembo had dazzled her during his stay in Ferrara, passing through Court society like some meteor, haloed with breeding and eloquence. On his departure, he had left behind him the shadow of a doubt which was destined to continue down the ages: that concerning the nature of his attachment to Lucrezia. Was it platonic or not? The dedication of his *Asolani*, published at Venice in March 1505 by the press of Aldus Manu-tius, may have concealed the memory of passionate hours; alternatively, it may merely have been the expression of a sentiment which confined itself to the sphere of tender yearning.

What had more dangerous repercussions on her life, and her reputation, was the friendship she granted to Ercole Strozzi, the elegant Ferrarese poet who had entertained Bembo in his country-house. There was a good deal of covert talk about this relationship, too, since Strozzi was young and passionate, and in his imitations of Petrarch took scant trouble to dissimulate those ecstatic feelings which the Duchess aroused in him. The scandal redoubled when, one June morning in 1508—only a few days after his marriage to Barbara Torelli, the widow of a Bentivoglio—he was found dead at a street corner, wrapped in his cloak, with all his hair wrenched out, and his whole body one mass of dagger-wounds. It looks as though this murder was in fact the outcome of a plot hatched by Galeazzo Sforza—if not by the Bentivoglio themselves—over mundane matters relating to the dowry; but gossip did not hesitate to whisper Lucrezia's name in connection with it. Some thought that she herself had organized the deed, either because of jealous resentment at the poet, who, after tasting the fruits of her intimacy, had had the impudence to take a wife, or else in fear that he might reveal the favours she had bestowed upon Bembo. Others argued that Alfonso had been responsible for the ambush, caught between two equally compelling motives: marital jealousy and the fury of a lover scorned, though the truth was that no one had ever seen him evince the slightest interest in the beautiful widow.

Anti-Borgia propaganda was always imaginative in its libels, and now its viperish tongue began to flicker to some purpose. Lucrezia's name was further linked to that of her brother-in-law Francesco Gonzaga, a brutal, hairy, gloomy, but indubitably virile, figure. God alone knows what masterpieces of intrigue the rumour-mongers would have cooked up had they been able—as history now is able—to bring the names of Lucrezia, Gonzaga and Strozzi together as ingredients in the same unsavoury hotch-potch. It transpires, in fact, that Lucrezia—using one of her ladies-in-waiting as a go-between—conducted a clandestine correspondence with Gonzaga in which her husband was referred to as 'Camillo', and she herself as 'Barbara'; and the most interesting detail which emerges is that Ercole Strozzi figured as the go-between for a meeting which took place at Ferrara during Alfonso's absence. However, there are two considerations which militate against drawing too extreme an inference from this. One is the unswerving affection always lavished on Lucrezia by her sister-in-law Isabella, an anything but naive or gullible person; the other is the punctilious care which Lucrezia took to safeguard her own reputation as a faithful wife. No tangible facts ever emerged to cast a shadow on that reputation.

Alfonso, moreover, was a man given neither to humour nor to tolerance; and it was well-known that at the Court of Este, in certain situations, they employed methods which lost nothing by comparison with those more notorious tricks attributed to the Borgias. If Lucrezia was under the erroneous impression that her move from Rome to Ferrara had brought her out of a storm-tossed sea into some idyllically calm and peaceful harbour, one episode she witnessed there quickly banished all such illusions from her mind.

This drama had its beginning a few months after her husband succeeded Ercole (he having died in 1505) and she as a result became the reigning Duchess.

Both Giulio and Cardinal Ippolito—the first Duke Ercole's bastard, and the second his legitimate son—had fallen in love with Lucrezia's cousin Angela Borgia, whom she had brought with her from Rome. Giulio was remarkable for the extraordinary beauty of his eyes; and Angela had the ill-starred notion of singing their praises, with most untimely enthusiasm, at the very moment when Ippolito was clasping her to him in an effort to seduce her. To free himself from what was clearly a most damaging disadvantage, the reverend cardinal could find no better solution than to deprive his brother of these blackguardly eyes; and on 3 November 1505, on the way back from a hunting-party, he laid an ambush with this precise intention. Hired bullies, under his personal supervision, did their best; but so did the doctor who cared for Giulio afterwards, with the result that, though he lost one eye, the other survived—still as beautiful as ever.

Alfonso found it expedient to treat his brother the cardinal with a certain lenience, and merely exiled him to a safe distance from Ferrara. Giulio, his one surviving eye flashing fire, swore a vendetta, and set afoot a conspiracy for a *coup d'état*. Among his fellow-conspirators were yet another brother—Ferrante, who in December 1501 had been a member of the party that went to Rome to fetch back Lucrezia—and several members of the Ferrara aristocracy including Count Boschetti, as well as the wandering poet John of Gascony. Their plan did not lack a certain radical forcefulness: they aimed to stab Alfonso during a masked ball, poison Cardinal Ippolito, and proclaim Ferrante Duke.

In July 1506 the plot was discovered. Giulio stupidly sought refuge in Mantua, whence his sister and brother-in-law quickly restored him to Alfonso, who could barely wait to see him again. Ferrante, no less stupidly, flung himself at his brother's feet to implore forgiveness: Alfonso jerked one eye from its socket with the point of his sword, shouting that now he would be on an equal footing with his accomplice. Both Ferrante and Giulio were condemned to be hanged, and led in chains to the foot of two gibbets which had been set up facing a dais on which (at the Duke's most kind invitation) all the nobility was now assembled. Then, at a sign from Alfonso, the execution was postponed: a nasty joke, which caused both its one-eyed victims to faint. They were taken back to their cells in the castle-tower; Ferrante survived until 1540, while Giulio was released in 1559 after no less than fifty-three years of detention. It goes without saying that for the other conspirators, including Count Boschetti, there was no such reprieve *in extremis*. Parts of their quartered bodies were in fact impaled upon lances, like so many scarlet banners, and set up on the top of the castle tower. The wandering poet fled to Rome, and was sent back to Alfonso by Julius II with a recommendation that his life should be spared. He was shut up in a cage, and the cage hung from the same tower; a week later, he was found strangled.

So there was something rotten in Ferrara too; and Lucrezia's life did not always flow like a beautiful river, majestic and calm, beside that of Alfonso. This ultra-stern husband of hers might spend his leisure hours working at a lathe, or handling paint-brushes—not to mention casting the finest cannons in all Italy—but when a crisis arose, he showed just how deeply he was to be feared.

Lucrezia had much on her mind: domestic tragedies, anxieties arising from political events (which forced the Duke to steer a perilously tricky course between Venice, France, and Julius II), the whole weight of her remembered life in Rome, and the agony of being parted from her son, who was growing up far away, in the care of his aunt, Isabella of Aragon (Gian Galeazzo Sforza's widow). To all these worries—at times eclipsing them—there was now added the thought of Cesare as a prisoner.

From 1503 on Lucrezia never wearied of interceding on his behalf. She explored every possible avenue; she begged and pleaded not once, but again and again; she enlisted the aid of high Church dignitaries and monarchs and great lords in an effort to obtain his release; but all her efforts proved futile.

In April 1507 the news of his death in battle reached Ferrara. Alfonso was away at the time; out of consideration for her feelings Cardinal Ippolito merely informed her that Cesare had been wounded. Lucrezia had no peace until she had sent a trustworthy agent of her own to Navarre to find out the whole truth. Then she retired to a convent—something she was in the habit of doing at the most critical moments of her life—to seek help and comfort from prayer. Hardly had she returned to the castle when Cesare's groom, a young Spaniard named Juanito Grasica, appeared at the Court of Ferrara. He had been the first person to find his master's body on that accursed night, after following him through the dark and rain-lashed countryside. Now he reeled off a full account of Cesare's death. Lucrezia wept till she had no more tears left to shed.

Just as the news of Cesare's escape from the Castle of Mota had electrified all Italy—rekindling in the breasts of his countless supporters, and among the populace of the Romagna, the hope of seeing him come back sword in hand, and consternating his enemies—so now the announcement of his death made an immense impression, as contemporary correspondence and a number of poetic tributes very clearly show. The most eminent man of letters in the anti-Borgia party, Jacopo Sannazzaro, fabricated a dexterous and cynical little lampoon on the subject, addressed to Marino Caracciolo, and modelled directly on Catullus:

O dulce ac lepidum, Marine, factum,
dignum perpetuo ioco atque risu,
dignum versiculis facetiisque,
necnon et salibus, Marine, nostris . . .

Ercole Strozzi intoned a Latin elegy, in which, with heartfelt accents, he
lamented the sorrow of Lucrezia and Charlotte d'Albret, and celebrated
Cesare's heroic exploits.

In the popular mind this remote, imprisoned Duke had already achieved
legendary status. Various obscure rhapsodes faithfully interpreted this mood,
composing 'laments' in *terza rima* and mournful songs employing the octo-
syllabic line:

>All now weep and make lament for
>Cesar Borgia Valentino . . .

The years passed; grief subsided into resignation, taking on the hue of a
diffuse and not wholly disagreeable melancholy. Life pursued its usual daily
round of minor duties and modest events: feast-days, dances, theatrical spectacles (with the ingenious new stage-machinery of Biagio Rossetti), cultural
entertainments, visits from Isabella and her husband. There were less pleasant
things, such as the war, with its heartache, its partings and reunions. Punctu-
ating everything, there was the birth of children.

In eight years Lucrezia brought five offspring into the world. In 1508 she
bore Ercole, who at the age of twenty was to marry that ugly but highly intelligent, and somewhat disturbing girl, Renée of France, Louis XII's daughter,
thus bringing down a whole load of trouble on his own head from the Holy
See because of his wife's blatantly Protestant sympathies. In 1509 Ippolito was
born, the future diplomat and cardinal, a wealthy, luxury-loving gentleman,
and a passionate antique-collector, who was to be responsible for building the
Villa d'Este at Tivoli; in 1514 Alexander, doomed to die in early childhood;
in 1515 Eleonora, who became a Ferrara nun; and in 1516 Francesco.

Insensibly, the years began to change her. Her blonde beauty lost its bloom, her
lithe dancer's figure grew thicker. As she grew older she became more and more
like her father. She had always had a hidden streak of melancholy; now it became more serious, more profound. Time was when she had enjoyed expressing
this mood in Spanish verses, with affected *agudezas* and elegantly succinct anti-
theses:

Tan vivo es mi padecer
y tan muerto mi esperar
que ni lo un puedo prender,
ni lo otro quiero dejar . . .

Now such conceits were a thing of the past. The season of poetry had died in her. When she did leave her apartments, which were all draped in satin and velvet hangings, and full of cushions embroidered with the Borgia coat of arms, it was more often (and more willingly) to pass the day in the peaceful atmosphere of some convent than to take her leisure in the salons and gardens of the Palazzo di Schifanoia [the Este palace at Ferrara].

Now that Alexander VI and Cesare were both dead, she formed a focal point for what remained of Borgia society in Italy: a small world, still shattered and terrified by the catastrophe, whose children had no notion of the way in which their fathers—ambitious, guiltridden, filled with that blind presumption which ephemeral human power inspires—had planned and calculated for their futures. Close to her—though not in the ducal palace—there lived Cesare's two natural children. In 1509 Camilla, then seven years old, was legitimized by a gentleman of the Este Court, the CountPalatine Gerolamo Giglioli; the act of legitimization, which a notary named Bartolomeo Codegori drew up, declared her to be *filiam quondam Ill.mi Domini Valentini Borgiae Ducis, natam ex eo coniugato et matre coniugata.* The child was brought up and educated, to begin with, in the Ferrara convent of Corpus Christi, and afterwards in that of San Bernardino. In 1516, at the age of fourteen, she donned the monastic habit of the Poor Clares, taking the name of Sister Lucrezia (undoubtedly to show the gratitude and affection she bore her aunt). Her brother Gerolamo was entrusted to Alberto Pio, the Lord of Carpi, and grew up in the small but resplendent Court of Ariosto's protector, surrounded by all the attention due to the prince of a distinguished house. On him, as on Camilla, Lucrezia bestowed her loving and vigilant solicitude; at the same time she kept up an affectionate correspondence with Cesare's legitimate daughter Luisa.

The year 1512 was a bitter year for her. Her husband had been awarded a handsome laurel wreath after the victory of the Battle of Ravenna (which was soon to wither away); but finding himself excommunicated by the Pope, he had been obliged to endure his own small Canossalike humiliation in the Vatican before he could receive absolution. He got it in the end, but with a thunderous intimation that the dukedom of Ferrara would be taken from him; and had he not fled before worse befell, he would never have returned home again. All this took place in July. In August, with his aunt Isabella of Aragon at his side, there died Rodrigo, the young Duke of Bisceglie, the son born of Lucrezia's one great true love-affair. He was thirteen years old. 'I find myself still full of tears and bitterness over the death of the Duke of Biselli, my dearly beloved young son,' she wrote some time afterwards. Since the time of her third marriage she had never seen him again.

Fate did not spare Lucrezia its blows; she was afterwards to declare that it had only kept her alive by way of expiation. Without her sons, without the nephews who were all that remained to her in the world, above all without the comfort deriving from faith, she slowly sank into a state of total despair. Close acquaint-ances began to notice that she was gradually renouncing all worldly vanities. She had only just turned thirty, and she was still a beautiful woman. But she took no more care of her beauty than Court etiquette prescribed; and she always dressed austerely.

Death continued its work, weeding out character after character from a now remote and distant story, leaving behind nothing but plaintive memories. Early in 1517 news of Goffredo's demise reached Ferrara. He had passed away at the age of thirty-five, in his principality of Squillace: that principality which he had had so little chance to enjoy while his father and his brother still lived, and which he had, indeed, run a considerable risk of losing. At the time of the French occupation he was actually stripped of it, after charges of treason had been pre-ferred against him for his alleged collaboration with the enemy; and during this period the Aragonese Court had limited itself to paying him an allowance for the maintenance of his wife. In 1502 he had regained possession of Squillace (or Esquilanche, as the Spaniards called it), minus the County of Cariati, and those supplementary titles which in 1494 had been bestowed upon him in preparation for sovereignty. Sancia—the turbulent, indomitable, unhappy Sancia, who had passed like a raging wind through her own life and Borgia history—was already dead and buried by 1506, at the age of twenty-seven, leaving no issue. Goffredo had married again, his second wife being a Spanish noble woman named Milá de Aragón y de Villahermosa, King Ferdinand's niece, who had given him the progeny necessary to secure the continuation of the princely House of Squillace.[1]

In that same year (1517) there appeared, as though from some kingdom of the dead, a seventeen-year-old youth who, setting out from Naples to the Romagna by sea, had suffered shipwreck on the Adriatic coast, where his baggage was plundered by brigands from Pesaro. Shortly afterwards he appeared at the Court of Este, and Lucrezia asked the Duke's *oratore* to demand restitution of all he had lost through robbery. From then on the youth was often seen in Ferrara, introduced by Lucrezia as her brother, and treated with every kindness by Alfonso, who took active steps to look after his future. This was none other than the Roman Infante, Duke of Nepi and of Camerino.

The following year, weighted down with money, houses, and good works, the seventy-six-year-old Vannozza died in Rome. She and Lucrezia had kept up a desultory correspondence over these latter years; but the two of them had never actually met again. With her shining examples of piety and charitable works, Vannozza had almost succeeded in making people forget her long-past sins of love, and her rather more recent financial lawsuits. She was a ghost from a vanished world, in which Lucrezia's memory could recall, beside her own childhood self, so many dear and happy images—above all, that of Giulia Farnese.

After the tragedy of 1503, Giulia had returned to Bassanello, at her husband's side, with the sensible air of a woman who has decided to change her way of life. In November 1505 she married off her daughter Laura—whom many regarded as the fruit of her affair with Alexander VI—to a nephew of the present Pope, Julius II, author of the Borgias' downfall.

She could, indeed, leave this world without too many regrets, her face twisted in the bitter smile of the losing gambler. Nowadays Lucrezia, too, loved to pray, to help the poor, to support convents and churches with her charity. She confessed every morning, and received Communion several times a month. It was said that she wore a hair-shirt.

On 14 June 1519, after a most difficult and painful pregnancy, she produced a still-born child, a girl. The birth left her prostrate. Complication intervened, and her condition worsened. During those days it became clear how deeply Duke Alfonso loved her. He became gloomy and taciturn; when his duties compelled him to leave his wife's bedside, he seemed like one crushed by an incubus. In a few days he became skeleton-thin, as though suffering from some long illness.

On the 22nd, aware that her end was nigh, Lucrezia wrote to Pope Leo X, who six years previously had absolved her from the ecclesiastical censure laid upon her by Julius II. Her letter is a moving document, both through its resignation and because of the strength of mind which it reveals: 'Having by reason of a difficult pregnancy suffered great ill for more than two months, it pleased God that on the fourteenth instant I should be delivered of a girl; and I hoped, my delivery once accomplished, that my ills too would be alleviated; but it proved quite otherwise, in such degree that I must needs yield to nature. And our most merciful Maker has granted me this great boon, to recognize that the end of my life is at hand, and to know that within a few hours I shall have left it, after first receiving all the sacraments of the Church. And at this point, as a Christian, albeit a sinner, I am minded to beseech Your Holiness, that out of kindness Your Holiness would deign, from Your Holiness's spiritual treasure, to lend some help to my soul by giving it Your Holiness's blessing; and this I most devoutly pray. And to Your Holiness's grace I like-wise commend my lord consort and my children.'

She died during the night of the 24th. Immediately afterwards, as soon as her body had been laid out, Alfonso wrote to his nephew Federico Gonzaga: 'It has pleased Our Lord God at this hour to take to Himself the soul of Her Grace the Duchess, my most beloved consort . . . I cannot write without tears, so heavy a burden is it to find myself deprived of so sweet and dear a companion, for such she was to me, both through her excellent conduct and that tender love there was between us . . . And I would rather fain have my friends lament with me than offer me consolation. . . .'

These words—revealing unquestionably sincere grief, and full of such nobly proclaimed esteem, from the pen of a most rough-tempered warrior, for whom words truly meant what they said—formed the most reliable and authoritative foundation for all moral evaluation of this enchanting woman, so much dis-cussed, so greatly slandered and besmirched, who had now ended her earthly span.

Her death removed the last figure of note from the family in Italy. Concerning the other survivors we have only sparse and fragmentary evidence.

The Roman Infante, who at the time of Lucrezia's death was in France, came back to Rome for the last time (1530) over a lawsuit, as claimant to the dukedom of Camerino conferred on him by Alexander VI. Gian Maria Varano having died in 1527, there were three rivals for the succession: Giulia, the daughter of the deceased, who was still a minor; a bastard of the Varano family; and Giovanni Borgia himself, who from the records of the case is re-vealed to have been '*oratore* to the Pope', and a figure of some consequence. The Roman Rota gave its verdict in favour of Giulia; and the Roman Infante, who —to his own detriment—had dug out the two famous Bulls of Legitimization discussed earlier in this work, was ordered to pay the costs of the proceedings. He died at Genoa in 1547, without having made a will. We do not know who inherited his property in Italy. The fairly substantial heritage which he left in Spain would, in the absence of any specified legatee, be spent on charitable works: so the law prescribed. But Francis Borgia, a saint who did not rely solely on divine bounty when it came to providing for the future of his own offspring, lost no time in laying claim to the Spanish inheritance. His letter to the Pope on this subject emphasized the theme of poverty and want a shade more than was strictly necessary. 'Your Holiness,' he wrote, 'would not prefer that this property should fall into the hands of unknown and possibly ungrateful persons, rather than leave it to my sons, who are Your Holiness's servants, and poor.' The Pope (who was Paul III, formerly Cardinal Farnese, Giulia's brother) replied: 'In consideration of the fact that you, being the nephew of our predecessor Alexander, to whom we owe so much, have the responsibility for seven children, of whom the first-born son will succeed you; and that the others are too poor to live according to their noble birth and condition . . . we grant you permission to set aside for your son Juan, or another, rather than that it should go to the poor or to charitable works, the sum of twenty-five thousand gold ducats.' He imposed one condition, that Francis should erect a sepulchral monument to Alexander VI in the Basilica of Santa Maria Maggiore. The Dukes of Gandia duly collected their 25,000 ducats; but their progenitor never got his monument. It was decided to postpone its construction until somewhat later; the idea survived for a while, in a somewhat attenuated form, and finally vanished altogether.

Camilla, Valentino's illegitimate daughter, died in 1573, in the Poor Clares' convent of San Bernardino at Ferrara. She had risen to become its abbess, and had presumably dedicated a large part of her long life of isolation and prayer to intercessions for the soul of her father, whose very appearance she could not recall. She was seventy-one at the time of her death. From the *History of Bologna* written by her contemporary Cherubino Ghirardacci we learn that she herself was remembered as a woman of great brilliance and intelligence: so much so, the historian claims, that, had she chosen to give proof of her abilities in the world, 'she would have far outstripped her father'. And at the conclusion of his enthusiastic profile the writer added: 'She was revered and honoured by all as a mirror of glorious virtue, and died full of good works.'

The same could not seemingly be said of her brother Gerolamo, who in-herited all the Borgias' less desirable inclinations, together with their high-handed methods. The centre of his life remained Ferrara, where in 1537 he married a high-born girl from the Pizzabeccari family. Left a widower, in 1545 he contracted a second match, this time with Isabella Pio di Carpi, daughter of the gentleman who had brought him up at his Court. The one episode we know from his life—sufficient, nevertheless, to give an idea of the kind of man he was—is his organization of a band of cut-throats to waylay and murder one Castrone, an adherent of the Lambertini family. This was in February 1542, at Poggio Renatico. It was a purely political crime, which in any case proved abortive: Castrone got away. But as Gerolamo's father had said, 'what is not done at lunch can be done at dinner'. He himself must have said much the same on this occasion. Poor Castrone was rash enough to show his face in Ferrara some four years later, on 16 November 1546; and this time the hired assassins' daggers did not miss their mark. After this Caravaggio-like gleam of light—as sinister as it is lurid—the figure of Gerolamo Borgia vanishes into the shadows once more.

FRANCE: CHARLOTTE AND LUISA

The official betrothal, the drawing up of the marriage contract, and the wedding itself were all crammed into the same day in May 1499. There followed two months of happy travelling among the French châteaux, and then a separation which lasted, without interruption, for almost eight years, and was made permanent by death. Such is the story of Cesare Borgia's marriage to Charlotte d'Albret. During this separation there came the birth of a daughter whom he never saw.

It is an odd and somewhat disconcerting story. How in fact are we to explain this total absence of meetings between them—at least up to August 1503, during the period when Cesare enjoyed complete freedom of movement? To darken the mystery still further we also have the irreparable fact that all correspondence between husband and wife has been lost (or, better, has not yet come to light). Nevertheless, it may be possible to illuminate the problem to some extent by the use of indirect evidence.

This shows, first and foremost, that Cesare's thoughts were always turning to his distant wife. The letters he wrote to his lieutenant and procurator Charles Seytre, immediately after leaving France in 1499, show that he meant to rejoin his wife as soon as possible; that he was full of solicitous enquiries, begging her to choose a place of residence which really suited her (after visiting all their estates), and authorizing her to take whatever steps she pleased for the restoration and embellishment of the buildings; and that he wrote to her whenever he had the opportunity.

More important still is the picture which emerges from surviving diplomatic correspondence: constant insistence on Charlotte's part that Cesare should return to France, and on Cesare's part that Charlotte should join him in Italy. Episodes in what was clearly a classic tug-of-war crowd thick and fast on one another over the years. As early as January 1500 we find Alexander VI contracting a loan of several thousand ducats to send Cesare's wife, thus offering her the chance of coming to Rome in great comfort and dignity. And here, in a dispatch by the Venetian ambassador to Rome, we glimpse for a brief flash what was in all likelihood the truth. The official story was that Charlotte could not undertake such a journey because of her pregnancy. On the other hand, the shrewd diplomat of the Most Serene Republic asserted that the reason why she did not come was because the French Court had forbidden her to do so. It was for this reason that the Pope, having got wind of the secret veto, told his courier not to hand over the money until he was quite certain that permission for Charlotte's departure had been granted. In June 1500 a messenger from Alain d'Albret reached Rome, and informed Valentino that he now had a daughter, Luisa; his secondary purpose in coming was to persuade the Duke to return to France, since (he said) poor Charlotte hardly felt as though she were married at all. Cesare wavered, but in the end did not go. In January 1501 two friars brought him fresh and urgent representations from his father-in-law. He received them in bed, said he was ill, and told them (according to the Venetian ambassador, from whom this information derives) that 'he could make no reply whatsoever'.

On the other hand, Cesare was constantly—at times indeed, with a certain impatience—putting pressure on his wife to get her to come to Italy. On more than one occasion (in December 1501, when the idea was first mooted of betrothing Luisa to young Federico di Gonzaga, and Lucrezia's marriage to the Duke of Ferrara was in course of preparation; and in February 1502, when this union was being celebrated at Ferrara) it looks as though Charlotte came very close to making the journey. Yet in the end she never did.

Cesare did not give up. During the spring of 1502 he sent a specially trustworthy agent to try and extract her from Issoudun; in July of that same year he changed his tactics, and dispatched a messenger not to her, but to Louis XII, with the task of 'urgently requesting that his wife should be made to join him'. When, a month later, he met the French King in Milan, he was loud in his complaints, and kept insisting that his just request be granted.

And here one senses some devious and suspect ploy: the wife who, first with excuses of indisposition, then with plain obstinacy (no justification advanced at all), refuses to budge; the King who, first to Valentino's emissaries and then to Valentino himself, announces himself displeased by the lady's refusal, promises to intervene in person, actually says that if she remains stubborn he will not let her show her face at Court again, and, finally, undertakes to ensure that Cesare at least gets the child.

Now some facts cannot be gainsaid. Charlotte was in love with her husband, and most urgently wanted an end put to their separation: she made this quite clear by her solicitous efforts to lure him back to France. She was perfectly well aware that he could not break off the work he was doing in Italy, even for a moment, or leave the country without a risk of the whole enterprise collapsing.

He will certainly not have omitted, through letters and by embassies, to have clarified his situation on her behalf. She was a devoutly religious woman, well aware of her duties and far from unfeeling; so she must have known very well that her attitude as well as her refusal to bring or send Cesare the child were morally reprehensible.

Logic, then, forces us to assume the intervention of some external impedi- ment. In the light of that indiscretion which leaked out during January 1500, not to mention an earlier instance in 1499 (when Louis XII similarly pretended to be offended by Carlotta of Aragon's conduct, and to be on the point of banishing her from Court, whereas in fact he did not want her to marry Cesare) there can be only one possible explanation for the enigma. Charlotte was forcibly detained in France at the King's behest, if not as a hostage to be used at some opportune moment, then undoubtedly as a means of keeping Valentino under control. This way he could implement no unwelcome policy, and assume no really dangerous attitude. It was in fact well known that Louis XII distrusted him intensely, and had become more and more alarmed by the steady growth of Borgia power. Equally well known was the fact that the Duke of Romagna had numerous influential (and highly suspicious) enemies at the French Court.

Towards the end of 1502, Cesare gave the impression that he had thrown in his hand, and abandoned all attempts at bringing his wife and daughter to Italy. He cannot have reached this decision without much suffering, and a terrible inner embitterment against Louis XII and the French. A man with his temperament, capable of such coldly implacable hatreds, could not have re- acted otherwise. Perhaps it is not mere rash speculation to suggest that this furious resentment may have been the determining factor both in making him back the new political line which Alexander VI took during the final months of his pontificate, and in swinging his choice towards Spain during April 1503. Valentino was a rational calculator; but he also had an impulsive streak to his nature, besides the tendency to nurse hatreds and vendettas. In opting for Spain, his object—as he at once made clear with his scheme for an expedition against Tuscany—was to strike a blow at France. All the evidence suggests that he wanted to settle a personal score with Louis XII, and make the King pay dearly for the blackmailing restraint placed on his wife and daughter.

Charlotte resided more or less permanently at Issoudun, her favourite (and the most romantic) among all those French feudal estates which Cesare had turned over to her. A princess of the blood-royal, Duchess of Valence, and a noble- woman of the very highest rank in France, she led the life of a petty sovereign, her Court containing numerous gentlemen-in-waiting, and maids of honour, five equerries, a comptroller, and countless lesser household officials. Sometimes, she would linger on the (still surviving) white tower of the castle, as though waiting for something or someone, scanning the horizons of the quiet Berry countryside. She went out to visit the sick, succour the poor, and talk, in a simple, familiar manner, to the peasants on her estate. Sometimes she would go as far afield as Bourges, to the Convent of the Annunciation, where she would visit Louis's repudiated wife, Jeanne de Berry, once her Queen, in a period which must have seemed far distant to them both.

The fall and imprisonment of Cesare came as a stunning blow to her. For the first time, after all these years, she went back to Court, and pleaded with the King to intercede on Cesare's behalf. Louis, characteristically, sent her off with words of hopeful encouragement, but took good care not to assist his now ruined enemy in any way whatsoever. She tried to get help to her husband through the agency of her brother the King of Navarre, who applied himself to this task with the greatest conceivable diligence, though already very conscious of Ferdinand's covetous eye on his Kingdom. Personally, she could achieve nothing. Despite her impressive Court, she remained one weak woman. On top of this, the backwash of that malice which the King and the high nobility felt towards her husband inevitably affected Charlotte herself. This hostile atmosphere subsequently intensified when the imprisoned Duke, from his various castles in Spain, began asking (through Jean d'Albret) for payment of that dowry of 100,000 livres which Louis XII had guaranteed him in 1499, but never yet disbursed. The King's reply to this impertinent request was embodied in a decree of 18 February 1506, which ordained that the Duchy of Valence and the countship of Diois (previously assigned to Cesare and his descendants in perpetuity) should be taken back from him and reabsorbed into the Crown's dominions.

In 1504 Charlotte had abandoned Issoudun and moved to La Motte-Feuilly, a small fief which she had acquired: a grey castle set in a verdant landscape, a small farmhouse-like church with a steepled bell-tower. At La Motte-Feuilly Charlotte's life reached a state of almost complete isolation. She had her daughter with her, and dedicated herself to the girl's upbringing. By now she had re-duced her household staff to very modest proportions.

She was already in a very distressed state after the news of her husband's escape when her brother broke it to her that he had been killed during the Viana campaign. She had all the castle-walls draped in black, and prepared to spend her remaining days wholly cut off from the world. She was twenty-four or twenty-five years old. On 11 March 1514 she died of grief, at the age of thirty-two. She had made arrangements for her heart to be buried in the little church at La Motte-Feuilly, and her body in the Convent of the Annunciation at Bourges, beside the body of the Queen whose favourite lady-in-waiting she had been, and whose most faithful friend she latterly became.

Some years later, Luisa decided to have her mother's heart enclosed in a sepulchre worthy of it, and entrusted the commission to Martin Claustre, the sculptor. The base was of black marble, as were the columns, 'carved in the antique style to resemble candelabra'. The seven Virtues were placed around the sarcophagus, three down each side and one at the head. At its foot were carved the armorial bearings of the Duchy of Valence. Above the black columns was a slab of white marble, on which reposed the supine effigy of the Duchess, in alabaster, with a cushion beneath her head and two lap-dogs at her feet. The same artist was also to sculpt, for the chapel where the tomb stood, a statue of the Madonna of Loreto, likewise in alabaster.

During the most chaotic period of the French Revolution this stupendous tomb was destroyed. Afterwards it was reconstructed from the broken frag-ments, and can be seen in the little church to this day, set amid bare rough walls, with the light from a low window falling on the recumbent statue, hands folded across its breast. On the floor, as a covering for the recess in which her heart is buried, there now lies the stone which originally stood at the head of her sepulchre. Its inscription reads:

Là gît le coeur de très haulte et très puissante dame Charlotte d'Albret, en son vivant veufe du très hault et puissant domp César, duc de Valentinois, comte de Diois, seigneur d'Issoudun et de La Motte de Feuilly, laquelle trespassa à son lieu de La Motte au mois de mars l'an de grâce mill cinq cent quatorze.

Guardianship of the orphaned Luisa Borgia, at the time of her mother's death still only fourteen, was assumed by Louise of Savoy, Duchess of Angoulême and mother of the sovereign who, before many months were out, would succeed Louis XII under the name of Francis I. She still kept up a correspondence with her grandfather Alain d'Albret (who from his castle at Nérac kept a watchful eye on the estates she had inherited), and likewise with her aunt Lucrezia and with Isabella d'Este, to whom she turned to salvage what she could of the wealth her father had left in Italy.

Here is a letter she wrote to the Marchioness of Gongaza:

Lady, as humbly as I may, I commend myself to your good grace.

Lady, the thing I desire most in the whole world is to learn what prosperity my good kinsfolk and friends enjoy. To be informed concerning your own,

and that of Madame the Duchess of Ferrara, my aunt, I now charge and dispatch the present bearer, to see you and bring me back your news. I beseech
you, lady, to send me, through his good offices, a full and detailed account
thereof. And if it please you to hear mine, I will tell you it in ample measure.

Lady, I have also charged him to tell you one further thing on my behalf.
I beg you to heed his words, and to aid me in my affairs, of which I will
speak to you. And by so doing you will lay me under an eternal obligation of
gratitude. With the help of Our Lord, whom I pray, Madame, to grant you
a long and happy life.

Written at Auxonne, the ninth day of June.

Your most humble niece and good friend. LOUISE DE VALENTINOIS.

Vast riches were at stake: the sums which her father had on deposit with
various bankers, and the *objets d'art*—to a value of 150,000 ducats—which, at
the time of his downfall, he had entrusted to Cardinal Juan Vera de Ercilla,
with instructions (in the event of some mishap befalling him) that they should
be passed on to Charlotte. The cardinal had died in 1507, two months after
Cesare himself. Luisa, in all likelihood, never got so much as a penny from all these
treasures; it would seem that Julius II found some way of appropriating them.

Now that Valentino had disappeared from the scene, there was no more talk
of betrothing her to Federico Gonzaga. When, in 1516, he was sent to Paris,
the two young people met, and probably, as they stared at each other in mutual
curiosity, smiled to recall the union projected between them when both were
little more than toddlers.

In April 1517 (even then she was barely out of her adolescence) Luisa wed
the husband chosen for her by the Duchess of Angoulême: Louis de la Trémouille, Prince of Talmont and Viscount of Thouars, a famous soldier,
formerly married to Gabrielle de Bourbon Montpensier, and now a widower of
almost sixty. An honourable match, but scarcely an exciting one. It seems
probable that she shed no more tears than decency required when, in 1525, news
reached her that this doughty warrior had fallen during the Battle of Pavia.

Widowed at twenty-five, she remarried at thirty: her second husband likewise
was a distinguished scion of the higher French nobility, Philippe de Bourbon,
and similarly destined to meet a glorious death in another famous battle, that of
St Quentin. She bore him six children, and then, in 1553, she died. Though
both her husbands carried many lofty titles, she had always continued to sign
herself *duchesse de Valentinois et comtesse de Diois*—a typical touch of Borgia pride.
The ducal title of Valence fell vacant on her death, and so remained until 1652,
when Louis XIV assigned it to the Grimaldi of Monaco.

SPAIN: THE DUKES OF GANDIA

Though struck down by a thunderbolt in Italy—where, when all is said and done, it was merely a transplant—the good fortune of the Borgias prospered and spread majestically in Spain, on their own native soil. There, clearly, it found the waters which best suited it, and breathed the air which it found most stimulating.

At the time of the Roman catastrophe, during the summer of 1503, the palace of Gandia was occupied by Maria Enriquez, now a widow of about twenty-five, and her two children: Juan, who was eight, and the seven-year-old Isabel. In the hands of these three lay the family's future.

The parallels which exist between Maria Enriquez's destiny and that of Charlotte d'Albret are quite astonishing. Married to two brothers, they both, while still in the flower of their youth, received news that their husbands had died a tragic and violent death far away from them; both reacted to their misfortune by taking refuge in ardent religiosity and an impassioned devotion to their children. The story of one seems based on that of the other.

Yet their moral features are so dissimilar that the comparison resolves itself into the establishment of a contrast. Nothing, in fact, could be more remote from the melancholy mildness of Charlotte d'Albret, with her passive submission to the will of those who for so many years kept her far from Cesare's side, and her sorrowful surrender to the tides of circumstance, than the drive, passion and energy of Maria Enriquez, that most splendid embodiment of the 'strong woman'.

Her impetuous spirit, her robust will, her tireless and courageous enterprise reveal in her the temperament of those heroines who combine spirituality with action, and who have nowhere flourished so remarkably as in the Spain of her day, their supreme exemplar being Teresa of Avila. The Duchess of Gandia certainly did not attain the stature of the Carmelite saint, but, within her limitations, she was of the same breed: a breed, I would maintain, that is quintessentially Iberian. The memories of her which still survive in the Valencia region—oddly vivid memories, as of a far more recent figure—offer the most convincing testimony to her exceptional character. The people of Gandia without even needing to mention her name distinguish her from all the many other overlords of the Duchy: *la duquesa*, the descendants of her ancient subjects still say, with unmistakable pride. I once made an unpremeditated, but fortunate, stop, during a journey on the trail of the Borgias, in the parlour of an enclosed convent at Moncada (Valencia). I shall not readily forget the light of fervour, enthusiasm and veneration I saw glow in the Spanish eyes of the Mother

Superior and another sister, as they sat there on the far side of the grille, out of the blazing August sun, and recalled her personality.

A strong woman indeed. From the moment her husband had left her, to go and get himself ambushed and killed on a dark night in Rome, she had grasped the reins of power, and kept a strikingly firm hold on them. Both its size and the nature of its environment made the Duchy a tough proposition, calling for solid nerves and a well-balanced mind. Though they had not yet attained the de-velopment that was to come some forty or fifty years later—when they also embraced the Marquisate of Lombay and fourteen baronies, and their subjects numbered over 3,000 families—the Borgia domains already constituted a State in miniature, with a large number of anything but superficial problems. The very composition of the population made it difficult to govern. On the one hand there was a small nobility, as poor as it was proud, sometimes rebellious and frequently turbulent; on the other, a common populace in which the *moriscos* constituted by far the most influential element. There were not more than about thirty 'old Christian' families in Gandia; all the rest were (more or less) converted Moors and Jews. *Quien tiene moro, tiene oro,* said a Spanish proverb; but to amalgamate so hybrid a population, and discipline it into some sort of viable coexistence—relying solely on the authority and responsibilities which the laws of the period conferred on the lord of a vast feudal estate—was no small undertaking. However, the Duchy—set as it was in one of Spain's most glorious regions—prospered exceedingly. The fertility of the *huerta,* with its luxuriant African vegetation, made it a privileged domain. The cultivation of the sugar-cane and the orange-tree, a flourishing trade, and various forms of local craftsmanship all helped to guarantee a reasonable level of general econ-omic conditions.

Those ambitions which, in another woman of Maria Enriquez's social standing, would have taken the banal form of personal ostentation, in her were directed, with drive and enthusiasm, towards the embellishment and endowment of the recently-built parish church. She asked Alexander VI to promote it to collegiate status; and he not only showed himself very willing to oblige her (with a decree dated 24 October 1499), but also enriched the church by making it personal gifts of furnishings and sacred vessels. Even Lucrezia, knowing of her sister-in-law's passionate addiction to this cause, sent her an extremely valuable monstrance. With the passing of time, Maria had the sacred edifice en-larged, gave it a magnificent west door bearing the Borgia and Enriquez coats of arms, and commissioned various distinguished painters and sculptors to execute the works of art which afterwards shone in splendour above its altars—thus exercising a talent for patronage by no means unworthy of mention.

Amongst the artists of whose services she availed herself, one who stood out particularly was the Valencia sculptor Damian Forment, to whom she entrusted the west door and the antependium of the high altar, and the Italian painter Paolo da San Leocadio, who had possibly come to Spain in 1472 with Cardinal Rodrigo Borgia (as he then was) on his mission as Legate for the crusade, and been commissioned by him to paint the ceiling of Valencia Cathedral. Summoned to Gandia by the Duchess in about 1501, he proceeded to execute numerous works for her, including the triptych for the main altar, and, most notably, a 'Sacred Family' now preserved in the Museo Provincial de Bellas Artes of Valencia. By a contract drawn up in 1507 he bound himself to remain permanently at her disposal.

After Cesare's death, Maria Enriquez commissioned a very odd painting from him, now lodged in Valencia's Colegio del Patriarca, built between 1586 and 1610 for the Archbishop and Viceroy Juan de Ribera. This edifice is rich in works of art, and famous for a highly picturesque ceremony known as the *Miserere*, celebrated every Friday in the church of the Colegio.

The picture itself is an altarpiece of indifferent aesthetic value, but highly suggestive for the student of Borgia history. The centre is dominated by a Madonna and Child, standing on a crescent moon between St Dominic and St Catherine. In the right foreground is Duke Giovanni of Gandia on his knees, with a hired thug behind him, about to plunge a dagger into his back. In the left foreground we see Cesare. He stands there, holding the blade of his own dagger by the point, and extending it downwards as though to hand it over. Beside him is Goffredo, watching him with an expression of open affection.

This scene is an enigma. Some have tried to interpret it as an act of accusation. Personally, I feel we must see something very different in it: the symbolic projection of peace attained—what we might call the sublimation and catharsis of the drama. One detail which particularly encourages me in this assumption is the serene expression and humbly resigned gesture of Cesare, who lifts his eyes towards the crucifix held up for him by St Catherine. Maria Enriquez, even though she was convinced of Cesare's guilt, and for a while persecuted him through the King and Queen of Spain, had too noble (and too profoundly Christian) a mind not to succeed in freeing herself—faced with Cesare's death, especially such a death—from that choking knot of rancour. The picture, in my opinion, bears witness to an inner liberation achieved through forgiveness. The atmosphere surrounding the figure of the three brothers conveys, to me, a sense of piety melting the harshness of anguish in enlightened sorrow.

During Julius II's pontificate, Maria asked permission to have the remains of Pier Luigi and Giovanni removed from Rome to Gandia: her fiancé and her husband, the first and second Duke. The Brief still survives in which the Pope —no friend to the Borgias—ordered the Augustinians of Santa Maria del Popolo, under pain of excommunication, to allow this double exhumation, so that the mortal remains *quondam Petri Ludovici de Borgia et Johannis etiam de Borgia, fratrum et ducum Gandiae,* could return *ad locum originis et sepulcra suorum maiorum.* The threat of excommunication in the event of disobedience leads one to infer some resistance on the part of the friars who had the two tombs in their custody.

The poor of Gandia had, in the Duchess, an assiduous and extraordinarily generous helper: when she sold, to Ferdinand the Catholic, those feudal do-mains which her husband had formerly owned in the Kingdom of Naples, she applied the entire sum thus realized to the alleviation of their misery and want. Her children, moreover, were indebted to her for their sound and enlightened education.

At Valladolid, on the last day of January 1509, the fifteen-year-old Duke Juan married Doña Juana of Aragon, niece to the King. A little rummaging into this girl's past origins dredges up various unsavoury details. We have to look back forty years, to a time when Ferdinand, by his mistress Aldonza Roig, Viscountess of Evol, had a son named Alfonso. At the age of nine this boy was appointed Archbishop of Saragossa, an office he continued to discharge for the next forty-two years. In his leisure moments between more serious tasks, he found time to sire four children on Doña Ana de Gurrea: Juan and Fer-nando, who both in turn afterwards occupied the same archiepiscopal see (one of them also held the title to the abbey of Veruela, founded by that remote figure Pedro de Atarés), and two girls, the first of whom entered the annals of Spain's highest nobility as the Duchess of Medina Sidonia, while the second (with whom we are here concerned) married the young Duke of Gandia. To round off the story, one may add that on the death of Alfonso—who celebrated Mass once only in his life, on the day he was ordained, nineteen years before departing this world—Ana de Gurrea continued to occupy his archbishop's palace, surrounded by the affectionate veneration of her children. She is buried in Saragossa Cathedral; her tombstone bears a Latin epitaph extolling her virtue.

This marriage, by strengthening the ties of blood which already existed be-tween the royal House and that of Gandia, not only extended the Borgias' influence, but also increased their wealth. As time went on, their position in Spain seemed to become steadily more outstanding and distinguished. Its economic foundations, solid *ab initio* thanks to Church funds and the dowry brought by Maria Enriquez, were strengthened still further by the revenues of the fief, and the capital realized on the selling-up of the estates in Italy. The ducal palace on the banks of the Serpis was overflowing with the treasures— jewellery, arms, furnishings, works of art, precious fabrics—acquired by Pier Luigi and Giovanni, and subsequently augmented by generous gifts from Alexander VI and Cesare.

Everyone in Gandia benefited to some extent from this wealth, especially the religious foundations. Maria Enriquez made regular visits—and most generous subventions—to a convent of *damas pobres*, or Poor Clares; these were French by origin, but during the reign of King John had settled in this small city. When she went there, she generally took her daughter Isabel with her.

Now it came about that one fine day in 1507 the girl entered the nunnery to accompany the viaticum, and could not by any means be induced to come out again. She imprisoned herself there for the term of her natural life. In September 1513, at eighteen years of age, she made her brother heir to her possessions, assumed the name of Sor Francisca de Jesús, and thereafter, in the felicity of renunciation, followed a life of prayer and austerity. Her retreat lasted fifty years: she did not die until 25 October 1557.

But the most surprising decision was still to come. Four years after her daughter's courageous gesture, Maria Enriquez herself crossed the same thres- hold. Her health was delicate, and the doctors had advised her against taking such a step; she would not, they predicted, be able to bear the rigours of the Franciscan rule for more than a year. She bore them for twenty-six.

On 24 March 1512 she made her profession. Under the name of Sor Gabri- ela, this cousin to the greatest and most powerful sovereign of the age, this woman who for fifteen years had ruled a Duchy, now exchanged her magnifi- cent attire for a grey habit, and day in day out performed the convent's most lowly tasks. For many long years she owed obedience to her own daughter, who had been made Abbess; later in 1530, she herself was chosen to bear the 'cross' of authority, and did not relinquish it until 1535. Sor Francisca de Jesús per- haps never fully understood the task of oblation and expiation to which, in redemption of the Borgias' sins, her mother dedicated her life.

If the son of Maria Enriquez had been a sovereign ruler rather than a mere duke, his contemporaries would undoubtedly have dubbed him Juan the Prolific. By his first wife, whose pedigree we traced above, he had seven children: Francisco (whom from now on I shall refer to as Francis, since this was the future saint), Alfonso, Maria, Ana, Isabel, Enrique and Luisa. The poor girl died while still in the flower of her youth, having borne these seven offspring in eleven years of married life.

The Duke's second wife was Francisca de Castro y de Pinos, the Viscount of Evol's daughter, who could claim descent from James the Conquistador. Juan must have found her at least as attractive as her predecessor, since during the twenty years of their union she bore him five sons (Rodrigo, Pedro Luis, Felipe, Diego, Tomás), and five daughters (a second Maria, a second Ana, Magdalena, Leonor and Margarita).

He had got his eye in for this wide-ranging display of paternity very early on. In 1507, that is to say when he was a mere thirteen, he produced an illegitimate son by the name of Cristóbal, the fruit of a love-affair with a high-born damsel named Catalina Díaz. He was in no great hurry to acknowledge the boy, though he did so in his will, before he died. *Mas vale año tardío que vacío*, they used to say in Spain during this period.

Seventeen legitimate children could constitute something of a problem, even for a Duke of Gandia. Juan solved this problem according to the custom of his day, though he took it to its logical extreme; all the boys (except for Francis, the first-born) were to enter the priesthood, while all the girls were to become nuns. The latter were packed off on the road to the convent at a very tender age, and only Luisa, out of all those born to Juan's first marriage, escaped the fate decreed for them by this autocrat in the ducal palace.

So it was that Juan II, with some dispatch, contrived to empty his own house —and in so doing to fill up the Convent of the Poor Clares, transforming it into a kind of creche. There, moreover, the children would be under the wing of their grandmother and aunt. And since his son, and his son's descendants, all followed the example he had set, it is not to be wondered at that no less than thirty-five female members of the family lie buried within the walls of this Gandia nunnery. At the same time, the boys went off, one after the other, to swell the ranks of the Spanish clergy—the higher clergy, naturally. All this was done, simply and solely, to maintain the family's wealth intact, and concentrate it in the hands of the heir to the dukedom. It was a curious fact that the above-mentioned Luisa, who actually had a strong vocation for the religious life, should have been the one led, by force of circumstance, to live in the world and become the Duchess of Villahermosa. However, this did not stop her striving diligently to perfect her nature; she left behind so dazzling a record of virtuous living that she became known as the *santa duquesa*. Equally paradoxical was the fact that Francis—for whose rights and privileges of primogeniture his sisters and brothers had thus been sacrificed—one day divested himself of these privileges in order to enter the priesthood.

The most notable episode to take place at Gandia during Juan's period was a violent popular uprising. In 1519 an epidemic broke out, and the nobility from the Valencia area took off in search of somewhere more salubrious, leaving the inhabitants exposed to the incursions of the Moors, which at this time were a regular scourge along the Mediterranean coast. In July of the following year, the populace took its revenge for this shameful act of desertion, organizing (allegedly for defence) the so-called *Germanía*, an armed league against the nobility. Encouraged by the simultaneous emergence of the *comuneros* in Castile, this insurrectionary movement soon spread through the greater part of Spain. Though drastically repressed in Aragon and Andalusia, in the area round Valencia it developed with aggressive virulence, forcing the aristocrats into headlong flight. The Duke of Gandia, however, firmly stood his ground; and when, on 12 March 1521, a group of twenty-one rebel leaders nailed a defiant manifesto to the coat of arms adorning the west door of the collegiate church, he replied by confiscating their possessions, and condemning them to death *in absentia*. He sent his mother, sister and children to the impregnable fortress of Peñíscola (formerly, as the reader will recall, a place of refuge for Benedict XIII), keeping only Francis with him in the palace, and prepared to continue the struggle *à outrance*.

Carlos V, to whom the aristocracy of the Valencia region turned at the first hint of trouble, in the hope of getting a decisive military intervention from him, had feigned not to hear their urgent solicitations; for certain private reasons of his own, he was by no means displeased by the fix in which they now found themselves. The insurgents disposed of 8,000 well-armed men, and rejected all compromise offers. To try conclusions with them, all that was available were the meagre forces of the Viceroy: about a thousand foot-soldiers and a mere handful of cavalry, who on 23 July were concentrated in Gandia. Juan sallied forth from the palace in battle array, followed by his troops, and preceded by an ensign bearing a standard draped in black, the Duchess having just died. The army now marched off. The rebels, under the command of that formidable figure Vincent Peris, were waiting for him a league or so from the city, on an uneven plateau near La Vernisa. The treachery of the Viceroy's gunners—who suddenly abandoned their artillery-train in order to go off and plunder Gandia—brought about a mass desertion by his Moorish troops, who likewise quit the field of battle, and hurried away after them. We cannot even talk in terms of a rout, since all that remained facing the rebels were the leaders; the army itself had vanished. Even these, were forced to save themselves by relying on the speed and energy of their horses. The ducal palace was sacked in true barbarian fashion; the eleven-year-old Francis only escaped the violence of the rebels (and perhaps death) thanks to prompt action by one of his tutors, who hurried him through a side-door into the gardens. Thence they made their way through open countryside till they reached and crossed the Serpis. Here the tutor mounted a horse, took Francis up in the saddle with him, and galloped away to the sea. They got a boat to carry them as far as Denia, some nineteen miles south of Gandia, where they found the fugitives from the battlefield piling aboard a Genoese vessel, and joined them. While they sailed away in the direction of Peñíscola the rebels occupied almost all the main key-points in the Valencia region.

It was not until the following year that the insurrection was quelled, and Juan, sword in hand, recovered his dukedom. He never forgave Carlos V for the malicious inertia he had shown. Already unsociable and intolerant by nature, he now withdrew into complete isolation from the Court, and the out-side world. He was one of the grandees of the Kingdom; his family was among those twenty which, in a decree dated 1520, the sovereign recognized as belong-ing to the *primera grandeza*, members of which were entitled to describe them-selves as cousins to the King. But such prerogatives he never exercised in the slightest degree. He had no wish for honours, or flattering pomp and show, or friends in high places; he refused all those 'services' which were the bread, the cross and the delight of those aristocratic circles which revolved and fluttered around the divinity of the sovereign. He remained a permanent and unshiftable feature of Gandia, ruling his subjects, supervising the cultivation of his estates, improving and augmenting his sugar-refinery installations, strengthening the city's defences (eventually he had no less than sixty guns set up on the ramparts) and stocking his palace arsenal, where he accumulated enough arms and equip-ment to fit out fifty men-at-arms and six hundred arquebusiers. His taste for independence made him misanthropic.

One episode among many may be described here to illustrate his tempera-ment. When Carlos V decided that Francis should marry Leonor de Castro, a Portuguese girl who was the favourite lady-in-waiting (and fellow-country-woman) of the Empress Isabella (or Elisabetta), he foresaw a certain amount of trouble from Duke Juan. The Duke, true to the traditions of the Aragonese nobility, did not look kindly on marriages with outsiders. Carlos sent a messen-ger to inform him of the decision that had been taken; at the same time he wrote him a most considerate and cordial letter, in which he guaranteed a splendid future for the young man himself, who during a brief sojourn at Court had already won golden opinions from the sovereign and his empress.

Juan replied in a few brief lines. He was most grateful to the Emperor, he said; but he himself, when he judged the time to be ripe, would make personal arrangements for his son's marriage, choosing him a suitable bride from the ranks of the Aragonese nobility. Carlos V, who had never succeeded in taking

the measure of this eccentric recluse, was flabbergasted. It was left for Francis—
who knew his father well, and had already begun to show hints of the subtle
psychologist and skilled diplomat he afterwards became—to suggest (with a
mischievous smile) what proved the correct gambit. A second messenger left
for Gandia, bringing the Duke an invitation from his sovereign. Why not come
to Court, where they could have a friendly discussion about the matter?
Terrified by such a proposal, Juan begged the Emperor to excuse him: his son,
he said, could marry Leonor de Castro without more ado, he no longer had
any objections to the match.

Francis Borgia's life and achievements belong more properly to the sphere of
hagiography. His history is one which goes beyond a purely Spanish context,
to achieve European dimensions. Any attempt to recapitulate it, cramming its
vast material and countless characters into the few pages still left of this book,
would be absurdly presumptuous. I shall therefore restrict myself to sketching
no more than its bare outlines, indicating only the most important moments on
the journey which led Cesare Borgia's great-nephew to achieve fame and glory
so different from that won by his forefathers.

Born on 28 October 1510, from earliest childhood (somewhat to his father's
disappointment) he showed signs of that religious vocation to which he would
one day commit himself, thus marking a clear break between two quite separate
'periods' of his life. He grew up more at home in the spiritual atmosphere of the
Santa Chiara convent than in the aristocratic-cum-military environment of the
palace; he was more influenced by his grandmother Maria Enriquez and his
aunt Isabel than by his own mother. Yet the shock he suffered when he saw the
latter in her death-agony was extremely violent; he withdrew to a private
chamber, wept for hours on end, and inflicted severe flagellation on himself to
save her from the tortures of the hereafter. One scarcely needs a profound
knowledge of psychoanalysis to appreciate the importance of this episode.

At the age of eleven, as a result of the *Germanía* insurrection, he, together with
his young sister Luisa, was entrusted to his maternal uncle, Juan of Aragon,
Archbishop of Saragossa and to Ana de Gurrea (discussed earlier in these
pages). In the Archbishop's princely palace he received the education befitting
a perfect gentleman: literature, music, fencing, riding, conversation and deport-
ment—all the skills needed to produce a complete and impeccable 'courtier'.

From the palace of his uncle the Archbishop he was transferred, the following year, in the capacity of *menino* or page, to the royal residence of Tordesillas,
where the Infanta Caterina (youngest daughter of Joanna the Mad, and sister
to the young Emperor) spent her days in the depressing company of her mother.

One may legitimately wonder whether the appearance of this Borgia child did not rouse dormant memories in the cloudy mind of Philip the Fair's widow, recalling the period at Medina del Campo, when she had the imprisoned Cesare for a neighbour.

Francis stayed three years with the Infanta. When in 1525 she married King John III, Juan refused to let his son follow her to Portugal. The sorrow which Caterina experienced at this separation pays tribute to the charm of her page.

After another three-year spell at Saragossa, mainly devoted to the study of philosophy, Francis entered the Emperor's service. On his journey to Valla-dolid, some biographers have emphasized an incident which, though suggest-ive, has scant claim to be considered historical; while riding through Alcalá de Henares, Francis saw a man of thirty-six being haled off to prison, escorted by the minions of the Inquisition, and was so profoundly struck by the nobility of his bearing, and the expression in his eyes, that he drew rein and kept watching him, as though rooted to the spot. The man was Iñigo López de Recalde, better known as Ignatius of Loyola. He was a gentleman from the North, who had earlier experienced some sort of blinding revelation, like Saul's on the road to Damascus. A brilliant, proud, and gallant officer, on 21 May 1521 he was fighting with the troops of Spain, under the walls of Pamplona, against a French force commanded by Jean d'Albret—Cesare's brother-in-law, who had lost Navarre and was now trying to win it back again—when a shot from a falconet took off one of his legs. Borne home to his Basque castle on a stretcher, he spent a long period in complete seclusion. It was during this period that he was touched by Grace. Afterwards he travelled in Spain, Italy and Palestine, secretly developing his plan for a 'company' (in the military sense) of men of the Church who would be ready to make any sacrifice *ad maiorem Dei gloriam.*

At the Imperial Court Francis passed from adolescence to the full flower of young manhood. Tall, vigorous, extremely good-looking, with a passion for horses and hunting, and a record of victories in tourney and tiltyard, he recalled the twenty-year-old Valentino; his figure had not yet acquired that obesity which was later to become legendary, and for many years transformed him into an impressive but hulking giant. He accompanied his King on an ill-fated military expedition in Provence, where he nevertheless gave splendid proof of the blue blood which flowed in his veins. Near Fréjus his friend Garcilaso de la Vega, the great soldier-poet, was fatally wounded while with quite incredible courage attempting to storm a tower defended by some fifty arquebusiers. Under enemy fire, Francis climbed down into the ditch, slung his friend across his shoulders, and struggled back the way he had come. After this he carried him off the battlefield, accompanied him as far as Nice, and stayed with him until he breathed his last.

After his return to Spain, a long illness immobilized him at Segovia. He spent this interval of leisure deepening his already quite exceptional musical knowledge. It is certain that, had he made music the dominant interest of his life, his name would now be written, in letters a foot high, across the history of sixteenth-century polyphony. Contact with Flemish composers at the Imperial Court had encouraged in him the development of extraordinary gifts which, disciplined and refined by study, come out in activities which cannot be dismissed. Though they might perhaps be labelled dilettante in terms of the marginal position (though not always) which they occupied in his life, their results—which were those of an inspired and technically most brilliant artist—merit a far higher evaluation. Regarding his virtuoso qualities as a performer, whose voice was powerful, harmonious, and of great flexibility, we obviously cannot do other than accept the evidence of contemporary witnesses. But what little has survived from his polyphonic compositions—a love-song which in his own day could be heard all over Spain, and was in fact known as the *Canción del duque de Borja*, besides various Masses, motets and psalms which for long years were performed in all the great cathedrals, and which choirmasters vied with one another to obtain—offers even the most severe musical critic notable instances of taste, fertility of invention, and contrapuntal expertise. Even when he was General of the Jesuits, in Rome, Francis still went on composing in his spare moments. A learned Benedictine musicologist has unearthed, from the archives of the collegiate church in Gandia, a Mass and eight motets which are certainly by him, and presumably written in his own hand. His, too, beyond any shadow of doubt, is a Mass with organ accompaniment, lacking the *Gloria* and *Credo*, which for centuries was sung in the same collegiate church on Sundays during Advent and Lent. This is the *Missa sine nomine* generally ascribed to Orlando di Lasso, who in fact did no more than add the two missing sections, and include the whole opus among his own works.

Francis had been at Court for some time when, on the evening of 1 May 1539, right in the middle of the Toledo celebrations for the opening of the Cortes Generales, the Empress died. It was later alleged that he had been in love with her: this legend was picked up by writers of romantic inclinations such as Angel de Saavedra, Duke of Rivas, and Ramón de Campoamor, and still survives today among the common people of Spain. At all events, he was given the task of escorting her body to Granada (where it would receive burial in the newly-built cathedral), and of attending the official inspection and identification, to be held in the crypt of the Chapel Royal before she was entombed. The

Empress had forbidden the embalming of her corpse; the journey, under a blazing Spanish sun, had taken fourteen days, and since then the cadaver had spent another two stretched out on its catafalque while the various rituals were gone through. It is easier to imagine than to describe the monstrous horror which Francis found confronting him when he stepped forward from the semi-circle of gentlemen gathered round the bier, approached the lead coffin, and lifted the veil which covered the Empress's face. In a hoarse voice he swore to the dead woman's identity. Then he moved back and rejoined the rest of the company, and slowly walked up out of the crypt with them. When he emerged in the bright evening air he was shivering.

It was 17 May 1539, a date he was never to forget, when, with agonizing travail, he was born again. The following day he heard John of Avila (afterwards to be beatified) preach in the Cathedral, and asked for an interview with him. This meeting made his decision to change his way of life final and inevitable. But the time for the actual break had not yet come.

For four years, from 1539 to 1543, Francis was Viceroy of Catalonia, a region noted for rampant brigandage and scandalous collusion between criminals and the so-called representatives of justice; a region where tyranny went unpunished and violence reigned triumphant. Francis ruled Catalonia with an iron hand, unmasking complicity even when it lurked in high places, firmly refusing to budge when officials who were corrupt to the very core did their level best to spirit the guilty away from his grasp and set them free once more. This was what happened in the case of Gaspar de Lordat, a notorious bandit leader whom Francis had captured; the Bishop of Barcelona, Gaspar's 'protector', managed to gain custody of him with assurances that he would be punished. Francis made angry representations about the matter to the King: 'It is my belief that the Bishop's idea of punishing this fellow will be merely to sprinkle him with holy water. . . .' One has to read his letters from this period: they are masterpieces of spontaneity, studded with flashes of wit and dry epigrams, with outbursts and threats against this or that scoundrel—'*Si Dios lo pone in my manos!*' No compromises, no indulgence, no needless compassion: lay the axe to the root of the tree. '*Ahora voy a cazar con la justicia de Dios!*' It proved the most eventful chapter of his life, as romantic and as fascinating as any adventure story. By the time it was over, many things had been changed in Catalonia, where, at last, people saw what manner of thing a strong and incorrupt system of justice could be. It would be a long time before the Catalans forgot the image of that gigantic figure on horseback, his troops behind him, riding across plain and sierra in pursuit of malefactors. Nor would there easily be quenched in their hearts the gratitude they felt towards a man who had recognized the want and misery of the people as a root cause of so many ills, and had laboured indefatigably to alleviate them.

The death of his father (1543) brought him back to the palace on the banks of the Serpis to assume the succession, and be translated from Marquis of Lom⁄bay into the fourth Duke of Gandia. He arrived with the intention of staying a month, and remained for seven years.

No one in his immediate circle knew the secret behind this delay. Nothing gave any hint of the *coup de théâtre* with which he was to astonish the world. He had reached the peak of his career: loaded with titles and dignities, friend of the Emperor and of young Prince Philip, wealthy and powerful, he projected the dazzling prestige of his mighty person throughout the length and breadth of Spain. To see him going about his ducal palace, bearing himself like the great nobleman he was, with those formidably heavy shoulders of his, and that ex⁄cessive *bodriga* about which he himself was wont to make jokes—a belly so great that he had been forced to cut a semi⁄circle out of the dinner⁄table before he could sit down and eat (though austerity and fasting very soon reduced it)—one could never have imagined the metamorphosis for which he was preparing himself. Perhaps even he himself had no very clear idea of it as yet.

It was a time of absorption and meditation, but also of more practical pro⁄jects. During the course of this lengthy sojourn he founded a Dominican monastery at Gandia, for missionary work among those of his subjects who were *moriscos* (which in four districts of the Marquisate of Lombay meant virtually the whole population); a college for the education of boys (which he entrusted to the first Jesuits, sent to him by Ignatius of Loyola), and, finally, a university. This institution received the Pope's approval in 1547, and that of the Emperor three years later; but it very soon foundered for lack of students, this being due to the close vicinity and overwhelming competition of the University of Valencia.

During his period as Viceroy of Catalonia the Duke had met Ignatius of Loyola, and at once acknowledged him as an extraordinary master of the spiritual life. A regular and lengthy correspondence now kept the relationship between them alive and fruitful. From afar, by means of letters and messengers, the founder of the Company (now the Society) of Jesus inspired and directed not only his every action, but his every thought and design. The Duke, with the docility and enthusiasm that form the hallmark of the neophyte, was en⁄tirely in his hands.

On 15 November 1543, at Salamanca, the sixteen⁄year⁄old Prince Philip had married Princess Maria of Portugal; on 12 July the following year the Princess died, four days after giving birth to a child who grew up to be the ill-starred Don Carlos. This event profoundly disturbed the Duke, helping to accentuate his drift away from the Court and all that it had once meant to him.

But the decisive factor, which broke his last ties with the past, was the death of his wife. His beloved Leonor expired on 27 March 1546, while, at her request, they were reading her those passages in the Gospels which describe Christ's Passion. From the cruel anguish of that loss the new man emerged victorious.

One thought alone now dominated Francis's mind: to put all his affairs in order, with that scrupulous thoroughness which his sense of honour imposed upon him, so that he could 'leave the dead to bury their dead' and embrace what was, for him, the one true life.

He asked, and obtained, from Pope Paul III permission to pronounce his solemn vows, though still remaining another three years in the world. So, on 2 February 1548, he made his religious profession, in Gandia: 'I, Francis Borgia, being an abominable sinner, unworthy of Our Lord's vocation and of this profession, do hereby take a vow of poverty, obedience, and chastity. . . .'

He was still 'in the world'; but his spirit was already soaring far away. He participated in the meetings of the Cortes of Aragon, but did not bother to conceal his delight when they were over, and he could take his leave. He busied himself with the future welfare of his eight sons. His first-born, Carlos—so named in honour of the Emperor—he married off to Magdalena de Centelles y Foch, niece of that Cherubín who had been the first suitor for the hand of Lucrezia Borgia. For his eldest daughter, Isabel, he procured a most brilliant match, bestowing her upon the Count of Lerma; his second eldest girl he married to the third Marquis of Alcañices. The youngest, Dorotea, was in a convent. His younger sons—Juan, Alvaro, Fernando and Alfonso—now became the responsibility of Carlos, the new successor to the dukedom.[2]

On the morning of 31 August 1550 he mounted his horse and, accompanied by his son Juan, some Jesuits, and an escort of nineteen household servants, set off for Rome. The official reason for his journey was the Jubilee. His real motive was to have a meeting with Ignatius of Loyola, and work out the pattern of his future life.

When he reached a crossroads not far from the city-gate of Gandia he drew rein for a moment, and turned round. He gazed at the walls, glowing red now in the morning sunlight. '*In exitu Israël de Aegypto* . . .' he murmured, his voice trembling with joy, and added: 'The noose is broken and we are free, in the name of the Lord.' Then he set spurs to his horse and rode on towards the sea.

The twenty-two years still left to him until his death at Rome on 28 September

1572, after the last of his innumerable journeys, form a monument which dominates the horizons of Church history during the second half of the century, and the shadow of which reaches not only to us but to ages we shall never see.

At first he was an isolated labourer in God's fields, dispatched to the harsh, semi-wild Basque province of Guipúzcoa, where in May 1551 he celebrated his first Mass in the chapel attached to the castle of Loyola, and his second in the open air, before 20,000 people, all drawn by the sensational news of his changed life. Ignatius's prediction—'The world will not have ears enough to hear so great a sound!'—was all too true.

For eleven years, between 1554 and 1565, he was Commissioner-General for the provinces of Spain and Portugal, and the overseas territories in the East and West Indies; from 1565 until his death he held the helm of the Company, as its third General. When he took up this office he told the assembled Fathers: 'I beseech you not to refuse me that which is granted to beasts of burden. Men not only claim the right to load them, but demand that they carry their burdens on journeys. If they falter, then, their load is lightened; if they walk slowly, they are pricked with the goad; if they fall, they are helped to their feet again; if they are too weary, the weight of their burden is taken from them altogether. I am your beast of burden; therefore treat me with compassion . . . And that my words may remain impressed on your hearts, as proof of the love I bear you, I humbly kiss your feet.'

A whole library of documents, scores of houses and colleges all over Europe, missions in Mexico, Peru, and Brazil—these remain as evidence for the vast range and scope of his activities, which spanned a huge portion of the globe, involved the greatest figures of the age in their development, and brought him into contact with the memories—living or dead—of Callistus III, Alexander VI, and Cesare.[3]

In contrast to that proud lust for domination which had stamped the period of his family's history, he made a heroic effort to gain the mastery over himself, to repress those instincts he carried in his Borgia blood, to prostrate himself in utter humility. Perhaps no one ever knew what a victory his meekness (which was regarded as the basic feature of his personality) represented in such a man.

One day a letter was delivered to him from the King of Sardinia, which bore the following by way of address: *To His Grace Don Francesco Borgia, Duke of Gandia.* He looked at it, shook his head, and gave it back to the bearer, saying with a smile: 'I have no idea where in the world this person, His Grace Don Francesco Borgia, Duke of Gandia, is now to be found.' It was as though he wanted to forget, not only that he had been Duke, but also that he bore the renowned name of that family which, in him, had produced the last of its great representatives.

Just as the era of Callistus III had been the radiant dawn, and that of Alexander VI the high noon of a story fated—like all human adventures—to have a beginning and an end, so Francis's formed its sunset: a sunset which, in the splendour of his sanctity, gathered and released all the power of the last dying light, yet also heralded the slowly spreading shadows.

After him, the family continued for over a century and a half to produce figures of the highest social distinction, and to enjoy immense prestige; but it had, essentially, dropped to the level of fashionable gossip, and never reattained the high roads of history. It was living on the inherited capital of its past, amid the echoes and memories of vanished greatness. In 1740 the last Duke of Gandia died without issue. He was the eleventh of his line, and bore two significant names: Luís, which recalled the first Duke, Alexander VI's son, and Ignacio, which evoked recollections of the saint from Loyola. The two lines were in fact related by marriage. In 1743 there died Maria Ana de Borja, last descendant of the Spanish branch. When they shut her in the tomb it was as though the waters had closed over a sunken galleon.

NOTES

by a dispatch of the Venetian *oratore* Paolo Cappello, who referred to it as 'a
all Rome found most impressive'.

a dispatch by the Mantuan *oratore* Giovanni Lucido Catanei, dated 8 July 1500.

rt of 21 September 1500 to the Consiglio dei Pregadi (the Venetian Senate) by
in *oratore*, to whom Alexander had earlier (23 August) remarked, apropos this
ie Duke says he did not do it; but even if he had, it would be no more than he
di Bisceglie] deserves.'

ter from Pandolfo Collenuccio to Ercole d'Este, 29 October 1500.

risina belonged to the Malatesta family of Rimini; at the age of fourteen she married
II d'Este, Lord of Ferrara, an elderly widower. She fell in love with her husband's
ate son Ugo: they were caught in bed together, and both executed (1425). The
alluded to by Byron and D'Annunzio.

Of the dispatches sent from Urbino to the Signoria during the course of this legation,
he first two are by Machiavelli (though even these bear Soderini's signature). The
ated 22 June, was written before the meetings with Valentino, and refers, in notably
ing terms, to the tactics which Cesare employed for the capture of Urbino; the second
composed on the 25th, that is, the day after his companion had left for Florence. In
diplomatic correspondence we find the well-known and warmly enthusiastic portrait
Valentino drawn by Machiavelli: 'This gentleman is most splendid and magnificent,
is so doughty in arms that it is no great matter that his exploits cost him dear. In the
st for glory, and to acquire a State, he never rests, nor does he acknowledge effort or
nger. He reaches a place before those where he previously was realize that he has gone;
has earned the loyalty and good wishes of his soldiers; he has picked the best men in all
aly. And these things, allied with perfect fortune, make him both victorious and for-
nidable.'

25. Letter from Cesare Borgia to the Doge Leonardo Loredan, 31 December 1502.

26. Letter to the Elders of Forlí.

27. Discussions with the Venetian *oratore* Antonio Giustinian, November 1503.

28. Evidence for this meeting and discussion is provided by a letter written from Rome
to Urbino, reproduced by F. Ugolini in *Storia dei conti e duchi di Urbino* (Florence, 1859,
Vol. II), and a manuscript chronicle (*Cenni storici su Urbino*) in the Biblioteca Vaticana, no.
N. 7943, fol. 108.

29. Contemporary MS, published by A. Rodriguez Villa: *Crónica del Gran Capitano*,
Madrid, 1908.

ORIGINS

1. See Béthencourt, *Historia genealógica y heráldica de la monarquía española*, Madrid, 1902. We
must, moreover, recognize that Pellicer's aim was clearly commemorative: his *Seyano
Germánico* is, in fact, dedicated to Cardinal Gaspar de Borja (of the House of Gandia).
However, this does not prevent his assertion reflecting a version of events which, at the time,
was undisputed.

THE AGE OF CALLISTUS III

1. This prediction is taken, verbatim, from Pietro Ranzano da Palermo's *Vita S. Vincentii*
(v. Bzovius, *Annali*, XV, 1419).

2. Alfonso's brothers were taken prisoner at the same time as he was. On the anti-Aragonese fury of Genoa during these manoeuvres, and the double game played by the Duke of
Milan (one agreement, on 21 September, with the representatives of René of Anjou, and the
other, on 8 October, with Alfonso) see F. Cognasso, *I Visconti*, Milan, dall'Oglio, 1966,
pp. 445-7.

3. Alfonso's sensibility to the influence of Italian humanism, and the new direction which
his cultural interests assumed, can both be confirmed by comparing the catalogues of books
which he owned in Spain, prior to the conquest of Naples (Barcelona, 1412; Valencia,
1417) with the inventory acquired in Italy. On this topic, see T. De Marinis, *La biblioteca
napoletana dei re d'Aragona* (4 vols., Milan, 1943-53), where there is also reproduced a dedica-
tory epistle by Giacomo Curlo, Alfonso's Genoese secretary, which provides an outline
of the cultural situation in Naples, and of the sovereign's activities in this field. A sober,
authoritative, and accurate treatment of the subject is that by E. Garin, 'Alfonso d'Aragona
e l'umanesimo a Napoli', in *Storia della letteratura italiana*, Milan, 1966, Vol. III, pp. 159-64.

4. Nevertheless, certain ancient *testimonia* can be adduced in support of the case alleging
paternity, including the *Vitae et res gestae pontificum romanorum* by the Spanish Dominican
Alonso Chacón (or Ciaconio), who lived at Rome during the second half of the sixteenth
century, and specifically identifies Francesco as *filius notus Alphonsi Borgia cardinalis*.

5. On Gaspare of Verona, who during Callistus III's pontificate served as Apostolic
Secretary, see G. Zippel, *Un umanista in villa*, Pistoia, 1900. The portrait which he draws of
Paul II is in sharp contrast to the bile-ridden one by Platina, a clear libel which Burck-
hardt does not hesitate to describe as 'a caricature of biography'.

6. A. Mai, *Spicilegium Romanorum*, Rome, 1839-44.

7. The appointment of Pedro Luís as Prefect of Rome and Vicar of the places named above took place on 19 August 1457 and was followed, that same evening, by the Pontiff's meeting with Rome's civic authorities. Evidence for the speeches made on this occasion, and the much-vaunted 'Italian sentiments' (italianità) of Pedro Luís, is provided in a dispatch by Ottone del Carretto, dated 20 August.

8. O. Raynald, *Annales ecclesiastici* (1458, n. 41).

9. This episode took place in the summer of 1458. Antonio da Pistoia informed Francesco Sforza of it in a letter dated 24 July.

10. The phrase is reported by Aeneas Silvius Piccolomini in his *De Europa*, p. 58.

11. Dispatch dated 22 July 1455.

12. Dispatch dated 4 July 1458.

13. Dispatch from Ottone del Carretto to Francesco Sforza, dated 24 July 1458. During this same discussion Callistus III expressed the confident hope that the Duke of Milan would allow him full liberty of action against Ferrante, adding that, when victory was won, he would give ample proof of his gratitude.

THE AGE OF ALEXANDER VI AND CESARE

1. Andrea Schivenoglio, 'Cronaca di Mantova (1445–1484)', in *Raccolta di cronisti e documenti storici lombardi inediti*, Milan, 1857.

2. From a speech delivered at the consistory of 23 September 1463 (see Pastor, *Storia dei Papi*, 1961, Vol. II, pp. 239–41).

3. Charles the Bold was the last Duke of Burgundy. After his death Louis XI (son of Charles VII, 'the Victorious', immortalized as the Dauphin by Joan of Arc) took over not only Burgundy, but also Picardy. The territory which Maximilian acquired through his marriage to Marie of Burgundy was the Tyrol.

4. Letter from Cesare Borgia to the Priors of Perugia, dated 2 January 1503.

5. This shouting-match between Cardinals Rodrigo and Giuliano is alluded to by the Mantuan envoy Antonello da Salerno, in a letter dated 21 July 1492.

6. *The Prince*, Ch. XI.

7. The letter, written from Châtillon on 18 Octo[ber] was already looking Francewards as regards Cesa[re] a certain touch of peremptoriness, informs Cesa[re] act as mediator and advocate of Briçonnet's interest[s] to remain his intercessor at the French Court: 'Et *avoir. Et fault bien que vous soyez le sien a Rome envers façon que lui plaise le faire et creer cardinal le plus brief que j[*

8. The date of 7 May, which some historians refer to a[s] in fact that on which the marriage contract was drawn u[p]

9. Dispatch by Benedetto Capilupi to the Court of Ma[ntua] 1494.

10. The conjectural date 'end of October 1494' assigned to Appendix to Vol. III of his *Storia dei Papi*, 1959, is clearly a[

11. The phrase is taken from Zurita (see Bibliography) wh[o] before him the reports of the Spanish embassy'.

12. For a full exposition of the factual data and those critical con[clusions] opinion, make the fratricide thesis unacceptable, I may refer the r[eader] *Borgia*, Milan, 1958, pp. 116–28.

13. 'Sink, O avenging Tiber, the bull-calves in your raging bill[ows] fall, a mighty victim offered to the God of the Underworld.'

14. Sanudo, *Diaries*, Vol. II, p. 217.

15. Sanudo, ibid., Vol. II, p. 279; Zurita, Vol. V, pp. 159–60.

16. Sanudo, *Diaries*, Vol. II, p. 822.

17. *Translator's note*: The Italian phrase, though it literally means 'queen [of] signifies 'Queen of Spades' in the Neapolitan or Venetian (as opposed t[o] French) pack of playing-cards.

18. Andrea Bernardi *Cronache forlivesi dal 1476 al 1517*, Vol. I, pp. 245 ff.

19. During a famous *corrida* held in St Peter's Square on 24 June that year (150[ ] appeared in the arena wearing a plain jerkin, and dispatched six bulls in quick su[ccession] beheading the last one at a single stroke. The astonishment which this exhibition pr[

is confirmed
thing which

20. From

21. Rep
the Veneti
crime: 'T
[Alfonso

22. L

23. P
Nicolò
illegitin
story is

24.
only t
first,
admi
was
this
of
and
qu
da
he
It
n

THE DECLINE OF THE FAMILY

1. Goffredo's heir, Prince Francesco, married Anna Piccolomini. He was succeeded by his son Giovanni Battista, who in July 1547 founded, some four miles north of Squillace, the city which bears the family's name, granting it 'titles, privileges, and immunities'. From him the overlordship passed to his son Pietro, of whom a memorial survives in the pink marble coping of the Chapel of Sant'Agazio, built inside the Cathedral of Squillace. Pietro, though he married three times, had no male issue. His eldest daughter, Anna, brought the title and fief as a dowry to a member of the House of Gandia: Francisco (the saint's nephew), warrior, diplomat, poet, and Viceroy of Peru. (This genealogical sequence is taken from the unpublished manuscript *Squillacii redivivi*, by P. Giuseppe Lottelli da Squillace, Bk. I, Ch. 16, a work written in the mid-eighteenth century, and now in the possession of Professor Guido Rhodio. I am much indebted to this keen student of local history for his courtesy in bringing it to my notice.)

2. Juan—Francis's favourite son, and undoubtedly the most talented—had a dazzling career as diplomat and courtier, which let him mingle with all the greatest personages of his era. He was gentleman-in-waiting to Don Carlos, Philip II's ambassador in Portugal, and *mayordomo mayor* to Queen Margaret of Austria, Philip III's wife. His second wife was Francesca of Aragon, by whom he had four children. He died in the Escurial on 3 September 1606. One of his sons married that Anna Borgia (a descendant of Goffredo's, and referred to in a previous note), thus becoming Prince of Squillace.

3. In Italy he had frequent correspondence and contact with Lucrezia's son and nephew, Ercole II and Alfonso II d'Este, and stayed on more than one occasion at Ferrara. Further-more, some very touching letters still exist which were written to him by Valentino's daughter Suor Lucrezia, who died a year after he did. In September 1565, lastly, he received a humble petition, composed with a wealth of pious expressions, from a Cesare Borgia who was dragging out a highly obscure existence in Naples. This singular character, who had sunk to being a kind of out-at-elbows adventurer, subsequently (1567) found the where-withal to make his way into Spain. He landed at Valencia; from here he travelled to Gandia, with the intention of presenting himself in the palace, and making an appeal to ties of blood in the hope of getting sufficient assistance to embark on a way of life less unworthy of the name he bore. Duke Carlos was absent, and the pilgrim found himself driven out, to use his own expression, '*como si fuera hereje o turco*'.

BIBLIOGRAPHY

1. ORIGINS AND GENEALOGY

ALVAREZ, GABRIEL, *Historia de la provincia de Aragón*, 1607 and ff.

BÉTHENCOURT, FRANCISCO FERNANDEZ DE, *Historia genealógica y heráldica de la monarquía española, Casa real y Grandes de España* (Vol. IV: 'Gandía, Casa de Borja'), Madrid, 1902

CITTADELLA, L. N., *Saggio di albero genealogico e di memorie sulla famiglia Borgia, specialmente in relazione a Ferrara*, Ferrara, 1872

ESPINA, ATILANO DE LA, *Registro universal de todas las escrituras que se hallan en el archivo del monasterio de Veruela*, 1671

HÖFLER, C. R. VON, 'Don Rodrigo de Borja und seine Söhne' in *Denkschriften der kaiserliche Akademie des Wissenschaften*, XXXVII, Vienna, 1889

ORTIZ, JOSÉ MARIANO, 'Epitome o Historia de la ilustre familia de Borja' in *Archivos Osuna*, Madrid

DE PUT, A. VAN, *The Aragonese Double Crown and the Borja or Borgia device*, London, 1920

VILLANUEVA, JOAQUÍN LORENZO, *Viaje literario a las iglesias de España*, Madrid, 1803–52

ZURITA Y CASTRO, JÉRONIMO, *Anales de la corona de Aragón*, Saragossa, 1610

2. THE BORGIAS — GENERAL

COLLISON-MORLEY, L., *The History of the Borgias*, London, 1932

FYVIE, J., *The Story of the Borgias*, London, 1912

MENOTTI, M., *I Borgia, storia e iconografia*, Rome, 1917

ROLFE, F. W., *Chronicles of the House of Borgia*, London, 1901

SCHUBERT SOLDERN, V. VON, *Die Borgia und ihre Zeit*, Dresden, 1902

SCHÜLLER PIROLI, S., *Die Borgia. Die Zerstörung einer Legende; der Geschichte einer Dynastie*, Freiburg, 1963.

WHITFIELD, J. H., 'New Views upon the Borgias' in *History*, XXVIII, 1943

YRIARTE, CHARLES, *Autour des Borgias*, Paris, 1891

3. CALLISTUS III AND HIS TIMES

ALTISENT JOVE, J. B., *Alonso de Borja en Lérida (1408–23) despues papa Calixto III*, Lerida, 1924

AMETLLER Y VINYAS, *Alfonso V en Italia y la crisis religiosa del siglo XV*, Gerona, 1903–4

ANDRÉ, J. F., *Histoire politique de la monarchie pontificale au XIVᵉ siècle, ou la Papauté à Avignon*, Paris, 1845

BISTICCI, VESPASIANO DA, *Vite di uomini illustri del secolo XV*, Bologna, 1892–3

BORGIA, STEFANO, *Istoria del dominio temporale della Sede Apostolica nelle Due Sicilie*, Rome, 1788

BRUNI, LEONARDO, 'Rerum suo tempore in Italia gestarum commentarius' in *Rerum Italicarum Scriptores*, XIX, Milan, 1731

CIACONIO, ALFONSO, *Vitae et res gestae pontificum romanorum et S.R.E. cardinalium*, Rome, 1677.

CREIGHTON, M., *A History of the Papacy from the Great Schism to the Sack of Rome*, London, 1897

CROCE, BENEDETTO, *Storia del regno di Napoli*, Bari, 1924.

CUENCA CREUS, *San Vicente Ferrer. Su influencia social y política*, Madrid, 1919

DANIEL-ROPS, *L'Eglise de la Renaissance et de la Réforme*, Paris, 1955

FAGES, *Histoire de Saint Vincent Ferrer*, 2 vols., Paris, 1894

GUIRAUD, J., *L'Etat pontifical après le Grand Schisme*, Paris, 1896

JORGA, N., *Notes et extraits pour servir à l'histoire des croisades au XVe siècle*, Paris, 1889

MIRET Y SANS, J., *La política oriental de Alfonso V de Aragón*, Barcelona, 1904

PICCOLOMINI, AENEAS SILVIUS, *Commentarii rerum memorabilium quae temporibus suis contigerunt*, Frankfurt, 1614

RAYNALD, O., *Annales ecclesiastici*, Vols. VII–X, Lucca, 1752

RENOUARD, YVES, *La Papauté à Avignon*, Paris, 1954

RIUS SERRA, J., 'Alfonso de Borja' in *Analecta sacra Taraconensia*, VI, 1930

—— 'Catalanes y Aragoneses en la corte de Calixto III' in *Analecta sacra Taraconensia*, III, Barcelona, 1927

RODOCANACHI, EMMANUEL, *Histoire de Rome de 1354 à 1471*, Paris, 1922

SAMPSON, R. A., 'Halley's comet and Pope Calixtus' in *Journal of the British Astronomical Association*, XVIII, 1908

SANCHIS Y SIVERA, J., 'El obispo de Valencia, don Alfonso de Borja' in *Boletin de la Real Academia de la Histoire*, LXXXVIII, 1926

SCHWENKE, P., *Die Türkenbulle Papst Kalixtus III*, Berlin, 1911

SCHWOEKEL, R., *The Shadow of the Crescent: the Renaissance Image of the Turk (1453–1517)*, Nieukoop, 1967

SORANZO, GIOVANNI, *La lega italica, 1454–1455*, Milan, 1924

STEIN, J., *Calixte III et la Comète de Halley*, Rome, 1909

TOMMASEO, NICCOLÒ, *Le lettere de Santa Caterina da Siena*, 4 vols., Florence, 1860

VALOIS, NOËL, *La crise religieuse du XVe siècle. Le Pape et le Concile: 1418–1450*, 2 vols., Paris, 1909

4. ALEXANDER VI, HIS DESCENDANTS AND THEIR ERA

ADEMOLLO, A., *Alessandro VI, Giulio II e Leone X nel carnevale di Roma*, Florence, 1886

BATLLORI, M., *Alejardro VI y la Casa Real de Aragón*, Madrid, 1958

BEMBO, PIETRO, *Lettere*, Verona, 1743

BERNARDI, ANDREA, *Cronache forlivesi*, 2 vols., Bologna, 1895–7

BERTAUX, EMILE, 'Monuments et souvenirs des Borgias dans le Royaume de Valencia' in *Gazette des Beaux Arts*, II–III, 1908

BRANCA, SEBASTIANO DE' TADELLINI, 'Diario romano dal maggio 1485 al giugno 1524' in *Rerum Italicarum Scriptores*, XXIII, 1907

BUONACCORSI, BIAGIO, *Diario dei successi più importanti seguiti in Italia dall'anno 1498 all'anno 1512*, Florence, 1508

BURCHARD, JOHANNES, *Diarium*, ed. L. Thuasne, Paris, 1883–5

CERRI, DOMENICO, *Borgia, ossia Alessandro VI papa e i suoi contemporanei*, Turin, 1873–4

CHABAS, R., 'Alexandro VI y el duque de Gandia' in *Archive*, III, Valencia, 1893

———, 'Don Jofré de Borja y Dona Sancha de Aragon' in *Revue Hispanique*, XI, 1902

CLÉMENT, H., *Les Borgia. Histoire du pape Alexandre VI, de César et de Lucrèce Borgia*, Paris, 1882

COMMYNES, PHILIPPE DE, *Mémoires*, Paris, 1845

CONTI, SIGISMONDO DE', *Storie dei suoi tempi, dal 1475 al 1510*, Rome, 1883

DELABORDE, H. F., *L'expédition de Charles VIII en Italie*, Paris, 1888

DELL'ORO, I., *Papa Alessandro VI, Rodrigo Borgia*, Milan, 1940

DE ROO, PETER, *Material for a History of Pope Alexander VI*, 5 vols., Bruges, 1924

EHRLE, F., and STEVENSON, E., *Gli affreschi del Pinturicchio nell'Appartamento Borgia*, Rome, 1897

FEDELE, P., 'I gioielli di Vannozza' in *Archivio della Società Romana di Storia Patria*, XXVIII, 1905

FERRARA, ORESTE, *The Borgia Pope* (translated from the Spanish), London, 1942

FERRUA, A., 'Ritrovamento dell' epitaffio di Vannozza Cattaneo' in *Archivio della Società Romana di Storia Patria*, LXXI, 1948

FUMI, L., *Alessandro VI e il Valentino in Orvieto*, Siena, 1872

GASCA QIUERAZZA, G., *Gli scritti autografi di Alessandro VI nell'Archivum Arcis*, Turin, 1959

GENNARELLI, A. (ed.), *Giovanni Burchardi Diarum*, Florence, 1854

GIOVIO, PAOLO, *Illustrium virorum vitae*, Florence, 1551

GIUSTINIAN, ANTONIO, *Dispacci*, ed. P. Villari, 3 vols., Florence, 1886

GNOLI, U., 'Una figlia sconosciuta di Alessandro VI' in *L'Urbe*, II, 1937

GORDON, A., *The Lives of Pope Alexander VI and his son Cesare Borgia*, London, 1729

GUICCARDINI, FRANCESCO, *Storia d'Italia*, Bari, 1929 (translated by G. Grayson, London, 1966)

HALE, J. R., *Machiavelli and Renaissance Italy*, New York, 1960

INFESSURA, STEFANO, *Diario della città di Roma*, Rome, 1890

LA TORRE, FERDINANDO, *Del conclave di Alessandro VI*, Florence, 1933

LEONETTI, A., *Papa Alessandro VI, secondo documenti e carteggi del tempo*, 3 vols., Bologna, 1880

LUZIO, ALESSANDRO, *Isabella d'Este e i Borgia*, Milan, 1915

MACHIAVELLI, NICCOLÒ, *Le legazioni e commissarie*, ed. Sergio Bertelli, Milan, 1964

———, *Ie Principe*, ed. G. Sasso, Florence, 1963

MENOTTI, MARIO, 'Vannozza Cattanei' in *Nuova Antologia*, December 1916

OLLIVIER, M. I. H., *Le Pape Alexandre VI et les Borgia*, Paris, 1870

OLMOS Y CANADA, D. ELIAS, *Revindicacion de Alejandro VI*, Valencia, 1954

PASINI-FRASSONI, F., 'Lo stemma di Vannozza Borgia' in *Rivista araldica*, 1909

PASTOR, LUDWIG VON, *History of the Popes from the Close of the Middle Ages*, translated by F. L. Antrobus, London, 1923 (5th ed.)

PELICIER, P., *Lettres de Charles VIII*, Vol. v, Paris, 1898

PEPE, GUGLIELMO, *La politica dei Borgia*, Naples, 1945

PICOTTI, G. B., 'Nuovi studi e documenti intorno a papa Alessandro VI' in *Rerum Italicarum Scriptores*, v, 1951

PORTIGLIOTTI, GIUSEPPE, *The Borgias. Alexander VI, Cesare and Lucrezia*, translated from the Italian, London, 1928

RIDOLFI, ROBERTO, *Le lettere di Gerolamo Savonarola*, Florence, 1933

RODRIGUEZ VILLA, ANTONIO, *Crónica del Gran Capitano*, Madrid, 1908

SCHWEITZER, W., 'Zur Wahl Alexanders VI' in *Historisches Jahrbuch*, xxx, 1909

SORANZO, G., *Il tempo di Alessandro VI e di Girolamo Savonarola*, Milan, 1960

———, *Studi intorno a papa Alessandro VI Borgia*, Milan, 1951

TRUC, G., *Rome et les Borgias*, Paris, 1939

VANDERLINDEN, H., 'Alexander VI and the demarcation of the maritime and colonial domains of Spain and Portugal' in *American Historical Review*, xxii, 1917

VILLARI, PASQUALE, *Niccolò Machiavelli e i suoi tempi*, Milan, 1927 (4th ed.)

———, *La storia di Gerolamo Savonarola e dei suoi tempi*, Florence, 1926 (4th ed.)

VOLTERRA, GIACOMO DA, 'Diario romano' in *Rerum Italicum Scriptores*, xxiii, 1733

5. CESARE BORGIA

ALVISI, E., *Cesare Borgia, Duca di Romagna*, Imola, 1878

BELTRAMI, L., *Leonardo da Vinci e Cesare Borgia*, Milan, 1916

BENOIST, CHARLES, 'César Borgia, l'original du Prince', in *Revue des Deux Mondes*, xxxvi, 1906

BERNARDI, A. A., *Cesare Borgia e la Repubblica di San Marino, 1500–1504*, Florence, 1905

BEUF, C., *Cesare Borgia, the Machiavellian Prince*, Toronto, 1942

CARRACCIOLO, AMBROGINO, *Un ratto di Cesare Borgia*, Naples, 1921

CHIERICI, G., 'L'idea di Roma nel ducato della Romagna di Cesare Borgia' in *Istituto di studi romani: sezione emiliana*, II, 1944

CLOUGH, C., 'Niccolò Machiavelli, Cesare Borgia and the Francesco Troche episode' in *Medievalia e umanistica*, xvii, 1966

DIONISOTTI, C., 'Machiavelli, Cesare Borgia e Don Michelotto' in *Rivista storica italiana*, lxxix, 1967

FERRATO, P., *L'entrata del Valentino nel 1499 al Chinone*, Venice, 1866

GALLIER, ANATOLE DE, 'César Borgia. Documents sur son séjour en France' in *Bulletin de la Société d'Archéologie de la Drôme*, xxix, 1895

GARNETT, R., 'Contemporary Poems on Cesare Borgia' in *English Historical Review*, I, 1886

GASTINE, LOUIS, *César Borgia*, Paris, 1911

HAGEN, T., 'Caesar Borgia und die Ermordung des Herzogs von Biselli' in *Zeitschrift für Katholics Theologie*, X

LA SIZERANNE, R. DE, *César Borgia et le duc d'Urbino*, Paris, 1924

LARNER, J., 'Cesare Borgia, Machiavelli and the Romagnol militia' in *Studi Romagnoli* XVII, 1966

LETI, G., *La Vita di Cesare Borgia*, ed. M. Fabi, Milan, 1885

LEVY, R., *César Borgia*, Paris, 1930

LISINI, ALESSANDRO, 'Relazioni fra Cesare Borgia e la repubblica di Siena' in *Bulletino senese di storia patria*, VII, 1900

MEDIN, A., 'Il duca Valentino nella mente di Niccolò Machiavelli' in *Rivista europea*, XXXIX, 1883

ONIEVA, A. J., *Cesar Borgia: su vida, su muerte y sus restos*, Madrid, 1945

PEREZ, G., 'Cesar Borgia, obispo de Pamplona', in *Razon y Fe*, 1934

RICHEPIN, J., *Les debuts de César Borgia*, Paris, 1891

ROBERTSON, SIR CHARLES G., *Caesar Borgia*, The Stanhope Essay, Oxford, 1891

SABATINI, RAFAEL, *The Life of Cesare Borgia*, London, 1912

SACERDOTE, G., *La vita di Cesare Borgia*, Milan, 1950

SCHLUMBERGER, G. L., *Charlotte d'Albret: femme de César Borgia*, Paris, 1913

WOODWARD, W. H., *Cesare Borgia*, London, 1913

YRIARTE, C., *César Borgia*, Paris, 1889

6. LUCREZIA BORGIA

BELLONCI, M., *Lucrezia Borgia: sua vite e suoi tempi*, rev. ed., Milan, 1960 (abridged English edition, London, 1948)

BELTRAMI, LUCA, *La guardaroba di Lucrezia Borgia*, Milan, 1903

BERENCE, F., *Lucrèce Borgia*, Paris, 1951

BROSCH, M., 'Alexander VI und Lucrezia Borgia' in *Historische Zeitschrift*, XXXIII, 1875

BUGGELLI, MARIO, *Lucrezia Borgia*, Milan, 1963

CAMPORI, G., 'Lucrezia Borgia; una vittima della storia' in *Nuova Antologia*, 1866

CAPPALLETTI, *Lucrezia Borgia e la storia*, Pisa, 1876

CATALANO, M., *Lucrezia Borgia, duchessa di Ferrara*, Ferrara, 1921

DE HEVESY, 'Bartolomeo Veneto et les portraits de Lucrezia Borgia' in *Arts Quarterly of the Detroit Institute of Arts*, II, 1939

DE UHAGON, F. R., *Relacion de los festines que se celebraron en el Vaticano con motivo de las bodas de Lucrecia Borgia, con Alonso de Aragon*, Madrid, 1896

FELICIANGELI, B., *Un episodio nel nepotismo borgiano: il matrimonio di Lucrezia Borgia con Giovanni Sforza, signore di Pesaro*, Turin, 1901

FUNCK-BRENTANO, F., *Lucrèce Borgia*, Paris, 1930

GILBERT, W., *Lucrezia Borgia, duchess of Ferrara*, London, 1869

GREGOROVIUS, F., *Lucrezia Borgia*, Stuttgart, 1874 (English edition, London 1948)

MANCINI, F., 'Lucrezia Borgia, governatrice di Spoleto' in *Archivio storico italiana*, CXV, 1957

MORSOLIN, B., 'Pietro Bembo e Lucrezia Borgia' in *Nuova antologia*, XV, 1885.

ONIEVA, A. J., *Lucrezia Borgia*, Barcelona, 1959

VILLA-URRUTIA, W. RAMIREZ DE, *Lucrezia Borgia*, Madrid, 1922

ZUCCHETTI, C., *Lucrezia Borgia*, Mantua, 1860

7. THE DUKES OF GANDIA AND ST FRANCIS BORGIA

AMOROS, L., 'El monasterio de Santa Clara de Gandía y la familia ducal de los Borjas' in *Archivo Ibero-Americano*, XX–XXI, 1960–1

'Archivos de Osuna', Madrid. (Ancient archives of the ducal House of Gandia, so called because of the name of their last owner, the Duke of Osuna and consisting of a collection of rare documents most of which are unpublished)

BAIXAULI, MARIANO, 'Las obras musicales de Francisco de Borja' in *Razon y fe*, October and November, 1902

BATLLORI, M., 'De borgiae patris' in *Archivum Historica Societatis Jesu*, XXVI, 1957

CERVOS, F., and SOLA, J. M., *El palacio ducal de Gandía,* Barcelona, 1904

GARZON, F., *Vida de San Francisco de Borja*, Madrid, 1953

KARRER, O., *Der heilige Franz von Borja, General der Gesellschaft Jesu*, Freiburg, 1921

MARTINDALE, *In God's Army*, Vol. II, 'St Francis Borgia', London, 1916

'Monumenta Borgiana' in *Monumenta historica Societatis Jesu*, Madrid, 1904–9

RIBADENEIRA, P., *S. Francis Borgia*, Rome, 1596

SAINT-PAULIEN, *Saint François Borgia, l'expiateur*, Paris, 1959

SANCHIS Y RIVERA, JOSÉ, *Algunos documentos y cartas que pertenecieron al segundo duque de Gandía, don Juan de Borja*, Valencia, 1919

GENEALOGICAL CHARTS

TABLE I

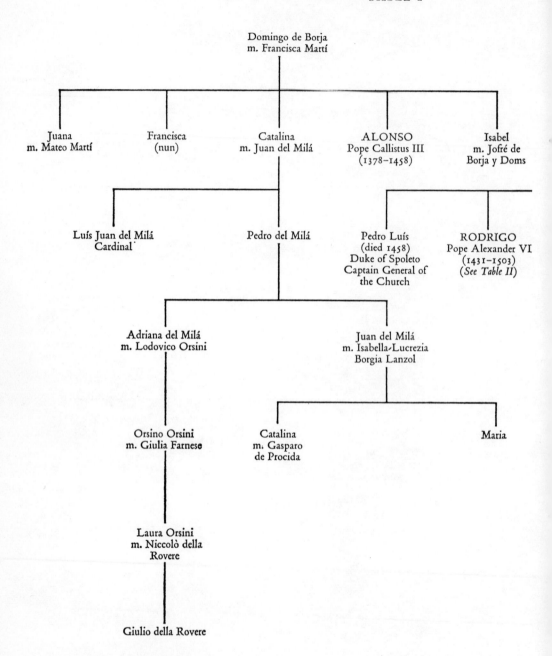

Domingo de Borja
m. Francisca Martí

Juana
m. Mateo Martí

Francisca
(nun)

Catalina
m. Juan del Milá

ALONSO
Pope Callistus III
(1378–1458)

Isabel
m. Jofré de
Borja y Doms

Luís Juan del Milá
Cardinal

Pedro del Milá

Pedro Luís
(died 1458)
Duke of Spoleto
Captain General of
the Church

RODRIGO
Pope Alexander VI
(1431–1503)
(See Table II)

Adriana del Milá
m. Lodovico Orsini

Juan del Milá
m. Isabella Lucrezia
Borgia Lanzol

Orsino Orsini
m. Giulia Farnese

Catalina
m. Gasparo
de Procida

Maria

Laura Orsini
m. Niccolò della
Rovere

Giulio della Rovere

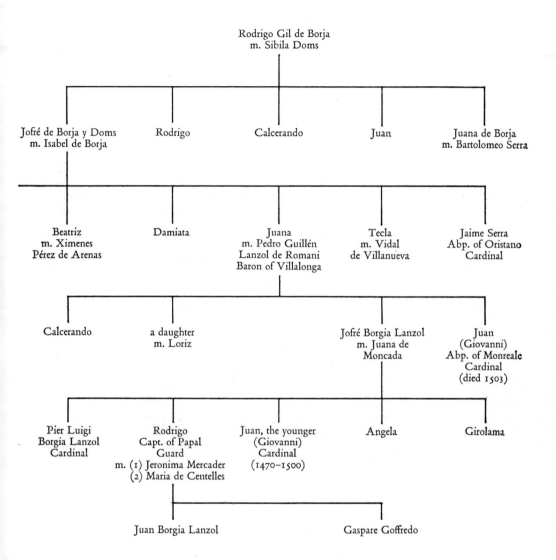

TABLE II   THE FAMILY

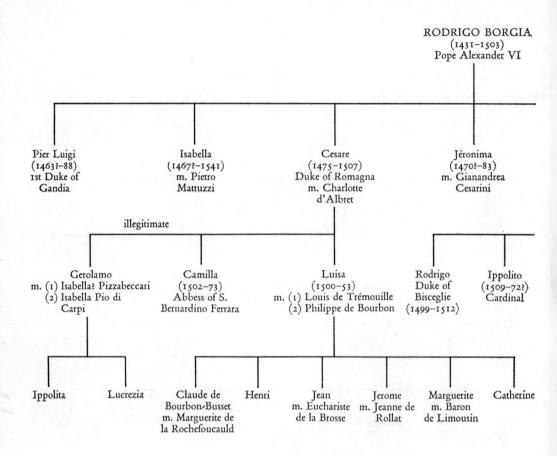

RODRIGO BORGIA
(1431-1503)
Pope Alexander VI

Pier Luigi
(1463?-88)
1st Duke of
Gandia

Isabella
(1467?-1541)
m. Pietro
Mattuzzi

Cesare
(1475-1507)
Duke of Romagna
m. Charlotte
d'Albret

Jéronima
(1470?-83)
m. Gianandrea
Cesarini

illegitimate

Gerolamo
m. (1) Isabella? Pizzabeccari
(2) Isabella Pio di
Carpi

Camilla
(1502-73)
Abbess of S.
Bernardino Ferrara

Luisa
(1500-53)
m. (1) Louis de Trémouille
(2) Philippe de Bourbon

Rodrigo
Duke of
Bisceglie
(1499-1512)

Ippolito
(1509-72?)
Cardinal

Ippolita

Lucrezia

Claude de
Bourbon-Busset
m. Marguerite de
la Rochefoucauld

Henri

Jean
m. Euchariste
de la Brosse

Jerome
m. Jeanne de
Rollat

Marguerite
m. Baron
de Limousin

Catherine

336

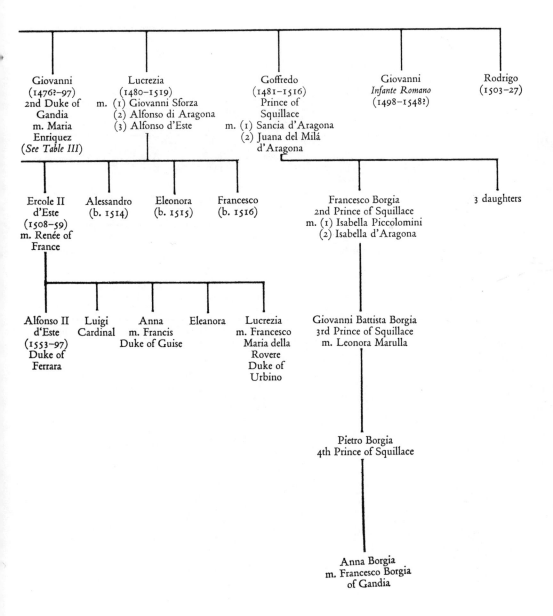

TABLE III

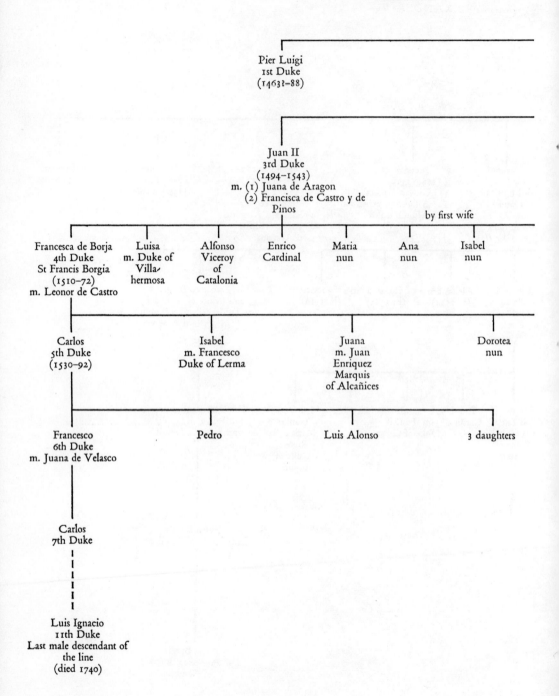

Pier Luigi
1st Duke
(1463?–88)

Juan II
3rd Duke
(1494–1543)
m. (1) Juana de Aragon
(2) Francisca de Castro y de
Pinos
by first wife

| Francesca de Borja 4th Duke St Francis Borgia (1510–72) m. Leonor de Castro | Luisa m. Duke of Villa- hermosa | Alfonso Viceroy of Catalonia | Enrico Cardinal | Maria nun | Ana nun | Isabel nun |

| Carlos 5th Duke (1530–92) | Isabel m. Francesco Duke of Lerma | Juana m. Juan Enriquez Marquis of Alcañices | Dorotea nun |

| Francesco 6th Duke m. Juana de Velasco | Pedro | Luis Alonso | 3 daughters |

Carlos
7th Duke
|
|
|
|
|

Luis Ignacio
11th Duke
Last male descendant of
the line
(died 1740)

338

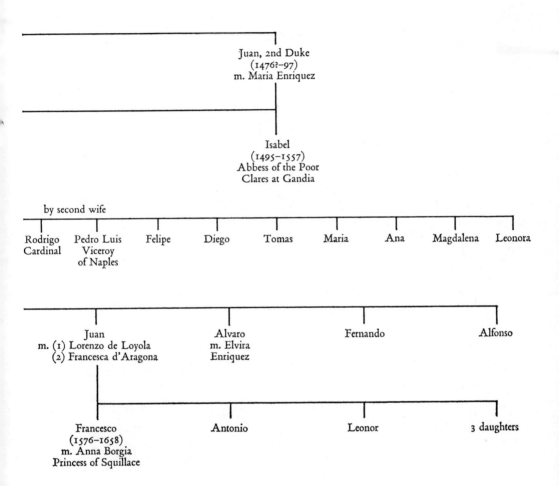

Juan, 2nd Duke
(1476?–97)
m. Maria Enriquez

Isabel
(1495–1557)
Abbess of the Poor
Clares at Gandia

by second wife

| Rodrigo Cardinal | Pedro Luis Viceroy of Naples | Felipe | Diego | Tomas | Maria | Ana | Magdalena | Leonora |

Juan
m. (1) Lorenzo de Loyola
(2) Francesca d'Aragona

Alvaro
m. Elvira
Enriquez

Fernando

Alfonso

Francesco
(1576–1658)
m. Anna Borgia
Princess of Squillace

Antonio

Leonor

3 daughters

LIST OF ILLUSTRATIONS

The Publishers wish to thank Mrs G. Calmann who supplied and set the titles and initials by hand in Cancelaresca Bastarda.

1. Urban VI, from a fifteenth-century wood-cut. Photo Mansell Collection.
2. Saint Peter's and the Vatican from a fifteenth-century engraving. Photo John R. Freeman and Co. Ltd.
3. Callistus III by Sano di Pietro. Accademia di Belle Arti, Siena. Photo Alinari.
4. Eugenius IV by Salviati. Palazzo Farnese, Rome. Photo Mansell Collection.
5. Cesare Borgia as a young boy by Pinturicchio. Dresden Pinacoteca. Photo Alinari.
6. Alfonso of Aragon, medal by Francesco di Giorgio. Photo courtesy the Ashmolean Museum, Oxford.
7. The bulls, emblem of the Borgias, and a portrait of Alexander VI. Vatican, Borgia Apartments, Sala dei Santi. Photo Alinari.
8. Alexander VI, portrait bust by Pasquale da Caravaggio. Berlin Museum. Photo Phaidon Archives.
9. Giulia Farnese, detail from the *Transfiguration* by Raphael. Vatican Museum. Photo Alinari.
10. Charles VIII of France by Jean Perréal. Photo courtesy the Bibliothèque Nationale, Paris.
11. Giovanni, Duke of Gandia, detail from the *Disputation of Saint Catherine* by Pinturicchio. Vatican, Borgia Apartments. Photo Alinari.
12. The Castello Estense, Ferrara. Photo Alinari.
13. Lucrezia Borgia, detail from the *Disputation of Saint Catherine* by Pinturicchio. Vatican, Borgia Apartments. Photo Alinari.
14. Alfonso d'Este by Dosso Dossi. Galleria Estense, Modena. Photo Alinari.
15. Goffredo Borgia and Sancia d'Aragona, detail from the *Disputation of Saint Catherine* by Pinturicchio. Vatican, Borgia Apartments. Photo Alinari.
16. Castel Sant'Angelo, Rome. Anonymous pen and ink drawing about 1540. Private Collection. Photo Warburg Institute, London.
17. View of Rome, wood-cut. From Jacopo Fillippo Foresti da Bergamo, *Supplementum Chronicarum*, Venice 1486. Photo Phaidon Archives.
18. Presumed portrait of Cesare Borgia by an unknown painter (formerly attributed to Leonardo da Vinci). Museo Civico, Venice. Photo Alinari.
19. Niccolò Machiavelli, terracotta bust of the fifteenth century. Società Colombaria, Florence. Photo Mansell Collection.
20. Lorenzo de Medici by Vasari. Uffizi Gallery, Florence. Photo Mansell Collection.
21. Alexander VI, detail from the *Resurrection* by Pinturicchio. Vatican, Borgia Apartments. Photo Mansell Collection.
22. Savonarola by Fra Bartolomeo. Museo di San Marco, Florence. Photo Alinari.
23. Guidobaldo I, Duke of Urbino, bas-relief of the fifteenth century. Palazzo Ducale, Urbino. Photo Mansell Collection.
24. Mounting a gun, drawing by Leonardo da Vinci. Windsor Castle Library. By Gracious Permission of Her Majesty the Queen.
25. Julius II by Raphael. Uffizi Gallery, Florence. Photo Alinari.
26. The Colonna family by Scipione Pulzone. Colonna Gallery, Rome. Photo Phaidon Archives.

27. Louis XII of France, attributed to Jean Perréal. Windsor Castle. Photo by Gracious Permission of Her Majesty the Queen.
28. The *Virgen de Los Caballeros* by Paolo da San Leocadio. Giovanni Borgia, Duke of Gandia is kneeling on the right and on the left are Cesare and Goffredo. Collegio del Corpus Christi, Valencia. Photo MAS.
29. Palazzo Sforza Cesarini, Rome. Photo Alinari.

Map of the Papal States in the fifteenth century. Drawn by Patrick Leeson.

The Publishers also wish to thank The Bodley Head Ltd. for permission to base the genealogical charts in this book on those appearing in *The Borgias: The Rise and Fall of a Renaissance Dynasty* by Michael Mallet.

INDEX